The
Gardener's
Year

The Gardener's Year

The ultimate month-by-month gardening handbook from
ALAN TITCHMARSH
Photographs by Jonathan Buckley

BBC
BOOKS

CONTENTS

INTRODUCTION

It doesn't matter how long you've been gardening, there always comes a time when you need a reminder about this and that. A memory jogger. A book that will say 'Yes, you can do this now' or, 'Hang on a bit, you'd be better off doing that at another time of year'. 'Oh, and here's how to do it.' Welcome to *The Gardener's Year*.

What I hope this book will do is take the worry out of gardening rather than putting it in. The last thing I want to do is make you feel guilty. The bottom line in gardening is that it should be enjoyable, not a chore. I know that weeding, painting a fence with preservative and cleaning out a garden pool might not be high on anyone's list of favourite jobs, but at least you can gain reassurance from knowing when is the best time to do any of them, even if you then decide to do it tomorrow and have a lie in instead.

It is the seasons that affect the changing routines of our gardening year, and it is the seasons that form the backbone of *The Gardener's Year*. It's divided up into months and further divided into sections dealing with different parts of the garden – like the patio, the pond and the greenhouse – and different groups of plants – like flowers, vegetables and fruits – so that you can see what is going on around you in your garden and what you should be doing throughout the year. There are also checklists in each month that will make it easy to find any particular task you are looking for, and plenty of suggestions of plants that are at their best in each month so that if you have a gap in your garden's interest you can see at a glance how to brighten it up.

Don't let the book's comprehensiveness put you off. You're not expected to do everything, but I'm anxious that anything you do choose to do is covered thoroughly and clearly so that you can dip in and out of the book with ease. It's designed to be a comfort, not a nag, simply someone by your side advising you what to do, when, how and why.

Obviously it doesn't always work quite as easily as that, because varying temperatures and climate differences mean that garden jobs will have to be done at slightly different times of the year all over the country.

For example, if you live in the north of England, your April may be the equivalent of March in the south. If you're not too familiar with your local climate, talk to your neighbours, garden centres or local gardeners. And changes in weather patterns alter the beginning and end of each year's growing season. Once upon a time the frosts would come in September and tender plants would be blackened. Nowadays our summers are much longer and bedding plants can last into November. Our winters are often wetter than they used to be, and not nearly so cold, which means plants that were once regarded as unreliably hardy in British winters will often survive. The climate of the UK has changed over the past twenty years, and *The Gardener's Year* takes account of that.

I'm an organic gardener and you won't find long lists of chemical sprays and potions within these pages. There are several reasons for this. The first is that I think a garden is best run like a garden, not a farm. I enjoy butterflies, bees and birds, and all kinds of insects. Many of them are beneficial; they are as much a part of my garden life as dahlias and hostas. I have offered organic means of pest and disease control where possible, and been honest in describing their effectiveness. Slugs and snails are as prominent in gardens where poisonous pellets are used as they are in one run on organic lines, and so many chemicals formerly available to gardeners are now being withdrawn from the shelves. It seems to me that it makes sense to find alternative means of pest and disease control since in the long term we are likely to have no other option.

I hope *The Gardener's Year* becomes a book you'll keep pulling down off the shelf. Better still, keep it in your shed, until its pages are fingerprinted with mud and the spine falls apart. That way, you'll know that it's been worth having by your side.

JANUARY

January brings the snow, or at least it used to before the climate warmed up. Whether it snows or not, you can't help being aware how sparse the garden looks now that Christmas is over and we're resigned to a couple of long, cold months before things start to perk up again. For now, the stars of the January landscape are tree trunks, coloured stems and twiggy shapes. They show up quite well on their own against an uncluttered background, but they look best combined with strategically placed evergreens, especially those with unusual foliage colours or textures.

There's always something to do in January, even if it's indoors. And because now is the only bit of slack in the gardening year to take stock and plan ahead, make the most of it. Maintenance may not be the most glamorous job in the garden but it has to be done, and in winter – when the garden is a skeleton of its usual self – it's much easier to reach the bits that need attention. By the time you've finished, you'll really feel you've achieved something. Honestly.

THE BIG PICTURE attractive bark and stems

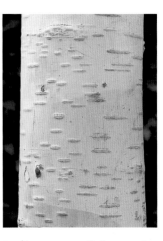

Prunus serrula, Tibetan cherry (above), is a cherry tree with a difference – its main feature is not the blossom but the bark, which is as smooth and shiny as a conker, and about the same colour. The tree does carry white flowers in spring, though, and these are followed by small oval fruits – regard them as a bonus. Don't plant one of these if you plan to move house in the next few years, because it needs to be reasonably mature before the girth is wide enough to show an impressive shine. Also, it's not a tree for a small patch as it makes a medium-size dome shape, reaching 6 × 5m (20 × 15ft). But in the right garden, it's hard to keep your hands off it.

PEAK SEASON October–March.
GROWING CONDITIONS
  Reasonable soil and good light, but also tolerates poor chalky soil and clay.

Acer griseum, paperbark maple (above), has brilliant autumn colour as the leaves prepare to drop; once they've fallen, the trunk and branches stand out vividly in the winter landscape, as they are covered in copious shaggy chestnut flakes curling back from the greyish bark. A good tree looks as if it's just had a perm. Paperbark maple is a slow-growing tree, reaching about 5 × 4m

(15 × 12ft). Although its size makes it suitable for a small garden, it is a woodland species that is happiest in the company of others rather than on its own.

PEAK SEASON October–March.
GROWING CONDITIONS Prefers woodland, but tolerates sun or light shade. Needs humus-rich soil that doesn't dry out badly or become waterlogged.

Birches come in all shapes and sizes but the one thing they all have in common is sensational bark. Even the common silver birch, *Betula pendula*, 10 × 5m (30 × 15ft), has pure white bark on all but the youngest specimens. There are also several more unusual species. *Betula utilis* var. *jacquemontii* (above), 10 × 5m (30 × 15ft plus), is particularly luminous in its whiteness and good when planted in threes. The canoe-bark birch, *Betula papyrifera*, 8 × 5m (25 × 15ft), is a white-barked kind that North American Indians make boats from; if left on the tree, the bark peels to show a faintly golden skin beneath. Most colourful of all is the Chinese red-barked birch, *Betula albosinensis* var. *septentrionalis*, 8 × 5m (25 × 15ft), as its bark peels back to reveal pink, cream, orange or cinnamon-coloured blotches arranged in patterns. All birches have golden autumn tints to their leaves, and since they only make a light canopy of leaves they won't plunge the garden into deep shade.

PEAK SEASON October–March.
GROWING CONDITIONS
  Common silver birch is not too fussy about soil and grows in sun or light shade. Choicer species need fertile soil and reasonable drainage. All are tolerant of wind.

Bamboos, it's fair to say, look stemmy all year round – you just notice them more in winter, when there are few other distractions. It also depends how you grow them, because as they get older they naturally grow twiggy sideshoots all along the main stems. In the case of thicket-forming species with lots of thin stems, such as *Fargesia nitida*, 3 × 1.2m (10 × 4ft), the shape of the thicket is the main attraction. However, if you grow one with fewer, tall, thick, coloured stems, such as the yellow *Phyllostachys aurea*, or the ebony-black *Phyllostachys nigra*, both of which are capable of making 5 × 1m (15 × 3ft), trim off the sideshoots to leave just a flag of foliage flying for the top few feet to see them at their best. Do it in autumn to reap the benefit all winter. Both the latter are popular for growing in tubs, which restricts their activities quite a bit. My favourite bamboo of all time is the one with a real mouthful of a name: *Phyllostachys aureosulcata* f. *aureocaulis* (above). It is tall, at around 3m (10ft) high, but tidily clump-forming and has the most wonderful golden-orange canes. Try spotlighting it at night – wow!

PEAK SEASON October–March.
GROWING CONDITIONS Fertile
soil but dislikes wet; prefers a
sheltered site in sun or light
shade.

Dogwoods have some of the most colourful stems to be found in the sort of shrubs that suit small gardens. *Cornus alba* 'Sibirica' (above) is the old classic with sealing-wax red stems, while the newer *Cornus sanguinea* 'Midwinter Fire' has orange and almost luminous pink stems that look like flickering flames. Both are very tolerant of wet soil, so they are useful for planting in clay soil, bog gardens or along riverbanks, as well as normal gardens. All are easy to grow, but what you must do is cut out the oldest stems at the end of each winter; the new shoots that replace them have the brightest bark. Stemmy dogwoods reach roughly 1.2 × 1.2m (4 × 4ft).

PEAK SEASON October–March.
GROWING CONDITIONS Any soil
including wet and clay. Regular
manuring will keep young stems
coming. The stems colour best
in full sun.

Eucalyptus have outstanding trunks with peeling bark, or multicoloured patterns of greys, browns and creams as irregular-shaped pieces flake off, but the snag is the patterning only occurs when the plants are allowed to grow into fair-sized trees. One of the hardiest and most reliable to grow this way in British gardens is the snow gum, *Eucalyptus pauciflora* subsp. *niphophila* (above), which will easily reach 6 × 5m (20 × 15ft). But when grown the way most people with small gardens have to grow it – cutting it hard back every few years to keep the stems short and bushy – you'll have grey-green stems and more rounded evergreen juvenile leaves instead of the scimitar-shaped adult foliage of an untrimmed tree, but without the trunk patterns. With eucalyptus, you can't have it both ways.

PEAK SEASON All year round.
GROWING CONDITIONS Well-
drained soil; dislikes chalk.

Salix alba var. vitellina cultivars, golden willow, also have coloured young stems. Left to their own devices, they'll grow into trees, but in the garden you can keep them to a shrubby 2–2.5m × 1.2m (6–8 × 4ft) by cutting them back hard each spring the same way as dogwoods. They'll grow in all the same difficult places. The two to go for are *Salix alba* var. *vitellina* 'Britzensis' (above), which has scarlet stems, and *Salix alba* var. *vitellina* 'Chermesina', which is bright red. *Salix daphnoides* has pewtery purple stems. Use the buff-coloured *Salix alba* var. *vitellina*, which is more vigorous, if you want to harvest your own willow wands for making baskets, large willow screens or elaborate garden sculptures.

PEAK SEASON October–March.
GROWING CONDITIONS Any soil
including wet and clay. The
stems colour best in full sun.

OLD FAITHFULS

***Mahonia × media* 'Lionel Fortescue'** (above) is a real trouper. It is a rather upright, architectural sort of shrub, which is decorated from midwinter to spring with long, yellow 'shuttlecock' flowers at the tips of the stems, all set off against leathery, holly-like leaves arranged in formal double rows along wiry midribs. There are other mahonias, but this hardy, showy, strongly fragrant plant has it all. Allow it to reach about 2 × 2m (6 × 6ft), then prune out a few of the oldest stems close to ground level each spring to keep it youthful-looking, as old plants sometimes have unsightly bare 'legs'.

PEAK SEASON January–March.
GROWING CONDITIONS
Reasonably fertile soil, light shade and a sheltered site.

Viburnum tinus, laurustinus, is a real winter standby. It forms a bushy evergreen, studded with bunches of buds that sit still until the weather warms up, then suddenly burst open in late winter. It's the sort of shrub you often inherit with an old garden, but if you're thinking of buying one I'd always go for a form with pink buds, such as ***Viburnum tinus* 'Eve Price'** or ***Viburnum tinus* 'Gwenllian'** (above), because they look so much warmer in cold weather than ice-white. A lot of people think the buds look better than the flowers. At 2.5 × 2.5m (8 × 8ft), *Viburnum tinus* is big enough to block off a bad view when other things have lost their leaves. It is also a good shrub to place behind birches or dogwoods, as it makes a good background for winter trunks and stems.

PEAK SEASON December–March.
GROWING CONDITIONS Grows in any site including shade.

Jasminum nudiflorum, winter jasmine (above), is unstoppable. It is not the most beautiful of plants, I grant you – with those floppy green stems and trifoliate leaves from April to October – but it looks much better if you grow it up through evergreen shrubs, support it with rustic trellis or team it with ivies, and its yellow flowers bring welcome cheer in winter. It also puts up with pretty dreadful soil, neglect and shade; about the only thing it won't tolerate is early morning sun, which defrosts the flowers too fast and burns the petals. Winter jasmine is the answer to the problem of what to grow on a north-facing wall; if you train it out neatly, it will reach 2.5 × 2.5m (8 × 8ft).

PEAK SEASON November–March.
GROWING CONDITIONS Any reasonable soil. It is best in shade, and avoid an east-facing site.

SOMETHING SPECIAL

Iris unguicularis, Algerian iris (above), flowers in milder spells from now into spring. You'll sometimes see the buds pushing up through snow, but if the weather forecast predicts a severe spell, it's worth going out to pick them as they'll last a lot better indoors in a vase. This plant leads an unusually Spartan lifestyle, making it a good choice for a difficult hot spot with very dry soil. Its slender evergreen leaves survive all year; don't be tempted to cut them off to 'tidy up', just remove the dead ones. It also dislikes being moved, and takes a couple of years to settle down into flowering mode, so only split the clumps when you really have to, and then do the job in spring. Space the divisions 30cm (1ft) apart.

PEAK SEASON January–March.
GROWING CONDITIONS Poor, dry soil at the foot of a sunny, south-facing wall.

Witch hazel never fails to excite any onlooker early in the year, with its citrus-scented, spidery flowers that are carried on the bare, leafless branches. About the best yellow is still the old favourite *Hamamelis × intermedia* 'Pallida', whose flowers are pale sulphur-yellow, but there are others, such as *Hamamelis × intermedia* 'Jelena', which is coppery orange, and *Hamamelis × intermedia* 'Diane' (above), which is rich red. Both are lovely but neither stands out quite so well in dull weather. In time, the shrubs will make a large shuttlecock 3 × 3m (10 × 10ft), but they are relatively slow-growing and can even be planted in containers. Rather neatly, the autumn colour of the leaves (which appear as the spiders fade) matches the colour of the flowers – red in the red varieties, butter-yellow with the yellows.

PEAK SEASON
    December–February.
GROWING CONDITIONS
    Reasonably rich soil, preferably not chalky, in sun or light shade.

OTHER PLANTS IN THEIR PRIME IN JANUARY

- **Trees** *Prunus × subhirtella* 'Autumnalis' (see p.267)
- **Shrubs** *Chimonanthus praecox* (see p.292), *Lonicera fragrantissima, Lonicera × purpusii* (see p.292), *Viburnum × bodnantense* (see p.268), *Viburnum farreri*
- **Evergreens** *Daphne bholua, Erica carnea* (see p.267), *Mahonia japonica, Rhododendron* 'Christmas Cheer' (see p.293), *Sarcococca hookeriana* var. *digyna* (see p.290), *Skimmia japonica* 'Rubella' (see p.270), *Viburnum rhytidophyllum* (see p.268)
- **Climbers/wall shrubs** *Clematis cirrhosa* 'Freckles' (see p.270)
- **Berries/fruits** *Cotoneaster, Ilex* (see p.290), *Gaultheria procumbens* (see p.270), *Malus × robusta* 'Red Sentinel' (see p.244), *Pernettya, Pyracantha* (see p.244), *Skimmia reevesiana, Stranvaesia japonica* subsp. *davidiana, Viburnum davidii* (see p.268)
- **Perennials** *Helleborus niger* (see p.290), *Iris foetidissima* (berries) (see p.267)
- **Bulbs** *Crocus tommasinianus* (see p.48), *Cyclamen coum* (see p.33), *Eranthis* (see p.32), *Galanthus* (see p.32), *Iris histrioides*
- **Bedding** Ornamental cabbages and kales (see p.269), winter-flowering pansies (see p.269)

JANUARY at-a-glance checklist

GENERAL GARDEN TASKS (p.15)
✔ Carry out repair jobs.
✔ Treat and repaint fences, sheds, greenhouses, canes, stakes and garden furniture.
✔ Clean, oil and sharpen the metal blades of garden tools; maintain mowers and other machinery.
✔ Deal with slippery paths: wash paving and grit paths in icy weather.
✔ Reorganize your storage space – make room for tools, barbecue accessories and gardening gear.
✔ Sort out the Christmas tree.
✔ Clear up around the garden.
✔ Prepare new beds and borders.
✔ Redesign parts of the garden that aren't up to par.

LAWNS (p.20)
✔ Keep off the grass or make a temporary path for walking on.

TREES, SHRUBS AND CLIMBERS (p.20)
✔ Brush snow off the greenhouse roof, also conifers, large evergreens and hedges to avoid splaying or breaking.
✔ Prune wisteria.
✔ Renewal-prune old shrubs, cut back overgrown deciduous hedges, prune out-of-control climbers, e.g. ivies, Virginia creeper, Boston ivy and climbing hydrangea.
✔ Move deciduous trees and shrubs (although ideally do this in November or early March).

FLOWERS (p.21)
✔ Order seed from mail order seed catalogues.
✔ Cut old leaves off Lenten hellebores.

PATIOS AND CONTAINERS (p.22)
✔ Check to see if containers need watering about once a week.
✔ Protect plants and containers from frost.
✔ Deadhead pansies.

VEGETABLES AND HERBS (p.22)
✔ Plan your veg patch.
✔ Cover soil with black polythene in mild locations in preparation for early sowings.

FRUIT (p.23)
✔ Prune standard apple and pear trees.
✔ Prepare planting hole for outdoor grapes and figs and prune vines and fig trees.
✔ Rejuvenate old overgrown soft fruit bushes.
✔ Protect fruit cages from snowfall.

UNDER COVER (p.25)
✔ Keep an eye on the greenhouse – brush off heavy snow, check the temperature regularly and adjust the heater thermostat, if necessary, to maintain frost-free conditions. Water plants sparingly.
✔ Wash pots and seed trays.
✔ Force rhubarb, chicory, strawberries.
✔ Chit first early seed potatoes for forcing in pots under glass for the very earliest new baby spuds.
✔ Harvest stored fruit and vegetables from the shed.
✔ Sow extra-early crops under glass if greenhouse is frost-free or heated, as well as seeds of houseplants, tuberous begonias, tender perennials and slow-germinating greenhouse exotics.

WATER GARDEN (p.28)
✔ Protect pond against icing over.
✔ Make a new pond (see project, p.29).

Watch out for
○ Snow damage.
○ The pond freezing over.

Get ahead
○ Chit first early seed potatoes for forcing in pots under glass for the very earliest new baby spuds.
○ Wash pots and seed trays and store in plastic carrier bags.
○ Prepare the soil for new beds and borders when it is diggable.

Last chance
○ Order seeds from catalogues to make sure you get the pick of the crop.

GENERAL GARDEN TASKS

WINTER DIGGING

If you haven't done your winter digging yet, and the soil is in workable condition, i.e. not too wet and not too frosty, you can do it now (see November, pp.271–3). If you garden on very wet ground you may have to wait until March or even April.

CARRY OUT REPAIR JOBS

Mending is a major job to get out of the way this month. Broken fence panels are best replaced, but if they only have a broken post or arris rail you can easily mend them using a metal bracket sold specially for the job in DIY shops. If your shed roof needs re-felting, pick a still day when it's not due to rain to get the job done – if you don't feel like doing it yourself, get someone in to do it for you. And at the risk of sounding obvious, do any repairs *before* painting or treating wood, or you'll only have to go over it again afterwards.

TREAT AND REPAINT TIMBER

Outdoor timber needs treating every year with a preservative, such as a combined wood stain and anti-rot product. Keep these products off plants, even when dormant. It goes without saying that dry weather is needed for any painting and wood-preserving job, and a still day is a must if you use a sprayer, otherwise the droplets go everywhere.

Sheds, greenhouses and fencing

You can paint on timber preservatives with a brush, and some brands can be applied using a roller, which is a time-saver for large, flat areas. If you have fiddly things such as woven hazel or willow panels to tackle, it's much quicker to use a sprayer; a lot of people simply leave them untreated, but then they don't last so long. If you re-treat every year you might get away with one initial coat that you top up the following year, but for best results apply two coats, as this will give a deeper, richer colour and will withstand the weather better.

Canes and stakes

While you've got the can of wood preserver out, you might like to give your garden canes and wooden plant stakes a coat. I know a lot of people don't bother but it's worth doing the ends that go into the ground, even if you leave the top, because it's the buried part that rots first, causing canes to break off – always as your prize delphinium is approaching its peak.

- Half fill a metal bucket or old tin can with wood preservative and stand the canes up in it overnight, so they soak up as much of the treatment as they can. Prop the tops up against a wall so they don't fall over.

Garden furniture

Wooden garden tables and seats can also be treated with coloured or natural wood preservative, but good-quality furniture warrants a more specialized product – the kind of thing you'd use on hardwood window frames. Your DIY shop will be able to advise. Pay particular attention to the base of the legs, as that's the first place rot will set in. When you have wooden furniture that's left permanently outdoors, it pays to stand the feet on bricks sunk into the ground, with a gravel base all round the seat itself so you aren't sitting with your feet in puddles.

Aluminium furniture
Cast aluminium garden tables and chairs also look a bit battered after several years out in the open, so remove any flaking paint with a stiff wire brush, and then paint them with a suitable outdoor-quality metal paint. Aerosol versions are easier to use on furniture that has convoluted patterns.

TIMBER PRESERVATIVES
Coloured wood preservatives are very fashionable. They are available in a huge range of shades including blue, terracotta and lavender – some brands have matching metal and/or all-surface paints so you can colour co-ordinate your fences and shed with plant containers, decking and trellis. Water-based timber preservatives are more environmentally friendly than those with an oil base, but they tend not to be as long lasting.

HOW TO SHARPEN TOOLS

Keeping a good edge on tools makes them much more effective at their job and makes gardening easier too. Blunt knives can let in infection, and blunt hoes are just plain hard work!

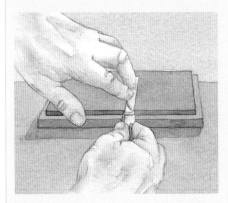

Knives

When I was an apprentice gardener, we used a carborundum stone to keep a good edge on our pocket knives. There's a knack to doing it right:

- For flat-bladed knives, place the sharpening stone flat on the bench and moisten it with a few drops of oil. Only one side of the knife should be sharpened – the other remains flat. Hold the knife at right angles to the stone so that the side of the blade to be sharpened rests on it with the cutting edge facing away from you. Raise the blade to an angle of 35 degrees and draw the blade towards you from the farthest end

of the stone. Do this repeatedly until the blade has a good edge.

- For curve-bladed knives, the stone will need to be on the edge of the bench. Start with the bottom of the cutting edge at the farthest end of the stone, drawing the edge of the knife along the edge of the stone so you end with the tip of the knife blade at the nearest end of the stone.

If you don't want the bother of sharpening garden knives, keep a pen-knife for odd jobs, and for cuttings use a craft knife with replaceable blades.

Secateurs

Sharpening secateurs sounds more complicated than sharpening knives, but it's the same principle. Some of the more expensive, professional-type brands can be taken apart for sharpening – you remove the cutting blade and sharpen it on a carborundum stone in the same way as a knife (see above). The blades usually have a flat surface and an angled surface. Place the angled edge parallel to the surface of your stone to sharpen it, and do the flat side the same as a knife blade. An occasional rub over with emery paper keeps them free of dried sap.

Hoes and spades

Rougher items, such as hoe and spade blades, can be sharpened with a metal file. Nowadays, you can buy special files that look more like the sort of thing you'd find in a

manicurist's parlour, made with tiny industrial diamonds, which are dead easy to use and produce a good, sharp edge in a lot less time than old-fashioned sharpening stones and traditional metal files. These come in various sizes to suit different jobs, so you don't have to dismantle your secateurs to sharpen them properly. Watch an expert demonstrating them on a garden-tool stand at a garden show – once you know how, it's so easy you'll wonder why you never found out before.

- Holding the tool blade firmly in a vice, oil the surface lightly, then rasp it gently using the file parallel to the angle of the blade. Do both sides of the blade and ensure you clean off any rough bits of metal sticking out afterwards.

Lawn mowers

On a rotary mower it's usually quite easy to take the blade out – it's just a case of undoing a nut (the makers often supply a suitable spanner with the machine). Once you've removed the blade, sharpen it with a metal file or the coarse blade of a diamond file in exactly the same way as when sharpening a hoe blade (above). Do both sides as before, and keep going until you've removed the worst of the burrs and chips, then put the blade back in the machine.

Safety warning: Make sure the lawn mower isn't plugged in when you take the blade out, and remove the spark plugs of a motor mower before dabbling with anything.

MAINTAIN GARDEN TOOLS AND EQUIPMENT

Garden tools should, in theory at least, be cleaned and put away properly each time you use them, but when you're busy there's never time. It's easier just to use them and shove them back. If this is the case, you'll need to give them a good going over once a year, ideally in winter.

Clean and lubricate tools

Regular cleaning and oiling will prolong the life of your tools.

- Wash tools down and scrub or scrape off hard-set soil.

- Wipe wooden shafts and handles over with a clean rag dipped in boiled linseed oil.

- Paint the metal blades with motor oil. We always used to use the old oil salvaged from the mower when we did its annual service, but it's a lot more convenient to use an aerosol oil these days – the sort used for 1001 odd lubricating and un-jamming jobs round the house. While the can is out, go round oiling all your locks, latches and hinges – on garden gates, the shed, and anything else you can think of.

Sharpen tools

One little job a lot of people forget about is sharpening garden tools. A good edge is essential if you're going to get a clean cut from pocket knives and secateurs, but it also makes all the difference to shears, hoes and mower blade (see box opposite).

Lawn mower care

Most modern mowers don't need to be sent away for routine servicing, but that's not to say they don't need a little regular attention, and winter is a good time to do it. First, find the manual (this is always worth keeping in a safe place along with other instruction books) and just do what it says. The details will vary for each different model, but as a general rule you'll need to do the following:

● Clean off dried or decomposing grass, which sets solid in hard-to-reach places.

● Clean or replace the spongy air filters.

● Change the oil and spark plugs if it's a motor mower.

● Sharpen the blades. When you actually take the time to look at them, you often find after a year's use they are so bashed and chipped it's amazing they ever cut anything at all. You can usually sharpen them yourself (see box opposite).

● Replace really badly battered blades. Parts for all the popular models are available in large garden centres, DIY shops and most other places that sell garden machinery. If you have no luck, refer to the service book, which may list stockists, or call the manufacturer's customer service department, who should have the information or may even supply the parts direct.

REORGANIZE YOUR STORAGE SPACE

Storage space – or lack of it – can be a right pain in summer, when there's no time to do anything about it, so the winter break is a good time to put up some tool racks on your shed or

garage wall so you can hang up your gardening tools. You don't need anything fancy – a small piece of wood, 5 × 2.5cm (2 × 1in), screwed to the wall with some hooks or nails to hang your fork and spade handles from does the job. If you want something more professional-looking, DIY shops stock ready-made tool racks that only need putting up.

HAVE A CLEAR UP

Take advantage of fine weather and spare time to do any clearing up around the shed, garage and garden so that things are shipshape by the time the serious gardening season starts again. Organize compost bins or heaps, tidy up debris that might house snails and other pests, and clear out junk underneath greenhouse staging or ivy and other weeds invading the bottoms of hedges.

PREPARE NEW BEDS AND BORDERS

If your soil is in workable condition, you can get ahead now and prepare new beds and borders.

Faded perennials that are no longer attractive or useful to birds can be cut down.

Winter is the ideal time to sharpen the blades on your mower.

- Strip turf or clear existing plants, builder's rubble or other debris, then dig the ground incorporating as much organic matter as you can. Leave it rough for the rest of the winter.

- Since old grassland is notorious for harbouring wireworms and other soil pests, fork it over several times if possible so that birds can feed on them. This is especially advisable if you are making a new vegetable garden or a bed for bedding plants, both of which are very prone to root pests.

DEAL WITH SLIPPERY PATHS

Slippery paths and paving are a seasonal hazard, and with the seriously cold season in sight, now is the time to do something about it. Real York stone paving is the worst offender – yes, I know it looks lovely, but when it's wet it's like walking on ice. Stately homes normally put up poles and strings to keep visitors right out of the danger zone in wet conditions, and that's frankly the safest option. Modern reconstituted stone slabs have a slight texture that gives your

shoes something to grip on to, but even those can be tricky to negotiate when they have a coating of green slime.

- You can spray hard paths with winter tar oil wash, of the sort used for fruit trees, to deter slimy algae, moss and liverworts from growing, but it's messy old stuff. Nowadays, it's cleaner, greener – and it has to be said, more fun – to keep paths and paving clean with an occasional going-over with a pressure washer, which blasts all the nooks and crannies clean and removes organic debris that nourishes the slimy stuff.

- Keep a bag of gritty sand on standby in the shed so that it's ready to sprinkle generously over an icy path without your having to make a special trip out. Don't use salt, which is what people think of first because it's what councils use on the road. It costs more, and it doesn't do your plants any good when the thaw comes, and the salt runs into nearby flowerbeds and on to the lawn. It's also disastrous if salt gets into your pond.

- The first fall of snow usually sees everyone rushing to clear the front path but it is often better left alone. While it's soft and fluffy, it's not especially slippery. If a snow fall looks like it's going to last a long time it's worth clearing your regular route to the front door, as a well-trodden path turns hard and icy.

WRAP INSULATION AROUND TAPS

January is often the coldest month so if you've not already insulated outdoor taps, do so now (see November, p.274).

AFTER-CHRISTMAS TREE CARE

If you had a real live Christmas tree, stand it outside in its pot in a sheltered part of the garden to keep growing so it can be used again next year. If you had the sort without roots, let it dry out thoroughly, then remove the branches to use in a wood-burning stove, or save them to use as twiggy supports for herbaceous plants in spring. If you have no use for the tree, take it to a council recycling centre for shredding.

RE-DESIGN PART OF THE GARDEN

Garden design is an on-going process. Oh I know, when you first move to a new house you are desperate to 'do the garden', but after that first flush of creativity things grow at different rates, some beds become overcrowded, or you just look at an area and think 'could do better'. We all feel like that sometimes, and that's when a part of the garden is ready for refreshing. Winter is the time to work out what you want, and to do any construction and preparation so that it's ready for planting in spring. Even if it's only a small area or a single bed, it pays to start with a plan.

- Take some squared graph paper and draw a plan of the patch, to scale. On your plan, indicate north and south so you can see which parts are in sun and which will be shady. Show anything in the surrounding area that has a bearing on the border, such as tall fences or large overhanging trees, and mark in anything that's already there that you want to keep.

- Choose a theme for your border, as it helps everything to 'hang together' better. Decide on the effect you wish to create and fill it with the appropriate plants:

  For a border filled with summer flowers, major on annuals and perennials in an island bed.

  Do you want something all the year round? If so, have a mixed border with some spring bulbs, shrubs, a few perennials and a good backing of evergreens; choose your mixture so there's something different coming to the fore every month.

  If you want an easy-to-care-for, family-friendly border, major on reliable and resilient shrubs such as ribes, forsythia, spiraea and philadelphus with plenty of weed-smothering ground cover.

  To attract butterflies and bees, go for sedums, buddleia, and lots of old-fashioned hardy annuals, herbs and lavender.

  If you wish to encourage birds, go heavy on the fruit and berries, with lots of twiggy trees and dense shrubs or, best of all, a mixed country hedge to provide them with bed and board.

- Push a few ideas around on paper, and do your homework – this is where the plant pages in this book will help. Study photos to see which plants look good together, and check out vital statistics to find out how big they will grow, what conditions they need, when they flower, and if they have other attractions at different times of year so you can start to visualize how the new bed will look through the seasons. If you want a year-round feature, try to include a few plants that are at their best each month of the year – full lists are included at the start of each chapter, especially to help anyone doing garden planning. Take your time – it's one thing you have plenty of in winter.

LAWNS

KEEP OFF THE LAWN

'Keep off' is my lawn-care tip of the month. If you don't – especially if you have some serious barrowing to do, or you have to walk the same route to the shed all the time – you'll simply wear the grass out and leave what look like sheep tracks all over it.

MAKE A PATH

If you simply can't avoid using the lawn, then unroll a temporary path of heavy-duty wire mesh or interconnected wooden slats where you need to walk, so you don't wreck the surface. But really, you'd be far better off putting in a solid path or stepping stones leading anywhere you need to go all the time (see September Project, p.239).

TREAT SLIMY, MUDDY LAWNS

If you garden on heavy clay soil, sprinkle gritty horticultural sand on any areas where the lawn is soft and gooey and your feet sink in, particularly where patches of green slime (which is a form of algae) or the overlapping green platelets of liverwort are appearing. They make the lawn slippery and kill off the grass by covering it so it can't see the light, and when you tread them indoors they wreck your carpets.

   If you have a lawn like this, make a note to treat it to some intensive care in spring and autumn, when the ground is in a more workable state. The key things to do are to spike and top-dress with gritty sand (see September, pp.224 and 225–7); you will also need to feed the lawn, but not until April (see p.88). You only need to do this for a couple of years to see a big improvement – the lawn stays firmer and flatter, and as surface drainage improves, mud and green slime disappear.

Wisteria needs pruning twice a year – in mid-summer and winter. Trim the whole plant in winter, cutting back sideshoots to about 8–10cm (3–4in), leaving two or three buds. Tie in any long stems that are needed to extend the plant's territory.

TREES, SHRUBS AND CLIMBERS

PROTECT AGAINST SNOW

When it snows hard, large evergreens, conifers, and even hedges can sometimes be so weighed down that the top branches splay out and never spring back afterwards. Use an old broom to knock the snow off before it thaws, as thawing snow becomes doubly heavy. If it's too late, support splayed-out branches using very thick fencing wire to suspend them from the trunk. Thread the wire through a 45cm (18in) length cut from a plastic garden hosepipe to cushion the branch where the wire loops around it.

PRUNE WISTERIA

Even if you did the right thing and pruned your wisteria thoroughly in midsummer (see July, p.185) it will have spent the rest of the season squirting new growth out in all directions, so it'll probably need a second dose now.

● Go over the whole plant systematically, cutting back all the sideshoots to finger-length. Easier said than done, I know, and it will take hours. Choose a fine day, fix your ladder safely, dress warmly, and get stuck in. You'll feel tremendously virtuous when you've finished.

MOVE DECIDUOUS TREES AND SHRUBS

You can move deciduous shrubs at any time throughout the dormant season (see November, p.276). However, the very best times are shortly after leaf fall and just before the start of the spring growing season (early March).

PLANTING OR HEELING IN TREES AND SHRUBS

You can plant bare-root trees and shrubs now if conditions allow (see November, p.276). However, if the ground is frozen or too wet to plant them properly, heel them in for now. Heeling in doesn't just mean bunging the roots into a hole in the ground – it needs to be done properly (see box opposite). Woody plants will 'keep' like this until early March if necessary, provided the right steps have been taken.

SORTING OUT AN OVERGROWN GARDEN

If you've inherited a garden full of overgrown plants, or things have just got out of control, the depth of the dormant season is the time to cut them back. January is the time to renewal-prune shrubs, cut back overgrown deciduous hedges, and prune out-of-control climbers such as ivies, Virginia creeper, Boston ivy and climbing hydrangea. These climbers don't need regular pruning, but when they spread too far or start hanging down off walls it's time to cut them back and thin them out.

How to renewal-prune a shrub

The obvious temptation when faced with an overgrown shrub is to charge in with the secateurs and give them the haircut of a lifetime to try and clear some space, but that really doesn't work. When you chop a big old shrub down hard, all that happens is it sends out masses of long, straight, sappy shoots that won't flower for years. Growth always follows the knife, and rampant growth follows butchery. The trick is to take the job in easy stages, and aim to remove a few of the oldest and grottiest branches every winter, so that the plant slowly replaces itself with a new one over several years. Then it never looks butchered and you won't miss out on flowering. Clever stuff.

- Choose two or three of the oldest branches and cut them out as close to the base of the shrub as you can. The oldest branches will be those that are the thickest, with the darkest bark, and which look the most gnarled and arthritic. If you can remember what they looked like in summer, they'll also have been the ones with the fewest flowers and the smallest, sickest-looking leaves. Get them out, and the shrub will look much better.

- Leave the other branches for now. Over the next year, the shrub will hopefully send out some nice new shoots, full of vigour, then this time next year you can remove a few more of the oldest branches entirely. In 3 or 4 years' time you'll have replaced the whole plant with strong, healthy, flowering young growth. To help things along, feed and mulch shrubs undergoing rejuvenation generously each spring (see April, p.91).

How to prune an ornamental vine

If you're going to prune a vine, it needs doing early in the month while it's safely dormant – at any other time of year vines 'bleed' badly. There's no need to be too fussy about it, simply reduce long leaders and thin out unwanted stems so the plant covers the area where you want it without looking messy.

FLOWERS

This is a good time to order seeds of hardy annuals like eschscholzia (orange) and nigella (blue).

ORDER SEED FROM CATALOGUES

Garden centres stock popular flower seeds, but for a wider choice of new, traditional and unusual varieties read the seed catalogues sent out by specialist firms. Look for copies in gardening magazines or simply respond to their adverts.

CUT OLD LEAVES OFF HELLEBORES

Lenten hellebores (*Helleborus orientalis* and *Helleborus* × *hybridus* varieties) will be starting to push up their flower stems. Cut off old leaves at ground level so they can be more easily seen.

HOW TO HEEL IN TREES AND SHRUBS

1 Unwrap the plants from their packaging and remove any strings securing branches. Pile up some soil into a wedge shape, roughly 30cm (12in) high and 60cm (24in) long, sloping down into a trench large enough to take the plant's roots.

2 Lay the plants down with their roots in the trench and the trunks or stems laying on the soil 'wedge' so that they are supported. Cover the roots with a good layer of well-drained soil, so they are protected from extreme cold and can't dry out.

In winter, keep containers close to house walls for warmth. If frost is likely, wrap the pots in bubble wrap or horticultural fleece. Alternatively, bring them under cover.

Below: After a frosty spell, remove dead pansy flowers and stems and the plants should flower again.

Right: Black polythene warms up the soil for early vegetables, and suppresses weeds as well.

PATIO AND CONTAINERS

WATER OCCASIONALLY

It's easy to think, just because it's winter, that there's no need to bother about containers. Oh, I know they don't need the daily attention they do in summer, but they may still need watering occasionally because the walls of your house keep a lot of the rain off – it's the umbrella effect. Check them about once a week, and water them when they need it. Don't be tempted to feed anything at this time of year, even if the weather is fine and sunny, as there's worse to come – the last thing you want is to encourage lots of weak, soft growth that'll just get clobbered by frosts.

PROTECT AGAINST FROST

Even the hardiest plants drop stone dead when all the water in their compost turns to ice for a few days. It's not the cold that does the damage, it's the lack of liquid water – plants can't 'drink' ice. It is well worth taking a few precautions:

- Keep containers close to walls in winter, as a solid chunk of brickwork provides shelter and acts in a small way as a storage radiator.

- If a sharp spell of cold, frosty weather is forecast, shift your containers under cover, or truss the plants up in horticultural fleece and the containers in bubble wrap, before the lot freezes solid.

DEADHEAD PANSIES

If there's a long, cold spell even the best winter-flowering pansies may 'shut down' temporarily. If that happens, after the worst of the cold spell is over snip off the dead heads and trim back any stems that have died back. They should soon recover and be back in business as usual.

PATIO PRECAUTIONS

Patios can be very slippery in winter, so if you're going to walk on the paving you'll need to clean and grit it when necessary to prevent accidents (see General Garden Tasks, p.15).

VEGETABLES AND HERBS

PLAN YOUR VEGETABLE PATCH

Plan out your vegetable garden on paper before working out what seed you want to order from the catalogues, so you don't over-order or end up with too much of the same things. Depending on what your family likes to eat, try to include some examples from each of the main crop groups – roots, brassicas, legumes (peas and beans) and leafy salads. The idea is to plant each in a patch of its own and rotate them each year. This is the best way to ensure you don't grow the same thing in the same bit of ground more than one year in four, which means you avoid lots of root pests and diseases, and can avoid putting root crops into newly manured ground, which sometimes makes them 'fork'.

PREPARE FOR EARLY SOWINGS

If you've already done your winter digging (see November, p.272), and your garden is in a mild location with well-drained soil, you can cover the soil with black polythene to warm it up ready for sowing early vegetables and salads in spring.

FRUIT

PRUNE STANDARD APPLE AND PEAR TREES

Just when you thought there wasn't much to do down the garden, suddenly it's pruning time for standard apple and pear trees, by which I mean the traditional tree-shaped sort rather than fancy forms such as cordons and espaliers. Now is the time to prune if you are going to at all, as they are completely dormant.

You don't absolutely *have* to prune standard apples and pear trees. However, the aim of pruning is to thin the tree out, which lets more light in and reduces the amount of fruit it carries. The result is bigger, better-quality fruit that develops more flavour and colour. An unpruned apple or pear tree may bear more fruit, but it may remain small, greenish and sharper tasting because of the delayed ripening.

- When you first buy a young fruit tree from a nursery or garden centre, the basic shape will already have been formed. If you select a good example – one with four or five strong, evenly spaced branches growing out all around the top of the trunk – it is unlikely to need any pruning for the first few years. Thereafter, cut out any shoots that cross over each other or rub together in windy weather, any that are dead, diseased or dying, and any that point back into the middle of the tree instead of outwards (see box below).

- If an older tree develops cankers (large, thick, warty-looking lumps), you can cut out the cankered parts of the branches tidily – it doesn't make all that much difference, it's just good housekeeping. With a really old tree, a lot of cankers are to be expected, so forget about them and regard them as part of the character.

GROW OUTDOOR GRAPES AND FIGS

Now that so many people are making Mediterranean-style gardens, there are a lot more grapevines and fig trees being grown. The foliage is extremely handsome, but if you want fruit, grapes and figs are best grown against a south-facing wall with their roots slightly restricted.

Prepare for planting

If you're thinking of planting outdoor grapes and figs, now is the time to prepare the spot and order the plants for planting in March or April (see April, p.105).

- Dig a large planting pocket, about 1m (3ft) square, and line it with bricks. This acts as an underground 'container' that keeps the plants compact so they produce more fruit and less green, leafy growth. Fill it with good-quality topsoil enriched with plenty of compost.

Pruning

When you're growing grapes and figs for fun, I wouldn't attempt to go in for complicated pruning in the way that a professional fruit-grower would, since you want them to look good on your wall as well as producing a crop. In the garden, they are dual-purpose rather than seriously productive. But you do need to do *some* pruning (see box below), otherwise they'll try and take over, and you won't have much to eat at all.

HOW TO PRUNE A STANDARD TREE

When you prune a standard fruit tree, don't snip around taking off lots of little bits and pieces, there's really no point. A few good-sized branches make a much better job of it. Use sharp secateurs for shoots up to 1cm (¹/₂in) thick, loppers for branches up to 2.5cm (1in) thick, and a pruning saw for anything thicker. A well-pruned standard should resemble the shape of a wine glass, with the branches forming a hollow-centred cup shape and the trunk forming the stem of the glass.

- When cutting off a shoot, take it right back to the point where it grows out of a thicker branch and cut if off very nearly flush, so there's no 'snag' to die off and act as a breeding ground for disease.

- If you want to remove a really large branch, cut it off roughly 45cm (18in) from its base first to reduce the weight, and then make a second cut to remove the remaining stump cleanly. Saw it off just beyond the swollen 'collar' that you'll see around the base of the branch, as that way the bark will soon grow over and heal the wound naturally. Pruning paint is 'out' in tree circles these days. Nature is the best healer.

HOW TO PRUNE OUTDOOR GRAPES

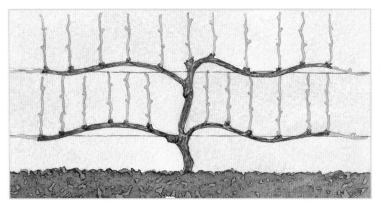

1 Cut off the ends of the 'framework' stems to stop them growing longer than you want.

2 Cut off all the sideshoots that grow out of the framework, pruning them back to a couple of buds from the main stems.

Pruning outdoor grapes

Think of a grapevine as a plant in two parts – a permanent framework of thick, old woody stems, and the thin green 'annual' stems, which carry the leaves and bunches of grapes and are cut out and replaced every year. After planting a new vine, you need to tie it in (see April, p.105). Once the framework is in place, all you do is to prune the vine each winter.

Pruning outdoor figs

When planting the fig in spring (see April, p.105), train the main branches out flat against the wall to create a rough fan shape, like the spokes of half a wagon wheel. Thereafter, prune each winter, but don't be too fussy about it, and don't worry about making a mistake – the great thing about fast-growing plants like these is that missing bits soon grow back.

- In the first few years, start by tying the main stems up to the wall and then cut out any shoots that grow straight out from them.

- As the fan becomes older and starts to look cluttered, thin out some of the stems so they are nicely spaced. You can also cut out any long, old stems to a convenient height.

REJUVENATE OLD OVERGROWN SOFT FRUIT BUSHES

Follow the same technique as for rejuvenating geriatric shrubs (see Trees, Shrubs and Climbers, p.20); the idea is to take out one or two of the oldest (i.e. the thickest, craggiest and inevitably least productive) branches every year, as close to the base of the plant as possible, to encourage vigorous new shoots to take over. For exactly the same reason as with shrubs, don't be tempted to chop the whole plant back down low or you'll only encourage masses of vigorous, soft, sappy shoots that won't flower or fruit for years.

PROTECT FRUIT CAGES FROM SNOWFALL

If a heavy snowfall settles on top of your fruit cage, remove the worst of it with a broom so the weight doesn't break or bend the uprights holding the netting in place. A lot of people living in areas with regular heavy snowfalls will remove the netting from the roof every autumn and replace it in spring, to avoid snow damage.

HEEL IN FRUIT TREES AND BUSHES

If bare-root fruit trees and bushes are delivered now, heel them as for trees and shrubs (see Trees, Shrubs and Climbers, p.20) and plant in early March (see p.72).

WHAT NOT TO PRUNE

Espalier- and cordon-trained apples and pears
Don't prune espalier- and cordon-trained apples and pears now; they are to be pruned in summer, which is the best time to encourage the development of fruiting 'spurs' (see August, p.214).

Stone fruit
Don't prune stone fruit (cherries, plums, peaches or nectarines) or flowering cherries and plums now. If you prune them at all, do it lightly between April and June (see p.106), when the sap is flowing freely, as this bleeding prevents the organism responsible for silver leaf disease entering the sap-stream. If that happens you've only a few years before the disease kills the tree. Don't risk it.

UNDER COVER

PROTECT STRUCTURES FROM SNOW

A light covering of snow won't do your shed or greenhouse any harm, and in fact can make useful insulation, but if it's more than 5cm (2in) or so, play safe and brush it off to reduce the weight.

CHECK THE GREENHOUSE

Continue watering greenhouse plants as sparingly as possible (see October, p.259) and pick them over regularly to remove dead leaves, fallen petals, etc. before fungal disease can take hold. With a heated greenhouse, check your max./min. thermometer regularly to make sure the heater is maintaining the right temperature, and ventilate for a few hours on fine days.

WASH POTS AND SEED TRAYS

Regular cleaning of pots and seed trays keeps pests and diseases at bay.

- Use an old washing-up brush and a bucket of warm soapy water to clean off old compost residues and other dirt, then rinse in clean water with a dash of garden disinfectant (organic versions based on citrus extracts are available). Dry then put them away.

SOW SWEET PEAS

If you want early flowers but didn't get around to sowing in autumn, you can put some seeds in now – but most people prefer to wait until March (see pp.62–3), when the conditions are better and there's less chance of seeds rotting or young plants being affected by fungal disease.

SOW IN A HEATED PROPAGATOR

If you have space in a heated propagator, now's a good time to sow seeds of houseplants, tuberous begonias and slow-germinating greenhouse exotics, such as bird of paradise flower (*Strelitzia reginae*). It's also worth sowing slow-growing tender perennials such as geraniums now, so they start flowering in time for the start of the summer. And although it's not commonly done, if you want to grow hardy perennial flowers from seed, sowing them now, in the warmth of a heated propagator, means you should get a few flowers from them this season, since plants will be well ahead of those sown outdoors in summer.

CROPS UNDER GLASS

Greengrocers aren't the only source of out-of-season fruit and veg. There are some you can bring on early at home. It's fun to do, when you have the raw materials, and makes you feel useful when you can't grow anything much in

Scrub and disinfect pots and seed trays – good hygiene is vital.

Storing pots and seed trays
To keep disinfected pots and seed trays clean until you're ready to use them, pack them into plastic carrier bags, knot the top, and hang them from a nail in the shed.

HOW TO FORCE RHUBARB

1 Dig up a root of rhubarb that's been growing in the garden for a couple of years or more – new plants don't have enough oomph.

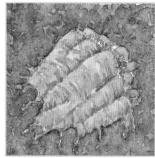

2 Leave the root out in the open for 2–3 weeks for the frost to act on, then pop it into a pot that's just big enough to hold it. Tuck potting compost or soil around the roots.

3 Stand the pot in a warm, dark place such as an airing cupboard. Water just enough to stop the soil drying out but no more.

4 About 6 weeks later, the tender young sticks of forced rhubarb should be ready for pulling. Keep pulling until the plants look like pegging out.

HOW TO GROW STRAWBERRIES

1 Stand young strawberry plants outside in the open for 4–6 weeks in January – they need a cold spell before they're forced. Move them under glass in February. Water sparingly at first, but step it up as they grow more strongly and you can see new growth.

2 When the first flowers appear in April/May, start liquid feeding with quarter-strength liquid tomato feed once a fortnight. Hand-pollinate the flowers by dabbing a soft watercolour brush into the centre of each one every day, transferring the pollen from one flower to another.

Forcing rhubarb and chicory

When forcing rhubarb or chicory, second-hand potting compost or garden soil is fine for the job. The pot should be kept in a warm, dark place. An airing cupboard is ideal (provided it is not heated to tropical temperatures above 24°C/75°F), or a cupboard under the stairs. You could put the plants in the greenhouse, but they grow considerably faster in warmer conditions. If plants aren't in a place that is naturally dark, cover them with an upturned bucket or thick black bin liner.

the vegetable patch outside. Plus you score double brownie points when friends come to dinner; the warm glow makes you feel positively flush.

Forcing rhubarb

The long, thin, ultra-tender pink early rhubarb stems that you buy from the greengrocer come from special varieties grown in 'forcing houses', which are kept warm and dark like mushroom sheds, but you can do a pretty good job yourself at home (see box, left). Plants you've once used for forcing aren't much cop afterwards; if you re-plant them in the garden they'll recover after a year or so but I wouldn't force them again for a few years. (For planting rhubarb outdoors, see March, p.71.)

Forcing chicory

Chicory is fast becoming a must-have salad leaf, and it's easy to force for winter use. Forcing sounds like a lot of effort, but there's nothing to it, and the sense of satisfaction to be had out of doing something that gives such a big return from such a small area, and so out of season, is quite something. Plant a new pot of chicory roots every 2 weeks, and you'll have a

continuous supply of chicons through the rest of winter starting in about 6 weeks' time.

Serious veg fanciers will grow forcing varieties of chicory especially for the job (see box below). These are sown in May or June (see May, p.136) and left until autumn, when the roots are dug up and stored in the shed until you want to force them. If you grew raddichio or other salad-leaf varieties that didn't form a heart in autumn, and if the roots are still in the ground, you can use those. Either way, dig them out now.

- Twist off what's left of the leafy tops of the chicory plants.

- Put about 6 of the large, bare roots into a pot, the right way up. Pack them with enough moist soil or potting compost to bury them up to their necks.

- Stand the pot in a warm, dark place at room temperature. Check every few days – water very lightly if the compost seems dry, and evict any slugs and snails.

- After 4–6 weeks, when the chicons are about 8–12cm (3–5in) tall and torpedo-shaped, cut them off at soil level with a sharp knife. Make sure you cut your chicons early enough. If you leave them too long they 'explode' into a load of loose leaves that aren't half so nice to eat.

Growing strawberries

Bought strawberries are quite tasteless compared to the home-grown sort, so if you fancy fruit that's ready to eat in June, around Wimbledon Fortnight, start with pot-grown plants now (see box above). You'll be lucky to find strawberry plants at the garden centre this early, so unless you planned ahead and bought some last autumn, it's a case of using your own home-grown runners that you rooted into individual pots last summer.

Growing extra early potatoes

Of all vegetables, the ones I look forward to most are the very first baby new potatoes, and

do part of their growing in the warm so they get off to a much faster start and are streets ahead of seed potatoes planted outside when dormant. It takes a few weeks for them to grow sprouts, so they aren't ready to pot up until next month (see February, p.44).

CHECK STORED CROPS

Use stored fruit and veg from the shed, and check remaining stored crops regularly for signs of rotting – remove any that are infected before it spreads to all the rest.

SOW EXTRA-EARLY CROPS UNDER GLASS

If you want very early crops and have a well-prepared but vacant soil border in a frost-free greenhouse, it's worth making use of the space by sowing a few fast-growing crops, such as lettuce, radishes, early carrots and spinach. If you have a heated house or one with a heated propagator you can sow early varieties of summer cabbage, cauliflowers, peas, broad beans, and sow seed of maincrop onions, so you have strong healthy plants ready to put outside in March. If you don't have any background heat there's no point starting sowing anything so soon as the seeds will just sit there without germinating; wait until next month when it's warmer (see February, p.40).

Left: If you want to start off early potatoes now, they will need chitting. This encourages them to sprout so that, once planted out, they will grow faster.

the earliest of the lot are the ones I grow in pots in the greenhouse. You'll find seed potatoes turning up in garden centres some time this month, and though there's no great rush to buy them for planting out in the garden – which you can't do until late March (see pp. 68–9) or April (see p.100) – now is the time to buy the extra-early varieties for starting off under glass. Good kinds for forcing include 'Rocket', 'Swift' and 'Sharpe's Express'. If you have the choice, choose seed potatoes that are about the size of a bantam's egg.

When starting off any early potatoes at this time of year, it's essential to 'chit' them, which just means encouraging them to sprout before you plant them (see box below). That way, they

---

HOW TO CHIT POTATOES

1 In a clean seed tray lined with newspaper, or in a compartment of an egg box, place seed potatoes up on end with the tiny buds facing upwards.

2 Stand the box in a warm, dry place in the house, ideally where the spuds will receive a reasonable amount of light.

3 When the shoots are 2.5–4cm (1–1¹/₂in) long, the potato tubers are chitted. Planting won't take place until next month (see p.44) as it takes the shoots time to develop.

WATER GARDEN

MAKE A POND
Winter is the ideal time to do any construction jobs while you aren't tied up with routine chores or seasonal 'rushes', such as the spring planting bonanza. January is the ideal time to create a water feature.

PROTECT AGAINST ICE
Watch out for your pond in the cold weather. If the surface freezes right over and doesn't thaw enough to expose a small patch of open water within 24 hours, it's essential to make a hole in the ice. Even in winter, fish, hibernating frogs and other pond-life including micro-organisms and water plants will still be ticking over, so you need to let in some oxygen and let out waste gases (created by decomposition of organic matter and respiration). Whatever you do, don't crack the ice with a hammer as the underwater shock waves aren't good for your fish.

- Some people like to float a rubber ball or a piece of polystyrene on the water (see December, p.300). This can be lifted out leaving open water, but in a severely cold spell it'll soon freeze over again.

- Another method is to stand a saucepan of hot water on the ice until it melts its way through to open water. In a long cold spell, you might need to do that daily.

A frozen pond is a beautiful sight, but if it freezes solid you will need to make a hole in the ice so that pond-life can survive.

PROJECT Make a pond

Choose an open sunny site, which should ideally be on the level – otherwise you'll need to level it, to avoid all the water ending up at one end.

The big advantage of building a pond at this time of year, besides staggering your workload, is that you can leave it to mature for several months before introducing plants – this gives the water time to develop a natural micro-flora and fauna, and for chemicals from tap water to disperse. Water plants are not usually available until late spring, so don't worry about planting a new pond until then, and give them at least 6 weeks to settle down before introducing fish.

1 Clear the area and mark out the shape of the pond with spray paint or dry sand, remembering to include sloping beaches, planting shelves and deep areas.

2 Dig out the shape of the pond. Remove the soil, unless you plan on mounding it up to make a rockery or wildflower bank. Check the edges of the pond are level, using a spirit level laid over a long plank.

3 Remove sharp stones or roots sticking out of the pond surface and place a layer of pond underlay over the floor and sides of the excavated area.

HOW DEEP SHOULD THE POND BE?

The deepest areas of the pond, which are in the middle, should be at least 60cm (2ft) deep. This central area is for deep-water plants, and is also a retreat for fish; it needs to be about 15 per cent of the total area of the pond. Planting pockets around the edge, for standing baskets of waterside plants on, should be 22cm (9in) deep, and the average depth of the rest of the pond should be approximately 45cm (18in). 'Beaches' for pebbles should slope gently down to the floor of the pond and include a ridge to retain the pebbles, so they don't just run away into the middle. Leave flat surfaces firm and level, and make slopes and horizontal surfaces sharply defined, not vague.

4 Lower your butyl rubber pond liner loosely into place. Run water from the hose into the bottom – this makes the liner 'cling' closely to the soil, which acts like a mould. Tweak the liner slightly so that folds fall evenly around corners and curves.

5 When the water reaches the top, and the liner has sunk as far into the hollow pond shape as possible, trim off excess butyl from around the edge, leaving a fringe 30cm (12in) wide all round for 'finishing off'.

6 Cover the exposed area with paving, decking or turf. Don't just leave a visible ring of black rubber showing – and don't rely on waterside plants to hide it because they aren't there all year round.

What you need

Spray paint or dry sand

Pond underlay

Butyl rubber pond liner

Hose

Paving, decking or turf

HOW MUCH POND LINER?
When working out how much pond liner to buy, to be on the safe side measure the length and breadth of the pond, then add twice the maximum depth to each measurement.

FEBRUARY

February brings the thaw, or that's the rumour, anyway. Either way, it's nearly always wet, but the first signs of spring are starting to appear if you don't mind going out to look for them. The effect this month is subtle rather than startling, with the first bulbs, catkins and early flowers making a cautious debut.

February finds gardeners desperately looking for some real gardening to do. Once spring arrives, everything will need doing at once, so make the most of your last chance to finish winter work and push ahead with anything you can. But do leave time to watch spring creeping slowly over the garden.

THE BIG PICTURE the first signs of spring

OLD FAITHFULS

Galanthus nivalis, snowdrops, are just about the first popular spring bulbs to open, but they have a dead heat with the not-so-well-known winter aconites, *Eranthis hyemalis*, which look like large yellow buttercups wearing green frilly collars. The two are roughly the same size (10 × 5cm/4 × 2in). They look very good growing together and enjoy the same growing conditions. Both do well under deciduous trees or shrubs in a border or in light woodland, but there's no reason why you shouldn't naturalize them anywhere in the garden where conditions are not too extreme. There are many good varieties of snowdrop. Look out for *Galanthus* 'S. Arnott' and also *G. nivalis* 'Viridapice' (above), which has green tips to the flowers.

PEAK SEASON February.
GROWING CONDITIONS Moist, fertile soil with organic matter, in light shade.

Primula vulgaris, primroses (above), are some of the earliest wildflowers to open in the countryside, and if you have a grassy bank in light shade then they look lovely naturalized in a wild garden at home. The cultivated kind that you will be offered as spring bedding grow 15 × 15cm (6 × 6in), and come in a huge range of colours – bold reds, blues, pinks and tangerine shades as well as a bright golden yellow. Those sold as pot plants in greengrocers and supermarkets, usually with larger flowers, are nowhere near as tough as their wild cousins. If you buy these in flower now, use them as spring pot plants for your porch, conservatory or cold greenhouse. In another month's time, when conditions are kinder, it'll be okay to plant them out in containers and gaps around the garden. If in doubt, check with your local garden centre or nursery.

PEAK SEASON February–March.
GROWING CONDITIONS Fertile soil in a sheltered site. Happy in dappled shade.

Corylus avellana 'Contorta', corkscrew hazel or Harry Lauder's walking stick (above), is a good indicator of the state of the season. In winter, its main claim to fame is as a horticultural contortionist, with its extravagantly convoluted stems, which only show up properly after leaf fall in November or December. The twirly look lasts all winter, then, late this month or early next, depending on the weather, the plant breaks out into fluffy yellow catkins that tremble in the breeze before the leaves reappear; very jolly. Corkscrew hazel grows slowly to start with, but by the time it's 2.5 × 2m (8 × 6ft) you'll probably feel like pruning it to stop the spread, so take out whole branches over the winter. Use them to make short, curly supports for perennials or tall, rustic tripods for climbers to grow up – sticks like these are too good to waste.

PEAK SEASON February–March.
GROWING CONDITIONS Anywhere, even wet or clay soil and windy areas.

Garrya elliptica is a large evergreen shrub that, at 3 × 2m (10 × 6ft), almost counts as a tree. In a cold area it is often trained flat against a wall for protection. It's not the most exciting plant for much of the year, but for the next 8–10 weeks it will be dripping with long grey-green catkins that aren't phased by wintry weather. *Garrya elliptica* 'James Roof' (above) is especially outstanding, with catkins often reaching 30cm (12in) or more long. It's the sort of shrub you ache to plant a clematis through to perk it up outside its peak season. If you give in to the urge, go for one of the texensis or viticella types – these can be cut down to the ground in winter, enabling the garrya to bloom without the distraction of faded clematis stems.

PEAK SEASON February–March.
GROWING CONDITIONS Any reasonable soil in a sheltered situation in sun or partial shade, including north-facing.

Bergenia is what we used to call elephant's ears, which describes the shape of the leathery leaves to a T, although they are actually more the size of a Great Dane's. You can choose various shades of pink, mauve or red, but for my money those whose leaves take on red, purple or bronze tinges in cold weather, such as *Bergenia* 'Sunningdale' (above) with its pink flowers and purple-bronzy leaves, or *Bergenia cordata* 'Purpurea' with its magenta flowers and red leaves, are the ones to go for as they pack much more of a punch. Don't mess about planting them in ones and twos, even though they make cabbage-shaped plants about 38 × 38cm (15 × 15in) – no, the way to grow bergenias is in decent groups or as a carpet under big shrubs or trees.

PEAK SEASON February–May.
GROWING CONDITIONS Any reasonable soil in sun or dappled shade.

Iris reticulata is the little rockery iris, whose 10cm (4in) high flowers in shades of blue or maroon appear – as if by magic – weeks ahead of the stiff, thread-like leaves that make grassy tufts about 30cm (12in) high. Plant the bulbs in late autumn in a sunny, well-drained spot such as a rockery, raised bed or scree – they are also good bulbs for pots. The flowers don't last long, and the old bulbs rarely do so well second-time round, so lots of people throw them away afterwards – but after a year off, they'll usually come good again, so it's worth being patient. Good hybrids include *Iris* 'Harmony' (above), which is blue, and *I.* 'J.S. Dijt', which is purple.

PEAK SEASON February–April.
GROWING CONDITIONS Very well-drained soil in a sunny spot.

Cyclamen coum (above, in its variety 'Maurice Dryden') is the hardy cyclamen that flowers in late winter and early spring and whose flowers are out at the same time as the leaves. Little charmers, which grow from flattish round tubers at or just below the soil surface, they'll self seed where they are happy and go on to form good-sized colonies in time. Individual plants are only 5 × 10cm (2 × 4in), so you need lots of them.

PEAK SEASON February–March.
GROWING CONDITIONS Well-drained soil containing plenty of organic matter, in light shade.

SOMETHING SPECIAL

Daphne mezereum, or mezereon as it's sometimes known (above), is often thought of as difficult to grow, but if the conditions are right it's not a problem. The straight stems of deep mauve 'bobbles' are an inspiring sight in spring, and the scent is to die for. And at 90 × 60cm (3 × 2ft) it won't outgrow even a small garden.

PEAK SEASON February–March.
GROWING CONDITIONS Cool, sheltered but sunny spot with fertile, well-drained soil containing plenty of organic matter; avoid chalky ground. Plants can fizzle out after a few years.

Abeliophyllum distichum, white forsythia (above), is quite an unusual shrub that deserves to be better known, not least for its strongly almond-scented white blossom. With an ungainly habit, something like a cross between forsythia and winter jasmine, this is one to grow up against a sunny wall. It'll cover an area about 2 × 2m (6 × 6ft) – train it out tidily somewhere you walk past often in winter to really reap the benefit.

PEAK SEASON February–March.
GROWING CONDITIONS Well-drained soil and a sheltered, sunny wall, but not east-facing.

Sempervivums (above) and silver-encrusted saxifrages provide early evergreen interest in the rock garden, alpine scree beds and rocky-themed containers long before even the earliest flowers spring into action. They both qualify for my description of 'little treasures', as most species measure only a few inches in any direction. As the season goes on, their sculptural rosettes make a shapely background for later-flowering species. They are very collectable, and good for growing in pots to create winter displays in an unheated greenhouse.

PEAK SEASON All year round.
GROWING CONDITIONS Well-drained soil and a sunny spot.

Hellebores, particularly the fashionable Lenten hellebore, ***Helleborus orientalis*** (above) and ***Helleborus × hybridus***, are real garden must-haves these days, and those with fancy names from specialist nurseries are all the rage. Still, if you invest in decent stock there's every chance the self-sown seedlings that turn up will be well worth having – especially if you mulch the older plants with chipped bark to make an effective nursery into which they can drop their seeds. Hellebores grow to about 45 × 45cm (18 × 18in).

PEAK SEASON February–March.
GROWING CONDITIONS Reasonable soil, with some organic matter added, in a sheltered spot in sun or light shade.

OTHER PLANTS IN THEIR PRIME IN FEBRUARY

- **Trees** *Prunus × subhirtella* 'Autumnalis' (see p.267)
- **Shrubs** *Chimonanthus praecox* (see p.292), *Hamamelis* (see p.13), *Lonicera fragrantissima*, *Lonicera × purpusii* (see p.292), *Viburnum × bodnantense* (see p.268), *Viburnum farreri*
- **Evergreens** *Daphne bholua*, *Erica carnea* (see p.267), *Erica × darleyensis*, *Mahonia × media* 'Lionel Fortescue' (see p.12), *Mahonia japonica*, *Pachysandra terminalis*, *Rhododendron* 'Christmas Cheer' (see p.293), *Rhododendron* 'Praecox', *Sarcococca confusa*, *Sarcococca hookeriana* var. *digyna* (see p.290), *Skimmia japonica* 'Rubella' (see p.270), *Viburnum tinus* (see p.12), *Viburnum rhytidophyllum* (see p.268)
- **Climbers/wall shrubs** *Clematis cirrhosa* 'Freckles' (see p.270), *Jasminum nudiflorum* (see p.12)
- **Berries/fruits** *Gaultheria procumbens* (see p.270), *Malus × robusta* 'Red Sentinel' (see p.244)
- **Perennials** *Helleborus niger* (see p.290), *Iris unguicularis* (see p.13)
- **Bulbs** *Chionodoxa*, *Crocus chrysanthus*, *Crocus tommasinianus* (see p.48), *Iris histrioides*, *Narcissus bulbocodium*, *Narcissus cyclamineus*, *Narcissus* 'February Gold' (see p.48), *Scilla mischtschenkoana* 'Tubergeniana'
- **Bedding** Ornamental cabbages and kales (see p.269), winter-flowering pansies (see p.269)
- **Rock plants** *Anemone blanda*, *Saxifraga apiculata*

Stachyurus praecox (above) is a large shrub or small tree, 2.5 × 2.5m (8 × 8ft), that you won't see all that often, but at its peak it looks as if the branches are dripping with long yellow catkins – these are actually strings of small, bell-like yellow flowers hanging from the bare branches. Fascinating.

PEAK SEASON February–March.
GROWING CONDITIONS Fertile, well-drained soil with plenty of organic matter, in a sheltered spot with reasonable light.

FEBRUARY at-a-glance checklist

GENERAL GARDEN TASKS (p.36)
- ✔ Finish off winter digging.
- ✔ Make new beds and borders.
- ✔ Order plug plants.

LAWNS (p.37)
- ✔ Keep off the lawn, or make or buy a temporary path.
- ✔ If mild and dry, mow the grass and prepare the ground for a new lawn.

TREES, SHRUBS AND CLIMBERS (p.38)
- ✔ Prune certain kinds of clematis.
- ✔ Brush snow off conifers, large evergreens and hedges to avoid splaying or breaking.
- ✔ Renewal-prune old shrubs, deciduous hedges and climbers.
- ✔ Move deciduous trees and shrubs (ideally do this in November or early March).

FLOWERS (p.39)
- ✔ In mild, dry conditions you could plant out early spring bulbs and polyanthus.
- ✔ Plant lily-of-the-valley crowns.

PATIOS AND CONTAINERS (p.39)
- ✔ Don't rush into planting – if you become impatient while waiting to plant spring bedding, treat yourself to a pot-grown spring-flowering shrub.
- ✔ Harden off polyanthus before putting them out once the weather turns milder.
- ✔ Tidy up and deadhead your winter-flowering pansies in tubs and hanging baskets.
- ✔ Water and top-dress plants in year-round tubs.

VEGETABLES AND HERBS (p.40)
- ✔ Prepare soil ready for sowing, covering it with polythene sheeting to warm it up for early vegetables.
- ✔ Sow extra-early crops of vegetables and salads if appropriate, and cover the crops with horticultural fleece.
- ✔ Plant shallots and Jerusalem artichokes.
- ✔ Top-dress container-grown herbs.

FRUIT (p.41)
- ✔ Prune autumn-fruiting raspberries now, and plant new canes between now and mid-March.
- ✔ Protect strawberries with horticultural fleece.
- ✔ Continue planting soft fruit bushes, bare-rooted fruit trees and summer-fruiting raspberry canes.
- ✔ Finish winter-pruning standard apple and pear trees (up to mid-March).

UNDER COVER (p.42)
- ✔ Ventilate the greenhouse at every opportunity, but water as little as you can get away with.
- ✔ Sow tuberous begonias, busy Lizzies and sweet peas.
- ✔ Pot up stored dahlia tubers and lily bulbs.
- ✔ Prick out seedlings.
- ✔ Spray fuchsias with water on fine days to start them back into growth.
- ✔ Sow early vegetables in the greenhouse borders (French beans, baby carrots, beetroot, radish, spinach).
- ✔ Sow vegetables in pots (lettuce, leeks, onions, early brassicas, peas, broad beans, extra-early new potatoes).
- ✔ Chit potatoes, if you didn't last month.
- ✔ Water strawberries.
- ✔ Harvest Brussels sprouts, sprouting broccoli, the last of the leeks, and winter lettuce from the greenhouse.

WATER GARDEN (p.44)
- ✔ Create a new pond.
- ✔ Take precautions to ensure your pond never freezes over entirely.

Watch out for
- Early greenfly – but only take action if there's a serious infestation – outdoors it's best left to bluetits.

Get ahead
- Prepare the soil ready for sowing. Cover it with polythene sheeting to warm it up for early vegetables.
- Prepare the greenhouse before the start of the propagating season – clean water storage barrels, watering cans, pots and seed trays, and propagator and greenhouse glass.

Last chance
- Sprout early seed potatoes for planting out next month.

GENERAL GARDEN TASKS

WINTER DIGGING

If you haven't done your winter digging yet (see November, p.272), now is the time to do it, unless you garden on very wet ground, in which case you can wait until March or even April.

MAKE NEW BEDS AND BORDERS FROM SCRATCH

If you're going to create new beds and borders starting with previously untamed land, it pays to start preparing the ground as early in the season as possible so the ground is in decent condition by the time you're ready to start putting plants in. If you prepare the soil thoroughly in the first place, you will reap the benefits later. Don't worry about delaying progress, as you don't want to start planting until March or April, when the soil has warmed up and plants are just starting to grow again.

- Mark out the shape of the border. Some people like to lay a hosepipe down on the ground, since it's easy to move if you want to try out several shapes before committing yourself, but at this time of year you'll have to run warm water through it to make it flexible! Landscapers will often trickle dry sand out of an old soft drink bottle, as this leaves the ground free of obstacles so it's easier to dig the shape out with your spade. Special building-site marker aerosols are also available from builders' merchants.

- Skim the ground clear of whatever's currently growing on it, such as weeds and/or grass.

- Dig over the soil, incorporating as much well-rotted organic matter as you can lay your spade on. Just turn the ground over with a spade or a fork, a row at a time, and spread a generous amount of organic matter along the base of each 'furrow' as you work so it is automatically buried as you dig your way across the area.

If the soil is workable, you can prepare the ground now for planting later. Remove weeds, dig in plenty of organic matter and fork over the soil.

- Keep lightly turning over the surface of the ground regularly, every couple of weeks. This simple soil preparation technique kills off a lot of weeds, and gets rid of soil pests the natural way. By bringing the seeds to the surface and exposing them to the light, they start to germinate, whereupon you bury the seedlings. You'll also be able to spot and remove bits of root as they start growing.

Cutting a new bed in the lawn

If you're cutting a new bed in the lawn, don't even think about digging the turf in. You might think it saves time, but it'll just keep re-growing so you spend the next 5 years fighting it back. You could wait until the weather is warmer and kill the grass off with weedkiller, but that's not very 'green', so strip the turf off and stack it up down the garden – this both gets rid of the roots and leaves you with a valuable by-product – home-made loam (see box opposite).

When you make new beds on ground that has previously been down to grass, the one thing you can expect to find are soil pests, such as leatherjackets and wireworms. They shouldn't be a problem where you will be planting trees and shrubs, as the roots are pretty tough, but flowers and vegetables are likely to be chewed off unless you tackle the problem. Short of using soil pesticides, the best remedy is to fork the soil over several times (see above) to expose grubs to birds, hedgehogs and other beneficial wildlife who'll enjoy a good feed, and be happy to act as free biological control. If you keep chickens and ducks, they'll have great fun ferreting them out – my modest flock really earns its keep.

ORDER PLUG PLANTS

A good range of patio plants is available as plugs at garden centres from March right through the spring, but by ordering from specialist young plant catalogues in winter you can have access to an enormous range of plug vegetable plants, bedding, patio and garden plants, including quite unusual varieties.

LAWNS

KEEP OFF THE LAWN

February is a quiet month for lawns, and the very best thing you can do is to keep off the grass as much as possible. Oh, I know it sounds a bit park-keeper-ish, but this is the soggy season, and if you go hoofing about, your boots will leave deep indentations that make the surface impossible to mow properly later. The same is true of ruts left by wheelbarrows, so if you can't avoid shoving barrowloads of heavy stuff across the lawn, for goodness sake lay a row of planks down first, or buy yourself one of those portable paths – a series of linked wooden slats that unroll – and run your barrow over that.

MOW IN MILD WEATHER

If the weather is mild, you'll very likely find the grass is already growing again. If you can choose a day when the ground is firm and the grass is fairly dry, then go ahead and give it a light cut. Raise the mower blades up to their highest cutting position so the grass is only topped instead of scalped – in this way it will have more resilience to frost and poor growing conditions. However, most people will need to wait until conditions underfoot are firmer and

drier, even if it means turning a blind eye to the odd seasonal crop of moss, wormcasts or weeds. Sort them out later, when you can walk on the lawn without your feet sinking in.

NEW LAWNS

If you plan on making a new lawn this spring (see March, p.55 and April, p.89), wait until the ground has dried out enough before completing soil preparations (see September, pp.226–7) or laying turf (see October, p.250). Don't even think about it when it's cold and soggy or in a spell of frosty weather.

Left: Keep the turf removed when cutting a new bed in a lawn, and stack it, so that it turns into useful, crumbly loam.

TURNING TURF INTO LOAM

Never let old, unwanted turf go to waste – it breaks down into brilliant fibrous loam, the like of which you can never buy. Good-quality loam like that is invaluable for topping up garden beds, filling raised beds or even making your own potting compost, if you don't mind sterilizing it in the oven.

How to turn turf into loam

1 Strip the turf off the soil, with about 5cm (1in) of soil, so that you take up all the roots. You can skim it off with a spade or hire a turf-stripping machine, which is worth it if there's a large area to do.

2 Stack the turves in a solid heap, rather like making a brick wall, with the grass-side down. That way the grass dies off, leaving the dead root fibre acting as 'roughage' to produce superb, weed-free topsoil, which is ready to use a year later.

MAKING YOUR OWN POTTING COMPOST

To sterilize soil in the oven, use large roasting bags and an old baking tray or roasting tin you won't be using for its original purpose again. Half-fill the roasting bags with the loam (after checking it's free from stones, dead leaves weeds or other rubbish). Press out all the air and fix the neck of the bag with the sealing ties provided. Lay the bags flat on the trays and put them in the oven, on its lowest setting, for 45 minutes, and leave to go cold before removing from the oven. Leave the loam in the sealed bag until you want to use it for making potting mixture, to prevent unwanted organisms from getting in.

TREES, SHRUBS AND CLIMBERS

PRUNE CLEMATIS

February is clematis-pruning time, but before you run amok with the secateurs I should point out it's only some of them that need pruning now (see box below).

The easiest way to tell which type of clematis you have is to keep the label that comes with a new plant when you buy it from a garden centre. The pruning instructions will be on the back. If you've lost the label and can't remember the name of the plant, all you need to know is roughly what type of clematis it is and when it flowers.

If you have clematis of any kind growing up through trees or over an arbour or pergola, there's no need to worry about pruning – just leave them alone.

PROTECT PLANTS FROM SNOW

Brush snow off conifers, large evergreens and hedges (see January, p.20).

PLANTING OR HEELING IN TREES AND SHRUBS

You can plant bare-root trees and shrubs now if conditions allow (see November, p.276). However, if the ground is frozen or too wet, heel them in for now (see January, p.20).

REJUVENATE OLD SHRUBS

There is still time to renewal-prune old shrubs, as well as prune overgrown deciduous hedges and out-of-control climbers (see January, p.21).

MOVE DECIDUOUS TREES OR SHRUBS

You can move deciduous shrubs at any time throughout the dormant season (see November, p.277). However, the very best times are shortly after leaf fall and just before the start of the spring growing season (early March).

WHICH CLEMATIS TO PRUNE NOW?

Clematis

Clematis species may have flowers shaped like bells, flared cups or wide-open saucers, less than 4cm (1¹/₂in) across. As a general rule, these don't have to be pruned at all. If they look a bit untidy, tuck wayward stems back into the body of the plant, or train them where you want them to go and tie them in, which you can do at any time of year. But if you want to do a bit more, you can give a light tidy up – by which I mean snipping off the worst of the sticking-out bits to neaten the shape. The best time to do that is after flowering, which is now in the case of late summer- or autumn-flowering species, and summer or autumn in the case of spring- or early summer-flowering species.

The species that flower early in the year can't be pruned now, as you'd cut off the bits that would otherwise flower; use the tidy-up technique above if needed for these. *Clematis montana* makes an absolute mattress of growth and doesn't need pruning until it gets really out of hand; then you can butcher it quite severely as soon as it's finished flowering, provided you are prepared to sacrifice flowers for a year or two. Clematis that flower after July, such as Viticella and Texensis types, can be pruned very hard. Cut off everything you can see now, in February – the new shoots will shoot up vigorously from the base and produce flowers in the summer.

Large-flowered hybrids

Large-flowered hybrids are easily recognized, as they're the ones that have typical clematis flowers – wide open saucers, about 10–15cm (4–6in) across. With these, you need to know when they flower to tell how hard they can be pruned.

The sort that flower in early and late summer, with a break in between, are best just lightly tidied up – if you hard prune them you'll miss out on your early flowers. Cut back any untidy top growth to a fat pair of buds. The ones that really must be pruned now are those that don't start flowering until June and keep going until September or so. The reason is simple: they make very vigorous growth and only flower on the very ends of the shoots, so if you don't prune them the flowers end up way out of sight. With this type, be ruthless and cut the whole plant down to 60cm (2ft) from the ground. It looks drastic at the time, but the plant will be all the better for it, and new shoots will start growing up strongly in another month or so, so don't worry.

FLOWERS

PLANT OUT EARLY FLOWERS IF MILD AND DRY

The end of the winter sees the garden looking rather barren, but hang on in there: it will all start to change next month. If the weather is mild, and the ground isn't inhospitably soggy, you can introduce splashes of colour into key places close to the house or in gaps between shrubs, by planting out pots of the very earliest spring bulbs and polyanthus, as soon as they appear on sale in nurseries and garden centres. But leave it for another few weeks if conditions are not very plant-friendly – even the toughest plants can't take too much of a battering when they've just come out from the shelter of nursery beds. Tip the plants cleanly out of their pots, and plant them without breaking up the rootball, after fluffing up the soil.

PLANT LILY-OF-THE-VALLEY CROWNS

Plant dormant crowns of lily-of-the-valley between shrubs in well-drained soil enriched with plenty of organic matter; the plants should be in light dappled shade during the summer.

PATIOS AND CONTAINERS

DON'T RUSH INTO PLANTING

The first shafts of weak spring sun are all it takes for container-fever to strike, but bide your time. Responsible nurseries and garden centres won't risk selling spring bedding before the weather has improved enough to plant it out. If you can't wait, make the most of evergreens for now, or treat yourself to a good, pot-grown spring-flowering shrub from a nursery and stand it inside a large patio tub temporarily, before planting it out in the garden later.

If you insist on making an early start, polyanthus are a whole lot tougher than most spring bedding, but even so they won't want shoving out in the cold when they've just come out of a sheltered greenhouse, so harden them off a bit first (see April, p.108) and wait for a mild spell to put them out. If it turns cold, be ready with some horticultural fleece to wrap them in for instant protection (see Vegetables and Herbs, p.40).

AFTERCARE FOR YEAR-ROUND TUBS

Keep an eye on containers planted for year-round effect, since even in the wet season tubs of shrubs or evergreens can dry out, especially when they are in the lee of a wall. Also, take the opportunity to go round top-dressing year-round tubs (see March, p.67).

Left: In relatively mild, dry conditions you can start filling gaps in the border with hardier bedding plants and very early spring bulbs.

A pot of winter-flowering bulbs, such as these irises and crocuses, brings cheer to the patio at an otherwise sparse time of year.

Right: Woody herbs, such as this bay tree, benefit from annual top-dressing. Remove the top 2.5cm (1in) of old potting compost and replace it with new compost mixed with slow-release fertilizer.

Black polythene
When warming up the soil for extra-early crops, black plastic polythene is best since it suppresses weeds; you can use clear plastic but then you'll need to hoe off the rash of weed seedlings immediately before sowing.

VEGETABLES AND HERBS

SOW EXTRA-EARLY CROPS
If you have a sunny, sheltered spot with fertile, well-drained soil that has previously had a good helping of organic matter dug in, you can use it to start producing some extra-early crops. Only early varieties of vegetables and salads are suitable. Normal summer varieties will just bolt or else the seed will rot if it's put in too early. Good choices include early peas, broad bean 'Aquadulce Claudia', lettuce varieties suitable for spring sowing such as 'Little Gem', and varieties of radish, carrot and turnip described as suitable for forcing.

- Fork the ground over early this month, rake it well, and cover it with a sheet of polythene, to warm it up (see p.22). Leave the plastic in place for at least 2 weeks, but 4 weeks is better and it won't do any harm to leave it longer if the weather is bad or you aren't ready to start.

- Choose a fine day to uncover the ground, then sow as usual, in shallow drills (see March, p.68). Water and cover the area you've just sown with a sheet of horticultural fleece for protection, holding the edges down with stones (see box below).

PLANT SHALLOTS
If the weather is mild and the soil is dry enough to work, you can plant shallots. Plant them like onion sets, with a trowel, just below the surface, in well-prepared and raked ground, about 20cm (8in) apart (see March, p.69). If soil conditions aren't good, wait until March.

PLANT JERUSALEM ARTICHOKES
Jerusalem artichokes are a bit of an oddity. The plants look like tall sunflowers, but the edible parts are the knobbly tubers that form on the roots underground during the summer; in late autumn you harvest and store the tubers to use as a winter vegetable. Although they aren't exactly mainstream vegetables, they make a very attractive screen to partition the veg patch off from your decorative garden, or plant them along the north side of an exposed veg patch to make an edible shelter belt. They make great soup!

- To plant, bury the tubers in a row in well-prepared ground, 2.5cm (1in) deep and 30–45cm (12–18in) apart. You can wait until next month if the soil isn't in workable condition yet.

TOP-DRESS CONTAINER-GROWN HERBS
Top-dress shrubby herbs in pots, for example bay and rosemary, as you would other plants in year-round tubs (see Patios and Containers, p.39).

HORTICULTURAL FLEECE
Horticultural fleece has really revolutionized vegetable growing. It looks like a thin, woven, white opaque plastic-fibre sheet, which is simply draped over a newly sown or planted bed of vegetables. Place a few bricks to hold the edges and corners down so it doesn't blow away. A single layer of fleece is enough to give a few degrees worth of insulation from cold, although don't rely on it to protect plants from freezing in seriously cold spells. In addition, fleece also shelters early crops from wind and hail, keeps the pigeons off your seedlings, and lets light and rain through, which means you don't need to keep taking it off and putting it back, except for hoeing off weeds.

FRUIT

PLANT AND PRUNE AUTUMN-FRUITING RASPBERRIES

The great thing about growing autumn-fruiting raspberries – apart from the fact that they ripen in autumn, when raspberries cost a fortune in the shops – is that the canes only grow 1.1m (3½ft) tall. That means you don't need to put up posts and wires to hold them up, or grow them in polite rows. Just leave them to spread and make a bed approximately 0.4 square metres (4 square feet), which will be packed solid with short, stocky raspberry canes. That's what I call a good use of space – very productive.

Planting raspberries

If you want to grow autumn-fruiting raspberries, you can sometimes buy potted plants in a garden centre, but most people order bare-rooted canes through the post, for delivery some time during the winter. If the soil is too wet when they are delivered, stand the roots in a tub of potting compost to stop them drying out until conditions are suitable, but do get them in before the start of the growing season, in mid-March.

- Prepare the ground as usual, and plant the canes 30cm (1ft) apart, in rows 60cm (2ft) apart. Firm them in and water. That's all there is to it – you don't need any supports. If the plants arrive with long stems, prune them down to ground level immediately after planting.

Pruning raspberries

If you already grow autumn-fruiting raspberries, the one thing you must do now is prune them. It's delightfully easy. There are no decisions to make or sorting out to do.

- Cut all the fruited canes down to about 2.5cm (1in) above ground level no later than the end of the month – it's like the summer sales, everything must go.

- Pull out any weeds, and while the ground is clear take the opportunity to mulch the bed thickly with well-rotted compost. In another 4–6 weeks from now the new shoots will be pushing through, and you don't want to risk damaging them.

PROTECT STRAWBERRIES

Drape containers of strawberry plants and strawberries growing in the ground (if you only have a few) with horticultural fleece for protection from cold and wind, and to encourage them to flower and fruit earlier than usual. Don't forget to water them when necessary, and uncover them when the first flowers start opening – otherwise insects won't be able to reach them for pollination. No bees, no crop!

CONTINUE PLANTING

Continue to plant soft fruit bushes, bare-rooted fruit trees (see November, p.276) and summer-fruiting raspberry canes (see November, p.284). If you can't find the bare-root plants you want, wait until spring to buy pot-grown plants.

FINISH WINTER-PRUNING

Finish pruning standard and bush apple and pear trees before the leaf buds burst in mid-March (see January, p.23).

Now is the time to plant autumn raspberries. Dig a trench, add plenty of organic matter, and insert the canes 30cm (1ft) apart, in rows 60cm (2ft) apart, using a taut line to mark the row.

UNDER COVER

PREPARE THE GREENHOUSE

A rainy February day is just the job for preparing the greenhouse for the start of the propagating season.

- Start by cleaning the inside of the glass, which has usually managed to grow a light film of algae over the winter, even when the greenhouse was well cleaned out in autumn – you need all the light that is going at this time of year. Use greenhouse disinfectant (see October, p.258).

- Scrub out pots, seed trays and anything else you'll be using for growing seeds, since good hygiene is vital – you can waste weeks of work, not to mention a fortune on expensive seed, through neglecting this simple and very obvious-sounding job.

- While you're at it, wash out your watering cans. And if you save rainwater in a water butt, empty it and scrub it out with greenhouse disinfectant, then rinse it out well before leaving it to refill. All sorts of gremlins live in dirty watering equipment given half a chance.

- If you have a heated propagator, wash that out too, and give it a final rinse with greenhouse disinfectant – use the type derived from citrus peels as a natural alternative to chemicals. Spread 2.5cm (1in) of silver sand over the base, and damp it slightly to even out the heat, then you are ready to make a start.

- Ventilate the greenhouse whenever you can, but water as little as you can get away with.

- Check greenhouse plants for early greenfly, which can build up quickly – wipe them off between your fingers or use damp tissue.

- Buy pots of early spring-flowering alpines, such as saxifrages, and dwarf rockery bulbs, such as *Iris danfordiae,* to beef up ornamental displays on the greenhouse staging.

Above: Use greenhouse disinfectant and a clean rag to wash the inside of the greenhouse glass.

Above: Dahlia tubers that were stored over winter can be potted up now.

SOW TUBEROUS BEGONIAS

Tuberous begonias are no trouble to grow from seed, provided you give them a long growing season in which to form a large enough tuber to enable them to survive their dormant period next winter. So an early start is essential.

- With very fine seeds like these, spread a fine layer of horticultural vermiculite over the surface of your pot of seed compost, then sprinkle the dust-like seeds thinly over – don't cover them. Water them by standing the pot in a dish of water for 10 minutes, as overhead watering will just wash them away. Keep them in a heated propagator, at a temperature of 18–24°C (65–75°F).

SOW BUSY LIZZIES AND SWEET PEAS

If you're heating the propagator anyway, and you want to fill unused space, sow seed of busy Lizzies. If there's room in the propagator, you could also put in pots of hardy annuals, including sweet peas (these will also be perfectly okay coming up on the staging of a cold or frost-free greenhouse). Alternatively, you could wait until next month to sow (see March, pp.62–3).

BOX OR POT UP STORED DAHLIA TUBERS

Plant stored dahlia tubers in pots or boxes filled with potting compost in a frost-free greenhouse, to get them off to an early start. This is especially worthwhile doing with patio dahlias, where you want them to start flowering as soon as possible after it's safe to put them outside. It's also worth doing when you want to force soft young shoots of dahlias to take as cuttings. Dahlia cuttings need taking early, as they need time to make good plants that will flower reasonably well this year. Several tubers can be fitted into a box, or one into a 15-cm (6-in) pot. The tuber should sit just below the surface of the compost.

POT UP LILY BULBS

If you want to have lilies to put out on the patio early this summer, plant three or five bulbs half-way down a 25–30cm (10–12in) pot and stand them in an unheated or frost-free greenhouse, to bring them on early. Assuming the potting compost is slightly moist, don't water until it starts to look dry or the first shoots appear above the surface – whichever happens first. Whatever you do, don't over-water, as the big fat bulbs rot easily, particularly when conditions are cold, dull and damp. Wait until you can see strong growth before starting to increase the watering.

PRICK OUT SEEDLINGS

Prick out seedlings as soon as they are big enough to handle (see April, pp.107–8).

SPRAY FUCHSIAS

Spray fuchsias in heated greenhouses and conservatories with water on fine days to start them gently back into growth.

EARLY VEG IN THE GREENHOUSE BORDER

If you have a soil border in the greenhouse, you can use it for growing very early crops that spend their entire life under cover. This is especially worth doing with French beans, baby beetroot and new carrots, as you'll be eating them months ahead of the same crops grown outside in the garden, and while they are still expensive in the shops. If you need space for tomatoes, which you'll need to plant in late April or early May (see May, p.141), or peppers and aubergines or melons, which are planted in late May or early June (see May, p.141), make sure you leave enough room for them, as beans, carrots and beetroot will occupy the ground until June or July. When you need all the ground for summer crops, such as tomatoes, it's better to stick to fast crops, such as radish or spinach, which you'll have eaten by tomato-planting time.

French beans

Choose your varieties carefully, checking the details on the back of the packets or seed catalogue before buying, as only a few are recommended for growing under glass. You'll have a choice of climbing or dwarf varieties. Climbing beans are the most worthwhile under glass, as they give by far the biggest crop, and the same plants keep cropping far longer than dwarf varieties – but against that there is the nuisance of putting in canes for them to climb up.

- Sow two bean seeds per small pot, and stand them on the staging of a frost-free greenhouse to germinate. (They'll come up faster on a warm windowsill indoors, but in a heated propagator they very often rot due to the high humidity).

- When the plants fill their pots with roots, plant them 20cm (8in) apart in rows in a greenhouse border that's previously been generously enriched with organic matter. Push a bamboo cane in alongside each plant, if using climbing beans. Once they get going, they will twine themselves round for support.

Baby root veg and salad crops

- Sow radishes and thin to about 2.5cm (1in) apart when they are big enough to handle; start pulling the largest a few at a time.

- Sow spinach thinly, and don't bother thinning the row as the plants develop. Pick baby spinach leaves for salads, leaving the plants to keep growing to provide bigger leaves for cooking later.

- Sow lettuce seed thinly in well-prepared soil in the greenhouse border, making shallow drills 30cm (12in) apart to maximize space. Thin the seedlings out when they are big enough to handle. Don't waste the small plants you thin out – use beets and lettuce seedlings as baby salad leaves.

SOW VEGETABLES IN POTS

When bad weather or unsuitable soil conditions make it impossible to sow early vegetables straight outdoors into the garden, you can always raise plants under glass in pots, to plant outside when the conditions are better. It's always worth protecting greenhouse-raised vegetables under a layer of horticultural fleece (see box, p.144) for at least the first few weeks after you first plant them out, as they are used to warm, sheltered conditions under cover.

Lettuce, leeks, onions and brassicas

- Sow lettuce, leeks, onions, and early brassicas such as summer cabbages and

To grow French beans, insert two seeds per small pot filled with compost and press them down into the compost until they just disappear.

cauliflowers now, sowing the seeds thinly into pots of seed compost in a cool propagator, set to about 10–15°C (50–60°F).

- When the seedlings are big enough to handle, prick them out into trays or individual small pots on the staging, and gradually lower the temperature to acclimatize them to conditions in the greenhouse.

- Keep them under cover, in frost-free conditions, until they are big enough to plant out and the weather outside is mild and soil conditions suitable.

Peas and broad beans
- Sow early peas and broad bean seeds into small, individual pots (three peas or one bean to a pot), or use seed trays, sowing the seeds 2.5cm (1in) apart and pressing them down into the compost until they just disappear.

- Stand the containers on the staging in a frost-free greenhouse, where the seeds germinate

Once a bean plant has filled its pot with roots, it is ready to plant in the greenhouse border or outside in the vegetable garden if mild and dry.

slowly – in the heated propagator they are far more likely to rot. But take precautions against mice, which are almost telepathic when it comes to pea and bean seeds. They make a good easy meal.

- Pea and bean plants are ready to go outside when they have filled their pots with roots, but choose a mild spell, when the soil is in good workable condition, and don't risk putting them out while it's cold or wet.

Extra-early new potatoes
You can also grow extra-early potatoes in pots, using tubers chitted last month (see January, p.27). These are well worth the effort – delicious to eat (you'll be picking your first baby spuds in May) and no bother to grow (see box below). Growing potatoes in pots means they are portable, so if you need the space for something else you can move them outside once the risk of frost has passed.

CHIT POTATOES
If you didn't chit your early seed potatoes last month, there is still time to sprout them now (see January, p.27).

WATER INDOOR STRAWBERRIES
Water indoor strawberries sparingly (see January, p.26), and remove any dead or mildewy-looking leaves.

HARVEST NOW
Harvest the Brussels sprouts, sprouting broccoli and the last of the leeks. Harvest winter lettuce from the greenhouse.

WATER GARDEN

CREATE A NEW POND
Winter is the time to make a new pond (see January Project, p.29).

CHECK THE POND
Take various precautions and check the pond regularly, to ensure the water never freezes over completely (see January, p.28).

HOW TO PLANT SEED POTATOES IN POTS

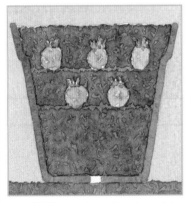

1 Half-fill several 30–38cm (12–15in) pots with potting compost, and plant three or four chitted seed potatoes of a very early variety (see January, p.27), spaced evenly apart, in each pot. Add another 8cm (3in) of compost and plant another three or four seed potatoes, then fill the pot to the rim with compost. Water the compost so it is just moist, not soggy.

2 Stand the pots in a frost-free greenhouse. Water sparingly until shoots appear out of the top, then slowly increase watering as the plants grow. As soon as the shoots reach 15cm (6in) tall, start liquid feeding every 2 weeks.

PROJECT Build a gazebo

A good garden is worth sitting in, and a gazebo has always been the traditional place to enjoy a good view at any time of year. There's no 'right' or 'wrong' type of construction: a gazebo can be a garden shed that's been converted with a coloured paint job and some decorative touches such as window boxes, shutters and decking into something closer to a summer house, or it can be little more than a seat with some uprights clothed in climbers making a green roof over it to give it a semi-enclosed feeling.

What you need

10 posts, 18 × 5 × 5cm (7 × 2 × 2in), pointed at the bottom

10 beanpoles

Stout but bendable garden wire

Gravel, bark chippings or paving slabs

Hardwood seats or bench

RUSTIC GAZEBO

If you want something quick and easy, you can knock up a lightweight rural gazebo from rustic posts and beanpoles in little more than an afternoon. The end result is more Heath Robinson than Capability Brown, but rickety is big in designer circles right now, so have a go and save yourself a fortune. If you want a bit of extra protection from sun, breeze or drips, there's no reason why you shouldn't open up a large garden parasol inside. In spring, when the soil is workable, you could plant three or four climbers, such as clematis, climbing roses, passionflower or jasmine, in well-prepared planting holes around the outside of the gazebo walls.

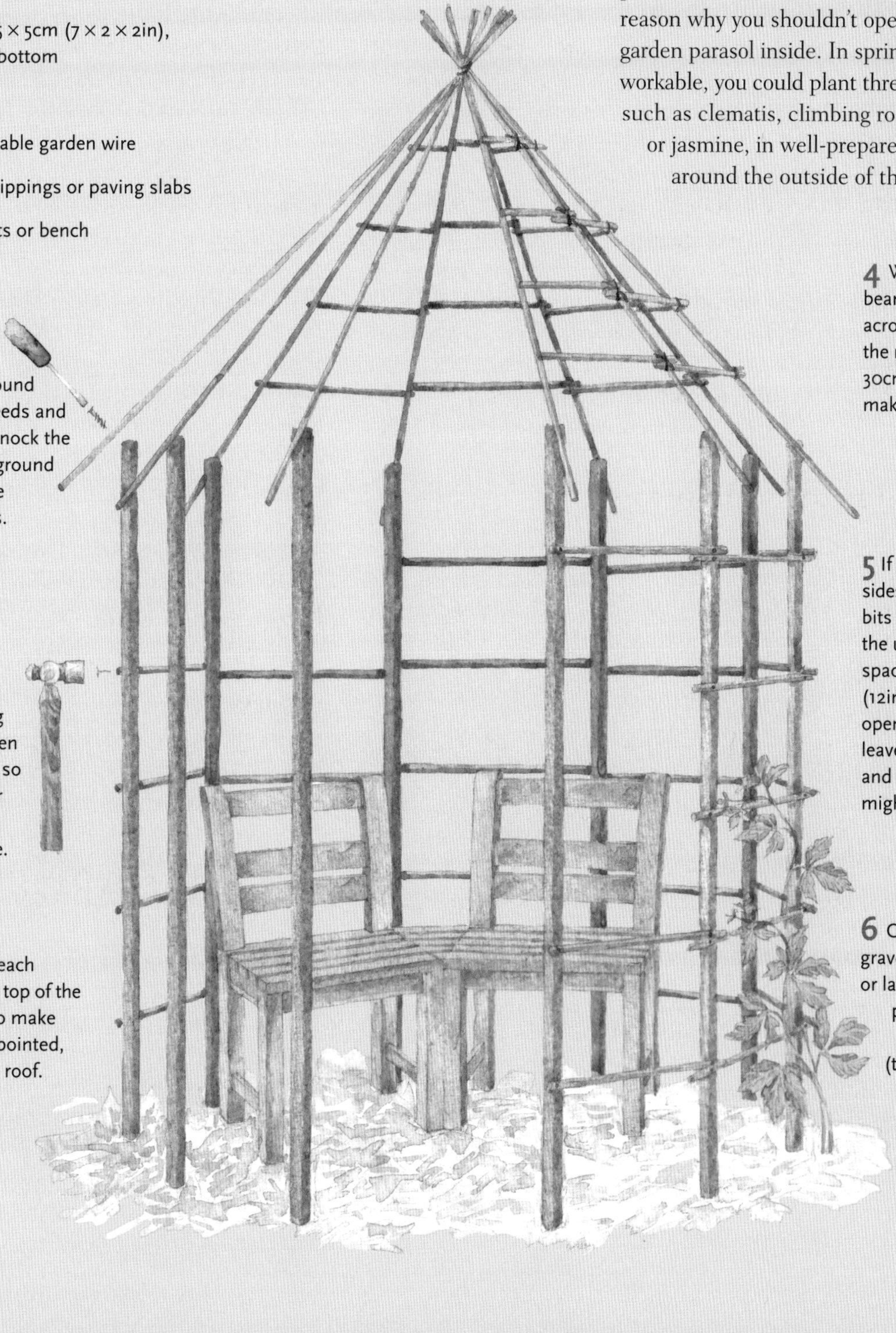

1 Level the ground and remove weeds and rubbish, then knock the posts into the ground to make a circle 2m (6ft) across.

2 Tie 10 beanpoles together at one end with strong garden wire, then splay them out so they look rather like a Native American tepee.

3 Wire or nail each beanpole to the top of the upright posts to make the bones of a pointed, jungle hut-style roof.

4 Wire lengths of beanpole, cut to size, across each section of the roof framework at 30cm (12in) intervals to make a cobweb pattern.

5 If you want to fill the sides in slightly, use more bits of beanpole to join the upright posts, again spacing them 30cm (12in) apart, forming an open trellis-work pattern; leave a gap for the door and any 'windows' you might want.

6 Cover the floor with gravel or bark chippings, or lay paving slabs, and put hardwood garden seats or a bench inside (these can be left out all year round).

MARCH

March is known to be windy ... remember the old rhyme about March winds and April showers bringing forth May flowers? Well, these days the May flowers are likely to be opening a month early, but the winds and rains you can certainly still count on – and a sharp frost can still catch you out. But, the sun often shines this month, spring bulbs are starting to come out in force, and you can almost see the new gardening season gathering steam daily.

In March, the days become longer, the ground is warming up, and the weeds are starting to grow. You don't need to be an expert at reading the 'natural signs' to know that the gardening season starts here – and March is all go. I don't want to nag, but if you let things slide now you could be in a mess for months. But by keeping on top of it all in early spring, the rest of the gardening year runs like clockwork. This is not the month to be taking a holiday.

THE BIG PICTURE spring bulbs

Daffodils, or narcissi if you want to be botanical about it, are *the* spring flowers in most people's minds. If you grow a selection of varieties, you can have daffs out in bloom from the end of February (*Narcissus* 'February Gold', 30 × 5cm/12 × 2in) to late April (*Narcissus* 'Winston Churchill', 38 × 10cm/15 × 4in) or early May (*Narcissus poeticus* cultivars, 38 × 10cm/15 × 4in), although the bulk of varieties will bloom over the next 6 weeks. Daffodils naturalize well, so you can plant them in drifts in the lawn, or grow them under trees and shrubs, as well as in borders. They are no bother, as you can just leave them where they are, without having to dig them up and re-plant them again each year. The shorter-stemmed cultivars, such as *Narcissus* 'Tête-à-tête', *Narcissus* 'Jetfire' (above) and *Narcissus* 'Jenny', all 25 × 8cm (10 × 3in), are the best bet as they stand up well to wet and windy weather, and are also good for planting in spring pots and tubs, whereas tall daffs just flop.

PEAK SEASON March–April.
GROWING CONDITIONS Any reasonable soil including clay, and even under big deciduous trees where it's dark and dry in summer. The flowers last longest in a sheltered spot.

Crocuses are also among the earliest of the spring flowers. *Crocus vernus*, the large Dutch crocus, and its cultivars – the ones with the purple, mauve-striped or orange-yellow flowers – bloom marginally ahead of most daffs. However, these are the ones the birds will often take a fancy to and shred. Don't try to protect them with black threads held up on sticks as some people recommend, as it looks awful and you'll feel justifiably guilty when birds become snagged, especially if the cat gets to them first. You could also enjoy slightly smaller-flowered species crocuses naturalized in short grass and borders. I especially love *Crocus tommasinianus*, 8 × 5cm (3 × 2in), which has impeccably dainty flowers of amethyst-purple from late winter to early spring. Its variety 'Whitewell Purple' (above) is darker and a good colonizer.

PEAK SEASON February–March.
GROWING CONDITIONS Reasonably fertile, well-drained soil in a sunny, sheltered spot.

Convallaria majalis, lily-of-the-valley (above), is a real joy if you have the right place for it. The pairs of leaves and stems of small, neatly spaced, white bell-shaped flowers have a geometric precision that always appeals, and the scent is classic. Victorians used to force plants in pots to bring into the living room, but once you have a decent patch it's much easier to pick a few flowers to put in a jar. Single plants are 10 × 5cm (4 × 2in) but they spread sideways to make a loose carpet. Slow to establish, lily-of-the-valley hates being moved once it's got going, so plant it and leave well alone. The variegated form *Convallaria majalis* 'Albostriata', with gold lines patterning the leaves, is a treasure, with a price tag to match.

PEAK SEASON March–April.
GROWING CONDITIONS Rich, fertile soil with lots of organic matter in shade.

OLD FAITHFULS

'**Botanical' tulips** are the earliest tulips to flower. They include the more popular 'true' species, such as *Tulipa batalinii*, *Tulipa tarda* and *Tulipa clusiana*, which are often naturalized in well-drained soil or are grown on a rockery. They also include the so-called waterlily tulips – hybrids of *Tulipa greigii*, *Tulipa fosteriana* (above) and *Tulipa kaufmanniana* – whose flowers open so wide that they resemble waterlily flowers – slightly. Well, you have to allow for a bit of poetic licence with common plant names. Shorter than 'garden' tulips, most 'botanical' tulips grow about 15–22 × 5cm (6–9 × 2in). (See also April, p.83, for other tulips.)

PEAK SEASON March–April.
GROWING CONDITIONS Sunny, well-drained soil.

Magnolia stellata, the star magnolia (above), looks too sensational to warrant the description 'old faithful', but in magnolia terms it's just that. Whereas most of the tribe demand special conditions and grow into small or even not-so-small trees, this one puts on a great show every year in just about any garden, in the space required by a shrub. Its average size is about 2 × 2m (6 × 6ft) in a normal garden. (See also April, p.81, for other magnolias.)

PEAK SEASON March–April.
GROWING CONDITIONS Any reasonable soil in a sunny or partially shady and sheltered spot.

Chaenomeles, also known as japonica or flowering quince (right), are medium-sized spiny shrubs. They tend to have a loose, untidy shape, so are often grown up against a wall and trained out flat to keep them neater – allow 2 × 2m (6 × 6ft). Several varieties are commonly available – *Chaenomeles speciosa* '**Moerloosei**' is white flushed with pink, '**Simonii**' is rich red, and '**Nivalis**' is pure white. All have large, colourful, single apple-blossom-like flowers in shades of pink, red, peach or white. These are followed by knobbly green, spotted fruits, which hang on the plants until late autumn and eventually ripen to golden yellow. These aren't the proper cooking quinces, although some people do use them as such.

PEAK SEASON March–May.
GROWING CONDITIONS Grow anywhere.

Forsythia is on my list of 'old indestructibles' – you really have to try hard to kill it. Well known for its blaze of spiky yellow flowers, *Forsythia* × *intermedia* 'Lynwood Variety' (above) is still one of the best cultivars. Plant it as a shrub for the back of a border, allowing 2.5 × 2m (8 × 6ft), or grow a row as a flowering hedge 2m (6ft) high, preferably where you have lots of room as it's not that exciting once the flowers are over.

PEAK SEASON March–April.
GROWING CONDITIONS Grows anywhere in anything; best in sun but tolerates light shade.

Camellias are wonderfully spectacular garden essentials. They are fair-sized evergreen shrubs, 2 × 2m (6 × 6ft), with big single or double powder-puff flowers in every known shade of pink and red, as well as white; however, be warned – white camellia flowers have a nasty habit of turning brown at the first sign of wet or windy weather. Even when not in flower, the neat glossy foliage of the camellia makes a handsome background for later-flowering plants. Hybrids of *Camellia* × *williamsii* are especially good garden plants. Look out for 'Donation' – pink, semi-double – 'J.C. Williams' – pale pink, single – and 'Francis Hanger' – white, single. *Camellia japonica* hybrids, such as 'Mercury' (above), are very spectacular but may need regular dead-heading.

PEAK SEASON March–May.
GROWING CONDITIONS Well-drained, fertile, lime-free soil with plenty of organic matter, in a sheltered site in light shade. A sunny spot will do if the ground stays moist in summer, but avoid east-facing situations. Also good for growing in tubs of ericaceous compost where the garden soil is not suitable.

Amelanchier lamarckii, the snowy mespilus (above), is the perfect early-flowering tree for a small garden, as it won't let you down in an 'iffy' season or outgrow its welcome, growing to about 5 × 5m (15 × 15ft). The small palest pink blossom smothers the bare branches and is joined by the first of the bronze-tinged young foliage once the flowers have been out for a while. In summer, the small red fruits are snapped up by blackbirds, and in autumn a great blast of fiery tints takes over, making this truly a tree for all seasons.

PEAK SEASON March–April.
GROWING CONDITIONS Any soil except chalk; best in a reasonably sunny spot and tolerates wind.

Aubrieta, usually called aubretia (above), is taken for granted, but when you want a tried and tested early-flowering rock plant to trail down over a low wall, gee up spring containers, or brighten up a dull rock feature, this is it. Available in all shades of magenta, red, lilac and pink, cheap and cheerful sums it up. Plants make low mats 5 × 30cm (2 × 12in).

PEAK SEASON March–May.
GROWING CONDITIONS Reasonably sunny spot in any soil unless poorly drained.

Polyanthus (above) are the natural sequel to coloured primroses for spring bedding. The plants look similar, except that polyanthus flowers grow in bunches at the top of the stem instead of singly, as in the case of primroses, so plants are taller, approximately 20 × 15cm (8 × 6in). They come in the same range of bright jewel colours – red, blue, orange, red and yellow – but they are a tad tougher than primroses. Use them in beds and borders or in containers. They team well with spring bulbs of all sorts.

PEAK SEASON March–April.
GROWING CONDITIONS Any reasonable soil in sun or dappled shade.

Primula rosea (above) is the first of the popular primulas to flower. The cerise-pink flowers appear slightly ahead of the bronzy-green young leaves. They are small plants at the best of times, 20 × 20cm (8 × 8in), so plant a tight group if you want them to show up well.

PEAK SEASON March.
GROWING CONDITIONS Fertile, wet to boggy soil in sun or light shade.

Erysimum cheiri, wallflowers, are classic spring bedding plants, growing 38 × 15cm (15 × 6in). Even if they seem a bit old hat these days when there is so much else on offer, it takes a lot to beat the scent of a bed of wallflowers. Dwarf modern varieties, 15 × 10cm (6 × 4in), are good for containers – something you could never do with the straggly older kinds. New varieties also offer autumn flowers, but keep them regularly deadheaded so they continue flowering. Wallflowers team particularly well with tulips. Good varieties include '**Orange Bedder**' and '**Blood Red**' (right).

PEAK SEASON March–May.
GROWING CONDITIONS Any good soil in sun.

SOMETHING SPECIAL

Azara microphylla (above) is not something to try growing if you live in a cold, exposed or northern garden, but in a mild, sheltered garden south of Watford it's well worth a shot. This medium to large evergreen shrub or small tree, 3 × 2.5ft (10 × 8ft), can also be trained against a wall for extra protection. In spring the stems break out into masses of fluffy yellow flowers that are strongly scented of marzipan.

PEAK SEASON March.
GROWING CONDITIONS Well-drained, fertile soil in a sheltered, sunny spot.

Cornus mas, Cornelian cherry (above), is a shrub that always turns up at garden clinics in spring, with the owner clutching a twig and asking 'What's this?' It is conspicuous for its balls of small yellow flowers that appear on bare twigs – flower arrangers love it. You get a second bite of the cherry (sorry!) later in the year as it also has good autumn foliage colours.

PEAK SEASON March.
GROWING CONDITIONS Grows in any reasonable soil in sun or shade.

Gold-laced polyanthus (above) are charmers with a foot in garden history, as they were one of the original 'florists' flowers', bred for showing by 17th-century artisans. Think of a polyanthus but with a cluster of small black or maroon flowers edged with gold or silver (in which case they are correctly called silver-laced). Once on the brink of extinction, they are now thriving again and you can occasionally buy plants at the garden centre in flower, or grow your own from seed.

PEAK SEASON March–April.
GROWING CONDITIONS Fertile, well-drained soil with plenty of organic matter in light shade with shelter. Alternatively, grow in pots and 'stage' a spring display on shelves against a sheltered wall.

OTHER PLANTS IN THEIR PRIME IN MARCH

- **Trees** *Parrotia persica, Prunus cerasifera, Prunus dulcis, Prunus × subhirtella* 'Autumnalis' (see p.267)
- **Shrubs** *Chimonanthus praecox* (see p.292), *Corylus avellana* 'Contorta' (see p.32), *Corylopsis, Daphne mezereum* (see p.34), *Lonicera fragrantissima, Prunus triloba, Ribes odorata, Ribes sanguineum* (see p.81), *Spiraea thunbergii, Stachyurus praecox* (see p.35), *Viburnum × bodnantense* (see p.268), *Viburnum tinus* (see p.12)
- **Evergreens** *Erica carnea* (see p.267), *Garrya elliptica* (see p.32), *Mahonia aquifolium, Mahonia × media* 'Lionel Fortescue' (see p.12), *Rhododendron* 'Praecox', *Skimmia japonica* 'Rubella' (see p.270), *Viburnum rhytidophyllum* (see p.268), *Viburnum tinus* (see p.12)
- **Climbers/wall shrubs** *Abeliophyllum distichum* (see p.34), *Clematis cirrhosa* 'Freckles' (see p.270), *Forsythia suspensa, Jasminum nudiflorum* (see p.12)
- **Berries/fruits** *Gaultheria procumbens* (see p.270), *Malus × robusta* 'Red Sentinel' (see p.244)
- **Perennials** *Bergenia* (see p.33), *Caltha palustris, Helleborus foetidus, Helleborus × hybridus* (see p.34), *Iris unguicularis* (see p.13), *Primula vulgaris* (see p.32), *Viola odorata*
- **Bulbs** *Chionodoxa, Convallaria, Cyclamen coum* (see p.33), *Iris histrioides, Iris reticulata* (see p.33), *Puschkinia, Scilla mischtschenkoona* 'Tubergeniana'
- **Bedding** *Bellis* daisies, *Primula* 'Wanda' and other coloured primroses, ornamental cabbages and kales (see p.269), winter-flowering pansies (see p.269)
- **Rock plants** *Anemone blanda, Arabis, Saxifraga*

MARCH at-a-glance checklist

GENERAL GARDEN TASKS (p.54)
✔ Spring clean the garden – fork over the soil in borders, weed and mulch, and dig up and divide overcrowded perennials.
✔ Remove weeds and moss on paths and drives.
✔ Order biological control nematodes to control vine weevil in the greenhouse sometime this month or next – timing is critical.

LAWNS (p.55)
✔ Deal with wormcasts and molehills.
✔ Make the first cut if it is dry enough and begin regular mowing.
✔ Redefine lawn edges.
✔ Lay turf before the end of the month if you didn't in autumn.

TREES, SHRUBS AND CLIMBERS (p.57)
✔ Plant pot-grown shrubs, roses and climbers.
✔ Prune modern bush roses, vigorous climbing roses, *Buddleja davidii*, coloured-stem dogwoods and willows, ornamental elders and coppice eucalyptus.
✔ Tidy up patio roses, ground-cover roses, and shrub roses and species roses grown for their hips.
✔ Move deciduous trees and shrubs and plant new bare-root plants before they start into growth.
✔ Prepare large deciduous shrubs for moving the following year.
✔ Renovate overgrown climbers.

FLOWERS (p.62)
✔ Tidy up the rock garden, alpine screes and sink gardens, top up stone chippings around plants and fill any gaps with new rock plants.
✔ Sow wildflowers and hardy annuals.
✔ Plant and divide perennials.
✔ Divide snowdrops 'in the green'.
✔ Plant gladiolus corms and lily bulbs.

PATIOS AND CONTAINERS (p.66)
✔ Scrub or pressure-wash patio slabs.
✔ Freshen up pots containing winter/spring bedding.
✔ Plant spring bedding, flowering spring bulbs, rock plants, compact perennials and small evergreens.

VEGETABLES AND HERBS (p.68)
✔ Prepare soil, then sow lettuce, rocket, radishes spring onions, leeks, onions, broad beans, parsnips, spinach, turnips, early varieties of carrots and peas.
✔ Plant onion sets, shallots, Jerusalem artichokes, autumn-sown brassicas and veg plants bought from garden centres.
✔ Plant early potatoes grown in pots undercover; plant outdoors at the end of the month.
✔ Harden off and protect early vegetables by covering them with horticultural fleece.
✔ Prepare an asparagus bed for planting next month.
✔ Harvest sprouting broccoli, Swiss chard left in the ground last year, the last of the Brussels sprouts.
✔ Sow hardy herbs and plant and divide perennial herbs.

FRUIT (p.71)
✔ Spring clean the fruit garden, weeding and mulching everywhere.
✔ Plant rhubarb, pot-grown fruit trees and bushes and strawberry plants.
✔ Water pot-grown fruit.
✔ If you've not already done so, prune standard apple and pear trees before the buds burst into growth.
✔ Hand-pollinate peaches, nectarines and apricots and protect early blossom with horticultural fleece.
✔ Plant pot-grown strawberry plants.

UNDER COVER (p.73)
✔ Clean the greenhouse.
✔ Keep heating the greenhouse and water plants very sparingly. On sunny days, cover the propagator in the greenhouse with a single sheet of newspaper and on cold nights cover with several layers for insulation.
✔ Sow tomatoes, chillies, sweet-peppers, aubergines and half-hardy annuals/bedding plants in a heated propagator.
✔ Sow hardy annuals including sweet peas, in pots in a cold greenhouse or in the ground outdoors; sow wildflowers as for hardy annuals.
✔ Pot up plug plants and young plants as soon as possible after delivery or purchase.
✔ Start dormant begonia and gloxinia tubers, arum lilies, canna, achimenes and dahlia tubers by potting them and keeping in a frost-free greenhouse.
✔ Start cacti and succulents by spraying with water, and dormant fuchsias and half-hardy perennials by splashing with water.
✔ Take cuttings of border perennials, corms and tubers.
✔ Plant early crops in pots – there's still time to plant extra-early new potatoes, as well as summer cabbages and summer cauliflowers.
✔ Water and hand-pollinate strawberry plants.

WATER GARDEN (p.76)
✔ Clear netting from ponds in time to stop emerging marginal plants becoming entangled, but if herons are a problem put a trip wire round the edge of the water to keep fish safe.
✔ Replace underwater lighting and submersible pumps for running fountains.
✔ Feed fish if weather is warm and fish are active.

Watch out for
- Slugs, snails, woodlice and greenfly under glass.
- On cold nights cover vulnerable plants with horticultural fleece and heat a frost-free greenhouse.

Get ahead
- This month you'll be lucky to keep your head above water, so don't even think about taking on something you can leave until next month.

Last chance
- Finish winter digging.
- Try to complete turf laying.
- Move deciduous trees and shrubs and plant bare-root plants before they start into growth in mid-March.
- Prepare large deciduous shrubs for moving the following year.
- Prune apple and pear standards.
- Plant extra-early potatoes in pots in the greenhouse.

53

GENERAL GARDEN TASKS

FINISH WINTER DIGGING
Ideally, complete any winter digging that still needs doing (see November, p.272). If you garden on wet or heavy, clay ground, don't worry about leaving the job this late because it's not until spring winds and sun start drying it out that you can start working on it. Don't risk digging it while it's soggy, or it'll just set like concrete in summer.

TIDY BORDERS
If you do nothing else this month, the one thing to tackle is the annual spring clean of beds and borders. It's all about putting the garden back to rights at the end of winter, so you start the season with everything in order and raring to go. Even if you're short of time, make this your top priority – anything else you can fit in will be a bonus.

- Go through your beds and borders systematically, forking out weeds and cutting down any dead stems of perennial plants left from last autumn. Cut them off as close to the base of the plant as you can, without damaging emerging buds or young foliage.

Besides looking tidier, it means there are no stubby stumps left to gather disease or spike your fingers when you're weeding later.

- Fork the soil over between plants to loosen it up. While you work, gather up and remove any odd bits of plant debris as well as slugs and snails.

- Dig up and divide any perennial plants that have spread too far or died out in the centre (see How to divide and replant perennials, p.64). Split the clump into several pieces and replant the best bits after working some well-rotted compost back into the ground.

- When clearing the garden, watch out for self-sown seedlings. It's worth transplanting or potting up any you can use elsewhere in the garden, and even if you can't use them they often come in handy for stocking plant stalls at charity events later. Look out especially for hellebores, nasturtiums, cerinthe and daphne.

MULCH THE SOIL
While the soil is still fluffy from its fork-over, cover it with a generous layer of organic matter, such as garden compost, manure, mushroom compost, or bark chippings, up to 5cm (2in) deep. Beware of burying plant labels under the mulch – it's easily done. Some people like to sprinkle general fertilizer over the soil before mulching, but if the weather is still cold and plants have hardly started to move it's much better to wait until next month to feed, since the last thing you want to do is encourage lots of soft lush growth that will be knocked for six by a hard frost.

Mulching is a good habit to get into as it benefits the garden in several ways, all of which will save you work for the rest of the season. It covers annual weed seeds, keeping them in the dark so they can't germinate. It reduces evaporation, so you save on watering, and it is the lazy way to add 'roughage' to ground that you can't dig because there are plants growing in it – by mulching, the worms do the job instead.

Don't make extra work for yourself
When tidying beds and borders start at the back and work your way to the front. In this way you can eradicate your footprints and avoid leaving the ground compacted, and you won't have to fork the same bit of ground over twice.

Improve the soil with a good covering of manure.

WATCH OUT FOR PESTS
Keep an eye open for early pests.

- Greenfly may already be around if the winter has been very mild, but there's no need to use pesticides – leave them for blue tits to deal with. If you've been feeding the birds all through the winter, the odds are you'll already have a good population of pest-collectors visiting the garden.

- If you've had trouble with vine weevil in the greenhouse, where it's most likely to attack pots of cyclamen, potted alpine plants or lurk in the soil ready to nip the roots off whatever you plant, then order the appropriate nematodes for biological control by mail order, so they are delivered in time to apply next month. (For outdoor vine weevil, order in April for delivery in May, as the pests are at work about a month later than under glass, owing to lower temperatures.)

REMOVE WEEDS AND MOSS ON PATHS AND DRIVES
- Remove weeds and moss from gravel paths, using an old hoe, and rake out tyre marks and footprints from a gravel drive to leave it looking tidy; top up with a few bags of fresh gravel if necessary.

- Weed the cracks between paving slabs with an old dinner knife or a proper weeding knife sold specially for this job. Unless you want to grow rock plants or other small flowers in the cracks, it's a good idea to 'grout' them to prevent weeds. Simply fill the gaps with a dry mortar mix (1 part cement, 5 parts sand), brush it into the cracks and damp the area very lightly with water – use a slow-running hose with your thumb over the end to produce a fine spray that soaks in instead of washing the powder away.

LAWNS

CREATING A NEW LAWN
If you're making a new lawn then spring is the second-best time to do it, autumn being by far the best, since the grass has all winter to establish so it's ready to use around now, when you want to start spending more time outdoors.

- If the soil is in a workable state – not too wet and soggy – you can prepare it from scratch now (see September, p.227) or if you rough-dug the ground in winter just give the lawn its final levelling and firming – allow time, as it's a long slow job to get right.

- Lay turf before the end of this month if you can (see October, p.250) or if you want to save money by growing a new lawn from seed, you can sow late this month if you live in a mild area with well drained soil (see September, pp.227–8). Otherwise, do it in April.

DEAL WITH MOSS AND THATCH
If you didn't do your lawn fitness training in autumn, or a mild, wet winter means a lot more moss has grown, give the lawn a good raking once it's been cut back to its usual height (see September, p.225). Don't try raking a long, shaggy lawn.

DEAL WITH WORMCASTS AND MOLEHILLS
Worms and moles can make a real mess of a lawn. Both are at their most active in spring, and you won't get rid of them, so it's a case of learning to live with them – the nuisance peaks now but it tends to subside as the year goes by. Before cutting the lawn do the following:

- Scoop up molehills and spread the soil on the borders, or sprinkle it thinly over the lawn as a top-dressing and work it in with a wire rake or besom broom, making sure it's no more than 5mm (¼in) thick or you'll smother the grass. If moles have undermined the lawn badly, use a hose to wash the soil back down

> **Use up biological controls**
> It's no good storing biological control agents. The contents of the packs need using within a few days of delivery as they are living organisms. For further information on biological controls, see May, p.125.

Weeds have a habit of popping up in the cracks between paving stones. You can dig them out using an old knife.

If the grass is too long to mow, give it a rough trim first using a rotary line trimmer (strimmer) or shears.

into the holes instead of removing it, to prevent the lawn sinking into the maze of underground cavities.

- On a dry day, break up wormcasts with a besom broom or wire rake and spread them over the lawn, where they act as a nourishing top-dressing. They are, after all, worm manure.

MAKE THE FIRST CUT

If you garden on heavy soil, you probably can't get near your lawn with a mower all winter. It's far too wet, and the ground is so soft that if you walk on it your feet sink in and slither about, churning it into a muddy mess. It's not until spring that the sun and wind dry it out enough to risk a first cut. The trouble is, the longer it's left, the taller it grows, and by the time conditions are right your average mower can't cope. If that's your problem, tackle the first cut in two stages:

- Top the grass roughly with shears or a rotary line trimmer, and rake up the bits. Then wait a day or so for the lawn to dry out the newly exposed damp under-layer.

- Mow the lawn with the cutting blades set as high as they'll go so the grass is left slightly longer than in summer. (All mowers have adjustable cutting heights for the blades; consult the handbook for details of how to adjust your particular model.) Giving a hay field a crew-cut would be too much of a

MOWING IN DIFFICULT AREAS

Mowing around spring bulbs naturalized in grass can be tricky. The easy way is to keep the bulbs in drifts (specific areas with definite shapes following the contours of the ground) so that you can mow around the edges.

The other big problem is trees growing in grass. If you want close-cropped grass right up to tree trunks, most people will use a rotary line trimmer to keep it short – but take great care, as it's all too easy to let the cord slice into the trunk, and if you bark-ring a tree it's certain to kill it. It's better to use hand shears, or surround the tree with some ground-cover planting to make a safe barrier for your trimmer.

CHOOSING A MOWER

This is probably the time more people buy a new mower than any other, as they find the old one won't start when they take it out of the shed. The things to look for when buying a new one are ease of altering the cutting height, the amount of storage space you'll need to house it, and most important – its cutting width. With a big lawn, you'll be going round all day unless you opt for a wide mower; with a small lawn it's not worth paying the extra, and in any case you'll find a narrower mower more manoeuvrable.

Different types of mower

Ride-on mowers are big, powerful machines with rotary cutters underneath a 'go cart' body, for large areas of uninterrupted grass. They often double as garden tractors, with a tow-hitch on the back to take a trailer, and an optional snow-plough attachment for the front.

Rotary mowers with petrol engines are powerful enough for long grass, even when it's a bit wet. Although they are more manoeuvrable than a ride-on, this type of mower is not ideal for fussy gardens with lots of complicated island beds to work round. Big mowers like these, with a wheel at each corner, are happiest going in straight lines.

Rotary electric mowers are ideal for small gardens but the grass must be dry when you cut it.

Electric hover mowers are the most manoeuvrable of all, as they move sideways as well as backwards and forwards, and they glide over the edge of beds, which you can't do with wheeled mowers. This makes hover mowers very handy for gardens with a lot of complicated curves or steep banks.

Cylinder mowers are the kind to go for if you want old-fashioned stripes, but a large, self-propelled motor version is an expensive piece of kit these days. If you can get hold of an old hand mower, it's ideal for anyone with only a pocket-hanky-sized patch to cut.

shock for long grass, and would leave it looking yellow. And even if you normally mow without using the grass box, to save time in summer, it's worth using it for the first few cuts of the season so the turf has a chance to dry out without being swamped by clippings.

MOW REGULARLY

Once you have the first couple of cuts under your belt the grass will look much better, even if winter has left it a bit below par. You can then gradually lower the cutting height of the blades slightly, but don't cut it too short just yet. Don't be tempted to green up a sickly looking post-winter lawn by ladling on the fertilizer, because that just encourages soft, lush growth that could still be clobbered by a proper frost. Wait until the middle of April, or even early May if you live in a cold area.

REDEFINE LAWN EDGES

Properly made lawn edges make a huge difference to the look of the lawn, and indeed the whole garden. They are the sort that make a sharp right angle where they meet the borders – the gardening equivalent of having properly pressed razor-sharp creases in your Dad's best weddings-and-funerals trousers.

In the case of the garden, edging isn't just for neatness. Properly made lawn edges are much quicker and easier to keep tidy. When you go round with the edging shears after mowing the grass, the bottom blade fits down the vertical 'channel' running right round the beds and borders, so you can scissor your way along them at normal walking speed. At least that's the idea – what usually happens over the winter is that soil washes down from your borders and makes the edges fuzzy so you can't use the shears. That's why they need redefining. An hour or two spent doing this now will save you hours of work for the rest of the year.

- Using a half-moon-shaped lawn-edging tool or spade, work your way along the edges of the lawn, wherever they meet a bed or border. Dig about 5cm (2in) deep and flick the soil back up into the border, leaving a shallow trench with a firm, vertical edge.

RENOVATE THE LAWN

Continue to repair and renovate established lawns if you didn't do it in autumn (see September, p.226).

TREES, SHRUBS AND CLIMBERS

PLANT POT-GROWN WOODY PLANTS

Nowadays you can plant woody plants (trees, shrubs, climbers, hedging plants and roses) at any time of year when the ground is in a workable state, provided they are grown in pots. Pot-grown plants come complete with all their roots, and as long as you are careful to keep the rootball fairly intact when you plant them, the plant hardly knows it's been moved and goes about its business as usual. Although you *can* plant virtually any time you like, strategically speaking, the very best times to plant woody subjects are at the beginning and end of the growing season, when the weather tends to take care of them for you. The advantage of planting during the growing season is that you can choose plants in full flower, so you can see exactly what you are buying and its effect on the garden instantly. The drawback is that you'll need to keep new plants watered during dry spells for the rest of the season, so they can establish themselves.

You can tidy up uneven lawn edges quickly using a half-moon-shaped tool (usually known as a half-moon iron). The lawn will be transformed, and maintenance will be easier.

WHEN TO PLANT?

Generally, autumn planting (see October, p.252) is best when you have light, well-drained soil, where roots can establish themselves without risk of a wet winter drowning them. Spring wins hands down in a cold, exposed spot, or anywhere with heavy clay soil or in a low-lying area where the water table comes up quite high in winter. But psychologically, more people plant new plants in spring than at any other time simply because it's the start of the growing season and you have the whole season to enjoy your new purchase.

Between now and through summer and autumn, plant pot-grown roses, hardy trees and shrubs, climbers and hedging plants. However, wait until April (see p.89) or September (see p.228) to plant conifers and evergreens, as they 'take' better then. Bare-root plants should only be planted in autumn or winter, when they are dormant (see November, p.276). They can be planted up to mid-March at the latest, just before the start of the growing season.

Rambler roses like 'American Pillar' can be planted bare-root or container-grown now.

Pot-grown roses

You can plant pot-grown roses any time you like, but if you plant them now, they'll have time to make enough new growth to put on a very acceptable show of flowers this season. What's more, new roses coming from a good nursery at the start of the season will almost certainly have been properly pruned before you buy them, so just put them in and leave them to it.

- Use the same planting technique as for shrubs (see below), but roses benefit from being planted very slightly deeper. That's because roses are actually two plants in one. The top bit with all the stems is the named variety, and the roots belong to a different species chosen

for its good growing qualities. The bulge you can often see where the stems and roots join is the union. Ensure that the union is buried under the surface when planting, in order to encourage stem rooting and to stop it looking as if it's climbing out of the ground. After planting, water, firm and mulch well.

Pot-grown wall plants and other climbers

Plant these in the same way as described for shrubs (see below), and at the usual planting depth (i.e. with the junction between the roots and shoots roughly level with the surface of the ground). However, the following factors need to be taken into account:

- If growing against a wall, you will need to prepare a double- or treble-sized planting hole; this is because a wall has hefty foundations that tend to absorb moisture. Place the plant at least 30cm (12in) or so away from the wall and lean it into position, so its roots won't be dehydrated in long, hot summers.

- The same goes for climbers being planted so as to grow up through a tree or large shrub – only in this case, competition for water and nutrients comes from the host plant. Again,

---

HOW TO PLANT A POT-GROWN TREE OR SHRUB

1 Dig a hole about twice the size of the pot the plant is growing in. Work a good helping of well-rotted garden compost or potting compost into the bottom of it. Sprinkle in half a handful of general-purpose organic fertilizer, and stir the lot together with a fork.

2 Water the plant well, then tip it out of its pot. If the roots look very solidly packed, tease a few gently out from the base and sides of the solid mass; don't break up the rootball more than you have to. (If the plant is pot-bound, see April, pp.95–6.)

3 Stand the plant in the hole, and check the planting depth; the top of the rootball should be roughly level with the surrounding soil. Use the spare soil mixed with extra organic matter to fill the gap around the edge of the rootball.

4 Firm the soil gently down with your heel, then water well and tuck a layer of compost (about 5cm/2in) around the plant as a mulch to keep the roots cool and moist.

the climbers need a large, well-prepared planting hole, and a planting distance of 45cm (18in) from the trunk is recommended.

Pot-grown clematis

Clematis is the odd one out when it comes to planting – it needs putting in very deeply. There are several reasons for this. Deep planting helps to keep clematis roots cool and moist in summer, which they like. But the main reason is as an insurance policy against clematis wilt. A clematis affected by wilt disease starts by flagging badly, then the lot gradually dies down to ground level. If you've planted it deeply, then, instead of being killed completely it can re-grow, because the underground portions of stem produce new shoots to replace what's missing. It's an easy way to save yourself the price of a new plant.

- Dig your planting hole in the same way as for planting shrubs (see p.60), but position the plant so that the top of the rootball is 10–15cm (4–6in) below ground level. After planting, firm lightly, water in and mulch well.

MOVE DECIDUOUS SHRUBS

You can move established deciduous shrubs at any time throughout the dormant season (see November, p.277). However, the very best times are shortly after leaf fall and early March, just before the start of the spring growing season.

PREPARE LARGE DECIDUOUS SHRUBS FOR PLANTING

This is your last chance to prepare large deciduous shrubs for moving the following year (see November, p.277).

LAST CHANCE TO PLANT BARE-ROOT PLANTS

If you still have bare-root trees, shrubs or roses to plant, do so as soon as possible (see November, p.276). Once the buds 'break' and new growth starts, usually around mid-March, there is too much demand on water reserves within the plant for it to cope happily when its roots have not yet started to get established.

HOW TO PRUNE MODERN BUSH ROSES

1 Start by taking out any dead or diseased shoots. Then remove any that are weak and feeble, or crossing the centre of the bush and causing congestion.

2 Cut back the main stems (the thickest, strongest looking ones) to about knee-high, cutting them off about 1cm (¹/₂in) above an outward-facing bud.

PRUNE ROSES

Although most people do their rose-pruning around mid-March, you can leave it as late as early April if the weather is very cold and frosty. The delay means the plants flower slightly later than usual, but it's better than having all the soft new growth nipped by frost. If you prune early you'll have to guess where the buds are going to appear – look for a scar on the stem showing where an old leaf fell off. By leaving pruning until a bit later, the buds start to develop into young shoots, so it's easy to see where to cut. However, don't leave it until the shoots are more than about 2.5cm (1in) long.

Modern bush roses

March is well known in gardening circles as rose-pruning time, but it's mostly modern bush roses that need doing now (see box below). These are the ones we always used to call Hybrid Teas and Floribundas. If you never go near anything else in your garden with secateurs, bush roses are the one group of plants you really *do* need to prune. The reason is simple – all the flowers grow at the tips of the stems, and if you don't prune the bushes they eventually grow so high the only way to enjoy the flowers is from your upstairs windows. In any case, an unpruned rose bush fills up with a clutter of dead twiggy bits like a rook's nest, which doesn't look too clever.

Clematis need to be planted deeper than other plants. The top of the rootball should be 10–15cm (4–6in) below ground level.

Dogwoods grown for their ornamental winter stems need pruning back hard in spring to achieve their full potential.

Patio and ground-cover roses

There are some roses that don't need much pruning at all. Patio roses and Ground-cover roses only need tidying up, but now is the time to do it.

- Use secateurs to nip off any ends of stems that have died back over the winter, and take out any weak, broken or overcrowded stems.

Shrub roses and species roses

Most shrub roses and species roses that are grown for their flowers are pruned in midsummer, just after they finish flowering (see July, p.184). However, those varieties (such as *Rosa rugosa* and *Rosa* 'Geranium') that are grown for their hips cannot be pruned then; instead, they can be trimmed lightly when necessary between late winter and mid-March.

Old fashioned roses, climbers and ramblers

These aren't pruned until later, just after they finish flowering (see July, p.184). However, some very vigorous climbers that are difficult to prune in summer (like *Rosa* 'Madame Alfred Carrière') can be tackled now, cutting back sideshoots to 15cm (6in) and tying in young and vigorous shoots to replace older ones, a few of which can be removed each year.

PRUNE COLOURED-STEMMED DOGWOODS AND WILLOWS

Prune *Cornus alba* cultivars (dogwoods), and *Salix alba* (shrubby willows) grown for their coloured winter stems.

- Cut the oldest stems off 15cm (6in) from the ground to encourage a good crop of new young stems, which have the brightest coloured bark.

PRUNE BUDDLEIA AND ORNAMENTAL ELDERS

Prune *Buddleja davidii* (butterfly bush) and *Sambucus nigra* and *Sambucus racemosa* cultivars (ornamental elders) by cutting last year's growth back to within 15cm (6in) of the main framework of old branches. This looks drastic, as it means removing quite long stems, and reduces the plant to about waist height, but don't let that put you off – it needs doing. An unpruned buddleia has all its flowers at the top where you can't see them, and an unpruned elder grows big and bushy but untidy – hard pruning reshapes it and encourages larger, more spectacular leaves, which is what you want in the case of gold, purple or variegated varieties grown for their foliage. With certain varieties, such as *Sambucus nigra* f. *porphyrophylla* 'Guincho Purple' and *Sambucus nigra* f. *porphyrophylla* 'Eva' (syn. 'Black Lace'), where the pink flowers are a major feature of the plant, prune much more lightly, so you merely reshape the bush, since very hard pruning favours foliage growth instead of flowers.

COPPICE EUCALYPTUS

Eucalyptus turn into very large trees – if you let them. But by cutting the plants hard back every few years they remain bushy, and they retain their attractive rounded juvenile foliage – beloved of flower arrangers – instead of developing the lance-shaped leaves of a mature tree.

- Using a saw, reduce the entire plant to 30–60cm (12–24in) towards the end of the month, or if the weather is very cold wait until April, so emerging shoots aren't hit by hard frosts.

RENOVATE OVERGROWN CLIMBERS

Renovate overgrown climbers by removing a few of the thickest old stems from the base of the plant. Instead of trying to heave them out from surrounding growth, it's easiest if you trace those stems back over and cut them into shorter lengths that can be 'unthreaded' more easily. With the decks cleared a bit, you can then tidy up what's left.

- Tidy up ivy, summer-flowering jasmine and honeysuckles, and if you still have large-flowered clematis un-pruned, then give them a very a light tidy up where you must, but nothing more or you'll miss out on some of this summer's flowers.

- In the case of overgrown rambler or climbing roses, select one or two of the oldest stems that form the main framework of the plant (these will be the most gnarled, woody ones that don't flower so well in summer) to cut out completely. Over the summer, look out for a couple of well-placed new shoots growing out from near the base of the plant, and tie them up to whatever the plant is growing on. Space them out so they fill the gap in the existing framework and cover the structure attractively.

LAYER SHRUBS

Layering is a good way of propagating shrubs when you only want one or two new plants for 'spares' or to give away to friends. It's easier than taking cuttings, since the whole idea is to encourage a stem to take root while it's still attached to the parent plant, which is already established and growing well in the garden. Since the parent looks after its offspring until the youngster has a reasonable set of roots and the two are separated, this technique is ideal for those shrubs that are difficult to root from cuttings, such as rhododendrons, viburnums and magnolias. It's also worth doing with easily rooted shrubs, such as cornus, when you want a really fuss-free propagation method.

Plants are usually ready after a year, although some, such as rhododendrons, may take two years before they are properly rooted. Move new plants produced by layering as if you were moving any bare-rooted shrub (deciduous shrubs from November to mid-March, while they are leafless, and evergreens in April or September, which is when they move best).

A pruning saw is useful for removing and cutting back thicker stems from rose bushes.

HOW TO LAYER A SHRUB

1 Choose a young, flexible shoot placed low down in the parent plant, so that you can bend it down to ground level. Work some well-rotted organic matter into the soil where the chosen shoots touch the ground.

2 Use a knife to make a shallow, sloping cut 2.5–5cm (1–2in) long, no more than one-third of the way through the stem, and about 15–23cm (6–9in) from the tip. Dust the cut surfaces with hormone rooting powder.

3 Bury the stem approximately 2.5–5cm (1–2in) deep along 15cm (6in) of its length, leaving 15cm (6in) of the tip sticking out of the soil. To stop the stem trying to spring back to its usual place, hold it down with a wire hairpin. Leave it for a year or two.

4 You'll know when the shoot has rooted because it starts to branch out and grow just like a freestanding young shrub. Dig the layer up carefully, sever the 'umbilical cord' to the parent and move the youngster to its new planting place.

MAKE A SCREE GARDEN FOR ROCK PLANTS

Rockeries are Victorian inventions that never really look right in today's gardens, to my way of thinking. They also need large amounts of natural stone, which is not 'green' as it is stripped from wild habitats. Water-worn limestone, which was the Victorian favourite, is particularly worth giving a miss as it is taken from irreplaceable natural limestone pavements that have taken millions of years for glaciers to grind into shape.

But if you have well-drained ground, or a slight bank or slope, you can recreate a different type of rock feature – a scree. This is what builds up where bits of stone roll down a mountainside and land up in a heap at the bottom of the slope. You can make a scree bed any shape and size – a formal square or oblong, or a more natural-looking 'teardrop' shape, especially if this fits into the contours of an undulating garden – and you can make it on the flat in a well-drained garden, or use it to fill a raised bed or large container. It's the perfect way to display a treasured collection of rock plants. A scree can look quite minimalist – you don't need to overcrowd it with rocks, pebbles or plants. Much of the appeal is the contrast between plants and gravel.

Improving drainage

If the soil isn't naturally well drained you can create a scree garden by building the soil up to make a raised bed. Outline the shape with dwarf walls of brick, stone or timber, place a 15cm (6in) layer of broken rubble or gravel in the bottom and infill with a mixture of 75 per cent good topsoil and 25 per cent gritty horticultural sand.

1 Clear the ground, then mark out the shape. Excavate it to about 15cm (6in) deep. Fill the hole with gravel and dig it into the soil to make a well-drained base.
2 Knock the rock plants out of their pots and plant them so the tops of the rootballs stand 5cm (2in) proud of the soil. Arrange them in small groups with gaps in between for a natural effect.
3 Mulch round them with a 5cm (2in) layer of pea shingle or granite chippings. You can use the odd chunk of rock or group of pebbles for decoration.

- **Saxifrages** (above left) – mossy and spreading, tussock-shaped with star-like flowers, or silvery mini-cabbages in clumps, all very collectable. Most are spring flowering.
- **Iris reticulata** – very early iris, 15cm (6in) high, with grassy foliage that persists after the flowers are over; grows from bulbs (see February, p.33).
- **Primula auricula** (alpine auricula) –

fat, round, succulent leaves with bull's-eye flowers in spring (see April, p.84).
- **Pulsatilla vulgaris** (Pasque flower – above centre) – feathery foliage with silky purple flowers in spring.
- **Armeria juniperifolia** (thrift) – tufts of green, thread-like leaves with pink pincushions on sticks for flowers, in early and midsummer.
- **Frankenia thymifolia** (sea heath) – thyme-like

carpets with yellow-centred pink summer flowers.
- **Lewisia cotyledon** hybrids (above right) – sophisticated, succulent rosettes of leaves with wavy-edged or stripy pink, magenta or apricot flowers on 15cm (6in) stalks in early summer.
- **Draba aizoides** (whitlow grass) – dense cushions studded with short-stemmed yellow flowers in spring.

FLOWERS

SORT OUT THE ROCK GARDEN

Rock gardens are like borders in miniature, and they need a similar going-over at the start of the season, as do alpine screes and sink gardens. Since everything is on a much smaller scale, use a hand fork instead of the big border version for weeding and titivating. The big difference about spring cleaning a rock feature is that it 'peaks' months earlier than your average flower border. Spring is the main rock plant season, so you'll find a lot of tiny treasures starting to bud up or break into flower now – work very carefully around them.

- After weeding and tidying, top up the mulch of stone chippings, choosing new pea gravel or granite chippings that match the original covering as closely as possible. Tuck it gently under the rosettes and around the necks of the plants. Besides looking good, it helps keep weeds down, discourages slugs and other pests and lets air circulate underneath low-lying leaves, which stops fragile plants rotting.

- If rock features look a bit gappy at the end of winter, now is the time to fill them up with new plants. You can plant pot-grown rock plants even when they're in flower, but keep the rootball intact. Water new plants carefully so the soil sinks down around the roots, and tuck gravel mulch well around them.

SOW HARDY ANNUALS

Hardy annuals are ideal for anyone with a garden to fill on a budget. They are also the kind to go for if you like lots of summer flowers for bedding, cutting or containers but you don't want to spend a fortune on plants or don't have a greenhouse in which to raise plants that need heat to grow from seed. What sets hardy annuals apart from the better-known bedding plants, which are half-hardy annuals, is that they stand the cold, so you can grow them outdoors from start to finish. Hardy annuals are particularly easy to grow on sandy soil, but

HARDY ANNUALS

Hardy annuals start flowering earlier than summer bedding plants (half-hardy annuals) but many of them finish sooner – they are often going over by the end of July – so don't regard them as a total substitute for bedding plants. But they are handy for people who go on holiday in summer and aren't bothered about having a garden full of flowers that need looking after while they aren't there to enjoy them anyway. In most years, hardy annuals will be in flower 12 weeks after sowing. Below are some of the most popular hardy annuals:

Agrostemma (corn cockle)	*Helianthus annuus* (sunflower)
Calendula (pot marigold)	*Iberis* (candytuft)
Centaurea cyanus (cornflower)	*Lathyrus odoratus* (sweet pea)
Cerinthe major 'Purpurascens'	*Limnanthes* (poached-egg flower)
Clarkia	*Nemophila* (baby blue-eyes)
Consolida (larkspur)	*Nigella* (love-in-a-mist)
Convolvulus tricolor (annual convolvulus)	*Tropaeolum majus* (nasturtium)

Sowing *in situ*

Some people like to sow their hardy annuals and wildflowers straight into the bed where they want them to flower (see box below). This can create a colourful, cottage-garden patchwork quilt effect, but if the soil is full of weed seeds, all your flower seedlings will be swamped before they're big enough for you to tell them apart. Where this is the case, you can sow them elsewhere and transplant them later (see below).

The transplanting method

A technique that works better for many gardeners is to sow flower seed in rows in a quiet corner of the garden. A spare row in the salad patch does fine, as the soil is usually good, and you won't need it for long.

● Prepare the soil as for sowing seed *in situ*.

● Sow seed in rows, making a 'drill' by scraping out a shallow depression with the corner of a rake, using a garden line or the side of a board to ensure a straight line. Sprinkle the seed thinly along it, then cover the seed to their own depth with more soil. On heavy ground, use horticultural vermiculite or sand instead of soil to cover the seed, as this improves drainage and prevents the soil 'crusting', so germination is better.

Dig up self-sown hellebore seedlings and pot up or plant elsewhere.

wherever you grow them the secret of success is well-prepared, well-drained earth. (For sowing seed of half-hardy annuals, hardy annuals in pots and tender perennials for summer bedding, see Under Cover, p.73.) Sow wildflowers as for hardy annuals.

HOW TO SOW SEEDS *IN SITU*

1 Fork over the soil. Remove weeds and stones, then sprinkle over general-purpose organic fertilizer. Add lots of garden compost and grit to heavy soil.

2 Rake over the soil well until it looks like well-combed cake crumbs. Mark out informal 'drifts' by trickling dry sand round the outlines of the shapes.

3 Sprinkle seed of a different variety over each patch, in shallow drills 10cm (4in) apart, and rake it in.

4 When the seedlings come up, thin out the overcrowded ones and let the rest grow where they are.

HOW TO DIVIDE AND REPLANT PERENNIALS

1 Work your fork under the clump, then lever it out of the ground with all its roots. If it's a very big clump, it often helps to cut all the way around the edge with a spade first.

2 Prise the clump apart with a spade or an old knife. Cut through where the plant looks less crowded, where there's a natural 'break'. Split the clump in two and get rid of the balding bits from the centre of the plant.

3 Divide what's left into reasonable-sized portions, a touch bigger than your fist, each with several good strong shoots and plenty of healthy-looking roots.

4 Refresh the soil by digging in a good bucketful of well-rotted organic matter, plus a sprinkling of general fertilizer, and replant the best divisions, preferably in groups of three to five. Water them in, and tuck your mulch back around them.

● When the seedlings are about 2.5cm (1in) or so high, thin them out. After a further few weeks of growing, move young plants to their final positions and water them in well. When you dig up the young plants, ensure you leave a little clump of soil clinging to their roots, as many of them resent root disturbance. A good puddling in should settle them into their new home.

PLANT PERENNIALS

Perennials are flowers that live for years, but die down each winter and pop back up each spring. Compared to bedding plants they have a relatively short flowering season, but they are used in quite different ways. These are the flowers to grow in herbaceous borders or in gaps between shrubs in a mixed border, and depending on which kinds you choose they'll flower in spring, summer or late summer/autumn.

The best time to plant new perennials is at the start of the growing season, so they have time to establish before they flower, although it's quite acceptable to plant pot-grown perennials from now until autumn, even when they are in flower, as long as you keep them watered for the rest of the season whenever the soil dries out.

Planting a new bed

Planting is simple. When you have a whole bed to do at once, prepare the ground thoroughly. Dig it over, work in lots of well-rotted compost or manure, and rake it so it's loose and fluffy. Stand your plants in their positions, still in their pots. Take each plant in turn and dig a hole the same size as the pot, tip the plant out and fit the rootball in the hole so its top is flush with the surrounding soil. Firm back the earth. Water the plants in and spread a mulch over the bare soil to seal in the moisture and suppress weeds.

Planting individually

If you are simply adding a new plant to an existing bed, you'll need to make a larger planting hole and work about half a bucketful of organic matter into the bottom, then plant as above and tuck compost-enriched soil in the gap all around the rootball. Firm the soil gently down, then water well and mulch.

DIVIDE PERENNIALS

As perennial plants grow, the clumps spread out from the centre. Once they look tatty and overgrown, fight for space with their neighbours, or start dying out in the middle, they need digging up and dividing. Some kinds spread faster than others, but you can usually expect

---

How to sow poppies
Don't try to transplant poppies, as they really hate root disturbance. They are best sown where you want them to flower. Alternatively, sow them thinly in small pots, thin out excess seedlings, then carefully tap out whole plants or small clumps so you transplant them with intact rootballs.

the job will need doing 3–6 years after planting. You can divide individual perennials at the same time as you tidy your borders (see General Garden Tasks, p.54), but if there are a lot of overgrown plants it's a good excuse to clear the whole bed, divide the lot and start from scratch.

The best time to divide perennials is in spring, when they are little more than clusters of small shoots pushing through the soil. If you wait until the young leaves have opened out, there's a bigger area for water loss, so your newly divided plants wilt and have a struggle to re-establish. A few very tough perennials, such as Michaelmas daisies and goldenrod, can be divided in autumn, but if you want to do the job all in one go, this is the time to do it.

CUT DOWN PERENNIALS

Cut back all dead growth of perennials after winter (see General Garden Tasks, p.54).

PROPAGATE PERENNIALS

Propagate perennials from basal cuttings and root under glass (see Under Cover, p.73).

DIVIDE AND PLANT BULBS

Snowdrops

Divide clumps of snowdrops now, after the flowers are over but before the leaves die down, while they are what's known as 'in the green'. Unlike most spring bulbs, snowdrops have a very short summer rest and the bulbs hate drying out, so they move best while they're still growing. Dig up clumps, separate them into clusters of three or four bulbs, then replant at 15cm (6in) spacings. Snowdrops normally like to be left undisturbed, so they only need dividing when they are so overcrowded that they no longer flower. You can also use this method to produce some new plants if you want some to put elsewhere in the garden.

Lilies

If you have large clumps of lilies that you want to split up, or want to plant new lilies, now is the time to do so. Dormant bulbs are available from garden centres, and bulb specialists supply them via their spring or autumn catalogues.

If you haven't grown lilies before, do check your soil is suitable as they are quite fussy. Lilies need deep, rich, fertile soil containing plenty of organic matter, but reasonably well drained or else they rot off in winter. Most need lime-free soil, meaning neutral or slightly acid when checked with a soil test kit – only a few species, such as the Madonna lily, *Lilium candidum*, will put up with lime. Lilies like to grow where their roots are shaded by surrounding plants but their stems and flowers can grow out into the sunlight. Mixed borders, where they can grow between shrubs and perennials, are perfect.

- To divide lilies, follow the same basic method as for perennials (see above), but be aware that the bulbs are very delicate, so prise them apart carefully. If you happen to slice one open then it's best detached from the group and thrown away, otherwise it'll rot and take its neighbours with it.

- Plant dormant bulbs, ensuring you plant deeply enough – most kinds need planting at three times their own depth. The only exception is the Madonna lily, which likes shallow planting, so put these in leaving their 'noses' just showing above the surface of the ground.

Gladioli

Gladioli may sound a tad old fashioned, but the smaller butterfly glads look good grouped in gaps in a border, woven among ornamental grasses. If you're going to cut them, plant a row in your vegetable patch, or a special 'cutting' garden. For a succession of glads over much of the summer, plant a few corms every 2 weeks between mid-March and mid-May.

- Plant the corms about 5cm (2in) deep – butterfly glads don't need staking as they only grow about 45cm (18in) high, but if you grow the big, heavy sort, you'll need to stake each flower stem as it grows to keep it straight. In autumn, when the foliage dies down, 'harvest' the dry corms to store in a frost-free place, as they don't always survive winter in the garden (see October, p.254).

Position container-grown plants thoughtfully – taking into account their height and spread – before planting them.

Lavish planting

In spring, you're planting for immediate results – the plants are usually already in flower, and as they won't last for more than 6 or 8 weeks they won't have time to grow. Plant them thickly so they put on a good show right from the start – one or two really flower-filled containers will make much more impact than half a dozen half-hearted tubs.

PATIOS AND CONTAINERS

CLEAN THE PATIO

The first spot of sun usually sees people casting a critical eye over their patio or decking. A combination of wet weather and lack of use means that by the time spring starts there's often a certain amount of mess to tackle.

- The first place to start is the hard surfaces, so remove any weeds or moss growing in awkward cracks in the paving – an old table knife is quite handy for this.

- Scrub paving slabs or wooden decking slats, or give them the once-over with a pressure washer. Most muck peels off quite easily given a bit of elbow-grease, but anything really tough usually responds to a dose of one of the proprietary patio or decking cleaning products now available. Don't risk using things like bleach, because they can remove the colour, and any run-off will almost certainly find its way on to plants.

FRESHEN UP CONTAINERS

If containers have evergreens or winter/spring bedding in them, the same plants will keep going for ages yet – all they need is freshening up. A quick weed-through, top up the compost, washing the outside of the containers if they've had muck splashed up them by winter rain, and you're about done.

PLANT NEW SPRING BEDDING

To plant new spring bedding, tip out last year's old compost, refill with new potting compost and start again with spring flowers (see illustration below). Don't worry if you didn't grow your own wallflowers, polyanthus and violas, because you'll have no trouble buying spring bedding and bulbs in pots, just coming into bloom now. You can also plant early-flowering perennials and rock plants to create instantly colourful spring container displays. When it's time to make way for summer bedding, shift the plants to a flowerbed to free up your containers and give you two-for-the-price-of-one planting.

Good garden centres and nurseries won't put spring bedding on sale until the weather is fit to plant it out, so in a cold season you may not see very many plants before April. But

HOW TO PLANT UP A CONTAINER

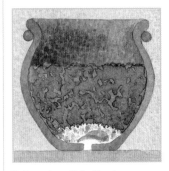

1 Put a handful of broken crocks or gravel in the bottom of the container for drainage. If there's a big drainage hole, cover it with a piece of broken clay pot. Fill the container with potting compost, until it's about three-quarters full.

2 Tip the plants out of their pots, planting them as close together as you can. Don't try to separate the roots, and leave the rootball intact, as any disturbance will set the plants back.

3 Fill around the plants with more compost, so that the top of the rootballs are roughly level with the surface of the compost. Make sure there is a gap of about 2.5cm (1in) between the rim of the container and the top of the compost to allow room for watering.

4 Water the plants in, but don't soak the compost. If there's a sharp spell of very cold weather – always a risk in spring – move the pot under cover temporarily, or wrap several layers of horticultural fleece around the top of the container like a turban to protect the plants.

watch out. If you are offered spring bedding that's standing outside in freezing conditions, so the pots have frozen to the ground, it's unlikely to be long for this world, so I'd wait until the better weather comes, and do my shopping elsewhere.

The initial range of spring bedding is relatively small, but as the season progresses a wider choice becomes available. The following list is just a selection of some of the plants that are available, including spring bulbs: *Bellis perennis* (double daisies), *Muscari* (grape hyacinths), *Myosotis* (forget-me-nots), *Narcissus* 'Jetfire', 'Jenny', 'Little Witch', 'Tête-à-tête' (dwarf daffodils), pansies, polyanthus, *Ranunculus* (turban buttercup), *Tulipa* (waterlily tulips and other short-stemmed tulips), and violas.

ALL-YEAR-ROUND CONTAINERS

If the idea of replanting your tubs and window boxes two or three times every year doesn't appeal, then forget about bedding plants and go for a permanent planting scheme instead. Compact evergreens are the best subjects, as they'll give you all-year-round interest, and they include quite a wide range of dwarf shrubs, herbs and alpines. The same plants can stay in the same container for 3–5 years, and as a bonus they don't usually need as much watering as bedding, which is notoriously thirsty, so you'll save yourself a fair bit of work.

Compost requirements

Use John Innes potting compost for all your year-round containers. Being made from soil, which is mineral in origin, it doesn't decompose and lose its open texture like a peat-based soil-less compost, which is why it's better for long-term use. There are several types of John Innes potting compost – ensure you use the right one for the job.

- Use John Innes No 2 or No 3 for shrubs and evergreens in large containers, as these contain more nutrients. John Innes No 1 is meant for young plants in small pots.
- For rock plants and anything else that needs particularly free drainage, mix up a gritty compost from 3 parts of John Innes No 2 potting compost to 1 part of potting grit.
- Lime-hating plants, such as dwarf rhododendrons and camellias, need an ericaceous potting compost – the John Innes version is best for year-round containers. If you can't find it, mix some lime-free grit into soil-less ericaceous compost to open up the texture, and make a mental note that you'll need to feed more often as soil-less compost doesn't hold nutrients as well as a soil mix.

Aftercare

Maintenance of year-round containers is easy. After planting, just treat them like houseplants that happen to live outdoors.

- During the growing season (roughly April to September), water them regularly whenever the compost feels dry to touch, and give them a dose of liquid feed every 2 weeks from April to late August.
- In winter, move them close to a wall for shelter. Although they won't need so much water you'll still need to check on them because you can't rely on rain to hit the spot – the foliage often acts as an 'umbrella' over the top of the tub. Water the plants if they appear dry.
- By the second spring, a year-round container will want freshening up. To top-dress, scrape off the top 5cm (2in) or so of old potting compost, removing any weeds or moss, and replace it with some new compost (see above) into which you've mixed some slow-release fertilizer. As long as you choose compact, slow-growing evergreens, you can follow the same routine for 3 or 4 years or more before the plants outgrow their tub or start to look jaded, which is a sure sign they need moving. When that happens, you have the choice – either repot them back into the same tub or a slightly larger one, with a complete change of compost, or plant them out in the garden.

The following are examples of plants that are good for year-round containers:

- **rock plants** – sempervivums, *Thymus* (creeping thymes), sedums, *Saxifraga* (silver-encrusted saxifrages)
- **herbs** – rosemary, lavenders, bushy thymes, winter savory, bay
- **shrubs** – hebes, camellias, dwarf rhododendrons
- **architectural plants** – *Buxus sempervirens* (box topiary), *Taxus baccata* 'Fastigiata' (fastigiate or clipped yew), *Ilex aquifolium* (standard or clipped holly)
- **plants for shade** – *Hedera* (ivies), evergreen hardy ferns, *Aucuba japonica* (spotted laurel), skimmias

VEGETABLES AND HERBS

Crops sown or planted outside in March need the protection of a cloche or horticultural fleece.

PREPARE THE SOIL FOR SOWING

The vegetable patch is coming out of hibernation this month. If you haven't got your winter digging done, it needs to be completed as soon as conditions permit (see November, p.272). A light, free-draining soil in a sunny spot produces the earliest crops, so choose your best patch for early growing. (If you have very heavy clay soil, there's no point even trying to make an early start outdoors, so either make an early start in your greenhouse border or be patient for another month or so.)

● Ground that's already been rough dug only needs final preparation to make it ready for sowing. Hoe off any last-minute weeds, take out any stones or bits of root and rubbish, sprinkle a light dressing of general-purpose organic fertilizer over the area, and rake the surface down to a fine tilth, leaving a seedbed the texture of cake crumbs. (For gardening on very wet or dry soil, see box opposite.)

SOW SEED FOR VEGETABLES

Although it's tempting to fill the vegetable garden up all at once, resist it for now. There are only a few things you can sow or plant this soon, and unless the weather is unusually kind you'll be well advised to cover early crops with horticultural fleece or cloches for protection – anything you can sow now will also wait until next month. In any case, leave plenty of room for crops that can't go in until later.

If you really must make a start outside, useful things to sow under cloches or fleece include lettuce, rocket, radish, spring onions, leeks, onions, broad beans, parsnips, spinach, turnips, early varieties of carrots and peas (see box below). You could also sow summer cabbage and summer cauliflowers, but it would be better to sow them in the greenhouse (see Under Cover, p.73) and transplant young plants later if you can.

PLANT NEW POTATOES

'Everyday' maincrop potatoes are not normally worth growing unless you have an allotment, but there's one kind you shouldn't pass up on and that's the first earlies. These are the varieties that produce wonderful baby new potatoes in June (see April, p.101, for recommended varieties). In a mild area, or an early spring,

---

HOW TO SOW SEED IN ROWS

1 Lay a straight edge, for example a garden line or a cane, on the ground as a guide and make a shallow groove (or drill) along it using a corner of a hoe or rake. The drill should be about 1cm (¹/₂in) deep.

2 Sprinkle your seeds thinly along the drill. After sowing, rake back the fine soil very lightly, just enough to barely bury the seeds.

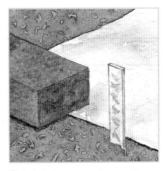

3 Label the row and cover it to keep the warmth in. The traditional way of raising extra-early vegetables was to grow them under cloches or in a cold frame, but these days it's cheaper and easier to use horticultural fleece (see February, p.40).

4 Once the seedlings come up, thin them out to the correct spacing. You'll find precise instructions for individual vegetables on the back of the seed packets, so don't throw them away (see also April, p.99, for recommended spacings).

they can go in at the end of this month – for the very earliest crops, cover the rows with horticultural fleece or cloches to speed them up. Elsewhere, wait until April – your new spuds will just be a bit later, but at least they'll be safe from frost.

- Dig a flat-bottomed trench 12cm (5in) deep and spread some well-rotted garden compost or manure along it. Plant seed potatoes that have been chitted (see January, p.27), with sprouts 2.5cm (1in) long. Space them 30cm (12in) apart along the row, with 45cm (1½ft) between the rows. Then fill the trench with soil, covering the tubers completely, and stick a label in the end of the row to mark the spot.

PLANT ONIONS AND SHALLOTS

Onions are a dreadful fiddle to grow from seed. Either you sow them under glass in January, prick them out into pots, then transplant them, or take a risk and sow them in rows in the garden, when – being small, slow-growing and grass-like – they are very often overwhelmed by weeds. That's why most people opt for planting onions sets instead of sowing seed, as it's a lot more straightforward (see box, right). Sets are like half-grown baby onions, but in a dormant state. Shallots are grown in exactly the same way as onions, the big difference being that each shallot you plant grows into a clump of several offsets instead of just one, so you need to space them out a bit more than onions.

PLANT GARLIC

If you don't get around to planting garlic in autumn (see November, p.283) you could plant it now, to use in September. However, November is preferable unless you live in a very cold area.

PLANT JERUSALEM ARTICHOKES

Plant your Jerusalem artichokes now, if you didn't in February (see February, p.40).

GROWING VEGETABLES IN WET OR DRY SOIL

Vegetable gardening is a doddle if you have perfect, deep, rich, loamy soil that's been previously well cultivated, with regular additions of well-rotted organic matter, but not everyone is that lucky.

- If you garden on wet, sticky, clay soil, be prepared to delay your vegetable gardening until next month, when the weather has warmed and dried the soil enough to make it workable. Sowing too soon on this type of soil simply means that seeds rot, especially big ones such as peas and beans. But clay can be improved if you really work at digging in garden compost and sharp grit at every opportunity. It also helps to trickle a little silver sand or potting grit along the drills before sowing seed, and then to cover the seed with a sprinkling of sand or grit, instead of soil, after sowing.
- Sandy soil is just the reverse: it drains quickly and warms up well, so you can usually start vegetable growing very early in the season. Also, provided you dig in lots of organic matter to beef the soil up and help it retain moisture, it's also the best type for bringing on early crops under cloches or horticultural fleece. To help retain enough moisture for seeds to germinate well, trickle some horticultural vermiculite or soil-less seed compost along the drills, and use more of the same to cover the seeds after you've sown them.

HOW TO PLANT ONION AND SHALLOT SETS

1 First, prepare the ground as if you were sowing seed (see facing page). Take out small holes with a trowel and lower the sets into the soil so that they just disappear from view (if you leave the tops showing, blackbirds will pull them out).

2 Space the onion sets about 10cm (4in) apart, in rows 30cm (12in) apart, so there's just enough room to run a hoe between them later. Space shallots 20 × 30cm (8 × 12in). Water well, and pop back occasionally to replant the odd one that the blackbird has tugged out.

To get greenhouse-raised plants used to cooler outdoor temperatures before planting out, place them outdoors on fine days but bring them indoors at night.

HARDEN OFF AND PLANT READY-GROWN VEGETABLE PLANTS AND AUTUMN-SOWN BRASSICAS

Young, ready-grown vegetable plants bought in garden centres and autumn-sown brassicas will have been kept under cover over the winter, so even though they are 'frost hardy' they need hardening off carefully before planting outside, to acclimatize them to the change of conditions.

● Stand the plants outside on fine days and bring them back under cover at night. After a couple of weeks, plant them out in rows at their final spacing, and if possible cover them with cloches or horticultural fleece for protection. But if the weather is cold and windy, and the soil wet and claggy, wait until next month.

PREPARE AN ASPARAGUS BED

One vegetable that's well worth growing, as it's such a high-value crop in the shops, is asparagus. Years ago, it was grown in a separate bed of its own, raised up on ridges, and heavily manured every winter, which made people think it was too much bother. But if you don't have room for a separate bed, it's now quite normal to grow a row of asparagus along one edge of a normal veg patch as long as you give it a sunny, sheltered, well-drained spot where the fleshy roots won't rot away in winter. Don't plant asparagus in the middle of a veg plot, because for most of the growing season it's a big, bushy perennial vegetable that would smother its neighbours.

Right: To increase your stock of perennial herbs, such as mint or chives, dig up a large plant, divide the clump, and replant the smaller sections.

● As asparagus is a perennial crop that stays in the same place for many years, it's essential to prepare the ground well. Dig deeply, burying as much well-rotted manure or other rich organic matter as you can spare. Add gritty horticultural sand to open up heavy ground.

● Plant asparagus in April (see pp.101–2).

HARVEST VEG

Harvest sprouting broccoli, the last of the Brussels sprouts, and Swiss chard (last year's plants that were left in the ground will be growing again now, and you'll have about 6 weeks of picking before they shoot up to seed and need pulling out).

SOW HARDY HERBS

If you're keen to get going, you can sow seeds of hardy herbs, such as parsley, chervil, coriander, fennel, dill and marjoram, in shallow drills outside, in the same way as for early vegetables (see p.68); protection from cloches or horticultural fleece is advisable in all but the mildest seasons. However, since most people only want one or two plants of each kind, it's often easier to sow them in pots on the kitchen windowsill or in the greenhouse, where they come up more quickly, and give you plants to put out in about 8 weeks' time. Sow the seeds sparingly in seed compost in 9-cm (3½-in) pots (see Under Cover, p.73), and don't bother thinning out excess seedlings unless they are badly overcrowded – simply plant out the whole clump.

PLANT AND DIVIDE PERENNIAL HERBS

Dig up large clumps of chives or mint that will by now be showing signs of life down the garden, and divide and replant them into well-prepared soil. Also, add to your herb collection by buying plants of perennial herbs, such as sage, tarragon and rosemary, to put in towards the end of the month. But don't risk non-hardy herbs outside just yet. And don't plant out pots of herbs bought from a supermarket, even hardy ones, since they'll have been brought on indoors in ideal conditions and won't be acclimatized to the rough and tumble of outdoor weather. Keep them on the kitchen windowsill, to use the way the growers intended, that is, immediately.

FRUIT

SPRING CLEAN THE FRUIT GARDEN

Compared to the vegetable patch, which is alive with early activity, the fruit garden is hardly waking up. However, there is still work to be done preparing for the months ahead.

● Go round your fruit trees, canes and bushes doing the same sort of pre-season tidy-up you've done in your ornamental borders, weeding and mulching everything with organic matter (see General Garden Tasks, p.54). However, don't feed until next month.

● Tidy up around strawberry plants, take out any weeds, remove dead leaves, and loosen up compacted soil with the points of a small border fork. Take care if you decide to use a hoe, as strawberries have notoriously shallow roots. Leave feeding until next month so as not to encourage a lot of early growth that will only be hit by late frosts.

● If the weather is very dry, start watering fruit in pots, plus any trained fruit trees or bushes growing against walls where the soil dries out quickly – give these a particularly generous mulch.

PLANT RHUBARB

Plant dormant rhubarb crowns now. Choose a sunny spot, as rhubarb stems turn rosy-red when they are exposed to plenty of sunlight; in the shade, rhubarb is an unattractive khaki-green.

● Rhubarb likes really rich soil, so dig a pit and fill it with as much well-rotted garden compost or composted stable manure as you can before planting the crowns into it. Buy pot-grown crowns and replant so the top of the rootball is level with the surface of the surrounding soil. If growing several rhubarb plants, space them 60–90cm (2–3ft) apart. Mulch generously. If you want to force rhubarb for long, thin, early, tender stems, leave new crowns for a couple of years to become well established before digging them up and forcing them (see January, p.26).

PROTECT PEACHES, NECTARINES AND APRICOTS

These are 'foreign' fruit trees that originate from warmer parts of the world, and flower much earlier than the usual apples and pears. As a result, the flowers need protection when the weather turns cold.

● Lower a curtain of horticultural fleece over the flowers to help protect them from frost. This will also reduce the likelihood of peach leaf curl by intercepting fungal spores.

HAND-POLLINATE PEACHES, NECTARINES AND APRICOTS

Because there aren't many bees about when these fruit trees flower, it pays to hand-pollinate them to be sure they set fruit.

● Dab the bristles of a small, soft brush (an artist's watercolour brush will do the job nicely) into the centre of all the open flowers to transfer the pollen from one flower to another. Do this every day, especially when the sun is out, and if possible around midday, but if that sounds like a tall order it's better to do it occasionally whenever it's convenient than not at all.

LAST CHANCE TO PRUNE APPLE AND PEAR TREES

Early March is the last chance to prune standard apple and pear trees, before the buds burst, otherwise leave it until next winter (see January, p.23).

TIE IN SHOOTS OF BLACKBERRIES AND LOGANBERRIES

Start tying in young shoots of blackberries and loganberries as soon as the plants start growing again.

You can remove weeds in the strawberry patch using a hoe, but be very careful as strawberry plants have extremely shallow roots.

LAST CHANCE TO PLANT BARE-ROOT FRUIT TREES AND BUSHES

Now is your last chance to plant bare-root fruit trees (see November, p.276) and soft fruit bushes. However, you can plant pot-grown ones from now right on through the summer, even when they are in flower or fruit (see below).

PLANT POT-GROWN FRUIT TREES

If you want to plant new fruit trees, canes or bushes, now is a good time to do so even though – strictly speaking – you can plant pot-grown fruit right through the summer. Doing it now means they can get established before the hot, dry weather starts. Choose a sheltered, sunny spot with deep, fertile, well-drained soil, avoiding anywhere with an easterly aspect, and plant them the same way as pot-grown trees or shrubs (see Trees, Shrubs and Climbers, p.55).

Very dwarfing rootstocks can't cope with competition from other plants for food and water, so fruit trees growing on them are no good for planting in the lawn or a flower border – they need at least 1m (3ft) of bare soil all round them. Choose trees on only moderately dwarfing rootstocks for those situations, but even so keep a circle of bare soil all round them for the first 3 years after planting so they have a chance to become well established before they have to face up to any competition.

STAKE FRUIT TREES AFTER PLANTING

Since fruit trees nowadays are grown on dwarfing rootstocks, which have weak root systems, they need firm staking and more support than your average ornamental tree.

- Use a 1.2m (4ft) long stake and hammer 45cm (18in) of it into the ground at an angle of 45 degrees so that it nestles alongside the trunk about 30cm (1ft) above ground level. Then use a proprietary tree tie to hold the trunk to the stake.

TRAIN FAN- AND ESPALIER-TRAINED TREES AFTER PLANTING

Fan- and espalier-trained trees are the best bet for planting against trellis at the back of your border, if you want a fruiting 'garden divider'. And of course they are brilliant for growing against walls – the wall acts like a storage radiator, so it's a particularly good place to plant warmth-loving fruit such as pears, plums, peaches, nectarines or apricots. After planting fan- and espalier-trained trees, tie the 'arms' out along canes fixed to horizontal wires, or to trellis for support.

PLANT STRAWBERRY PLANTS

You can still plant pot-grown strawberry plants (see October, p.257), although they'll only give a fairly light crop in their first year.

Insert an angled stake after planting a fruit tree.

Espalier-trained fruit ripens more quickly.

UNDER COVER

GENERAL GREENHOUSE MANAGEMENT

- Clean the greenhouse glass (see October, p.258).

- Continue heating a frost-free greenhouse since we can still have cold nights.

- If you don't have automatic ventilator openers fitted, put them in – they are well worth it for the time they save over the year.

- Pick plants over to remove dead leaves and spent flowers, and water plants sparingly, ideally in the morning of fine days so that plants are not left damp overnight.

- Keep an eye out for greenfly and wipe off plants by hand. Remove woodlice, slugs and snails (find them under staging and hiding among plants that have been left undisturbed for some time), especially if you'll be using the greenhouse for propagation – they'll make a bee-line for tender young seedlings.

- Order biological-control nematodes to tackle vine weevil if these have been a problem, and apply next month.

WAKE-UP CALL FOR DORMANT GREENHOUSE PLANTS AND TUBERS

- Start cacti and succulents back into growth by spraying them with tepid water on fine days. Don't risk watering them just yet. Wait a few weeks until they start growing again.

- Start dormant fuchsias and overwintered half-hardy perennials, such as tender shrubby salvias, into growth by splashing a little water on to the compost in their pots, just as a hint. Once new growth is visible at the base of the plant, cut off dead stems if you have not already done so.

- Start begonia and gloxinia tubers into growth by sitting them concave-side up on a tray of damp seed compost in a warm place, such as the propagator or windowsill indoors, and pot them up once growth buds are clearly visible, so you know they're the right way up. Pot them 2.5cm (1in) deep, for stability.

- Pot achimenes tubercles three or five per 10cm (4in) pot, so they make a good clump, planting them 2.5cm (1in) deep. Stand the pots in a heated propagator at 21°C (70°F).

- Pot dormant arum lilies, canna, and dahlia tubers and stand them on the bench of a frost-free greenhouse, watering only very gently until new growth is evident. Increase the watering and start light feeding when the stems are a few inches high, and keep them in good light.

SOW SEED IN POTS

Given a greenhouse heated sufficiently to keep it frost-free, plus a heated propagator, you can virtually have your own nursery raising a huge variety of plants – greenhouse pot plants, bedding plants you need for the garden and patio containers, tomatoes, peppers and aubergines, plus early, frost-tender vegetable plants for putting outside later. If you only need a few plants it's more cost-effective to grow pots of seeds on a warm windowsill indoors. (See illustration, p.74, for instructions on how to sow seed in pots.)

Hygiene tips
Good hygiene is vital for anything to do with seed and seedlings, so make sure seed trays and pots are scrupulously clean and start each season with a new bag of seed compost (don't risk using an old one that's been hanging around open since last year).

Start cacti and succulents into growth by spraying them with tepid water.

HOW TO SOW SEED IN POTS

1 Fill a new or well-washed pot to within 1cm (¹/₂in) of the rim with seed compost taken from a newly opened bag. Level the surface and firm the soil very lightly.

2 Sprinkle fine seeds very thinly over the surface and leave them uncovered (for larger seeds, see box, below). Stand the pot in 5cm (2in) of water until the moisture has soaked its way up to the surface of the compost. Allow to drain for a few minutes.

3 Stand the pots of seed in a propagator, on the windowsill or greenhouse benching at the correct temperature (see below), in good light but where the pots are shaded from bright sun. A single sheet of newspaper can be laid over the pots until the first seedlings start to show.

4 When seedlings come up and are large enough to handle (about 3–4 weeks after sowing), prick them out to give them more room to develop (see April, pp.107–8). In the case of large seeds sown two or three per pot, simply pull out all but the strongest seedling if several come up.

Medium and large seeds

Sow medium-sized seeds as for fine seeds, but after sowing cover with just enough compost to bury them, and no more. The easy way is to dust it through a coarse kitchen sieve. Water as in step 2 (above), or by using a fine rose on a watering can.

With large seeds, sow one or two per pot and push them into the compost with a pencil to roughly their own depth. Water with a gentle trickle from a watering can.

In the same way, you can also raise hardy annuals and wildflowers in pots in an unheated greenhouse or under the carport if there's enough light. The advantage of growing them under cover is that they'll be ready slightly ahead of outdoor-sown plants (see Flowers, p.63, for a list of hardy annuals). After a bit of hardening off (see April, p.108) they can go out into the garden as soon as they're big enough – but choose a moment when the weather isn't too cold, wet and windy. Although they're hardy, they aren't indestructible.

Ideal sowing conditions

The basic method for sowing seed in pots (see box above) works whether you're sowing tomatoes in a heated propagator, busy Lizzies on your spare bedroom windowsill, or hardy annuals and wildflower seeds in a frost-free or unheated greenhouse. Keep both germinating seed and young seedlings in reasonably good light, but shade them from the scorching effect of bright sunlight.

The backs of the packets give precise instructions for individual varieties of seeds, but as a rough guide, bear in mind the following:

- Bedding plants/half-hardy annuals, half-hardy perennials, tomatoes, peppers, chillies and aubergines need 21–24°C (70–75°F) to germinate.

- Early vegetable plants, such as summer cabbages and cauliflowers, require 10–13°C (50–55°F).

- Hardy annuals and wildflowers need 4–10°C (40–50°F).

POT UP PLUG PLANTS

If you don't want the bother of sowing seeds and pricking out seedlings, then you can cut down on work by buying plug plants and simply potting them up (see p.77). If you didn't order them through specialist catalogues in winter, you can buy a more limited range from garden centres throughout spring.

Nowadays, some distributors offer plugs in a choice of sizes from very small early in the season, to larger ones that are almost mini-plants later in the spring or early summer. These cost more but take less time to reach flowering size. The larger ones are best for beginners, as they aren't as fussy as the smaller semi-seedling types.

The one thing you must do with any plugs sent by post is unpack them straight away. Even if you don't have time to pot them up, stand them on a windowsill in the light – not strong sun – and give them a drop of water if they need it. That way, they'll stay in good condition until the weekend, when you have time to pot them properly. If you leave them in the parcel for a few days, they'll have started to turn slimy or at the very least they'll have been 'blanched' by lack of light and be difficult to get going.

HOW TO POT UP PLUGS

- Plant each plug plant individually into a 9cm (3½in) pot filled with seed or potting compost.

- Water carefully so the compost never dries out or becomes waterlogged, and keep the plants in good light but not strong sun.

- Nip the growing tips out of patio plants, such as fuchsias and pelargoniums, to make them branch.

- When the plants fill the pot with roots and are roughly the size of ready-to-plant subjects at the garden centre, plant them outdoors. In the case of tender species, such as patio plants and bedding plants, harden them off

Plug plants should be potted up as soon as possible. Plant each plug individually in a pot filled with seed or potting compost.

carefully (see April, p.108) and wait until after the last frost (usually some time in May).

TAKE CUTTINGS FROM BORDER PERENNIALS

When you don't want the bother of digging up and dividing the parent plant, you can propagate perennial border flowers from basal cuttings in the greenhouse (see box below). They are made in exactly the same way as cuttings of pelargoniums and fuchsias (see June, p.170), except you can't take them from the tips of long shoots – you have to use the young growth shortly after it emerges from the

Improvised propagator
If you haven't got a propagator, place a pot containing seeds inside a plastic bag to maintain humidity.

HOW TO PROPAGATE FROM BASAL CUTTINGS

1 Scrape away some of the surrounding soil to expose part of the blanched stem underground, then use secateurs to snip it off as deep below ground as you can.

2 Using a sharp knife, make a clean, straight cut across the base of the stem and remove the lower leaves, if any, so there are only a few unfurled leaves at the top.

3 Push in five cuttings around the edge of a 10cm (4in) pot filled with seed compost. Water lightly in. Place in a heated propagator at 16°C (60°F), or slip inside a plastic bag and keep on a shady windowsill indoors.

4 When the cuttings are well rooted and are clearly growing under their own steam, pot each one individually and grow it on in the greenhouse until it is big enough to plant outside.

Seed-potato tubers can be planted in black polythene bin liners, perforated in the based to allow drainage, and grown to produce an early crop in the greenhouse.

Right: A single trip wire, 23cm (9in) off the ground, will help to deter herons from fishing in your pond.

base of the plant. Not surprisingly, suitable shoots are only available in early spring, which is why it's now or never if you intend propagating perennials this way.

As soon as the first fat shoots of border perennials, such as delphiniums, lupins and hardy cranesbills, appear above ground and reach 5–8cm (2–3in) long, with a few opened-out leaves, they are ready to take as cuttings.

TAKE CUTTINGS FROM CORMS AND TUBERS

You can take cuttings of dahlias, gloxinias and begonias from tubers that you've potted up and started early in the greenhouse, using the same method as for propagating perennials from basal cuttings (see box, p.75). With plants that grow from corms and tubers, it's only worth taking cuttings early in the season as it takes all summer for them to produce a new tuber, which is essential if they are to survive the winter.

PLANT EARLY CROPS IN POTS

- If you haven't already done so, there's still time to plant sprouted tubers of early potato varieties in pots in a frost-free greenhouse (see February, p.44).

- For early crops, sow lettuce, summer cabbage and summer cauliflower varieties in pots in a propagator in the greenhouse to transplant outdoors later. If bad weather, wet soil or pests prevent you from sowing large seeds, such as broad beans and early peas outdoors, you can sow two or three seeds in 9cm (3½in) pots and put young plants out next month.

WATER AND HAND-POLLINATE FORCED STRAWBERRY PLANTS

Keep forced strawberry plants watered, and hand-pollinate the flowers with a soft artist's paintbrush (see January, p.26). Do not feed until the flowers have clearly set, in April/May (see April, p.112).

WATER GARDEN

START OF THE SEASON JOBS

Don't worry if the water looks green at this time of year; it should soon clear itself naturally once water plants start growing and the pond finds its 'natural balance'.

- Take netting off the pond to prevent emerging marginal plants from becoming entangled.

- Replace underwater lighting and submersible pumps for running fountains.

FISH CARE

- If the weather is warm and fish are active, begin feeding with wheatgerm pond fish food, which is very easily digestible. But it's usually best to wait until April, when the water is warmer.

- Put a trip wire around the edge of the water to keep fish safe if herons are a problem.

PROJECT Grow your own bonsai

If you fancy a novel feature, a small collection of bonsai trees is fun to grow and takes up very little room on a table on your patio or outside your gazebo. The plants are real characters, like pets in pots. But well-trained miniaturized trees can be very expensive to buy. It's much more creative to grow your own from seedlings, or cheat by converting pot-grown shrubs from the garden centre.

GROWING BONSAIS FROM SCRATCH

If you really want to start from scratch, sow your own pips from apples, cherries, or pears, or buy tree and shrub seeds. 'Bonsai seed' don't grow into bonsai specimens naturally – they are perfectly normal species that need training to miniaturize them. Sow the seed in pots sunk to their rim in the garden, and protect them from birds and mice with a cap of fine wire mesh. Some will come up this spring, but many need a cold spell before they will germinate, so they're unlikely to come up until after one or more winters outdoors – most people prefer to sow them in autumn.

It's much quicker to go to the garden and dig up self-sown tree or shrub seedlings, such as hawthorn, cotoneaster and oak, or buy small bare-root hedging plants, such as hornbeam, from a nursery and put them in pots (see below).

CONVERTING EXISTING POT-GROWN PLANTS

If you can't wait to grow a bonsai from a seedling, cheat. Buy a young plant of something vaguely oriental, such as *Ginkgo biloba*, *Acer palmatum* cultivars, or conifers, and choose a plant that looks slightly craggy or lopsided, as it'll lend itself better to bonsai than a perfectly symmetrical specimen. Repot into a shallow bonsai pot, trimming the roots (see below). Shape the top to accentuate the craggy shape you've already 'spotted'.

What you need

Tree or shrub seedling

10–12cm (4–5in) pot

Potting compost (John Innes No 1)

Secateurs or proper bonsai shears

Shallow bonsai pot

Copper wire, sold specially for bonsai

1 Plant a tree or shrub seedling in a 10–12cm (4–5in) pot containing John Innes No 1 potting compost for the first year or two.

2 One or two years later, at the start of the growing season (March), knock the plant out of its pot, shaking the old soil from the roots. Prune the roots back by about half and repot the plant into a shallow bonsai pot, again using John Innes No 1 potting compost.

3 Prune away one-third to half the shoots, leaving a craggy shape that will form the frame-work of your bonsai tree as it grows.

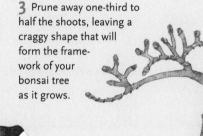

4 As new shoots grow and start to firm, wind copper wire around them and bend them gently into shape to produce a more intriguing-looking plant. Proper bonsai is trained into specific shapes, but when you are just having fun work freehand. Leave the wire in place for 1 or 2 years until the stems 'set' in position, then gently unwind it.

5 Water daily during the growing season, and twice daily in hot dry weather, as the small shallow pots dry out very quickly. Use a weak liquid feed every 3–4 weeks in summer.

6 Keep plants out of sun and wind, which make them dry out faster, and in winter stand them in a cold greenhouse or light carport for shelter, so the roots don't freeze solid.

APRIL

As if to prove that spring is really here, the blossom is out in force in April with everything from flowering cherries to common or garden fruit trees contributing to the show. On those perfect early spring days, when the air is clear, the sun is shining, and the blackbird is trilling away in the treetops, get out in the garden and enjoy it.

Mild sunny weather in April can make you think summer is here already. It isn't. Short, sharp frosts can still catch you out, giving newly opened leaves and buds a nasty nip in exposed places, and killing fruit tree blossom – which spells curtains for your crop. Don't let a few sunny days tempt you into planting tender bedding and patio flowers too soon. Oh, I know the garden centres have them in stock – but they need keeping under cover until you're completely sure of the weather, and that won't be until sometime next month. Unless you can keep plants under glass, for now, keep your money in your wallet.

THE BIG PICTURE spring blossom

Flowering cherries really smack you in the eye as you're out driving in April. Some of the subtler species start flowering earlier, but this is the peak cherry blossom time, when all the really over-the-top Japanese kinds are in full fig. About 35 years ago, local authorities loved to plant *Prunus* **'Kanzan'**, a large tree with a shuttlecock-shaped canopy, and double flowers of pink tulle that make you think of *Come Dancing*, circa 1950. Far more elegant is the Great White Cherry, *Prunus* **'Taihaku'** (above), 8 × 10m (25 × 30ft), with bronze young leaves, which eventually turn green, and double white blossom. But it does need space. For small gardens, the neater upright *Prunus* **'Spire'**, 8 × 5m (25 × 15ft), is a better bet and more pleasing in shape than the more frequently planted *Prunus* **'Amanogawa'**, which is just a bit too emaciated and columnar for my liking, although its flowers are a delightful soft pink.

PEAK SEASON April.
GROWING CONDITIONS
Sheltered, sunny spot with fertile, well-drained soil; in a windy spot the flowers don't last long.

Crab apples are another excellent choice for blossom, and the ornamental varieties with their long flowering season make useful pollinators for a lot of fruiting apple trees. To my mind, they make much better garden plants than flowering cherries, as the blossom lasts longer and is followed by colourful fruit. *Malus* 'John Downie' and 'Golden Hornet' (above) are two of the best for flower, with pink buds opening to large white flowers, but the purple-leaved crabs, such as *Malus × moerlandsii* 'Profusion', are the real spring stars, as the heavy crop of reddish blossom contrasts so well with the bronzy purple young foliage. All grow to about 5 × 3m (15 × 10ft). (For other crab apples, see October, p.244.)

PEAK SEASON April.
GROWING CONDITIONS
Reasonably well-drained, fertile soil in sun.

Fruit trees generally have billowing spring blossom, and even in tiny gardens there's room to grow **apple trees** on dwarfing rootstocks, which keep them a manageable 3 × 2m (10 × 6ft) or so. But if you aren't particularly bothered about growing serious crops, think about trying more unusual fruit trees such as *Cydonia oblonga*, edible quince, which has large pink blossoms and grows about 5 × 5m (15 × 15ft), or *Mespilus germanica*, medlar (above), which has attractive foliage and large white, pear-like blossom. In both cases the wonderful blossom is followed by extraordinary fruits, which are fun to watch growing even if you never use them for anything.

PEAK SEASON April.
GROWING CONDITIONS Deep, fertile soil with a sheltered, sunny site avoiding eastern exposures, since petals may be scorched by early sun during late frosts. Because bees avoid damaged flowers, they aren't pollinated and don't set fruit.

OLD FAITHFULS

Magnolia × soulangeana is the most popular of the magnolias, with large, pale pink, waxy, tulip-shaped flowers on bare branches. However, it tends to grow a bit big for smaller gardens (6 × 6m/ 20 × 20ft in time) and won't take kindly to being pruned. It's fussier about conditions than the easy-going *Magnolia stellata*, star magnolia, which flowers first (see March, p.49), but if you can meet its needs, give it a whirl. If you're on chalk, which most magnolias don't like, then try *Magnolia × loebneri* 'Merrill', a white-flowered kind with flowers somewhere between *Magnolia × soulangeana* and *Magnolia stellata* in shape. *Magnolia × loebneri* 'Leonard Messel' (above) is similar but is a delicious shade of soft pink. Magnolias make good specimen trees and are always a real head-turner, but they all resent root disturbance, so once established don't try to move them. Avoid teasing the fleshy roots at planting time, too, in case they snap.

PEAK SEASON April.
GROWING CONDITIONS
   Sheltered site in sun or partial shade, with fertile, lime-free soil containing plenty of organic matter.

***Spiraea* 'Arguta'**, bridal wreath (above), is a dense, bushy, 2 × 2m (6 × 6ft) shrub that totally vanishes under a froth of tiny white flowers. Flower arrangers love it as a 'filler', and you can cut plenty without wrecking the look of the plant. It is very reliable and stands up to anything the weather throws at it.

PEAK SEASON April–May.
GROWING CONDITIONS Not fussy. Most soils in sun or shade.

***Ribes sanguineum* 'Pulborough Scarlet'**, the flowering currant, is another very solid performer that withstands the weather well. Although it reaches 2.5 × 2m (8 × 6ft), it can be clipped to keep it smaller. It bears strings of reddish pink flowers and foliage that is blackcurrant-scented when bruised. *Ribes sanguineum* 'Tydeman's White' is a good white-flowered form, and *Ribes sanguineum* 'Porky's Pink' (above), a soft pink.

PEAK SEASON March–May.
GROWING CONDITIONS Not fussy. Most soils in sun or light shade.

Berberis, also known as barberry, are in flower around now, and they all tend to be prickly shrubs with clusters of orange, apricot or yellow flowers. Choose from deciduous or evergreen varieties, although to my mind the evergreen varieties are best for flower. A large range of sizes is available, so there's something for any spot. For intruder-proof hedging or a large specimen shrub, choose a tall evergreen species such as *Berberis darwinii*, 2.5 × 2m (8 × 6ft), with orange-yellow flowers followed by small black berries; the foliage makes a wall of small, tight-knit, holly-like leaves. *Berberis × stenophylla* 'Corallina Compacta', ideal for a small garden, is quite the opposite, making a 30cm- (12in-) high dome with apricot flowers. *Berberis* 'Goldilocks' (above), 4 × 3m (12 × 10ft), has evergreen leaves and bright yellow flowers carried in profusion. The deciduous *Berberis thunbergii* f. *atropurpurea*, 1.5 × 1.5m (5 × 5ft), has pale creamy yellow flowers that appear against the newly opening purple foliage.

PEAK SEASON April–May.
GROWING CONDITIONS Any reasonable soil in any site; tolerates dry shade under big deciduous trees.

Doronicum, leopard's bane (above), is one of the first upright border perennials to open, with large yellow, daisy-like flowers. Tough enough to stand up to indifferent weather, you can take amazing liberties with it, yet it still bounces back. Choose a relatively compact cultivar such as *Doronicum* 'Miss Mason', at 60 × 45cm (24 × 18in), in a windy spot to avoid broken stems.

PEAK SEASON April.
GROWING CONDITIONS Not fussy.

Pulmonaria, lungwort, gets its name from a quaint medieval method of allocating medicinal properties to plants based on their appearance. According to the *Doctrine of Signatures*, the large, spotty leaves were 'sent' to tell us to use the plant for curing lung diseases. Be that as it may, I'll stick to using pulmonaria as spring-flowering ground cover. The silvery white, spotted foliage sets off the short clusters of pink, white or blue flowers very elegantly, and the plants form clumps, 30 × 30cm (12 × 12in), which spread to make low, undulating carpets that look good under roses or towards the front of mixed or cottage-style borders. *Pulmonaria* 'Lewis Palmer' (above) has flowers that open pink and turn blue, hence the common name of 'soldiers and sailors'.

PEAK SEASON April–May.
GROWING CONDITIONS Any reasonable soil in light shade (it will wilt in hot sun).

***Rosa xanthina* 'Canary Bird'**
(above) is the first of the popular
shrub roses to flower, a good
6 weeks ahead of the usual
Hybrid Teas and Floribundas.
It has large, single, canary-yellow
flowers, attractive ferny foliage,
and is unusual in that it prefers
almost woodland conditions, in
complete contrast to the usual
rose-bed roses. Grown as a bush,
it makes a large shrub of about
2.5 × 2.5m (8 × 8ft), which is
difficult to weed around owing to
the extremely thorny stems. But
when grafted on to an upright stem
to make a standard, it becomes a
small flowering rose 'tree' that is
considerably easier to maintain
and also leaves room to plant
other things underneath it –
an important consideration in
a smallish garden.

PEAK SEASON April–May.
GROWING CONDITIONS Moist,
    fertile soil in light shade; it is
    particularly happy in dappled
    shade surrounded by a light
    canopy of trees.

Pieris are like outdoor poinsettias,
I often think. Their big red
'flowers' are actually coloured
young foliage growing at the tips
of the shoots, and they also have
sprays of white flowers, which
aren't always so noticeable. *Pieris
japonica* 'Firecrest' (above) is a
good choice for most gardens as
it only grows 2.5 × 2m (8 × 6ft),
unlike some that are whoppers
best left for woodland gardens
where there's more room.
They make good partners for
rhododendrons as they need
the same conditions.

PEAK SEASON April–May.
GROWING CONDITIONS Fertile,
    acid soil, in a partially shady,
    sheltered site.

Tulips (above) can start to
peak this month if the weather
is mild, otherwise the majority
will flower in May. Spread the
risk by growing a good mixture
of varieties. The traditional tulip-
shaped tulips include **Darwin** and
Cottage tulips, which come in a
huge range of colours including
black (which is really very dark
purple), and the popular flower
arrangers' variety '**Apeldoorn**',
which has cherry-red flowers.
Lily-flowered tulips, such as the
yellow '**West Point**', have nipped
in 'waists' around the middle of
each flower, giving them an hour-
glass figure; they strike me as the
sophisticated end of the market.
Parrot tulips are the gypsies,
with flamboyant, ruffled, swirling
petals often in loud colours,
such as the raspberry and white
'**Estella Rijnveld**' – the stuff of
Dutch master paintings. Heights
vary, but they average out at around
30–45 × 10cm (12–18 × 4in). (For
botanical tulips, see March, p.49.)

PEAK SEASON April–May.
GROWING CONDITIONS Well-
    drained, fertile soil in full sun.

SOMETHING SPECIAL

Primula auricula, commonly known as auricula (above), is one of the old 'florist's' flowers. It is grown for its cabbage-shaped rosette of farina-coated waxy leaves and bull's-eye flowers in reds, blues, yellows or greens, marked with concentric rings of floury 'paste'. Now, don't let me lead you up the garden path, because even the modern varieties of these little treasures can be tricky to cultivate. But if you want a challenge and a bit of fun, then treat yourself to a couple of plants and have a go. My best ever auriculas grew in an old sink, filled with well-drained soil that had been generously enriched with sharp sand and sieved leafmould. There they grew for years, happy and undisturbed, flowering their hats off each spring.

PEAK SEASON April–May.
GROWING CONDITIONS Well-drained soil enriched with leafmould and grit, or clay pots of rich organic compost, plunged in shady cold frames in winter (see also Patios and containers, p.94). Traditionally, auriculas were 'staged' on shelves in an 'auricula theatre' at flowering time (see Project, p.115).

***Viburnum × carlesii* 'Aurora'** is one of my all-time irresistible shrubs. It grows 2.5 × 2m (8 × 6ft) in time and, being deciduous, is nothing much to look at in winter. But in spring, its shoot tips open their large heads of white, pink-budded flowers that have the most heavenly scent. *Viburnum × burkwoodii* (above) is similar but evergreen and ever-so-slightly larger. I still have difficulty in resisting either of them whenever I see them pot-grown in a nursery, even though I have several already!

PEAK SEASON April–May.
GROWING CONDITIONS Well-drained soil in sun or dappled shade.

Fritillaria meleagris, snakeshead fritillary (above), is a 30cm (12in) native wildflower that we've domesticated for garden use as it's such a cracker. It has nodding, mauve or white heads with a checkerboard pattern. Good for naturalizing in orchards or a wildflower meadow.

PEAK SEASON April.
GROWING CONDITIONS Moist soil in sun or light shade.

Oxalis adenophylla and **O. enneaphylla** (above, in its variety 'Rosea') are little gems for the rock garden, scree or alpine containers, and are also good for growing in pots in an unheated greenhouse for an early display. Plants are tiny, making 8 × 15cm (3 × 6in) mounds of delicate, finely divided, grey-green foliage studded with pink and white flowers that only open in sunlight.

PEAK SEASON April–May.
GROWING CONDITIONS Well-drained soil in a sunny spot.

Brunnera macrophylla 'Jack Frost' (above) makes you think of perennial forget-me-nots with the added attraction of big leaves netted with silver grey. It is devastatingly beautiful grown as a ground-covering carpet under flowering trees or in an early perennial bed.

PEAK SEASON April–May.
GROWING CONDITIONS Fertile soil containing plenty of organic matter, in light shade.

Orontium aquaticum, golden club (above), is a little something for your pond. The name comes from the flowers, which resemble gold spikes sticking up in clusters among long oval leaves. The plant grows roughly 30 × 45cm (12 × 18in). Besides flowering streets ahead of all your usual waterlilies, it has oddity value because there's nothing else remotely like it, in or out of the water.

PEAK SEASON April–May.
GROWING CONDITIONS Grow in a planting basket of pond compost sunk in 20–45cm (8–18in) of water in a sunny spot.

OTHER PLANTS IN THEIR PRIME IN APRIL

- **Trees** *Amelanchier lamarckii* (see p.50)
- **Shrubs** *Chaenomeles* (see p.49), *Corylopsis, Forsythia* (see p.50), *Kerria japonica, Magnolia stellata* (see p.49), *Ribes odoratum, Spiraea thunbergii, Viburnum × juddii, Viburnum plicatum* 'Mariesii' (see p.119)
- **Evergreens** *Camellia* (see p.50), *Mahonia aquifolium*, dwarf rhododendrons, e.g. *Rhododendron* 'Bow Bells' (see p.118), *Viburnum × burkwoodii*
- **Climbers/wall shrubs** *Clematis alpina, Clematis macropetala, Forsythia suspensa*
- **Perennials** *Bergenia* (see p.33), *Caltha palustris, Darmera peltata, Epimedium, Helleborus foetidus, Lamium maculatum, Omphalodes cappadocica, Polygonatum, Primula denticulata*, gold-laced polyanthus (see p.52), *Viola odorata*
- **Bulbs** *Convallaria* (see p.48), *Erythronium, Fritillaria imperialis, Iris reticulata* (see p.33), *Leucojum, Muscari, Narcissus* (see p.48), *Trillium*
- **Bedding** *Bellis* daisies, *Erysimum cheiri* (see p.51), *Myosotis*, polyanthus (see p.51), *Ranunculus*, winter-flowering pansies (see p.269)
- **Rock plants** *Aethionema* 'Warley Rose', *Aurinia saxatilis, Anemone blanda, Arabis, Armeria juniperifolia, Aubrieta* (see p.50), *Erinus alpinus, Erysimum hieraciifolium, Ipheion, Narcissus* (dwarf) (see p.48), *Phlox subulata, Primula marginata, Pulsatilla vulgaris, Saxifraga, Tulipa* (dwarf botanical) (see p.49), *Waldsteinia*

APRIL at-a-glance checklist

GENERAL GARDEN TASKS (p.87)
✔ Spring clean borders, keep on top of weeding and hoeing.
✔ Feed roses, borders, hedges, trees, shrubs and spring bulbs with general-purpose fertilizer.

LAWNS (p.88)
✔ Feed grass if you live in the southern part of the country.
✔ Treat moss and weeds and re-seed bare patches.
✔ Sow grass seed to make a new lawn if you can't wait until autumn.
✔ Mow lawns at least once a fortnight or once a week in really mild weather.

TREES, SHRUBS AND CLIMBERS (p.89)
✔ Plant or move evergreen trees and shrubs.
✔ Feed acid-loving plants.
✔ Prune winter jasmine and hydrangea, and tie in shoots of climbing and rambling roses, wall-trained shrubs and newly planted climbers.
✔ Continue planting pot-grown woody plants.
✔ Tidy up hedges and clip if necessary, although usually this will be next month.
✔ Plant pot-grown evergreens for hedges.

FLOWERS (p.93)
✔ Wait for six weeks after flowers of spring bulbs are over before cutting the foliage down.
✔ Continue to plant perennials and finish dividing and replanting summer-flowering perennials.
✔ Towards the end of the month, plant dormant dahlia tubers outside.
✔ Plant new alpines and top up scree bed with gravel and grit.
✔ Continue to sow hardy annuals outside.
✔ Plant out hardy annuals sown in autumn.
✔ Pot up cuttings of tender perennials taken last year.
✔ Remove insulation from borderline-hardy plants.

PATIOS AND CONTAINERS (p.94)
✔ Plant spring bedding and summer bulbs in pots.
✔ Plant compact trees, shrubs and evergreens in pots.
✔ Plant alpine troughs.

VEGETABLES AND HERBS (p.97)
✔ Sow broad beans, summer cabbage, Brussels sprouts, early peas, calabrese, summer/autumn cauliflower, sprouting broccoli, leeks, beetroot, radish, spring onions, lettuce, rocket, turnips, kohl rabi, spinach, parsnips, Swiss chard, chicory, endive, carrots and onions.
✔ Plant first early, second early and maincrop potatoes; earth up shoots of early potatoes to protect them from frost.
✔ Plant asparagus crowns and globe artichokes. There is still time to plant Jerusalem artichokes.
✔ Look after your veg – water and hoe regularly, thin out and transplant seedlings, and give support to peas and beans sown earlier.
✔ Watch out for flea beetle, particularly on rocket, turnips, radishes, and some brassicas.
✔ Harvest the first overwintered spring onions, the last of the sprouting broccoli and Swiss chard.
✔ Sow hardy herbs (parsley, chervil, coriander, fennel, dill and marjoram).

FRUIT (p.105)
✔ Plant strawberries.
✔ Plant and tie in a new grapevine and figs.
✔ Check and harvest forced rhubarb.
✔ Feed blackcurrants, blackberries and hybrid berries.
✔ Prune stone fruit trees if necessary.

UNDER COVER (p.107)
✔ Ventilate the greenhouse on sunny days but shut it down mid-afternoon to retain the heat at night.
✔ Towards the end of the month, start standing bedding plants and frost-tender vegetables outside on fine days to harden them off gradually. Keep them in a frost-free greenhouse or frame for the rest of the time.
✔ Prick out seedlings, pot up cuttings rooted last year, repot any permanent greenhouse pot plants that need it, and pot on begonias and gloxinias.
✔ Top-dress and take cuttings from big old plants.
✔ Buy and pot up plug plants.
✔ Take stem-tip cuttings from pot-grown hydrangeas and leaf cuttings from Cape primroses.

✔ Rest amaryllis and cyclamen.
✔ Sow tomatoes.
✔ Sow frost-tender veg (greenhouse melons and cucumbers, sweetcorn, French and runner beans, marrows, pumpkins, squashes and courgettes) for planting outdoors later in a heated propagator.
✔ Prick out tomato seedlings into individual pots.
✔ Tie in vine rods.
✔ Pollinate and feed strawberry plants.
✔ Thin out vegetable and salad seedlings.

WATER GARDEN (p.113)
✔ Spring clean the pond.
✔ Divide overgrown plants and put in new water plants.
✔ Towards the end of the month, start feeding your fish.

Watch out for
○ Slugs and snails on newly emerged perennials and vegetable seedlings, flea beetle on vegetables and cats on newly prepared borders.
○ Cold damage.

Get ahead
○ Plant up outdoor tubs and hanging baskets but keep them in a frost-free greenhouse (you might get away with unheated glass towards the end of the month in a mild area).
○ Prepare ground for summer bedding.
○ Order biological controls for pests in greenhouse and garden for delivery next month – apply nematodes against vine weevil under glass later this month.

Last chance
○ Final opportunity to do winter digging.
○ Finish spring cleaning borders before herbaceous plants cover the ground so you can't clear and mulch easily.
○ Finish soil preparation.
○ Prune roses, before the middle of the month at the very latest.
○ Complete sowing of half-hardy annuals by the middle of the month at the very latest.
○ Take basal cuttings from border perennials.

GENERAL GARDEN TASKS

FINISH WINTER DIGGING

This is a very last call for those who didn't get their winter digging done earlier, perhaps because of wet, clay soil being unworkable (see November, p.272).

SPRING CLEAN THE BORDERS

Tidy up the borders before herbaceous plants cover the ground and you can't clear and mulch easily (see March, p.54). Keep on top of weeding and hoeing, and prepare the ground for summer bedding by forking over.

FEED THE BORDERS

Spring is feeding time out in the borders. Even if you have a low-fuss garden, it's worth going around with a bucket of general-purpose organic fertilizer now.

* Dust a light dressing over any bare soil in between shrubs, trees, roses, evergreens, conifers and climbers – particularly clematis, which are notoriously greedy – so they start the season properly topped up with nutrients. Lightly fork it in.

* You can use more of the same general fertilizer between perennials, on beds where you're preparing to put in bedding plants, and when you're breaking in virgin ground to make new beds and borders, so it's quite economical – one big bag does for everything. There's no need to buy something special for particular plants, unless you really want to.

PROTECT PLANTS

Protect at-risk plants from the following:

* Cold damage – Protect fruit tree blossom, new shoots and choice plants with horticultural fleece as necessary. Damage is most disastrous when there's been a mild winter that lulls plants into a false sense of security so they start growing early, in time to be clobbered by a late cold snap.

* Early pests, such as greenfly, and slugs and snails on newly emerged perennials and vegetable seedlings – order any biological control insects you want to use around the garden or greenhouse next month (see May, p.125).

* Cats using newly prepared soil as a latrine – dust at-risk areas with horticultural pepper or bury green plastic 'grids' between new plants; in real problem areas it may be worth considering an electronic device that emits a high-pitched noise when cats cross an invisible beam, or a gadget that squirts jets of water erratically at offenders.

Use fertilizer at the start of the growing season.

Tidy the garden regularly to keep it under control.

LAWNS

Lawn clippings

When space is in too short supply to build a compost bin that can cope with regular amounts of lawn clippings, you can mow 'little and often' and leave the clippings on the lawn, where they will usually be absorbed. But if they are more than 1cm (¹/₂in) long they can look messy and will tread into the house. It is often suggested that they help to feed the lawn, but I'm very dubious!

FEED THE LAWN

If you only want to feed your lawn once a year, April is the time to do it. A good feed at the start of the growing season sets the lawn up for the summer, so it looks green, grows strongly enough to fill gaps, smothers out weeds, and generally stands up to the rough and tumble of family life. To be slightly more accurate, April is the best time for a feed if you live in the southern half of the country, where you can safely expect seriously wintry weather to be over. If you live in a cold area, or we have a late spring with terrible weather, then play safe and wait until early May. This is because spring and summer lawn feeds contain a hefty dose of nitrogen, which makes grass grow lush and green; if the soft new growth is clobbered by prolonged freezing weather it turns black, which looks dreadful, and you'll actually set it back weeks.

LAWN PRODUCTS

Nowadays there are so many lawn-care products on the market that it's easy to be confused about which one you need. Spring and summer lawn feeds contain more nitrogen than an autumn grass feed, for leafier growth.

- *Inorganic lawn feeds* are available as powder or granules, which you apply by hand or through a fertilizer spreader. They give the grass a green-up that lasts about 3–4 weeks before slowly tailing off.
- *Organic lawn feeds* do much the same job but using natural ingredients, and they tend to last rather longer than the 'quick-fix' inorganic types.
- *Slow-release lawn feeds* are a good idea if you have a small lawn that takes a real hammering in the summer, as it 'drip feeds' the grass with nutrients little and often over the whole summer – you'll pay more, but the effects last longer.
- *Liquid lawn feeds* are fast food for grass, designed to give a short sharp burst. They are ideal if you want to have the lawn looking its best for a special event, or if it needs a quick tonic, but the effects aren't very long lasting.

DEAL WITH MOSS AND WEEDS

It's not until you start mowing the lawn regularly again that you notice problems such as moss or weeds that have crept in.

- You can buy liquid weedkillers or moss-killers that have to be diluted and put on through a watering can, but unless you have only a small isolated patch to treat it's far better to use a powder or granular product that combines fertilizer with a lawn treatment. That way, the grass has a boost that encourages it to spread and fill in the gaps left where patches of moss or clumps of weeds have been killed.

- If you don't like the idea of using chemicals, even on the lawn, then it just takes a bit more effort to dig out weeds by hand and scratch moss out with a wire rake or a mechanized lawn-raking machine.

- Remember, a well-fed lawn helps to fight off weeds and moss (see above). Because it is so thickly colonized with grass there is simply no room for anything else to work its

HOW TO OVERSEED THE LAWN

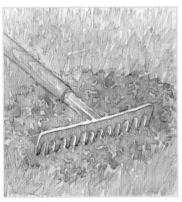

1 Prick the patch over with the points of a fork or have a good scrape with the teeth of a rake to loosen the compacted surface soil. Mix a handful of grass seed with half a bucket of seed compost and sprinkle it thinly over the area – half a bucket of the mix is enough to cover 1–2 square metres (1–2 square yards). You don't have to be too precise; it's not brain surgery.

2 Water the seed/compost mix well and mark the spot with sticks and string to keep people off – don't worry about birds. Keep it watered in dry spells. Mow around the area until the seed has come up. When the grass is about 4cm (1¹/₂in) high, treat it to a light haircut with the shears before mowing as usual. In a couple of months you'll hardy spot the join.

TREES, SHRUBS AND CLIMBERS

FEED WOODY PLANTS

The start of the growing season is when woody plants benefit from a good nutritional top-up. If you only feed once a year, now is the time to go around roses, trees, shrubs, climbers and hedges with a bag of general-purpose feed.

PLANT WOODY PLANTS

Continue to plant pot-grown roses, trees, shrubs, climbers and wall shrubs (see March, pp.57–9).

PLANT EVERGREENS AND CONIFERS

If you're thinking of planting evergreens and conifers, this is the time to do it. I know in theory that you can plant anything at virtually any time of year, so long as it's been grown in a pot and the ground is in a workable state, but evergreens establish very much better if you plant them in April or September; the beginning and end of their growing season seems to suit them best. The actual planting technique is exactly the same as for any pot-grown tree or shrub (see March, p.58). After planting, your evergreen needs watering in dry spells until it has rooted in well. If you skimp on this, the plant can go brown, and some never recover.

MOVE EVERGREENS AND CONIFERS

It's not just new evergreens and conifers in pots that benefit from planting now. If you have some in the garden that you want to move, now is the very best time to do it. The secret of success is to dig up your evergreen with a good, big ball of roots. On most soil types, you'll find the rootball is actually wider than it is deep, so you need to err on the generous side when starting to dig the plant up. The fine 'feeder' roots around the edge of the root mass are the ones that you really need to keep, as they're the ones that take water up into the plant – if you chop them off, you'll have a problem persuading the plant to re-establish itself.

Although the method of planting is exactly the same as when you plant a shrub from a pot

Left: A healthy lawn is often the centrepiece of a garden. Regular maintenance will reward you with a fine, green sward that will bring pleasure all year round.

way in, so feeding saves a whole lot of everyday lawn problems.

MOW THE LAWN

Mow the lawn at least once a fortnight now, and in mild weather once a week. Once you've given the grass its first couple of cuts, gradually lower the cutting height of the blades to their normal setting – between 1 and 2cm (½ and ¾in).

OVERSEED BARE PATCHES

Bare patches are bad news in a lawn, because they'll quickly be colonized by passing weed seeds, and in winter they're the first places to turn into mud-baths, so you're in a mess unless you do something about them.

If the grass is merely thinning it can usually be encouraged to thicken up quickly by feeding, but sometimes you'll find a patch where there isn't enough grass or no grass at all, and then the answer is to overseed the area (see box opposite).

WHEN TO SOW LAWN SEED
Autumn is usually the very best time to start a new lawn from seed (see September, pp.227–8), as it has all winter to establish before people want to start using it. However, in a cold area or on heavy or wet ground, spring is the best choice – and for some people it's simply more convenient to do the job now. On light soils or in a very dry spring and summer, you may need to keep spring-sown grass watered while it finds its feet. Turf should ideally have been laid by the end of March (see p.55).

Christmas tree spray
Christmas tree spray creates a biodegradable 'plastic' film over an evergreen's leaves. It prevents transpiration, and seals moisture into the plant, which is how it stops Christmas trees shedding their needles. You can also use it when transplanting conifers.

(see March, p.58), because there's been some root damage good aftercare is even more important. A newly moved evergreen or conifer will need regular watering for weeks, and in the case of a largish plant it's worth watering for the rest of the summer. Make sure the soil never dries out completely (see box below left).

MOVING LARGE EVERGREENS

Even quite large, established evergreen shrubs will often move well as they make relatively compact balls of fibrous roots around the base. There's always some risk involved with moving a large plant, but it's certainly worth a go.

To improve the success rate, it pays to improve on your normal re-planting technique. Start preparing a large evergreen for removal a year before you move it. Begin in April – the start of the evergreen growing season. By the following year you'll have what almost amounts to a container-grown plant in the ground that just needs to be dug out and shifted. Given a well-prepared spot, it should 'take' effortlessly.

- A year before you intend to transplant the evergreen, dig a trench as wide as your spade right around the plant, as far as the feeder roots reach – this is normally just under the edge of the leaf canopy. Dig down to the full depth of the fibrous roots, which may be as

little as 30–45cm (12–18in), or more on deep rich soil.

- Fill the trench with well-rotted compost or the contents of your old growing bags. Water well and apply a weak liquid feed. Keep your 'ditch' well watered all summer. By autumn the new roots should be well established, and rainfall will take care of the watering for you.

- To help reduce water loss through the leaves, 2 weeks before you plan to move the plant, spray the foliage evenly with Christmas tree spray (see box, p.89). Repeat this treatment on moving day and again a fortnight later.

- Transfer the evergreen from its original spot (see box, below) then plant as for any pot-grown tree or shrub (see March, pp.57–8). When replanting, turn it around so you plant it facing the same direction as it was in its original spot; evergreens don't like being re-orientated once growth is underway.

- Surround the plant with a screen of hessian sacking for the first month or two to act as a windbreak and sunshade, and damp the foliage over on dry days.

Watering a newly planted evergreen
To keep the soil around a newly planted evergreen moist, sink a plastic lemonade bottle with the bottom cut off, to make a funnel, alongside the plant, so you can channel the water straight down to the roots.

HOW TO TRANSPLANT AN EVERGREEN

1 Cut right around the plant with a spade, then run the spade underneath the ball of roots.

2 Lean the plant in one direction and slide a piece of sacking or polythene underneath the rootball. Then lean it in the opposite direction and pull the sacking through so that the whole rootball is supported.

3 If you're moving a plant some distance away, then it's worth tying the sacking up securely so the rootball holds together while it's shifted.

4 Move the shrub to its new, prepared planting hole. Remove the sacking and plant as for a pot-grown shrub (see March, p.58). Water thoroughly.

FEED ACID-LOVING PLANTS

Lime-hating plants, such as rhododendrons, are quite happy with general feed when they're on acid soil, but if you're growing them in marginally neutral conditions then it's worth giving them a dose of sequestered iron as well. This replaces the minerals that are locked up chemically where there's a hint of lime in the soil, and stops the leaves turning yellow and chlorotic. You can also acidify slightly iffy ground by mulching regularly with pine needles, either fresh or composted, and by working in some slow-release sulphur chips, which are sold specially for the job; they last 1–2 years before you need to repeat the treatment. I tend to grow my lime-haters in pots and tubs; it's a lot easier that way.

SPRING SHRUB PRUNING

The vast majority of shrubs never need any pruning at all, but a few species benefit from a bit of regular attention to keep them looking their best.

Prune winter jasmine

Winter jasmine grows notoriously straggly as it gets older, unless it's kept regularly in trim.

- When the plant is trained over a porch, or tied tightly in to a wall, the easiest way is to clip the plant back with shears. Trim it just enough to take off the dead flowerheads and to remove the tips of the shoots. Besides neatening the appearance you also encourage the plant to grow bushier, which will improve its looks no end.

- When winter jasmine is grown more informally, as a shrub or climbing up the trunk of a tree, use secateurs. Deal with each flowered shoot in turn; follow it back to its junction with a non-flowered shoot and cut just above it. You'll be taking off some longish shoots but don't let that worry you, because you'll be removing the old stems and making way for the new.

- If you've inherited an elderly and neglected winter jasmine, take the opportunity to cut a few of the thickest, woodiest old stems as close to the ground as you can each spring until, over several years, it's been totally rejuvenated. It'll flower all the better for the new growth that you encourage this way. But don't just chop the whole plant hard and hope it'll start again from scratch – that just makes it go berserk and produce clusters of strong, sappy young shoots that won't flower for years.

Prune hydrangeas

The other shrub that needs pruning now is the hydrangea. A lot of people prune hydrangeas too early or too hard, which can wreck their flowering chances later in the year. The way to prune a hydrangea is as lightly as possible – think of it as late deadheading.

- Look the plant over carefully before you cut anything. There are two kinds of shoots – the ones that carried last year's flowers, which may still have the remains of the old flowerheads at the end, and unflowered shoots, which will have a fat growth bud at the tip.

Winter jasmine needs pruning annually to keep it tidy. Remove the old flowered shoots to encourage new growth and better flowering next season.

Left: Acid-loving plants, such as rhododendrons, camellias and pieris, benefit from an application of sequestered iron at the start of the season to prevent the leaves from yellowing.

Rose-spraying
Avoid the temptation to spray roses. Leave aphids to blue tits and other birds, and learn to live with a modicum of blackspot. If roses are habitually disease-ridden, dig them out and replace them with varieties with in-bred resistance.

You may need to start clipping your hedge towards the end of this month. Hand shears are fine for most trimming jobs.

• Follow the flowered shoots back down to a strong, healthy sideshoot and cut just above it. That's all there is to it. Whatever you do, don't cut off the shoots with the fat green buds at the end, as they're the ones that should have this year's flowers.

• An old hydrangea that has a lot of woody congested 'sticks' in the middle can be thinned out slightly, removing the thickest 'sticks' close to the base of the plant. That will give you fewer but bigger and more spectacular flowers. A bit of rejuvenation goes a long way.

PRUNE ROSES

This is positively your last chance to prune modern bush roses and trim Patio and Ground-cover roses (see March, pp.59–60). Do it before the middle of the month at the latest.

TIE IN AND TRAIN SHOOTS

Tie in climbing and rambling roses and wall-trained shrubs, training them to be horizontal. Also, tie in shoots of newly planted climbers. Once the plants are established, the new growth of twiners, scramblers (such as clematis) and self-clinging species (such as ivy) will hold themselves on to their supports.

TRIM WINTER-FLOWERING HEATHERS

Clip over winter-flowering heathers lightly with shears now the last flowers are over, to tidy and deadhead the plants in one go.

HELPING HAND FOR HEDGES

Hedges are the part of the garden most people take for granted, so get the season off to a good start by giving yours a complete spring treat.

• Start by going along the bottom of the hedge, clearing out any ivy, weeds, snails and other rubbish, then sprinkle a generous helping of general fertilizer about 30cm (12in) or so from the stems. If you have some spare organic matter, follow up with a good mulch, while the soil is moist (see March, p.54).

• If you can go around the other side of the hedge and do the same thing there, so much the better. I know it smacks suspiciously of doing your neighbour's gardening for them, but there's method in my madness. By clearing out the junk under their side of the hedge, you stop a lot of unwanted weeds and pests creeping into yours. It's no problem when you have Mr Tidy living next door, but when it's an OAP with a frequent holiday habit or a busy Bridget Jones, they just won't have time.

• Although May is the start of the main hedge-clipping season, people with gardens in the south or otherwise 'early' gardens may find there's been enough growth to start clipping in late April (see May, pp.127–8).

PLANT EVERGREEN HEDGES

Plant pot-grown evergreens for new hedges or screens. (Bare-root hedges are to be planted in autumn or winter, see November, pp.276–7.)

FLOWERS

APPLY FERTILIZER
Sprinkle general fertilizer between perennials and on beds where you're preparing to put in bedding plants.

LEAVE THE DAFFS
Narcissi give gardeners a lot of grief when they've done their stuff for the year. Just when you're raring to get your borders tidied up and your lawn back in shape you find yourself lumbered with a load of tatty old daffodil foliage that you're aching to get shot of. Some people give in to the urge, and that's when you see little bundles of neatly knotted leaves trussed up with elastic bands, or lawns covered in green purée where someone has run the mower over drifts of what was once a flourishing patch of daffs. Don't do it.

Spring bulbs need time to recharge their batteries. Let the leaves finish their job; they take in sunlight and turn it into starch reserves stored in the bulb ready to power next year's flower show. Cut them off in their prime, or fasten the leaves together so that they're deprived of light, and the bulbs don't plump up so you won't have many flowers next year. I know it looks messy in the meantime, but the results are worth it.

- Wait at least 6 weeks before you tidy up, then snip all the foliage off at ground level and clear it away to the compost heap.

- As belt and braces, give the bulbs a jolly good feed to help things along, as soon as the flowers are over. Use a high-potash tomato feed or, failing that, a general-purpose organic feed sprinkled around.

PLANT PERENNIALS
Continue to plant perennials, and finish dividing and replanting summer-flowering perennials (see March, p.64).

PLANT OUT SUMMER-FLOWERING BULBS
Plant hardier summer bulbs, such as lilies and gladioli, but don't plant non-hardy kinds, such

---

TIPS FOR TIDIER DAFFS
- You can make things look a lot better by mowing around patches of bulbs naturalized in grass, so you leave 'islands' of what look like mini wildlife reserves.
- Next time you're naturalizing daffs in your borders, go for the dwarf kinds, such as *Narcissus* 'February Gold', 'Hawera', 'Jenny' and 'Jetfire' (see March, p.48) – they pack a good flowering punch, are seldom cowed by heavy rain, and since the foliage is half the normal size you'll hardly notice it while it dies down.

---

as tigridia or *Gladiolus murielae* (previously *Acidanthera bicolor*), until the end of April, or early May, so the emerging shoots avoid frost. And don't plant dry begonia corms outdoors yet – put growing plants out after mid-May.

Plant dormant dahlia tubers
Now is the time for planting dormant dahlia tubers outside. They need rich, fertile soil in a sunny spot. Mark each planting spot with a stake so you don't cut into them when you're hoeing, and if a late frost comes along when the first shoots stick their heads above ground, earth them up for protection. Don't plant rooted dahlia cuttings out until late May or early June.

ROCK GARDENS AND SCREES
Plant new alpines, and top up the grit and gravel of a scree bed if lost or moved by winter weather (see March, p.62).

SOW HARDY ANNUALS
Continue to sow hardy annuals outside (see March, pp.62–3).

PLANT OUT HARDY ANNUALS
Harden off and plant out hardy annuals sown in autumn (see p.108 and September, p.237).

REMOVE INSULATION FROM PLANTS
If you've trussed up borderline-hardy plants, such as tree ferns, left out in the garden all winter, and covered crowns of gunnera or hardy fuchsias with an insulating layer of leaves or other protective layers, it's time to let them out.

If you can't stand the sight of dead daffodil flowers, pick them off. As well as being tidy, you'll save the plants' energy, which would be used for producing unwanted seeds.

Right: Strawberries will grow very happily in a hanging basket in a sheltered spot.

It is well worth planting some lily bulbs now, in pots, to provide a splash of colour on the patio in summer.

PATIOS AND CONTAINERS

PERK UP CONTAINER DISPLAYS

As spring moves on, the very earliest spring bedding plants are going over, but the range of plants available is constantly being added to as the weather warms up, so you can be quite creative about perking up jaded container displays (see box below).

PLANT SUMMER BULBS

If you want to look ahead to summer colour, plant some summer bulbs. These are relatively new as patio plants, and what's made it possible to grow them this way is the 'invention' of short, stocky varieties – look for patio dahlias, dwarf gladioli, and compact lily bulbs, which grow about 45–60cm (18–24in) high. The tall kinds are fine for the garden but they are just too top-heavy for pots.

- Plant the dormant bulbs or tubers in 30–38cm (12–15in) containers. Put some broken crocks or gravel in the bottom for drainage, and fill the container with any good potting compost. If you plant the bulbs to the recommended depth (see box, left) there's no way shoots will surface while there's still any risk of frost.

PLANT STRAWBERRIES IN CONTAINERS

Strawberries are among the most successful fruits for containers. Container-growing is ideal when there's no room for a traditional strawberry bed, and it's very practical as plants are so accessible. It's also extremely easy to protect ripening fruit from the birds. The life expectancy of strawberry plants in containers is about 2–3 years.

- Plant half a dozen young plants in a 38cm (15in) pot or large tub filled with John Innes No 3 potting compost now, and you'll have quite an ornamental container for a sunny corner of the patio by June.

- Alternatively, plant five plants around the edge of a 35cm (14in) hanging basket and allow the runners to remain so they cascade down over the sides. By the second year, you'll have a positive waterfall of fruit, which looks stunning and gives you a large return from a small space. You'll have a fair crop this summer and more next year.

BEDDING PLANTS DOS AND DON'TS

- Do stick to spring bedding such as polyanthus, ranunculus, violas, forget-me-nots and pots of spring bulbs. Plant them early this month, and you'll have a good 6 weeks or more to enjoy them.
- Unless you have a greenhouse, don't fall for summer bedding that's already popping up in garden centres, because no matter how sunny the weather can be in April, the temperature drops pretty low at night and we can still have a serious frost, so play safe and leave summer bedding in the shops.
- If you have a greenhouse, then you can steal a march on everyone else by planting up your hanging baskets and tubs now and keeping them under cover (see p.109). By the time you can put them out, around the middle of next month, they will have filled out and be looking bloomin' marvellous.

PLANTING DEPTHS

Patio dahlias – plant one per pot, so the top of the tuber is 2.5–5cm (1–2in) below the surface of the compost.

Dwarf gladioli – plant corms 5–8cm (2–3in) apart, 2.5–5cm (1–2in) deep, for a good show in a pot.

Lilies – plant so the base of each bulb is just above the bottom of the container; plant one in a 23cm (9in) pot, but a group of three or five bulbs in a 30cm (12in) pot look better.

HOW TO GROW AURICULAS

A lot of people find auriculas challenging to grow, but if you understand the little darlings, and give them the conditions they like, they really aren't too bad at all.

Alpine auriculas are the tougher sort that will do well in a cool, shady part of the rock garden, in a pocket of humus-rich soil in well-drained surroundings. They'll also do well in pots, and it's as well to start with these while you gain experience.

Show auriculas are the real collectors' plants, and they include some genuine living antiques as well as modern varieties. These are the kinds that have perfect dartboard-patterned flowers with green, grey or white 'paste' in the centre, and powdery farina over the leaves, which is why the plants are spoiled by bad weather or careless handling.

Growing conditions

Grow auriculas in clay pots, in a compost made of roughly 3 parts John Innes No 1 potting compost, two parts fibrous peat-free compost or leafmould, and one part potting grit. For most of the year, when they are not actually on display, keep the plants in a cool, shady, north-facing cold frame, plunged to their rims in grit that is kept moist in summer and almost dry in winter. The porous pots take in moisture through their sides, helping to keep the compost inside at just the right state of dampness; aim to water the grit, not the plants, and avoid splashing the plants as water marks the farina on the leaves.

Protecting auriculas

Protect auriculas from pests, particularly vine weevil, which are a serious menace, and slugs and snails. Biological control, using nematodes mixed into the potting compost, is the most reliable method, and well worth the expense for little treasures like these. The plants are hardy, but put the lids over the cold frames in cold or rainy weather to stop the leaves being marked or damaged.

Dividing auriculas

A good show auricula should be a single rosette in a pot, but as the plants grow they naturally produce a clump of 'pups', which need separating to keep the plants looking symmetrical. The time to do this is in summer, shortly after they finish flowering – the young plants then have the best part of a year to reach flowering size, ready for next spring. Division is the way to propagate named auriculas, although real enthusiasts will have a go at raising their own new varieties from seed.

A lot of fuss? Yes, but sometimes it's worth making more of an effort to grow something this special.

PLANTING ALPINE TROUGHS

Old stone sinks and animal feeding troughs are traditional containers for alpines, but can cost a fortune at architectural salvage yards. Any wide, shallow container is fine as long as it has plenty of drainage holes in the bottom. Choose compact plants, in a mixture of contrasting mound and rosette shapes, with a few trailing kinds around the edges, but don't overdo the planting.

Before you plant, set the container on bricks so there's no risk of water-logging in a wet season – the finished container will be too heavy to move later if it's a fair size.

- Cover the base of the trough with a 2.5cm (1in) layer of stones, coarse gravel or crocks, for drainage. Fill the container to within 5cm (2in) of the rim with a mixture of John Innes No 1 potting compost and peat-free multi-purpose compost and potting grit (50:25:25).

- Place a few tasteful chunks of rock, or set some pieces of slate on edge to suggest natural rock strata, then stand your alpines in place – still in their pots – while you arrange them.

- When you're happy with the positioning, tip the plants out of their pots. Plant so that the rootballs stand slightly proud of the compost.

- Finish off with a top-dressing of granite chippings or smoothly rounded gravel that sets off the plants. Fill the container to the rim without swamping the plants (the reason for leaving the top of the rootballs standing out slightly above the planting mixture).

PLANTING POTTED TREES AND SHRUBS

Compact trees, including some kinds of fruit, and certain shrubs and evergreens, make good-looking plants to grow all year round in tubs on the patio, and they are easier to grow than you might think. Size won't be a problem because fruit trees are grown on dwarfing rootstocks nowadays, and the container acts as a 'corset', keeping a tree or shrub far more compact than it would be in the open ground. Ornamental trees, shrubs or evergreens are quite an easy option, especially if you go for the more drought-

A trough or sink planted up with alpines will guarantee a burst of spring colour.

HOW TO PLANT A FRUIT TREE IN A CONTAINER

  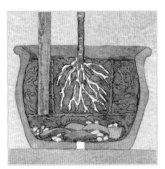 

1 Start with a pot-grown fruit tree or bush from the garden centre, and repot it into a larger tub or half-barrel. Choose a pot at least 38cm (15in) in diameter, but the bigger the better.

2 Place a handful of broken crocks or gravel in the bottom of the pot for drainage, then cover the base of the pot with John Innes No 3 potting compost.

3 Take the tree out of its pot, sit it in the centre and position a strong plant stake alongside it. Fill the gap around the edge of the rootball with more potting compost. Water well.

4 Tie the tree to the stake with tree ties at the top and bottom of the trunk. Choose a sheltered, sunny spot for the pot. A south- or west-facing patio is ideal – heat reflected by the walls creates a natural suntrap for fruit to thrive.

tolerant species, but potted fruit needs a lot of feeding and watering in summer, as the first sign of shortage sees it shedding all its developing fruit. However, it's no worse than looking after tubs of summer bedding.

Aftercare

- During the growing season, remove any weeds that appear in the pot, water regularly and use liquid tomato feed every week or two, diluted to normal tomato-strength.

- In late August, stop feeding and reduce watering as autumn draws on – but don't rely on natural rainfall to keep the compost moist in winter, as the house walls tend to act as an umbrella. Check at least every 2 weeks and water if the compost is too dry for comfort.

- In a wet winter, make sure the pot isn't standing in a puddle of water; if necessary, raise it up on bricks. To keep the pot from blowing over in windy weather, tie the plant up to a trellis or to a couple of vine eyes screwed into the wall to keep it upright.

- At this time each year, when potted fruit is starting to think about growing again, it's time for top-dressing. If it's top-dressed every spring, you can keep the same tree in the same pot for 3 or 4 years before repotting. To top-dress, scrape away the top 5cm (2in) of compost and replace it with a layer of fresh John Innes No 3 potting compost, leaving a 2.5cm (1in) gap between the compost and the rim of the pot so there's room for watering.

- Several years later, when the time comes for repotting, take out the plant and tease off the old compost from around the roots. If you don't want to buy a bigger tub, repot it back into the same container with fresh compost.

THE MOST SUCCESSFUL FRUIT FOR POTS

Some types of fruit are not worth bothering with in pots – cane fruit, such as raspberries and blackcurrants, are just too cumbersome and untidy and won't yield a worthwhile crop, even in large containers. Fruit trees generally need a fairly dwarfing rootstock to remain sufficiently compact for pots, so I don't suggest trying plums or pears, as very dwarfing rootstocks aren't available for them. There's nothing to stop you having a go if you really want to, but if you want a reasonable crop as well as good looks from a small space that's always on show, these are the best fruits to try:

Redcurrants – cordon trained

Gooseberries – cordon or standard trained

Patio peaches and nectarines – these are genetically dwarf plants, trained as bush or standard trees that need no pruning

Apricots – bush or standard tree

Figs – grown as a bush, or trained as a standard

Grapevines – trained up trellis

Apples – trained as upright cordon, or a small standard tree, growing on a very dwarfing rootstock

Cherries – trained as a tree, growing on a very dwarfing rootstock; choose a self-fertile variety for best results, as there's unlikely to be another one growing close enough nearby.

VEGETABLES AND HERBS

GROW YOUR OWN VEGETABLES

If you've never thought of 'growing your own' before, do have a go. There's an enormous sense of satisfaction to be had from picking and eating something you've grown for yourself – a touch of self-sufficiency really brings out the caveman in you. Dew-fresh vegetables and salads eaten straight from the garden don't just taste tons better, they are also healthier – bristling with vitamins – and it takes very little extra effort to grow them organically. You don't even need a lot of time or space – anyone can grow worthwhile amounts of salad leaves in containers or in a small, decorative potager bed, and what's more you can produce a much more varied and exciting selection than you can find in the supermarket.

But if you're growing your own for the first time, what I would say is start small and build up. The thing that puts most new vegetable-growers off is trying to grow far more than they can look after, then they find everything wants eating all at once – usually just as they go off on their summer holidays, so a lot of it runs to seed and spoils. And unless you have an allotment, don't bother trying to grow everyday vegetables such as maincrop spuds, swedes and onions – there's no real flavour benefit, and they take up too much space. No, the things to go for are leafy crops, things that taste best eaten fresh from the garden, and anything a bit 'special' – a gardening gourmet can live well off quite a small patch of land.

SOW AND PLANT CROPS

Anything that can be sown or planted in March (see pp.68–70) can still be put in during April. You won't have such early crops, but on the other hand you won't have to worry about cloches or horticultural fleece, or seeds rotting in cold, wet earth – just sow and go. In April there are lots of other vegetables that can go in as well.

- You can sow the following in April: broad beans, summer cabbage, Brussels sprouts, early peas, calabrese, summer/autumn cauliflower, sprouting broccoli, leeks, beetroot, radish, spring onions, lettuce, rocket, turnips, kohl rabi, spinach, parsley, Swiss chard, chicory, endive, parsnips, carrots and onions.

- You can still plant first early, second early and maincrop potatoes (see March, p.68) and Jerusalem artichokes (see February, p.40).

To make a seed drill, position a taut garden line on the soil, stand on it to keep it still, and draw the corner of a Dutch hoe along the line.

FAST-TRACK VEG

If you like an easy life, you can get away with one big burst of activity on your vegetable patch this month. Quite a few people find this the most convenient way of kitchen gardening. Just wait for a weekend when you can do all your soil preparation (see below) and virtually fill the whole vegetable patch up. Later, you will reap the rewards of a well-stocked greengrocery department down the garden.

One big benefit of getting all your vegetable-sowing done in one big go is that you don't need to give every row individual attention. Just treat the whole patch as one giant seedbed. Since everything will be at the same stage at the same time, you can do all your hoeing, thinning or whatever needs doing the same afternoon instead of constantly having to keep popping back for odd jobs here and there. Only with fast-maturing crops like lettuces, rocket and radishes would I sow 1m (3ft) of each row at weekly intervals for a succession rather than a glut.

Just-in-time soil preparation

Ideally you'll have done all your winter digging and soil preparation already (see March, p.68). If you leave preparing ground in your vegetable plot until this late, it's no good trying to dig in bulky organic matter, such as manure or garden compost, unless it is so thoroughly rotted that it almost looks like peat.

- To prepare the ground in your 'instant' vegetable patch for sowing, spread the compost (if any) over the area, sprinkle general-purpose organic fertilizer evenly, and fork it all in together. Then rake the ground over several times, leaving it smooth and level without any stones, roots or rubbish, and it's ready to go.
- Where you will be sowing seeds, and particularly root crops, use second-hand potting compost or the contents of last year's old growing bags to beef up the soil. And when you're pricking out seedlings in the greenhouse, save the seed compost left in the bottom of the pots to use for this job. It's too valuable to waste.
- If you have garden compost to get rid of, dig a trench and bury generous quantities under the places you've reserved for transplanting brassicas or planting out frost-tender vegetables later.

The only things you might want to leave some space for are frost-tender crops, such as French beans and courgettes, which can't be planted out until the middle of next month (see May, pp.135–6) as they can be killed by cold. Also, if you sow things that will need transplanting – such as Brussels sprouts and broccoli – you'll need to leave room to move them to wider spacings later.

ONGOING CARE

Whether you fill your vegetable patch all in one go, or you grow crops the traditional way by starting as early as you can and filling more of your patch every month, make regular time for upkeep. Vegetables need more attention than anything else in the garden.

Watering

Start watering straight away after sowing. In dry spells – of which there are many in April – it's essential to keep the surface moist. If seeds dry out half-way through germinating you don't have a second chance – they are stone dead and will never come up. Small seedlings are also very touchy about drying out as they only have shallow roots.

Hoeing

Regular hoeing is vital in the early stages. Run the hoe up and down between the rows *before* it is really necessary. That way you slice off tiny weed seedlings almost as soon as they germinate, before they clog up the rows and smother your emerging crops. It sounds like making work for yourself, I know, but it's very much quicker than waiting until you have to do a thorough job of weeding, with a hand fork, which takes a heck of a lot longer. The good news is that by the time vegetable crops cover the ground, you hardly need to do any more hoeing or weeding as their leaves shade the weeds out.

Thinning out

When rows of seedlings are just about big enough to handle, they will need thinning out. It's best done in two or three stages, so do a preliminary thin-out to leave them 2.5cm (1in) apart, so you have plenty of spares in case slugs

You will need to thin out seedlings (here, beetroot) when they are just large enough to handle. The idea is to remove weak plants and provide more space for the stronger ones.

TRANSPLANTING TIPS
- **Root crops** should not be transplanted. They should only be sown in the rows where you want them to crop, and thinned out to their final spacings (see box opposite). Unless you are lucky or careful, the roots fork or the plants run to seed, so you've wasted your time. Kohl rabi looks like a root crop but it's actually a brassica, and does best when it's transplanted.
- **Brassicas** need firm ground or they may fail to form solid hearts. When preparing the soil for planting, instead of forking it over, just hoe off surface weeds, and if the ground is fluffy firm it down by treading it first. It's quite normal to sow just a short row of brassicas, then thin the seedlings out and transplant them to their final growing positions later (see box opposite). Thin them out to 5–8cm (2–3in) apart and wait until they're proper young plants – roughly the same size as vegetable plants you buy in pots – before moving them to well-prepared soil.
- **Salad crops**, especially lettuce, must be transplanted before the beginning of June, as the combination of hot weather and a check in growth makes them less likely to survive the move; those that do will often 'bolt', or run to seed. Instead, sow seed in situ and thin out or plant out pot-grown plants so there's no root disturbance (see March, pp.68 and 76).
- **Parsley** can be transplanted, but without a lot of care it doesn't do very well. It's best sown in pots and planted out without breaking up the rootball. Alternatively, simply sow a short row and thin the plants out (see box opposite). It's slow to germinate, until the soil warms up.

have a nibble. A few weeks later, thin them out again, and give them another few weeks before thinning them to their final spacing (see box opposite).

Transplanting

Some vegetables, particularly brassicas and leeks, are sown close together in a seedbed for convenience. Later, fair-sized seedlings, usually when they are about 8–10cm (3–4in) high, are moved to their final planting positions. If you've grown pots of seedlings in the greenhouse, you'd also transplant those seedlings by tipping them out of their pots and separating the roots so each seedling can be planted out on its own.

Space your vegetable crops so that there is enough room between them to push a hoe, and to allow them to fill out.

Protect potatoes from frost
If a late frost is threatened, you can often save a row of potato foliage by covering it with a couple of thicknesses of horticultural fleece or even old newspaper, even after the foliage is too tall to cover with soil.

● Prepare the ground ready for transplanting vegetables in the same way as you would for sowing seeds (see March, p.68), and keep young plants well watered afterwards, while they find their feet.

● See box opposite for transplanting details of different kinds of vegetables and box below for final spacings of transplanted vegetables.

VEGETABLE SPACING GUIDE
When the seedlings of vegetables that were sown *in situ* earlier in the season are large enough to handle, thin them out, pulling out the weaklings and leaving the stronger plants spaced at the distances shown below.

Also, the seedlings that were sown and thinned out in a seedbed elsewhere (mainly brassicas) need to be planted in their final positions at the spacings shown below, as do plants raised earlier in pots under glass or those bought in a nursery. (See opposite and above for further information on thinning and transplanting seedlings.)

Broad beans – double rows, 20 × 20cm (8 × 8in), with 45cm (18in) between rows
Beetroot – 10cm (4in) apart, 30cm (12in) between rows
Calabrese – transplant 45 × 45cm (18 × 18in)

Carrots – 5cm (2in) apart (but best not thinned or carrot fly may be encouraged), with 15cm (6in) between rows
Chicory – 15–20cm (6–8in) apart, 30cm (12in) between rows
Endive – 30cm (12in) apart, 30–45cm (12–18in) between rows
Kohl rabi – 15cm (6in) apart, 30cm (12in) between rows
Leeks – 10cm (4in) apart, 30cm (12in) between rows
Lettuce – 15–30cm (6–12in) apart, 30cm (12in) between rows
Onions – 15cm (6in) apart, 30cm (12in) between rows
Parsley – 15cm (6in) apart, 15cm (6in) between rows
Parsnip – 15cm (6in) apart, 30cm (12in) between rows

Peas – double rows 15cm (6in) apart, 60cm (24in) between rows
Radish – 2.5cm (1in) apart, 15cm (6in) between rows
Rocket – 10cm (4in) apart, 15cm (6in) between rows
Spinach – 15cm (6in) apart, 30cm (12in) between rows
Spring onions – 2.5cm (1in) apart, 15cm (6in) between rows
Sprouting broccoli, Brussels sprouts – transplant 60 × 60cm (24 × 24in)
Summer cabbage – transplant 30 × 30cm (12 × 12in) or more depending on variety
Summer/autumn cauliflower – transplant 60 × 60cm (24 × 24in)
Swiss chard – 20cm (8in) apart, 30cm (12in) between rows
Turnips – 8cm (3in) apart, 15cm (6in) between rows

GROWING POTATOES

Potatoes fall into three groups: first earlies, second earlies and maincrop varieties (see box opposite, for recommended varieties). First earlies are your 'new potatoes'; they behave rather like baby veg, because they 'bulk up' faster. Second earlies are your serious summer spuds that you dig as you need them and leave the rest to keep growing. (When you start digging second earlies they are like large new potatoes, and as the summer progresses they'll grow bigger and more like the potatoes you buy from the greengrocer in winter.) Maincrop potatoes don't bulk up until late, but they store well – so leave them in the ground until autumn, then dig them all up in one go and keep them to use through the winter (see October, pp.255–6).

When and how to plant potatoes

Serious vegetable-growers traditionally plant each of the three groups of potatoes a few weeks apart, starting with earlies in March under cloches (see March, pp.68–9) or early April in the open, second earlies 2 weeks later, and maincrop varieties 2 weeks later again, at the end of the month. The potato crop would then be harvested in the same order, starting with the earlies from June onwards. But if you're only growing a few potatoes, there's no reason why you shouldn't just plant all your potatoes at once, at any convenient time in April.

● To plant any potatoes, follow the technique previously described for planting earlies (see March, p.69). All seed potatoes should be planted 12cm (5in) deep, but the spacings vary depending on the type: plant earlies 30cm (12in) apart, 45cm (1½ft) between rows; space second earlies and maincrop varieties 38cm (15in) apart, 60cm (2ft) between rows.

Earthing up

With all potatoes, aftercare consists almost entirely of earthing up (see box below). There are actually several good reasons for doing it.

The earlier you plant potatoes, the more chance there is that the first shoots will push up through the soil while there is still some risk of a late frost – you can tell when they've been nipped as the foliage turns black. Some varieties will eventually grow new foliage, but the frost is enough to kill many completely, so it pays to go around earthing up any shoots that appear above ground before the middle of May. Any potato tubers that push themselves out of the ground will quickly turn green – even a tinge on top is enough to make them taste horrible, but really green potatoes should never be eaten as they can be poisonous. It's also worth earthing up potatoes several times during the summer, as it increases your potato crop.

Earthing up also buries a lot of young weed seedlings, so it helps prevent your crop being

HOW TO EARTH UP

1 Using a draw hoe, pull earth up from each side of the row to form a low, mound-shaped ridge completely covering the line of potato foliage.

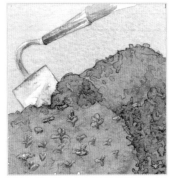

2 Each time you start to see any weeds, work your way along both sides of the rows, until the ridges are about 15–20cm (6–8in) high.

3 In summer, scrape up the soil around the stems of the plants only – the buried stems then take root, which boosts tuber production.

RECOMMENDED POTATO VARIETIES

If you're going to grow your own potatoes, it's worth choosing varieties for flavour and character. Unusual spuds are developing quite a cult following these days, in much the same way as tomatoes already have. Unless you have an allotment with bags of room there's really no point in growing 'everyday' maincrop potatoes – stick to a few of the more interesting kinds. These days, vendors cater for small-scale growers, so you can usually buy seed potatoes in small quantities, enough for a single row.

Earlies

'International Kidney' – A very old Victorian variety with superb ready-buttered flavour; when grown in Jersey it is known as 'Jersey Royal'.

'Red Duke of York' – A heritage variety with oval tubers, yellow flesh and a wonderful flavour.

Second earlies

'British Queen' – A heritage variety with a floury texture; makes the best mash ever.

'Charlotte' – A large, creamy-fleshed potato with a faint sweet potato flavour; good for salads.

'Edzell Blue' – A heritage variety with superb flavour and violet skin; wash and steam them whole to preserve the colour when they cook.

'Kestrel' – Beautiful tubers with violet 'eyes'; a regular winner on the show bench, so put a few into your local show; has a natural resistance to slugs and a very good flavour; good for roasting and chips.

Maincrop

'King Edward' – A classic old variety with a floury texture; good for mashing and boiling, but the best-ever roast potato.

'Pink Fir Apple' – A very old heritage variety, with knobbly pink-skinned tubers and yellow, waxy-textured flesh and outstanding flavour; steam whole to use for warm or cold potato salads. This is the latest potato to harvest; leave in the ground as long as possible to keep growing.

'Ratte' – An old French salad potato, tops for taste; ready to use before most maincrop potatoes.

'Sante' – Has good pest and disease resistance, so ideal for growing organically; fair flavour; a good all-rounder in the kitchen, use it for boiling and mashing.

swamped by weeds – it's like uphill hoeing. If you're old enough, you may remember that, if your Grandad had a weedy patch of ground, he'd plant potatoes to 'clean the land'. It works – but not due to any herbicidal properties in the spuds. It's all down to the regular earthing up, which gradually wears down the weed population. It's really the gardener's cultivations that clean the soil, rather than the potatoes themselves.

PERENNIAL VEGETABLES

Most vegetables are annual crops that are sown, grown and eaten all in the same year, but there are a few – asparagus and artichokes for example – that live for years, so it's no good growing those in the middle of your 'usual' vegetables as they don't fit into the same pattern of growing.

Perennial vegetables are not the mystery a lot of people make them out to be. They have a lot in common with the herbaceous perennial flowers you grow in your borders, as they die down each winter and reappear the following spring. They are usually grown in separate beds of their own, or in a row along one end of the vegetable patch. Perennial vegetables need a sunny, sheltered situation with fertile, well-drained soil and large quantities of well-rotted organic matter added and worked in deeply. This month is the best time to plant them; pot-grown plants can also go in during the summer.

Plant asparagus

Asparagus was traditionally planted on ridges, which allow the soil to drain faster and warm up quicker in spring for earlier crops. Nowadays, it is usually planted on well-drained, level ground, which makes working much easier (see box, p.102). Before planting, you need to prepare an asparagus bed thoroughly (see March, p.70).

I'd always recommend buying one of the modern, all-male, named varieties. Male plants have fatter and more succulent spears than females, but the main reason for choosing all-male asparagus is that it doesn't produce seeds. Females shed seeds, and unless you're very careful your high-yielding pedigree asparagus

HOW TO PLANT ASPARAGUS CROWNS

1 Dig a hole about 30cm (12in) deep and make a mound of soil in the middle, so you have an empty 'moat' around the edge. Sit the crown on top of the mound, and spread the roots out well all around it, going down into the 'moat'.

2 Cover the roots and crown with soil, but leave the top of the crown slightly above the level of the surrounding soil but thinly covered; crowns should be about 5–8cm (2–3in) below the surface. Water well and mulch thickly. Space asparagus crowns 75cm (30in) apart. If you're planting a double row, leave 75cm (30in) between rows.

Asparagus in the vegetable garden
Leave a margin of 1–1.2m (3–4ft) between asparagus and adjacent crops, since the stems and foliage grow quite big and floppy during the summer, and they'll smother anything else you plant too close.

patch can be slowly taken over by a lot of unproductive mongrels.

- In the first year, allow the plants to grow without cutting any spears, as it's essential to develop a strong underground root system.

- In the second year, some people permit themselves one or two spears per plant, taken in the middle of the asparagus season – some time in May – to minimize stress to the plant.

- It's not until the third year that a light crop of spears is cut, and from then on the golden rule is you can cut as much asparagus as you want from the time the first spears poke through in April until mid-June. This is when you need to apply fertilizer, and for the rest of the summer, leave the ferny foliage to develop unhindered. When the fern starts to yellow in autumn, cut it off close to ground level and tidy the beds (see September, p.234).

- Weed asparagus beds regularly, as the plants hate competition, but don't hoe. Always hand weed as asparagus plants are shallow-rooted, and in spring it's all too easy to damage emerging spears by hoeing or use of hand forks.

Plant globe artichokes

Globe artichokes are very easy to grow and don't need a bed of their own; you can either shoe-horn a plant or two into a flowerbed, or grow a row of them along one end of the vegetable patch. They make large, dramatic architectural plants with jagged, arching silver-green leaves. The part of the plant you eat is the flower bud, and as these can appear any time during the summer you will be cutting little and often for much of the season from July to September.

- Plant the artichokes, spacing them at least 1 × 1m (3 × 3ft) apart, as they need room to develop. Feed and mulch established plants generously each year in April, and keep them well weeded.

- Cut globe artichokes with a short stem when they are about fist-sized but before they start to open out into a flower. Pick as many as you like, from the first year onwards. If you miss some, they open out into purple 'thistle' heads that make good everlasting flowers for drying.

- As with perennial border flowers, you can dig up and divide globe artichokes in spring when the old plants become congested or unproductive. Instead of chopping the plant up with a spade, detach healthy young offsets from around the edge of the clump for replanting.

'GREEN' CROP PROTECTION

When you don't want to use pesticides, the best way to stop vegetables and salad crops being ruined is to exclude pests by covering the plants with a sheet of very fine insect-proof mesh, available from specialist organic gardening supply firms. This type of mesh screens out insect pests, such as greenfly, blackfly and carrot fly, and also keeps off larger predators such as birds and cats. Rain passes straight through the material, so watering is no problem, and it shelters crops from hail and wind, as well as reducing evaporation so the soil doesn't dry out so fast. The main drawback is that slugs, snails and other crawling pests can creep in underneath, particularly as you need to lift the mesh occasionally to hoe and weed.

Unlike horticultural fleece, insect-proof mesh does not trap heat underneath, so it can be used even in summer, whereas fleece needs removing as soon as the weather warms up, otherwise crops 'cook' underneath it. But you can have the best of both worlds by using fleece over newly sown crops for warmth at the start of the growing season, and then exchange it for insect-proof mesh later.

Using insect-proof mesh

- To use the mesh, lay the netting out over the crop and bury the edges, or hold them down with bricks to keep the sheet in place.
- For this method to work properly, you need to cover the crops from the start – if you cover half-grown crops, you're very likely to trap pests inside. When using mesh, sow all your root and leaf crops close together, as they can be left covered throughout their growing life.
- Tall-growing crops, such as Brussels sprouts and calabrese, clearly can't be protected for long with a blanket covering of mesh, so grow those away from low crops, such as lettuce, and make each plant an individual 'tent' to keep butterflies out so that crops are caterpillar-free.
- Plants that need pollination to produce a crop, such as beans, peas and courgettes, need to be uncovered once they start flowering or they won't 'set'.

You don't need a vegetable patch to grow globe artichokes. They are so architectural in form they look stunning in a herbaceous border combined with other ornamental plants.

GROWING BABY VEGETABLES

Tiny, tender baby vegetables are the last word in gourmet gardening. They are the same shape as full-sized vegetables, perfect in every detail, but less than half the usual size. Being genuine babies and not just stunted adults, they are ready to eat very much faster than usual.

You don't need much room to grow baby veg. Because they're spaced closer together than usual you'll pick huge quantities from a small space, and as they are picked very young you can replant the same area several times each season. To be successful, you need rich, fertile soil with regular weeding and watering so that baby veg can grow fast, without a check. Make some special beds, or use large containers completely filled with very well-rotted garden compost enriched with some general-purpose organic fertilizer. Sow your seeds into these, and use only half the normal spacing.

Varieties suitable for baby vegetables

Only certain crops are suitable for growing as baby veg, and even then you often need to grow the right varieties, because your average crop goes through a long 'teenage' stage, when it's little more than a long, lank, leafy seedling with little substance. For baby veg, it's essential that young plants form the mature shape a lot earlier than usual. Some seed catalogues have a page devoted specially to baby veg, so you don't have to wade through the complete vegetable section to find suitable varieties.

- *Normal vegetable varieties* – There are several normal vegetable varieties to grow at closer spacings and pick young. These include the following: spinach; leeks 'Kong Richard'; kohl rabi; lettuce 'Tom Thumb', 'Blush' and 'Little Gem'; beetroot; turnip 'Tokyo Cross' and 'Market Express'; parsnip 'Lancer'.

Some frost-tender vegetables also make good baby veg. These need sowing in a greenhouse around the middle of this month, to plant out mid-May (see pp.136–8). Look out for the following: pencil or filet-type French beans, such as 'Masai', 'Radar' and 'Aramis'; courgettes 'Sardane' and 'Defender' (cut them before the flower on the end is over); the type of summer squashes that are round with scalloped edges, such as 'Sunburst' and 'Green Buttons' (can be cut at 2.5cm/1in across). Cherry tomatoes are by far the best-known kind of baby veg, 'Gardener's Delight', in particular, being much appreciated for its superb flavour. Plants are readily available in garden centres at planting time. You can grow this variety in pots on the patio if you don't have a greenhouse.

- *Special varieties* – With some crops you need special varieties that only produce baby veg, even though the plants grow full size. For baby sweetcorn, as used in oriental stir-fries, you need special varieties such as 'Minor' and 'Mini Pop', but each plant produces two or three dozen 8cm (3in) baby cobs instead of the two or three normal full-sized varieties. There are also several varieties of mini-cauliflowers that produce fist-sized heads, and new varieties are coming along all the time.

Baby leaves

When you're thinning out vegetables and salad crops, such as lettuce, endive, rocket, herbs and oriental vegetables, don't throw away the seedlings you pull out. Instead, cut the roots off and wash them, and use them as early 'baby' salads.

WATCH OUT FOR FLEA BEETLE

Keep an eye out for flea beetle, which makes tiny holes in leaves – you'll sometimes see small, flea-like insects jumping around on or near the plants, hence the name. They only affect certain crops, particularly rocket, turnips, radishes, and some brassicas in early summer (and they can be the very devil on Chinese cabbage and pak choi, later in the season), but unfortunately there's not a great deal you can do about them short of spraying. The best defence is encouraging the plants to grow fast and outstrip any attack.

- When preparing the ground, use lots of organic matter and apply a general-purpose fertilizer. Keep plants well watered.

- You can also make organic flea beetle traps by putting pieces of rotten wood close to at-risk crops, in the hope the fleas will use the cool, damp area underneath as a nursery. With luck, beneficial insects will find them and do the necessary.

GIVE SUPPORT

Support peas and beans sown earlier.

HARVEST VEGETABLES

Now is the time to harvest the first overwintered spring onions, the last of the sprouting broccoli and Swiss chard.

SOW AND PLANT HERBS

You can plant or sow hardy herbs now, such as parsley, chervil, coriander, fennel, dill and marjoram (see March, p.70), but it is still too early to plant or sow frost-tender herbs such as basil.

FRUIT

ENJOY THE FRUIT GARDEN

There isn't a great deal to be done in the fruit garden in April, so sit back and enjoy the blossom while it's at its best. If you mulched around fruit in March (see p.71) there won't even be any routine hoeing or weeding to do, but do watch the weather forecasts – if a late frost threatens, cover any trees or bushes with open blossom in horticultural fleece, net curtains or old sheets to save your crop. If you don't have room for growing fruit trees or bushes the conventional way, in the ground, then it's worth thinking about growing some in pots (see Patios and Containers, pp.95–6).

PLANTING STRAWBERRIES

Nowadays, few people are prepared to give up the space for a traditional strawberry bed, but if you're a big fruit fan, with an area about 2.5 × 1m (8 × 3ft) to spare, a strawberry bed can be quite a good investment. If you didn't plant your home-grown runners in autumn, either plant those now or buy pot-grown plants. It's a good idea to grow three different varieties – an early, a mid-season and a late-season variety – to stretch the harvest. (For planting details, see October, p.257.)

PLANT AND TIE IN A NEW GRAPEVINE

Now is a good time to plant a new vine, although you can plant a pot-grown one at any time of year, even in summer.

● Plant as you would for any climber (see March, pp.58–9).

● After planting, train the stems out evenly all over the wall and tie them to a trellis or wall nails. That's your permanent framework, and those main stems will thicken up and produce sideshoots every year. Once the framework is in place, all you need to do is prune the vine each winter (see January, p.24).

PLANT AND TIE IN A FIG

You can plant a fig as for any tree or shrub (see March, pp.57–8), but if you want it to crop well instead of just looking architectural, it's best to restrict the roots slightly or it will grow big and leafy with less fruit.

How to plant a fig for fruit

Sink a large container to its rim in the ground (such as a black plastic water tank from a DIY store, after making some drainage holes in the bottom), fill with John Innes No 3 potting compost and plant into that. Alternatively, dig a large hole and line it with bricks or rubble, then fill it with good topsoil mixed with well-rotted organic matter and plant the fig into that.

Many fruit bushes and trees, such as this apple tree, are wreathed in blossom in April. If frost is forecast, you'll need to cover open blossom with horticultural fleece or another form of protection.

How to train a newly planted fig

- If the fig is grown against a wall, it needs training into a fan shape, with suitably placed branches tied to a trellis or wall nails (see January, p.24). Nip out growing tips of shoots as necessary to encourage them to branch out to produce the shoots needed to complete the shape and make best possible use of the wall space. Removal of unwanted branches is best left until the dormant season, ideally midwinter (see box below).

WHEN TO PRUNE A FIG
You can safely nip out the very tips of fig shoots during the growing season when the plant is in leaf without risk of 'bleeding', as you are only removing a tiny amount at the very end of the shoot, where it's not thick enough to do any harm. But do not cut out branches once the growing season has begun. Wait until midwinter to prune, when the fig is totally dormant (see January, p.24). If injured in the growing season the stems 'bleed' and severely weaken the plant.

- A freestanding fig can be left to grow naturally into a bushy shape, which can often look very craggy and attractive. Unless it grows too big you can get away without pruning it at all, although if the odd branch looks too lopsided or becomes broken, prune in midwinter.

- For a fig that looks more like a tree, train it as a standard. Start with an upright plant with a single stem, and when this reaches a suitable height (usually 1–1.5m/3–5ft) nip the top out to make it start branching, and keep nipping the tips out of the sideshoots produced until you form a good dense 'head'. It's much the same way as you'd form a standard fuchsia. To keep a standard fig tree compact and in shape, you'll need to cut back all the long stems that make up the head by about half – again, do this in midwinter when it's dormant.

CHECK AND HARVEST FORCED RHUBARB
Leave the forcer off once the rhubarb has been harvested and feed plants.

FEED FRUIT
Feed blackcurrants, blackberries and hybrid berries.

PRUNE STONE-FRUIT TREES
Stone-fruit trees, such as cherries, plums and nectarines, are happiest left alone as much as possible, and don't necessarily need pruning every year. However, if you are going to prune them, now is the time. Stone fruit are prone to silver leaf disease, which gradually kills the tree and spreads to others in the area. To avoid this, the trees should be pruned when they start making strong growth in spring, rather than the winter as with other fruit trees, as the bleeding sap prevents the organism responsible for the disease from entering the sap-stream.

Standard stone-fruit trees
With a standard tree, you can get away with virtually no pruning at all if you buy well-shaped trees in the first place – look for a strong, upright trunk with five strong branches evenly spaced all around the top of it. If you have inherited a lopsided tree, or one whose centre is badly congested with branches, don't snip lots of little bits here and there; instead, stand back and select an entire branch or two that you can remove to thin out the canopy, and prune those instead. And if a bottom branch is so low you can't get under it easily with the mower, take that off to raise the canopy slightly.

Fan-trained stone-fruit trees
With the ball of your thumb rub out any unwanted young shoots growing outwards from the main structure of branches. Left to grow, they'd clutter up the fan shape and shade the developing fruit during the summer. If fan-trained trees have previously been neglected, now is your chance to remedy the defects. Cut back all the unwanted shoots growing outwards from the fan-shaped framework of branches and into the path, avoiding short fruiting spurs that are carrying flowers.

UNDER COVER

TEMPERATURE CONTROL

Ventilate the greenhouse on sunny days but shut it down mid-afternoon to retain heat at night. Shade germinating seeds, seedlings, and young plants during sunny weather. When you have two-tier staging in the greenhouse, it's easiest to move 'sensitive' subjects such as these to the lower level, where they're automatically shaded by the top tier.

INTRODUCE BIOLOGICAL CONTROLS

Apply nematodes against vine weevil under glass later this month, since they need reliably warm conditions in which to live and work (see May, p.125).

GET RID OF WHITEFLY

Put out yellow sticky card to get rid of whitefly, but only as long as you aren't using a biological control, since sticky cards trap beneficial insects too.

PRICK OUT SEEDLINGS

Pricking out is a job that needs keeping on top of, but it's very therapeutic to sneak down to the greenhouse for half an hour after work and space out seedlings so they have room to grow into proper young plants.

Seedlings are ready for pricking out as soon as they're big enough to handle. Water them the day before you want to prick them out, so they're not under stress and the compost is moist – not dust dry or like porridge – so the roots lift out easily without breaking. There's a knack to pricking out, but it soon comes with practice. Use pots or seed trays, depending on the plants you're pricking out (see box, p.110).

Seed trays or individual pots?
If you're pricking out only a few plants, or intending to pot the plants on into larger containers, use small individual pots (9cm/3^{1}/$_{2}$in is a good size). For bedding plants, seed trays are a better option (in a standard-sized tray you can fit 8 rows of seedlings up the tray and 5 across).

A greenhouse provides the opportunity to grow a wider variety of plants and try out different propagation techniques.

ORGANIZE THE GREENHOUSE

A heated greenhouse is a hive of plant-raising activity in April. As fast as you take one batch of seedlings out of the propagator there are more seeds waiting to go in, and all those seeds you sowed last month will soon want pricking out. Geranium (pelargonium) and fuchsia cuttings rooted at the end of last summer or early autumn need potting up, and some of your existing greenhouse pot plants may also need repotting. There's lots to do, but it is pleasurable work and out of the way of foul weather.

A well-organized potting space really pays off at this time of year, but there's no need to splash out on a built-in potting bench that forms an integral part of the greenhouse staging – you're better off buying one of those inexpensive plastic potting trays with a raised back and flat front. You can rest it on the greenhouse staging while the potting frenzy is at its peak, then store it in the shed or garage when you aren't using it, so it's not occupying valuable growing space.

Park your potting tray at a comfortable working height (some people like to sit at a stool for potting and pricking out), pile your seed or potting compost up in the middle, pots to your left, tray of seedlings on the right, with plant labels and a pencil handy, and you're in business. When you're comfortable and well organized, spring greenhouse work runs like a well-oiled machine.

HOW TO PRICK OUT

1 Loosely fill clean pots or trays with seed compost and tap them down gently to consolidate the compost without pressing all the air out of it. Work a dibber or the point of a pencil under the roots and lift each seedling out individually, holding it by a seed leaf between your thumb and forefinger.

2 If your seedlings have been sown a tad too thickly, or left a few days too long, it's a lot easier – and less damaging – just to tip the whole potful out and divide the clump up with your fingers.

3 If using a seed tray, prick the seedlings out in rows. Make a seedling-sized hole in the compost with your dibber or pencil, feed the root down into it and lower the seedling until its seed leaves are just above compost level. Use the dibber to firm the compost around the roots. Water the seedlings using a very fine watering can rose or by standing the tray in water for a few minutes.

4 For pots, use the same pricking out technique as for trays, but you can cheat and plant a clump of three or more seedlings per pot if you want, to form a bushy plant faster. This is also a good way of using large tangled seedlings that can't be separated. Always hold a seedling by its leaf, not its fragile stem. Water well as for step 3.

Risk of frost

As a rough guide, when it comes to planting out frost-tender plants you're looking at the middle of May from the home counties southwards, but up to 3 weeks earlier at the tip of Cornwall and 3–4 weeks later in the north of Scotland. In the north of England and Wales, the end of May is usually safe. Harden plants off 2–3 weeks before planting.

SEEDLING AFTERCARE

After they've been pricked out and watered, seedlings need intensive care for a while – life in the outside world can come as a bit of a shock. Either put them back in the propagator for a few days, or stand them in a shady, humid part of the greenhouse – if you have two-storey staging, the bottom tier is ideal. Otherwise, make a 'tent' out of muslin and garden canes to cover them for the first week or so.

They'll need a rather light hand on the watering can until they get going. Keep the greenhouse heating on, so the temperature doesn't drop below 7–10°C (45–50°F) at night. Once you can see they're growing nicely, you can safely increase the light, ventilation and watering.

HARDEN OFF TENDER PLANTS

Anything that's been grown in a frost-free greenhouse, such as patio plants, bedding plants and frost-tender vegetables, will need hardening off before being planted outside. The idea is to acclimatize them slowly to outdoor conditions before you plant them, so that wind, rain and changing temperatures don't knock them for six. There's no point in even thinking about planting tender plants outside while there's still any risk of frost, so use the 2–3 weeks before your last expected frost for hardening off (see box, left).

- If you have a cold frame, which unfortunately not many of us have these days, the easy way is to move your frost-tender plants into the frame and simply open the lid on fine days, closing it again at night or when the weather is a bit iffy.

- Alternatively, move your plants out of the greenhouse for the day, and back inside at night. A few weeks of that, and with the last frost safely past, your bedding is ready to plant out. But don't rush it. There's no point in bunging tender plants out if conditions are rough, as they won't start growing in wild, wet and windy weather. Even if it means waiting a week, they'll then grow away much better without a check.

POTTING UP AND POTTING ON

Potting up, or potting off as some people call it, simply means putting a seedling or rooted cutting into its first pot. Potting on means moving a plant from a pot it's outgrown to a bigger one. The only real difference is that one plant is a baby with loose roots, so it needs a lot of TLC, while the other is older with roots that are already in a pot-shaped rootball for which a change of home is less of a wrench. The term 'potting' can be used loosely to describe either activity.

Potting up rooted cuttings

The first things that need potting up in most greenhouses are rooted cuttings. If you took cuttings of your own geraniums (pelargoniums), fuchsias and other frost-tender perennials in late summer or autumn, they'll have sat semi-dormant through the winter. Right now, they'll just be coming nicely back into growth and will need more root-room to expand into.

Treat newly potted cuttings the same way as newly pricked out seedlings (see Seedling Aftercare, opposite). After a couple of weeks you'll see them suddenly 'take off' and then you can gently acclimatize them to more light and lower humidity, and they'll start to need more watering.

Potting on greenhouse pot plants

While you're in the potting mood, take a look at the begonias and gloxinia tubers you started last month. When their original pot is full of roots and the plant starts to look a tad top-heavy, it's time to pot them on (see box, p.110).

Use the same technique to repot any of your permanent greenhouse plants that need it. It's a dead give-away when you can see roots growing out through the drainage holes in the bottom of the pot. If a plant simply looks top-heavy, it's often worth tipping it out of the pot to see if the rootball is packed solid – if so, then it's worth repotting. A pot-bound plant won't grow very well, and it'll always be short of water in summer, so it's much better off in a larger home (see box, p.110).

TOP-DRESS AND TAKE CUTTINGS FROM BIG, OLD PLANTS

If you keep the same greenhouse pot plants for several years, the day inevitably comes when the older ones are in the biggest pots that you want them to be in. When that happens, instead of repotting them, top-dress them instead. Plants will look and feel better for it.

- To top-dress, leave the plant in its original pot and scoop off about 2.5cm (1in) of the old compost and replace it with new stuff, after mixing in some slow-release feed granules to 'top-up' the nutrients.

- Every few years it's worth propagating replacements from seed (see March, pp.73–4) or cuttings (see June, p.171), as it's a mistake to keep the same greenhouse pot plants indefinitely – young plants grow and flower much better than woody geriatric specimens. Alternatively, treat yourself to a visit to a nursery. It might be just the excuse you need to try growing something different.

Choosing compost

Purists always keep to the same type of compost, either soil-less or soil-based, for both cuttings and potting, but I find that a mixture of half and half soil-less compost and John Innes No 1 potting compost makes a light yet stable mix that suits most things very well, whatever they were originally rooted into.

HOW TO POT UP CUTTINGS

1 Choose a pot slightly bigger than the plant's root system, so that it is not over-catered for but there's room to grow. Put enough compost into the pot (see box above) to cover the bottom. Lower the roots in, keeping them well spread out.

2 Fill the pot up with compost, almost to the rim, and firm it gently. Water lightly. To make plants grow bushy instead of long and leggy, nip out the growing tip at the top of each shoot. Sideshoots will start branching out within weeks.

POTTING ON A POT-BOUND SPECIMEN

It can sometimes be quite difficult to prise a badly pot-bound plant out of a tight-fitting container. When you have a plant that is badly pot-bound, you'll see a thick coil of roots forming a solid pot shape as soon as you extract it from its container. In that case, very gently prise a good number of roots from the solid mass so that they can grow into the surrounding soil.

How to repot a pot-bound plant

- Put your hand over the top of the compost, with your fingers each side of the plant, then tip it over carefully and tap the edge of the pot down on a hard surface. The vibration should loosen the plant, so you can slide the rootball out gently into your hand.

- A very badly pot-bound plant sometimes jams itself in so solidly that you have to break the pot to get it out. Crack clay pots gently and cut plastic ones away with a pair of scissors or a craft knife.

- Tease a few roots out from the rootball, then transfer the plant into its new pot, which should be one size larger than the last – no more – with a little compost covering the bottom.

- Sit the rootball in the centre so that the plant is standing upright, then fill the gap between the pot and the plant with more compost. Firm lightly and water. When potting is complete, the surface of the rootball should be just below the surface of the new compost – about 5mm (¹/₄in).

Repotting tip

It's a good idea to let plants dry out slightly before you repot them. That way the compost shrinks slightly so the rootball comes away from the sides of the pot more easily.

PLANT UP CONTAINERS

Plant up hanging baskets towards the end of the month and leave them in the greenhouse until late May or even early June, after the danger of frost has passed. You can also plant up tubs if there's room to keep them under glass for now.

BUY BEDDING PLANTS AS PLUGS

Buy and pot up plug plants (see March, pp.74–5), to plant out after danger of frost has passed (probably some time next month).

LAST CHANCE TO SOW HALF-HARDY ANNUALS

Complete the sowing of half-hardy annuals by the middle of the month at the very latest, or they won't start flowering until the summer is nearly over (see March, pp.73–4).

TAKE BASAL CUTTINGS

This is your last chance to take basal cuttings from border perennials (see March, pp.75–6). Leave it any later and the shoots will be too long to be of much use.

TAKE HYDRANGEA CUTTINGS

Take cuttings from pot-grown hydrangeas as for pelargoniums and fuchsias (see June, p.171), but avoid using shoots that are likely to produce flowers. Sideshoots lower down on the plant are usually suitable.

Right: If you have a greenhouse, you can plant up your hanging baskets now and leave them under cover until the danger of frost has passed.

REST CYCLAMEN AND HIPPEASTRUM

After flowering, both cyclamen and hippeastrum (often known, incorrectly, as amaryllis) benefit from a 'rest'.

Cyclamen

When the plants stop flowering and the leaves start turning yellow, which starts happening naturally sometime in March or April, reduce the watering gradually over several weeks until all the foliage falls off, leaving a dormant tuber in a pot. Store them for summer by laying the pots on their sides under the greenhouse staging, or stand them in a cool, shady place outdoors after mid-May when there's no more risk of frost.

Hippeastrum

You will have to play it by ear, as not all hippeastrum plants want to become dormant in the summer. Once the flowers are over, continue watering and liquid feeding them; if the foliage starts to look below par or starts turning yellow, reduce the watering and stop feeding, so that the bulbs gradually dry out over several weeks. Remove the dry, dead foliage and store the dormant bulbs in their pots in a cool, dry place until next autumn when they start growing again. A plant that shows no signs of turning dormant shouldn't be forced to do so – as long as it keeps growing and producing new foliage, continue feeding and watering as usual.

TAKE CUTTINGS FROM CAPE PRIMROSES

April is the time to take leaf cuttings of Cape primroses (*Streptocarpus*) (see box, below). Select a middle-aged leaf for cutting, meaning one that's fully opened and not damaged in any way; avoid the big old ones at the very outside edge of the plant.

SOW TOMATOES

Sow tomatoes early this month for planting outdoors in early June (see March, pp.73–4).

SOW SEED OF FROST-TENDER VEGETABLES

Seeds that must go in some time this month are all your frost-tender vegetables – French and runner beans, sweetcorn, courgettes, marrows, cucumbers, pumpkins, squashes and melons, including varieties suitable for baby veg (see Vegetables and Herbs, p.98). I sow mine in the middle of April, because I know they're going to take 4 or 5 weeks to make plants ready to put outside, and that way

Taking leaf cuttings
When taking leaf cuttings, results are slow so don't be impatient and chuck the lot out. If you're cutting across the midrib, make sure you know which is top and bottom on each cutting – the cut nearest to the base of the leaf is the bottom and needs to be covered by compost.

HOW TO TAKE LEAF CUTTINGS

1 Cut off the leaf, complete with its short stalk, using a sharp knife. If you only want one or two new plants, push the stalk into a pot of seed compost, leaving the rest of the leaf exposed.

2 If you want several plants, cut the leaf in half or into four if it's a large one, slicing it across the midrib in the middle. Push each section into the pot of compost so it is half in and half out.

3 Water the compost lightly and slip a large, loose plastic bag over the pot. Keep the cuttings on a warm windowsill, out of direct sun, and after a couple of months you'll see tiny plantlets growing up from the inserted edge of the leaf, where the midrib in the centre has been cut.

4 When the plantlets are several centimetres high, each one should have a big enough root system to live alone, so take them out and pot each one individually. If several plants grow from one leaf, as sometimes happens, divide them up carefully.

Well fed and kept free of weeds, border plants will grow away fast at this time of year.

Transfer pollen from one strawberry flower to another with a fine, soft paintbrush.

• Place pots of sweetcorn, cucumber and the marrow family into a propagator set at 21°C (70°F), where they come up fast and furious. If some seeds fail to germinate, sow another one in each blank pot. Bean seeds often rot in the propagator, so stand the pots on a shady bit of staging in a greenhouse that's heated to about 7°C (45°F).

• As soon as the first 'seed leaves' have just about unfolded, take tender vegetable plants out of the propagator, otherwise they grow weak and weedy. Stand them on the bench out of strong sun but in good indirect light, in a greenhouse heated to frost-free or slightly above. Water lightly, and after 4 weeks start weak liquid feeding every 2 weeks.

• Provided you hit the timing just right, young plants should be ready to plant out as soon as their pots are full of root. If there's a late cold spell, repot the plants in pots one size larger to keep them in good condition until they can be planted out safely.

PRICK OUT TOMATO SEEDLINGS

Prick out tomato seedlings sown last month (see March, pp.73–4). Put each one in a 9cm (3½in) pot of multipurpose compost. If you live in a mild area you can plant tomatoes in an unheated greenhouse at the end of the month (when plants are big enough), planting them into a well-prepared border, large pots, approximately 30–38cm (12–15in) in diameter, or growing bags. Tie up to supports and remove any sideshoots.

POLLINATE AND FEED STRAWBERRY PLANTS

Hand-pollinate flowers every morning they are open, using a fine artist's watercolour brush. Once fruits have clearly set, begin liquid feeding once a fortnight using tomato feed diluted down to a quarter of the normal strength.

they're timed just right to go out after the last frosts are safely over. If you live in a cold spot, leave it a week or two later, and you won't be caught with plants bursting out of their pots when you can't risk putting them outside. All the frost-tender vegetables have fairly large seeds, so I sow them singly in pots. You could sow them in trays, but the seedlings are so strong and grow so fast that the roots get tangled up and you can't help damaging them as you pull them apart.

• Ideally, soak the seeds in tepid water for 12 hours, maximum, before sowing in April, so they are fully hydrated right from the start. This isn't essential, but pre-soaked seeds do germinate more reliably.

• Sow the seed, preferably singly in pots (see March, p.74).

WATER GARDEN

SPRING CLEAN THE POND

Spring means spring-cleaning time for your pond, and the smaller the pond the more badly it will need attention. Start by clearing the decks:

- If you still have a net over the surface of the water to protect fish from herons and trap dead leaves in winter, take it off.

- Clear out any dead leaves or decaying bits of rubbish.

- Use a 'shrimping net' to skim off any duckweed that may be floating about already. Oh I know it looks pretty when there's only a bit, but as soon as the weather warms up it spreads like wildfire and covers the water with a suffocating mat of leaves that does no good at all. Don't be surprised if the water looks rather green and murky – that's fairly normal for the start of the season, and it will soon clear itself naturally if you're patient.

DIVIDE OVERGROWN WATER PLANTS

After your spring clean, turn your attention to the marginal plants, the sort that grow in net-sided pots and plastic baskets standing on the planting shelves around the edge of the water. They'll just be starting back into growth, and the timing is perfect for dividing up any that need it. You can also divide deep-water aquatics, which grow with their baskets standing on the floor of the pond – use the same technique (see box, below), you'll just get wetter dividing the latter.

ADD NEW PLANTS TO THE POND

If you want to add to your water plant collection, now is a good time to do so, although you'll probably find the full range isn't available until a bit later in summer, and waterlilies and irises may well not be on sale until May.

When you buy water plants they are often sold in very small pots, in which case they need repotting into planting baskets when you get them home. The square sort, 20 × 20cm (8 × 8in), are the best size to sit comfortably on the average planting shelf around a small pond, while for deep-water aquatics a round basket, 30cm (12in) in diameter, is often better. The technique is just the same as for potting water plants that you've divided (see below).

HOW TO DIVIDE MARGINAL AND DEEP-WATER AQUATIC PLANTS

 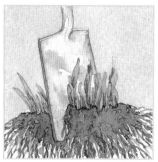  

1 Lift plants out of the water in their baskets.

2 Tip the plants out and divide them up with a sharp spade. Throw the unwanted pond plant pieces on to the compost heap.

3 Refill the basket with pond compost (see box, p.114) and replant the best part of the plant.

4 As the finishing touch, put a couple of handfuls of gravel or small pebbles all over the surface of your planted basket before lowering the pot slowly back into position (see box, p.114).

DIVIDING AND REPLANTING WATER PLANTS

When to divide aquatic plants?

Apart from growing knee-deep in water, aquatic plants behave just like herbaceous perennials in your borders, so they only need dividing when they are overcrowded and bursting out of their containers. Slow-growers may be fine for 5 years or more, but fast-spreaders may need splitting up every 2–3 years – ignore them at your peril. Overgrown marginal plants have a nasty habit of choking a pond, slowly turning it from open water into a bog garden.

Which plants should you divide this month?

You can divide and replant most marginal and deep-water aquatic plants this month, but don't divide waterlilies until next month (see May, p.145), as the tubers tend to rot if you take liberties with them while the water is cold – in any case, they don't start growing until later. The only other plants to leave for now are water irises, which are best divided a few weeks after they finish flowering (see July, p.196), otherwise you'll miss out on this year's show.

What soil should you use for planting aquatics?

Ideally you should use pond compost, which is like heavy loam without any fertilizer, for planting aquatic plants. You can use garden soil if you know for sure it's never had garden products used on it, but pond life and water plants are susceptible to even the tiniest trace of weedkiller, and any nutrients encourage algae, which turns the water green. On balance it's best to buy a bag of the right stuff.

Why top the compost with gravel?

Topping the surface of the basket with gravel or small pebbles looks good, but more importantly it stops the compost floating out when you put the plant in the water, and it also stops your fish digging your new plant out to see if there's anything tasty to eat lurking underneath.

Right: Use a large net to remove dead leaves, unwanted debris and any weeds that are floating about in the pond.

FINISHING TOUCHES

Once you've finished disturbing the water, put your pump, if you use one to power a fountain or waterfall, back into the pond (most people remove them for the winter). Even if the water has turned cloudy it'll soon settle. A quick titivate around the outside of the pond to remove weeds, and you'll be able to start the season with a well-turned-out water garden.

FEEDING FISH

It is fun to feed fish, as it brings them up to the surface where you can see them. But it isn't really essential in a well set-up pond, since the water will already support a wealth of tiny water life that fish will eat quite happily – they'll take water-snail eggs and mosquito larvae, which could otherwise build up to nuisance proportions. If you're going to feed your fish, start around late April, when the water has warmed up, and stop again around mid-September or October, depending on when it turns cold. When the water is cold they can't digest 'artificial' food, and they go off their grub in winter anyway.

PROJECT Make an auricula theatre

In the 17th century, auriculas (see p.84 and Patios and Containers, p.94) were grown by plant enthusiasts, or 'florists' as they were known. The plants were cultivated in pots so they could be taken to flower shows, which were actually an excuse for a great get-together at the pub, with a grand feast where the plants were shown off, followed by a lot of drinking and general debauchery. Today's flower shows are very genteel by comparison.

At posh houses of the time, auriculas were displayed in special outdoor 'theatres', which looked like tiered shelves with a backdrop of fabric, sometimes flanked by real curtains. Very few original auricula theatres remain today. There is one at Calke Abbey in Derbyshire, and you'll sometimes see a theatre-style auricula display staged by nurserymen specializing in auriculas at modern flower shows.

What you need

Pot-grown auriculas

Pine shelf unit or small backless bookcase, about 1m (3ft) high by 45cm (18in) wide and 15–20cm (6–8in) deep, with two or three shelves inside

Yacht varnish

Piece of dark velvet or dralon

Shelf fixings

1 Plant your auriculas in clay pots, in a compost made of roughly 3 parts John Innes No 1 potting compost, 2 parts fibrous peat-free compost or leafmould, and 1 part potting grit. Water carefully, wetting the grit rather than the plants. (See also Patios and Containers, p.94.)

2 To make the theatre, treat a pine shelf unit or small backless bookcase to a couple of coats of yacht varnish to help it stand up to outdoor weather, as it will be left out all year round.

TIERED DISPLAYS TODAY

The idea of a staged plant display lends itself very well to today's patio, and especially if you have a small garden it's a good way of showing off your special plants while they're at their best, and making more of a 'show' of them. Although auriculas are traditionally shown off in theatres, once you have built the structure it makes a good place to display all sorts of small potted plants after the auricula season – particularly those types that were historically grown and collected by 'florists', such as pelargoniums, pansies and polyanthus (see March, p.51), including the gold-laced kind. For a more modern slant, a tiered display like this would also suit pots of alpines, such as sempervivums and saxifrages (see February, p.34), and 'bonsai-style' plants (see Project, p.77).

3 Pin a piece of black (or green or dark blue) velvet or dralon across the back, with its best side facing forwards, so you can see it through the shelves. It won't last long outdoors, so you'll need to replace the material regularly. Alternatively, you can leave the back of the shelf unit in place and paint it matt black.

4 If you're feeling adventurous, you could make 'curtains' of matching fabric. They don't need to be big enough to draw across the front like a real theatre – simply hold them back with drapes so they frame the sides.

5 Fix the shelves to the wall of the patio. For auriculas, choose a sheltered, shady place where the plants won't be exposed to direct sun.

6 Select your best auriculas as they are just coming into flower. You only need a few plants to make a good display. Space them out well on the shelves so their shapes stand out clearly against the background. Check the plants daily and replace any whose flowers are going over.

MAY

May is the end of spring or the start of summer, depending on how you look at it. It's still too soon for most of the mainstream summer flowers, but if you live in an area with acid soil, you can't help noticing that rhododendron time is in full swing. May is, for me, one of the most exciting months in the garden, because you can see new flowers opening every time you step outdoors. Longer evenings and warmer weather bring the barbecues and outdoor furniture out, and it's hard to curb your impatience to get the bedding plants in.

Weather watching is a gardener's favourite sport at any time, but this month it's crucial, as is keeping tabs on the new rash of garden pests that start appearing as it warms up. Another top priority this month is to keep up to date with routine mowing, weeding and hoeing, because once those annuals and frost-tender vegetables are planted out, you'll be adding a whole lot of watering to your routine. But hey, it's pleasurable work in fine weather, and in May, the best of the year is to come. Relish it!

THE BIG PICTURE rhododendrons

Hardy hybrid rhododendrons are the popular evergreen kinds that are similar to and often hybrids of the *Rhododendron ponticum* that grows semi-wild in this country; they have flowers in a variety of colours. Not all of these rhododendrons are suitable for small gardens; some grow into huge shrubs or even trees in time, so don't just fall in love with the flowers when you're in the garden centre — look at the back of the label and find out how big the plant is going to grow. Some of the best known include **'Britannia'** (above), which has incredible scarlet flowers on squat plants, 1.5 × 2.2m (5 × 7ft), and **'Pink Pearl'**, with bright pink flowers verging towards magenta, 4 × 4m (12 × 12ft).

PEAK SEASON May–June.
GROWING CONDITIONS Well-drained, humus-rich, acid soil in dappled shade, such as woodland fringes or clearings. Will tolerate full sun for part of the day in a sheltered spot where the soil stays moist in summer.

Dwarf rhododendrons are also very hardy. Their compact mound shapes make these among the best rhododendrons for small gardens, even though the flowers tend to be smaller than those of other kinds. Varieties such as *Rhododendron* **'Blue Tit'**, 1 × 1m (3 × 3ft), with lavender-blue flowers, and **'Bow Bells'** (above), 1.5 × 1.5m (5 × 5ft), with pale pink bells and bronze-tinged young leaves, are charmers — rather like having a toy poodle instead of the standard, and you know they won't make a take-over bid for the garden. If you don't have acid soil, which is essential for rhododendrons, then they make very good plants for growing in tubs.

PEAK SEASON April–May.
GROWING CONDITIONS Humus-rich, acid soil in well-drained borders, raised beds, rock gardens and containers. These aren't shade lovers — they like sun, although not early morning sun. In tubs, grow them in ericaceous compost.

Rhododendron yakushimanum is a species rhododendron. Most rhododendron species are massive great brutes, but not this one. 'Yaks', as their fans call them, are neat and compact, with attractive semi-rounded leaves with brown flock undersides. A good range of 'yak' cultivars are available, flowering mainly in apricot-pink shades, including **'Ken Janeck'** (above), whose flowers are lined with pinkish purple. Some of the most popular are named after Snow White's seven dwarfs, such as **'Dopey'** (red flowers), **'Grumpy'** (pale yellow) and **'Sneezy'** (deep pink and red).

Most grow about 1 × 1m (3 × 3ft), and are first class for growing in tubs.

PEAK SEASON May–June.
GROWING CONDITIONS Well-drained, humus-rich, acid soil in sun, but not early morning sun. In pots, grow in ericaceous compost.

OLD FAITHFULS

Deciduous rhododendrons sound like a contradiction in terms, but these are what we used to call deciduous azaleas until a few years ago, and include all the Knap Hill, Ghent and Exbury hybrids. These are the kinds with large, exotic, trumpet-shaped flowers in wonderful rich tawny, yellow, red and orange shades growing on bare stems. The leaves follow later, and have glorious autumn colour. They are plants for a woodland garden, so if you have the right spot, make the most of them; expect them to fill a space about 1.5 × 1.5m (5 × 5ft).
Rhododendron luteum (above) is one of my favourites, with yellow flowers that have a divine scent, especially after rain. It grows to 2.5 × 2.5m (8 × 8ft) or a bit more in time.

PEAK SEASON May–June.
GROWING CONDITIONS Well-drained, humus-rich, acid soil in dappled shade such as woodland fringes or clearings.

Clematis **'Nelly Moser'** (above) is the first of the large-flowered clematis hybrids to open, and her pink and mauve pyjama-stripe flowers tell you that summer is nearly here. If the weather is a tad cold for her liking, the very first flowers will have a greenish tinge, which soon wears off. Expect this variety to reach 3m (10ft), although you can train her on trellis; it's one of the clematis it's best not to prune much, or you'll be cutting off the bits that ought to flower a little later. If you do want to tidy her up, cut out any dead or excessively tatty growth back to a pair of growing buds fairly high up the plant in February.

PEAK SEASON May–June and September.
GROWING CONDITIONS Fertile soil in any aspect except due south (which causes the flowers to fade), including light shade. Roots need to be cool and shady.

Clematis montana **var. *rubens*** (above) is one of the most popular clematis, and makes a much larger plant than the hybrids. The flowers are single, pink and only about 4cm (1½in) across, but there are lots of them and they look good against the bronze-tinged young foliage. This is one to let loose up an old tree or along a stone wall, where it has room to spread – it'll make 6–10m (20–30ft). It's very easy to grow, and doesn't need pruning unless it outgrows its welcome.

PEAK SEASON May–June.
GROWING CONDITIONS Fertile soil anywhere but in deep shade. Likes cool shade at the roots.

Viburnum plicatum **'Mariesii'** (above) makes a wonderful spreading shrub with tiered branches. The deeply veined, bright green leaves unfurl in spring and are followed by flat, creamy white heads of flowers – rather like a lacecap hydrangea – all along the branches. It's a lovely shrub, growing 2.5 × 2.5m (8 × 8ft) in time, and is spectacular in flower. Train a Viticella or Texensis clematis through the viburnum to brighten it up in summer (see July, p.180, and August, p.202).

PEAK SEASON April–June.
GROWING CONDITIONS Rich, well-drained soil and sun or dappled shade.

Dianthus barbatus, sweet Williams (above), and ***Campanula medium***, Canterbury bells, are old-fashioned biennials that behave a bit like annuals, except that they grow one year and flower the next. Although they aren't often seen nowadays, these two old favourites fill the natural break in the garden between spring and summer flowers, and since no-one much grows them, yours are bound to stand out. They are good for cutting, and sweet Williams have a terrific scent. Although you have to grow your own from seed, since plants don't often turn up in nurseries, it's really no bother to do.

PEAK SEASON May–June.
GROWING CONDITIONS Any well-cultivated soil in gaps between shrubs and under rose bushes, in sun or light shade.

Wisteria floribunda (above) is the classic early-summer-flowering climber, known for its long, trailing streamers of lilac-blue pea-like flowers, although there are many varieties in other colours. At 10m (30ft) or so, a huge twining climber can be a bit much for some houses – if you don't have room on the front wall, try training a wisteria out over a pergola, gazebo or around the edge of your carport roof. A wisteria can also be trained up a pole to make a weeping standard tree that can be either planted in the garden or grown in a large tub. New plants can be slow to come into growth the first spring after planting, and often take 5–7 years before flowering for the first time. Patience is needed, and the right pruning is essential for any wisteria (see January, p.20, and July, p.185). Buy a grafted plant of a named variety to make sure of proven flowering quality, and you may be surprised by flowers in 2 or 3 years.

PEAK SEASON May–June.
GROWING CONDITIONS Fertile soil (but not boggy in winter or bone dry in summer), in sun or light shade.

Euphorbia characias **subsp. *wulfenii*** (above) is an architectural plant that you'll find with the perennials at the garden centre, although it's evergreen and doesn't die down in winter. The grey-green leaves and bushy, dome-shaped plants are a must for a hot, dry, sunny, gravelly sort of garden, but it also seems happy on clay as long as it's not too wet in winter. The huge heads of lime green to chartreuse flowers dry out attractively on the plant, so it looks good over much of the summer. Like other euphorbias, the sap is an irritant, so take care when pruning out spent stems after flowering; also, it may be something to pass up on when you have young children.

PEAK SEASON May–June.
GROWING CONDITIONS Most well-drained soils, in sun.

SOMETHING SPECIAL

Geum 'Mrs J. Bradshaw'
(above) flowers reliably, her
double brick-red flowers papering
over the awkward gap between
spring flowers and summer
perennials. The leaves make
attractive ground cover under
the 45cm (18in) stems of flower,
which are wiry enough to stand
up to the weather. Good in
herbaceous borders or under
shrubs.

PEAK SEASON May–August.
GROWING CONDITIONS Any
   reasonable soil in sun or light
   shade.

Lonicera periclymenum
'Belgica' (above) is the Early
Dutch honeysuckle with fragrant
yellow, white and red flowers.
It's a variety of the wild woodbine
that grows in country hedges, and
twines around supports or up
trees when grown in the garden.
Delightfully scented.

PEAK SEASON May–July.
GROWING CONDITIONS Moist,
   fertile soil, where roots are in
   shade and the stems can grow
   out into sun.

Cercis siliquastrum, Judas tree
(above), isn't something to try in a
cold part of the country, but
where you have a mild garden this
is a tree with a difference. The
mauve-pink, pea-like flowers
appear ahead of the leaves,
growing straight out of the
branches and even the trunk.
The leaves are large, glaucous
and heart-shaped, and the tree
itself grows into naturally twisted,
craggy shapes – it's more of a
character actor than a bright
young thing. It'll make 4 × 3m
(12 × 10ft), but it can be cut
back hard or blown over at an
angle in gales and still springs
back, craggier than ever.

PEAK SEASON May.
GROWING CONDITIONS
   Reasonably well-drained soil,
   including chalk, in sun.

Crinodendron hookerianum (above) needs a special spot, but you would be pushed to find a more spectacular evergreen shrub, provided you have the right conditions. It makes a large shrub, 3 × 3m (10 × 10ft), with dark green linear leaves and large red, almost fluorescent, lantern-like flowers. Unless you live in an exceptionally mild area, it's best trained out flat against a wall, where it'll cover an area 2 × 3m (6 × 10ft) quite easily.

PEAK SEASON May–June, and sometimes has a second flush in late summer.

GROWING CONDITIONS Mild, sheltered spot in semi-shade, including north-facing walls, with moist, lime-free soil and organic enrichment.

Incarvillea delavayi, often called hardy gloxinia (above), is nothing of the sort. It's a very striking perennial, growing about 30 × 20cm (12 × 8in), with large, shocking-pink flowers whose chubby 'bunch-of-bells' shapes do suggest a gloxinia, although the two have little else in common. The ladder-like leaves appear as the flowers are coming to an end, but the whole plant doesn't stay above ground for long, making the fleshy taproot easy to spike with a fork when tidying, with terminal consequences.

PEAK SEASON May–June.
GROWING CONDITIONS Well-drained, fertile soil with plenty of organic matter, in sun or very light shade between shrubs.

Corydalis flexuosa (above) is one of those plants you must have – or at least it was one you had to have a few years ago, before everyone else had it. Think of a small maidenhair fern with slim, tubular, impossibly bright blue, spurred flowers resembling small, stretched aquilegias, and you just about have it. It's small, 20 × 20cm (8 × 8in), and grows from perennial fibrous roots, but since it dies down in summer a lot of people think it's dead and throw it out or plant something else over the top of it. It's a treasure, no doubt about it.

PEAK SEASON May–June.
GROWING CONDITIONS Well-drained, humus-rich soil in dappled shade.

Rosa banksiae 'Lutea' (above), has small, very double flowers, but hardly any scent. Its double-flowered cousin, **Rosa banksiae 'Lutescens'**, the Banksian rose, is something a bit special. A climber with clusters of small, single, pale yellow flowers, it has an incredibly powerful scent, which some people liken to violets. It's a large grower, 4 × 4m (12 × 12ft) and more, and you can't prune it without chopping out the bits that are supposed to flower next. But if you have the space, and a mild, sheltered spot, it is well worth having.

PEAK SEASON May.
GROWING CONDITIONS Rich, fertile soil in a warm, sunny, sheltered spot, ideally on a large, south-facing wall.

Tree peonies like *Paeonia suffruticosa* 'Kokuryû-nishiki' (above) are real stunners, with giant, crumpled-tissue-paper flowers, which can be as much as 30cm (12in) across, on small, elegant, woody trees that usually reach only 1.2 × 1.2m (4 × 4ft). The foliage is finely divided and is a feature in its own right when the flowers are over. Many have exotic names translated from the Japanese. You may find the odd plant in a garden centre, but generally this is a case for a specialist nursery, which will in any case stock the best selection. *Paeonia lutea* var. *ludlowii* makes a larger plant – to 1.5m (8ft) – with rich yellow flowers and handsome, finely cut foliage.

PEAK SEASON May.
GROWING CONDITIONS Very well-sheltered site in sun or partial shade, with deep, fertile, well-drained soil containing plenty of organic matter. Tree peonies can also be grown in pots and kept in the conservatory until after flowering.

Clianthus puniceus, better known as lobster claw or parrot's bill (above), is well named because that's just what the bunches of curved red flowers look like. The plant is neither a climber nor a wall shrub but something between the two; at any rate, it's extremely floppy in its natural state and needs the support of a trellis or netting.

PEAK SEASON May–June.
GROWING CONDITIONS Sheltered, sunny spot with well-drained soil; can also be grown in a large container in a conservatory and trained up a trellis on a wall, where it will flower a good 6 weeks earlier.

OTHER PLANTS IN THEIR PRIME IN MAY

- **Trees** *Caragana arborescens, Crataegus laevigata, Davidia involucrata, Embothrium lanceolatum, Laburnum, Mespilus germanica* 'Nottingham' (see p.80), *Paulownia tomentosa, Sorbus aria, Sorbus aucuparia*

- **Shrubs** *Berberis* (see p.82), *Chaenomeles japonica, Chaenomeles* (see p.49), *Cotoneaster, Enkianthus campanulatus, Exochorda racemosa, Halesia carolina, Kerria japonica, Kolkwitzia amabilis, Magnolia liliiflora, Piptanthus laburnifolius, Potentilla fruticosa, Ribes odoratum, Ribes sanguineum* (see p.81), *Ribes speciosum, Rosa xanthina* 'Canary Bird' (see p.83), *Sambucus nigra, Spiraea* 'Arguta' (see p.81), *Spiraea × vanhouttei, Syringa, Tamarix tetrandra, Viburnum × carlcephalum, Viburnum × carlesii* 'Aurora' (see p.84), *Viburnum × juddii, Weigela florida*

- **Evergreens** *Berberis* (see p.82), *Camellia* (see p.50), *Ceanothus thyrsiflorus* var. *repens, Choisya ternata, Cistus, Cytisus, Genista lydia, Genista hispanica, Hebe pinguifolia* 'Pagei', *Osmanthus delavayi, Osmanthus × burkwoodii, Pieris* (see p.83), *Pittosporum tenuifolium, Ulex europaeus* 'Flore Pleno', *Viburnum × burkwoodii, Vinca*

- **Climbers/wall shrubs** *Clematis alpina, Clematis* 'Barbara Jackman', *Clematis* 'Bees Jubilee', *Clematis* 'Duchess of Edinburgh', *Clematis macropetala, Clematis montana, Clematis* 'Proteus', *Clematis* 'Vyvyan Pennell'

- **Perennials** *Ajuga, Armeria, Bergenia* (see p.33), *Brunnera macrophylla* 'Jack Frost (see p.85), *Caltha palustris, Crambe cordifolia, Dicentra spectabilis, Epimedium, Eremurus stenophyllus, Euphorbia griffithii, Euphorbia myrsinites, Helianthemum, Iris* (Dwarf Bearded and Intermediate Bearded), *Lamium maculatum, Paeonia officinalis, Papaver orientale, Polygonatum multiflorum, Pulmonaria* (see p.82), *Saxifraga × urbium, Tiarella cordifolia, Trollius, Veronica gentianoides*

- **Bulbs** *Camassia, Hyacinthus, Leucojum, Ornithogalum, Scilla peruviana, Tulipa* (see p.83)

- **Bedding/biennials** *Aquilegia, Bellis* daisies, *Erysimum cheiri* (see p.51), *Matthiola incana, Myosotis, Ranunculus*, winter-flowering pansies (see p.269)

- **Rock plants** *Aurinia saxatilis, Armeria juniperifolia, Aubrieta* (see p.50), *Erysimum hieraciifolium, Erinus alpinus, Gentiana acaulis, Gentiana verna, Geranium cinereum, Iberis sempervirens, Ipheion, Lewisia cotyledon, Oxalis adenophylla* (see p.85), *Phlox douglasii, Phlox subulata, Primula auricula* (see p.84), *Pulsatilla vulgaris, Raoulia, Saxifraga, Viola*

MAY at-a-glance checklist

GENERAL GARDEN TASKS (p.125)
✔ From the middle of the month onwards plant bedding plants, tender exotics, pot-grown dahlias, frost-tender vegetables and sweet pea plants started off under glass.
✔ Prepare the soil for bedding plants.
✔ Keep on top of weeding and hoeing.
✔ Watch out for and deal with pests using biological controls and other organic remedies.

LAWNS (p.126)
✔ Feed established lawns if not done in April.
✔ Remove weeds.
✔ Mow lawns weekly.

TREES, SHRUBS AND CLIMBERS (p.127)
✔ Prune forsythia and flowering currant (*Ribes sanguineum*) after flowering.
✔ Tie in new growth of climbers and wall shrubs.
✔ Pinch out any green shoots appearing on variegated trees and shrubs.
✔ Water plants and protect new shoots with horticultural fleece.
✔ In mild climates, move tender conservatory shrubs in pots outside.
✔ Clip beech, hornbeam, box, thuja and Leyland cypress hedges late this month or early next.
✔ Cut privet and *Lonicera nitida* every 6 weeks or so throughout the summer.

FLOWERS (p.129)
✔ Support perennials.
✔ Divide clumps of polyanthus and primroses after flowering.
✔ Plant out dahlias and tender exotics.
✔ Sow seed of perennials.
✔ Cut back alyssum, arabis and aubrieta after flowering.
✔ Continue deadheading and feeding spring-flowering bulbs.
✔ Clear spring-flowering plants and prepare the ground for replanting.
✔ Plant and train sweet peas.

PATIOS AND CONTAINERS (p.131)
✔ Bring out nearly-hardy trees and shrubs from the conservatory once the danger of frost has passed.
✔ Plant tubs, troughs, windowboxes and hanging baskets in the middle of this month at the earliest.
✔ Check plants regularly to see if watering is necessary.

VEGETABLES AND HERBS (p.134)
✔ Water the vegetable patch regularly in dry weather.
✔ Sow swede, beetroot, maincrop carrots, autumn cabbage, autumn/winter cauliflowers, calabrese, peas, Swiss chard, radish, lettuce and spring onions.
✔ Direct-sow frost-tender vegetables, e.g. French and runner beans, sweetcorn, courgettes, squashes and pumpkins.
✔ Sow chicory for forcing in winter.
✔ Transplant brassicas grown in seedbeds.
✔ Plant frost-tender vegetables once the danger of frost has passed; harden them off first.
✔ Plant out leeks.
✔ Continue earthing up potatoes.
✔ Harvest asparagus, lettuce, radishes, rocket and overwintered onions.

FRUIT (p.138)
✔ Water soft fruit bushes with swelling fruit and newly planted fruit trees.
✔ Protect strawberries from grey mould and birds.

UNDER COVER (p.140)
✔ Ventilate the greenhouse well by day, and water plants more frequently.
✔ Apply shading paint to the greenhouse.
✔ Damp down regularly.
✔ Continue to prick out and pot on seedlings, cuttings and young plants.
✔ Continue hardening off bedding plants and frost-tender vegetables by standing them outside on fine days and returning them to the greenhouse at night.
✔ Take cuttings from pelargoniums, fuchsias and other tender perennials between now and mid-September.

✔ Plant tomatoes in early May and sweet peppers, chillies, aubergines, melons and cucumbers in late May.
✔ Water, feed, trim and train new plants regularly.
✔ Harvest baby potatoes.

WATER GARDEN (p.144)
✔ Add new floating plants.
✔ Divide overgrown waterlilies or put new waterlilies in the pond.
✔ Remove unwelcome weeds.
✔ Introduce new fish to the water garden and continue to feed fish.

Watch out for
- Late frosts – protect new shoots and fruit tree blossom with horticultural fleece, cover plants in an unheated greenhouse with newspaper, and don't plant bedding out too soon.
- Pests are everywhere at this time of year – in containers, in greenhouses, in the garden, and in conservatories.

Get ahead
- Dig up and dry off tulip bulbs once they have finished flowering, to make way for summer bedding plants.
- Identify any gaps in beds and borders and visit your local nursery or garden centre for new plants.

Last chance
- The beginning of the month is your last chance to sow a new lawn.

GENERAL GARDEN TASKS

PLANT HALF-HARDY AND FROST-TENDER PLANTS

Summer wouldn't be complete without dazzling displays of flowers in tubs and hanging baskets, and the big job to do this month is planting them up (see Patios and Containers, p.131). The same is true for all your frost-tender subjects; not just bedding plants, but pot-grown dahlias and tender exotics (see Flowers, p.129), and all those frost-tender vegetables such as courgettes, runner beans, sweetcorn and baby vegetables sown last month (see Vegetables and Herbs, p.136–8).

BE PATIENT AND PREPARE THE SOIL

Although you're probably feeling impatient to get on and plant, don't rush. If the weather looks iffy it's better to hang on for a few days. A late frost now can knock out all your bedding. Use your 'waiting time' to give the ground its final preparations, so that when it's finally safe to plant you can get straight on with the job.

- Clear your spring bedding or the last of the winter vegetables, winkle out any weeds, sprinkle general-purpose fertilizer over the soil and fork it in, removing any debris. Rake the ground over well leaving a fine tilth.

- If slugs and snails have been a problem in the past – they are particularly fond of the tender shoots of newly planted bedding and vegetables – start taking precautions a week before your start planting, to reduce their numbers *before* your plants go in. A reliable method, where slugs are the main problem, is biological control (see box below).

- From the middle of the month onwards, set aside a sensible time for planting so you don't rush it – it's worth doing properly.

WATCH OUT FOR PESTS

Watch out for pests, which can be troublesome this month, but try to avoid resorting to spraying – even organic remedies can upset the natural balance. For small outbreaks let nature take its course – it usually does so quite effectively.

Snails are a big problem in May. Pick them off plants as soon as you see them.

CONTROLLING GARDEN PESTS THE BIOLOGICAL WAY

The idea behind biological control is to use a beneficial insect to hunt down and destroy a species that's harmful to plants – a bit like employing a mini-gamekeeper to tackle micro-poachers. Biological control has become a very popular 'green' alternative to chemical pest control, but to be sure of good results it needs using properly. Being living organisms, biological controls can't be stored; they have to be bought by post and used shortly after delivery, although they will 'keep' in the fridge for up to 2 weeks. They are also quite expensive, as there is no single cure-all – you need a different 'gamekeeper' for each species of 'poacher'. On the plus side, they are entirely safe, harmless to children, pets and wildlife, and when used correctly they work very well, even against pests that have built up resistance to chemicals.

Several different biological control remedies are available for use under glass (see Under Cover, p.140), but two of the most effective for using outside in the garden are against slugs and vine weevil larvae. The 'gamekeepers' concerned are two different strains of beneficial nematodes, one that tackles slugs and another that takes on vine weevil larvae. They arrive as freeze-dried 'powder' that is diluted and watered on to the soil. Although the packs are a bit pricey, it's important to resist the temptation to economize by over-diluting them or watering them too thinly around to make the pack go further. To work successfully, the contents must be applied at the right strength, so buy as many as you need for the area to be treated.

Anti-slug treatment

The slug version can be used any time during the summer once the soil has warmed up, but strategically it's best applied in May to protect newly planted frost-tender vegetables and bedding, which are some of the most susceptible plants. It continues to work for several months, so it's good value

for money. Use a watering can with a fine rose and apply the 'nematode soup' evenly to the area. The little chaps are too small to see, but they seek out and destroy slugs by passing on a bacterial infection, which is what actually kills the pests. You'd think such an effective slug remedy would also work on snails, but because snails climb up into plants they manage to evade the nematodes, which only live in the soil.

Anti-vine weevil

The anti-vine-weevil nematodes must be applied when there are actually vine weevil larvae present in the soil, as without a source of food the nematodes just die. But if they find larvae, they breed and produce more nematodes, which keep up the good work. May is the key month to use this treatment outdoors. Expensive, yes, but if you've previously lost a lot of valuable plants to vine weevil, you'll probably agree that the expense is well justified.

LAWNS

Right: Lawns benefit from a good feed in April or May.

A daisy grubber is ideal for lifting weeds from a lawn, as it won't damage the turf. Remove as much of the root system as possible.

FEED ESTABLISHED LAWNS

Although April is usually lawn-feeding time (see p.88), in 'late' gardens – those in cold areas or with heavy or boggy ground – growing conditions may only become suitable for feeding the lawn early in May. Don't leave it any later – hot, dry conditions and lawn feed don't mix.

REMOVE WEEDS

Treat weeds in the lawn with weedkiller if you must (see April, p.88), although frankly it's just as easy to dig out occasional weeds by hand. Also, upright-growing species will be chopped off by the mower now you've started cutting regularly.

FINISH SOWING LAWNS

The beginning of the month is your last chance to sow a new lawn (see September, p.227–8).

MOWING THE LAWN

- If you have an established lawn, it will need mowing weekly by now.

- With newly laid turf, wait until it has rooted firmly into the underlying soil. Once rooted, you can use your mower as usual. If the grass has grown a bit tall, then raise the blades up to their highest setting to start with and reduce the height gradually over the space of a week or two.

- New grass that's grown from seed is a bit touchier. Wait until it has come up fairly evenly all over the area and the longest tufts are about 5cm (2in) tall, then use a pair of shears or a rotary line trimmer just to whisk the very tops off. This 'teaches' the grass to thicken out. Since new grass hasn't made strong roots yet, you have to avoid yanking great tufts out, which is what might happen if you used the mower. For the first real cut, make sure the blades are set quite high, at around 5cm (2in).

BEWARE OF ANTS' NESTS

Ants' nests often turn up in lawns sometime this month. They start as small patches of fine, dryish 'crumbs' of soil among the grass, and build up into crumbling hillocks that resemble tiny termite mounds. Sometimes the first indication you have of them is a woodpecker probing about in the grass for a snack, but that's about the only advantage of having a resident ants' nest. Black ants will swarm all over your feet, but red ants can bite ferociously, which ruins your afternoon sitting out in the garden, especially if you have any sweet, sticky food or drink with you – ants enjoy a picnic as much as anyone.

In rough grass you can afford to live and let live – ant colonies disperse naturally in August when they take wing and fly away. But if you like a smart lawn, ants' nests make a mess of it, so rather than putting down ant potions, deal with them as follows:

- As soon as the ants start excavating, flood the area with water. Keep doing so on a regular basis and they'll soon take the hint – it's no good waiting until their tunnels run down deep. Don't fall for the old tale about pouring boiling water down an ants' nest – it'll kill the ants, but it also kills the grass. No, stick to cold water and lots of it.

- Where an ants' nest is under patio paving or in a path, plant pennyroyal (*Mentha pulegium*) all around the area to ward them off. It acts like garlic to vampires.

TREES, SHRUBS AND CLIMBERS

CLIP THE HEDGES

May is the start of the serious hedge-clipping season. The amount of cutting you do during the year depends very much on the type of hedge you have (see box below).

Most people will clip a hedge by eye; if you stand back every now and then it's quite easy to keep a fairly good line, especially if you don't wait until the hedge is badly overgrown before giving it a haircut. The time to strike is while the hedge is still just fuzzy around the edges. Frankly, in a natural or wild style of garden, a few minor jinks and billows only make a hedge look better, so don't worry about it.

You should aim to make the sides of the hedge slope in very slightly so the base of the hedge is a tad wider than the top – that way you avoid creating shade that kills out a lot of the bottom of some older hedges. It always makes them look like bony-ankled spinsters holding their skirts up. Decide either to have a perfectly flat top, a gently rounded top or a pointed top – but whichever you choose be quite definite about it – don't have a half hearted, can't-make-up-my-mind look.

THE RIGHT KIT FOR THE JOB

There's a lot you can do to make hedge-clipping quicker and easier:

- If you have miles of hedge to clip, for goodness sake buy yourself a decent set of power hedge-clippers with a long blade. An electric model is fine if the cable reaches the full length of the hedge, otherwise you need the petrol version, which is quite a bit heavier and more tiring to use.
- Rechargeable battery clippers only last about half an hour before they need putting back on charge, which is fine for a small hedge, or for someone who likes to tackle the job in small stages. They are easy to use as there's no cable to lug about, and they're very lightweight.
- If you have tall hedges, a hedge-clipping platform will make a huge difference. It's a big improvement over the old pair of stepladders with a plank balanced over them, and far more stable. If you're standing on the ground it's really only practical to clip a hedge up to 1.5m (5ft) high.

WHICH HEDGE TO CLIP WHEN?

- Traditional hedges of thuja, box (above), beech and hornbeam want tackling early this month. If you give them a second trim in late August/early September, that'll be all they need for the year. Treat Leyland cypress in the same way; if you keep it regularly trimmed to a manageable height, it'll never be the menace it can be.

- If you have one of the fast-growing hedges, such as privet or the evergreen honeysuckle *Lonicera nitida* (above), there's nothing for it but to settle down to regular 6-weekly sessions from now for the rest of the summer, with the last cut no later than the middle of September.

- With box and yew (above) you can get away with a single clipping in late August/early September, although neat and tidy gardeners may prefer to give box an early trim in May/June, too, to keep the edges sharp all summer.

Dust sheets

A perfectionist will lay dust sheets at the foot of the hedge to make the mess easier to pick up, although it's not always possible, especially when there are beds of plants or other obstructions in the way.

HOW TO CLIP A HEDGE

1 If the hedge is any taller than shoulder height, you'll need a sturdy stepladder or, better still, a proper hedge-clipping platform to stand on. Have a helper at the bottom to hold steps steady, and take care of trailing cable if you're using electric hedge-clippers.

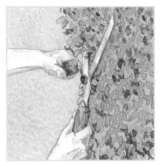

2 Start clipping at one end of the hedge, beginning at the bottom and working your way up; work on one section, about 1m (3ft) wide, at a time.

3 Repeat step 2 for the remaining sections of the hedge, until you have clipped all along the sides of the hedge. Leave the top until you have finished both sides of the hedge, as this makes it easier to get it completely level.

4 Trim the top by eye, or if you need a guide, bang a post in each end of the hedge and string a taut line between the two. Clear up the clippings.

EARLY SUMMER PRUNING

Now that forsythia and flowering currant (*Ribes sanguineum*) have finished flowering, they'll benefit from pruning. Young plants can be left untouched, but a few years down the line they really need a tidy up. The pruning technique for both plants is very similar to the one used for winter jasmine last month, but since forsythia and ribes are shorter and shrubbier it's a lot easier to see what needs doing. Basically, it's a glorified deadheading.

Now is the time to prune your flowering currant.

- Start with a shoot that has dead or dying flowers at the tip, follow it back until you find a young sideshoot that hasn't flowered, and then cut the main stem off just above it. Keep going until you've done the whole shrub.

- If it's an elderly plant, you can go a bit further to rejuvenate it. Take out one or two of the thickest and barest stems as close to the ground as you can, to encourage some strong young stems. This time next year, if there are more new shoots than you want, and if the centre of the shrub seems congested, thin them out to leave about four or five shoots that are well placed to improve the shape of the plant. After 3–4 years of this you'll have replaced all the old stems,

and instead of your original badly neglected old shrub you'll have a brand new one – for free.

TIE IN CLIMBERS AND WALL SHRUBS

Look out for climbers and wall shrubs that are making a lot of new growth. This needs dealing with before the weight pulls the whole plant down. Tie in the shoots that you want to keep to extend the framework, and cut back or prune out entirely any that are growing away from the wall, leaving only those that are well placed to thicken up the shape and produce flowers later.

DEAL WITH VARIEGATED SHRUBS

Pinch out any green shoots that appear on variegated trees and shrubs.

WATER AND PROTECT PLANTS

Water newly planted trees and shrubs regularly in dry spells, and protect new shoots or newly planted bedding with horticultural fleece in case of late frosts (see February, p.40).

BRING POTS OUTSIDE

In milder regions, tender conservatory shrubs in pots can be moved outside for summer.

FLOWERS

SUPPORT PERENNIALS

By now, a lot of summer perennials will be starting to grow well. Tall or floppy kinds will need supporting, but it takes a certain cunning to avoid ending up with a border full of sticks and bits of wire.

Generally, when you do the job properly, the supports don't show – all you see is natural-looking flowers. The trick is to put the supports in place slightly *before* they're needed, only to support the main weight-bearing stems, and to keep supports short enough that the mechanics are quickly hidden by leaves as the plants grow. As a rule of thumb, use supports that are one-third to a half the eventual height of the plant. (See also box below.)

If you don't mind seeing some of the superstructure, go for a taller, more artistic form of support, such as a wrought-iron obelisk or rustic poles, which will become a feature of your border.

DIVIDE CLUMPS OF POLYANTHUS AND PRIMROSES

Dig up and divide clumps of polyanthus or coloured primroses when they've finished flowering. The original plants have quite a short life, and division rejuvenates them. If you've used the plants as spring bedding and need the bed or container for summer flowers, plant the best of the divisions in a nursery bed (tucked away down the garden or at the end of your veg patch perhaps) and replant them in their flowering positions in the autumn when you take summer bedding out again.

Divide primroses and polyanthus after flowering.

PLANT SUPPORTS

You'll need to tailor the support you use to the type of flower, as some take more holding up than others. You also need to consider the style of the garden – flowers in formal gardens are well regimented, whereas in cottage gardens it's fashionable for them to be floppier.

Pea sticks or twigs
These are for bushy perennials that reach medium height and only need light support. Push half a dozen twiggy pea sticks in around the plants to prop up new growth. Or use your old tree prunings saved from last winter. Use secateurs to snip off twigs that stand up more than about two-thirds the eventual height of the plants if you don't want them to show.

Wire grids and interlinking metal supports
These are high-tech solutions, at a price. The wire-grid type look like metal stools with a grid where the seat should be; these you sit over an emerging clump of perennials, push the legs into the ground so the 'seat' is about one-third or at most a half the ultimate height of the plant. The idea is for the perennial stems to grow up through the grid, but you need to check several times while the stems grow up, as some need threading through if they want to escape round the edge.

The interlinking types are like T-shaped metal 'sticks' that you push in around a plant and then link the hooked bits together so they form a complete supporting circle. Again, they should be one-third to a half the ultimate height of the plant, but with this type you can put them in place after a plant is fairly well grown, so timing isn't as crucial.

In my own garden I cut sturdy wide-mesh 'stock fencing' into 1m (3ft) lengths and arch it over clumps of plants, pushing the edges into the earth. These make cheap and effective alternatives to proprietary supports.

Wide-mesh netting
If you want to support a whole border of herbaceous perennials on the cheap, hammer 2.5 × 2.5cm (1 × 1in) dahlia stakes in at 10cm (4in) intervals along the front and back of the border, and stretch wide-mesh plastic runner bean netting horizontally between them, about 45cm (18in) above ground level. The plants will grow through the mesh and eventually hide the support system.

Canes and stakes
These provide the strongest support for individual stems of tall plants with top-heavy flowers, such as dahlias and delphiniums. Knock one in alongside each main stem and tie in several places using soft, natural-fibre string in a loose figure of eight, to avoid cutting into the stem.

The green metal 'canes' coated in plastic are the least visible and also last much longer than wooden stakes or natural bamboo canes, which are only good for a few years unless treated (see January, p.15).

May is one of the most glorious months in the garden, with tulips pushing up among perennials to provide early colour.

Pot-grown dahlias can be planted out from mid-May onwards, if the danger of frost has passed.

PLANT OUT DAHLIAS AND TENDER EXOTICS

Plant out pot-grown dahlias and tender exotics after you're certain there's no longer a risk of frost – which usually means mid-May onwards for the south of the country. Prepare the ground in the same way as for bedding plants (see General Garden Tasks, p.125), and water plants in well afterwards. Don't plant rooted dahlia cuttings or dry begonia corms out until late May or early June.

SOW SEED OF PERENNIALS

Sow seed of perennials outside in a seedbed in your 'nursery' area at the end of the garden (see March, pp.62–4) or in the veg patch. Alternatively, use pots or trays and stand them in a sand bed, which helps to keep them watered during the summer.

CUT BACK PLANTS

Cut back alyssum, arabis and aubrieta when the flowers are over; trim the plants with snips or kitchen scissors to tidy them up.

BULB AFTERCARE

Continue deadheading and feeding spring-flowering bulbs (see April, p.93).

CLEAR AWAY PLANTS

Clear spring-flowering bedding plants and prepare the ground for replanting (see General Garden Tasks, p.125).

PLANT AND TRAIN SWEET PEAS

For general use as flowering climbers, plant sweet peas 15cm (6in) apart at the foot of trellis or netting. After tying in the first shoots the plants will hold themselves up by their tendrils.

If you want top-quality flowers for cutting, plant each one at the base of a 2m (6ft) cane, spacing them 20–30cm (8–12in) apart. Remove the tendrils (which can 'catch' the flower stems and make them kink) and tie the plant up to the canes every 15cm (6in) with soft string. Liquid feed and water regularly, and remove dead heads.

PATIO AND CONTAINERS

MOVE PLANTS OUTSIDE
Once the last frost is past, you can move nearly-hardy trees and shrubs out from the conservatory. It's a good way to stop pests building up without using chemicals, since they don't breed so fast outside, and it means less watering, as plants won't be so hot outdoors. Pots of olives, citrus, bottlebrush, bougainvillea and oleander give the patio a very South of France feel, and they team well with colourful bedding plants.

PLANT TUBS, TROUGHS AND WINDOWBOXES
If there's one thing that brings your patio to life overnight, it's filling your containers with colourful summer bedding plants. But don't be in too much of a hurry. Wait until the middle of the month, at the earliest, before planting outdoor containers up with frost-tender bedding and half-hardy perennials, as they're killed by cold. In colder regions, leave it until the end of the month, or even early June to be on the safe side. Once the weather is set fair, you'll see immediate results. Oh, I know we always used to be told never to plant things when they were in flower, but today's bedding is specially bred for the 'instant results' business.

- Whatever you do the rest of the year, make a clean start for the summer season. Empty the containers completely, and use the old compost on the garden. Ideally, wash tubs inside and out – well, you wouldn't make a cup of tea in yesterday's dirty cup.

- Use new potting compost, because unlike spring bedding, which only stays put for a few weeks, summer bedding is going to be growing for a good 5 months. Penny-pinching doesn't do you any good if your plants keel over halfway through the season from root disease or nutrient deficiency, all for want of the price of a bag of decent potting compost.

It also pays to be generous with plants, since containers are the summer showpieces of the garden.

- Plant up your container (see March, p.66). Plant them 'pot-thick', which means with their rootballs almost touching each other. I know it looks a lot, but then the container fills out fast and gives you a really cracking display right from the word go.

PLANT UP HANGING BASKETS
Planting hanging baskets can be a bit more complicated than other containers, depending on what type of basket you've bought. Again, for a traffic-stopping effect it pays to pack as many plants into the space as you can.

Bowl-shaped baskets
Big, bowl-shaped baskets with solid sides are like pots that just happen to hang up, except that you don't need to put any drainage material in the bottom – summer hanging baskets usually dry out too fast at the best of times. Fill the 'bowl' to within 5cm (2in) or so from the top with potting compost. Plant this type of basket mostly with trailing and bushy plants, with something taller in the centre, and perhaps a few annual climbers, such as morning glory, to scramble up the chains and over the brackets.

> **Planting rule**
> Always make sure that there's a gap of about 2.5cm (1in) between the rim of the container and the top of the compost to allow room for watering. If you over-fill containers with compost they'll simply overflow every time you water them and the only thing that will be soaked is you – the plants will always be drying out.

SUITING THE PLANT TO THE POT
- Upright, bushy plants tend to be the best type for tubs and troughs.
- For windowboxes, short, squat or trailing plants are best as they don't block your view and cut the light out of your rooms.
- Some people prefer a formal-style container filled with all the same kind of flowers; if you're going down that route I'd always stick to tried-and-tested 'stayers', such as pelargoniums or fuchsias, which you can rely on to last the summer if you look after them properly.
- If your tastes lean towards a jazzier mixture of flowers, choose varied shapes and sizes as well as colours, maybe a tastefully co-ordinated scheme of pastels – pinks, blues and mauves are the traditional favourites, with touches of silvery foliage – or a 'hot' orange, red and purple scheme for a more upbeat look.

HOW TO PLANT UP A WIRE HANGING BASKET

1 If your basket has a round bottom, sit it firmly in the top of a suitably sized pot or bucket to stop it rolling around while you work. Line the basket with a suitable material (see box below). If using a prefabricated or woollen liner, cut holes where you want to plant through the sides.

2 Cover the base of the basket with a layer of compost approximately 2.5cm (1in) deep. Plant a row of plants through the walls, pushing them through gaps in the moss or moss substitute, or through the holes cut earlier if using a liner. Do it from the outside, so the plant goes in roots-first so you don't bruise the leafy top.

3 Once you've made a ring of plants around the base of the container, pile another 5cm (2in) of compost inside. Repeat the process with a second layer of plants higher up the basket wall – think of it as a floral club sandwich. You'll probably have room for three layers of plants until you reach the top of the container.

4 Top the basket up with compost and plant your final few plants into the top as usual. In a short time the basket turns into a complete globe of flowers that would cost a fortune in the shops. Spectacular!

Traditional hanging baskets

Traditional wire-framed hanging baskets are a lot more trouble to plant up, and they need a generous amount of watering, as they have open mesh sides, which means they leak from every pore. However, they are worth the trouble as they look quite sensational. Use small plants for planting in the base of the basket – plugs are ideal as they come with a solid wedge of roots that pushes in through the moss or liner easily.

Patio dahlias

Look out for compact varieties of dahlias, so-called patio dahlias, which are very short and stocky. They are ideal for planting in pots or tubs as they have a long flowering season starting from late June onwards, and they aren't top heavy so there's little risk of pots toppling over.

Right: To liven up the patio, plant up containers with colourful bedding.

HANGING BASKET LINERS

Traditionalists use moss as a lining, but real moss is less popular nowadays for environmental reasons, so what I usually use is a woollen liner. You could cut up an old jumper that's too far gone even for gardening, or knit one to shape specially – I have several that have been sent in by kind viewers, and very good they are too. Otherwise, there are various synthetic-fibre nest shapes and loose moss substitutes sold specially for lining hanging baskets. As a general rule, choose a water-retentive liner for summer use (various sized liners made of thick, fibrous materials are available in garden centres) and a faster-draining one, such as the green fibrous moss-substitute, for winter baskets, where you want surplus water to run away faster.

GROWING PATIO VEGETABLES

Plenty of people who aren't particularly 'serious' about vegetable gardening will often grow a few runner beans, outdoor tomatoes or courgettes for summer meals. The plants are so productive you can grow worthwhile crops in nothing more than a few tubs on the patio, and they are so good looking that if you didn't know better you'd think they were chunky bedding plants. In fact, both runner beans and tomatoes were first grown as ornamentals, not as vegetables, when they were introduced to this country. Tomatoes were decidedly risqué, coming to the UK from South America via the flesh-pots of the Continent under the name of 'love apples'.

A wigwam of runner beans can be an attractive feature on a patio.

- In one growing bag, you'll fit 12 runner bean plants, or two bush courgettes, or three outdoor tomatoes. After planting, water them in well, and after 4 weeks start feeding with liquid tomato feed every 2 weeks. Once the plants fill the bag fairly well, you'll need to increase watering and up the feeding to once a week.
- Support tomato and bean plants with growing bag frames, or tie them up to nearby trellis – don't poke canes in, as they go through the bottom of the bag and make it leak.
- If you prefer growing in tubs, use 30–38cm (12–15in) pots filled with a 50/50 mixture of John Innes No 2 and peat-free potting compost. Plant one tomato or courgette, or five runner beans. Feed and water as before, but this time you can use canes, rustic sticks or decorative obelisks for support.

CONTAINER CARE

There's a lot to be said in favour of container gardening – there's no heavy work or weeding, and you don't have to bend down to do your deadheading. But because containers need to look 'special', it's essential to pay more attention than ever to detail. Naturally, you'll need to check newly planted containers regularly, but they won't need a lot of watering for a good few weeks yet. How often depends on the weather, so you'll have to play it by ear – or test the compost with your finger. The potting compost will contain enough feed for the first month.

LOOK OUT FOR PESTS

You will need to keep an eye out for pests in containers this month, particularly slugs and snails, vine weevil and ants.

Slugs and snails

Slugs and snails are easier to nobble in containers than in most other parts of the garden, since they have to glide up the vertical sides of tubs to reach the 'restaurant'. It makes containers a good way to cultivate notorious mollusc-bait, such as hostas and salads, which

are normally nibbled to shreds when they're grown in the ground. Aerial containers, such as hanging baskets and windowboxes, are relatively safe from slugs, as long as there aren't any lurking on your plants when you put them in, but snails will often climb walls if it means a free meal.

- If slugs or snails become a problem there's no need to fall back on slug pellets. They're easily put off by a 'barrier' of crop protection glue or jelly smeared around the top of the container. I've also had some success with copper collars placed around my hostas. They are sold as 'slug rings'. (For information on biological anti-slug treatments for the garden, see General Garden Tasks, p.125.)

Vine weevil

Another notorious pest is the vine weevil, which uses containers as a creche. The adult looks like a small, dark brown beetle with a conspicuous Y-shaped nose, and this is the beast responsible for nibbling notches around the edges of the leaves of plants, particularly evergreens, such as rhododendrons. The adult is not so much of a problem in containers,

The vine weevil (top) and its larvae (above) are major pests, destroying the leaves and roots of plants.

but if you see the adult beetles or their characteristic bite marks anywhere in the garden you can certainly expect to find their larvae, which look like fat, white, C-shaped grubs, in your containers.

May is the main problem season. You might not know you have a problem until it's too late. Vine weevil junior eats away at plant roots right down in the compost, where it's safely out of sight, and the first hint of trouble is when affected plants suddenly wilt and collapse. When you go to see what's wrong, the plant comes away in your hand because it's lost all of its roots. By then it's too late, and there's nothing you can do. The trick is to anticipate an attack, and act early this month.

- To keep vine weevil at bay, either use a special potting compost containing an anti-vine-weevil ingredient when you plant your containers, or dose your normal compost after planting with one of the new pesticides developed for fighting vine weevil. If you don't like the idea of using chemicals, go for biological control (see General Garden Tasks, p.125). If you had trouble with vine weevil last year, you can be almost certain it'll be back but worse this year, so be prepared.

Ants

One thing to watch out for in tubs and troughs that are standing on the ground is ants. Ants can be quite serious when they nest in containers. They don't attack the plants directly; instead, when nesting, they excavate the compost from inside the pots, which leaves plants literally dangling in thin air so that the roots can't take up any water, and the plant dies of thirst.

- If you see hordes of ants wandering in and out of a container, tip out the contents, remove the nest chamber, and repot the plants into more compost before it's too late. Stand the freshly planted pot in a plant-pot saucer with a ring of crop protection glue or pennyroyal smeared around the base to deter squatters.

VEGETABLES AND HERBS

ROUTINE JOBS

Down in the vegetable patch, it's a question of keeping your head above water. Planting and sowing is at its seasonal peak, and the more space you fill, the more watering, weeding, hoeing and thinning out there is to be done. This isn't the time of year to let things lapse as it takes forever to catch up, when everything is growing fit to bust.

Watering needs doing almost daily whenever the weather is dry, as most vegetables are very shallow-rooted and a lot will have problems if they dry out; newly germinated seeds and young seedlings are particularly at risk from drought. Aim to keep plants growing steadily from start to finish; vegetables that have suffered a check may become woody, as is the case with radishes, or else they 'bolt' like lettuce in their rush to set seed before they die of thirst. Finally, watch out for slugs and snails and deal with them as soon as possible (see box, p.125, and p.137).

SOW VEGETABLE SEED

Make regular sowings of things you need little and often, such as lettuce (see March, p.68). Most people go mad and sow a long row, then find themselves giving away dozens of lettuces they can't use before they think about making the next sowing, so they end up with a sort of feast-famine cycle. If you sow a short row each time you thin out the last one, you'll never be without a lettuce to cut all summer. Once the weather heats up from June onwards, it's a waste of time transplanting lettuce as they mostly shrivel up or bolt, so make a habit of sowing all your lettuces where you want them to grow. Sow them very thinly – if it helps, imagine each one as a small plant when you sow them – then thin out. You can't go wrong.

May is also the time to sow a lot of mainstream veg that only go in once and then take the rest of the season to reach maturity, for example swede, maincrop beetroots and carrots, autumn cabbage, and autumn and winter cauliflowers. But also put in some Swiss chard, calabrese and peas. There's still time to sow turnips, spring onions and a last batch of broad beans.

DIRECT-SOW FROST-TENDER VEGETABLES

Late this month or in June, anyone who doesn't have a greenhouse in which to raise their own frost-tender vegetables can sow them straight outside into the ground.

- You need a sunny spot with well-prepared, fertile, free-draining soil. Sow the seed where you want the plants to grow, so they don't need transplanting, which would check their growth and mean you wouldn't be picking the crops until much later.

- With large seeds, it's a help to soak them in tepid water for a couple of hours first, especially if the weather is hot, since dry soil makes it difficult for big seeds to absorb enough fluid to trigger germination. But water well after sowing in any case, and keep the area watered so they don't run dry at the crucial moment.

- When the seedlings are large enough to handle, thin them out, removing the weak seedlings and leaving the strong plants at the recommended spacings.

Sweetcorn

Sweetcorn is only worth growing if you're prepared to plant lots, as it's wind-pollinated and a couple of plants standing forlornly on their own stand no chance of producing any cobs. You need to grow at least a couple of dozen plants. To have plants spaced 45cm (18in) apart in each direction, plant two or three seeds at each 'station', pressing them down about 5mm (¼in) deep. If more than one seed grows, pull out the weakest seedlings, leaving only the best to grow.

Beans

Climbing beans produce far more edible crops than the short dwarf varieties, but in a windy area, or where you don't have room to put up a framework of poles for them, dwarf beans are the only real option. They like rich, well-manured soil that holds moisture well.

Sow French and runner beans in drills (see March, p.68). Thin seedlings of dwarf French

Remove weak sweetcorn seedlings, leaving a strong plant every 45cm (18in).

Traditionally, vegetables are grown in rows. The spaces between allow easy access for weeding and watering, and plants are easily covered by a cloche.

bean seeds to 8cm (3in) apart, and climbing French beans and runner beans to 10–12cm (4–5in) apart. Make a framework of canes or push beanpoles in as support for the climbing kinds later. Water plants in until they're well established, and if beans don't seem to be 'setting' later, it's often because the plants are too dry, so keep watering whenever the weather doesn't do it for you.

Squashes, pumpkins and courgettes

Pumpkins and squashes are big, trailing plants that need lots of room and really rich soil that holds plenty of moisture in summer. A lot of people plant them on top of the compost heap so they can feed off the rich, moist contents and scramble down over the sides, where they don't take up so much room. Alternatively, dig a pit 30cm (12in) square and as deep, and fill it with pure, well-rotted manure or garden compost, then cover it with good garden topsoil, mounding it up 15cm (6in) high in the

centre. Sow two or three seeds 1cm ($\frac{1}{2}$in) deep in the top of this. Again, if more than one seed grows, pull out the weakest leaving one seedling. Make a 'moat' around the base of the mound to use for watering. If you're growing several, space your pits-and-mounds 2m (6ft) or more apart for trailing varieties of courgettes, squashes and pumpkins, and 1m (3ft) apart for non-trailing courgettes. Feed and water generously all summer, and by the end of the season the ground will be covered in foliage dotted with big, colourful living 'lanterns'.

SOW CHICORY FOR FORCING IN WINTER

Sow witloof chicory (the sort grown specially for forcing) in rows and thin the seedlings out to about 30cm (12in) apart, then let them do their own thing over the summer. All the action takes place in autumn and winter (see October, p.257).

PLANT OUT GREENHOUSE-RAISED VEGETABLES

You can grow some frost-tender vegetables on the patio (see Patios and Containers, p.131) but if you have a vegetable patch you can go to town and fill all the remaining space with sweetcorn, pumpkins, summer and winter squashes, climbing or dwarf French beans and outdoor cucumbers, as well as tomatoes and courgettes. As ever, *don't* race to put them out before you are absolutely sure of the weather, and *do* harden them off carefully first (see April, p.108).

All the frost-tender vegetables need really rich, fertile soil that's had masses of organic matter worked in over the winter. Just before you're ready to plant, hoe off any newly emerged weeds and rake in a generous dressing of general-purpose organic fertilizer.

Sweetcorn, beans, courgettes, squashes and pumpkins

Below are the planting distances for sweetcorn, beans, courgettes, squashes and pumpkins:

- Sweetcorn – 45cm (18in) apart.

- Dwarf French beans – 8cm (3in) apart; climbing French beans and runner beans 10–12cm (4–5in) apart.

KEEPING LEFT-OVER SEED

By this time in the season, you'll have sown a lot of vegetables for which you only want one row of plants, and if you have only used part of a packet of seeds you may be wondering how to keep what's left in good condition so you can finish it next year. There are some seeds it's just not worth trying to keep, such as parsnips, which never come up next year. But others are worth hanging on to.

- Fold the top of the packet over firmly and re-seal it as well as you can using sticky tape. Place the packet in a screw-top jar and keep it in a cool, dark place at an even temperature as close to 4°C (40°F) as you can manage.
- You might think the fridge is the answer, since that's the temperature you find in the salad drawer, and in commercial seed-banks they do in fact store seed for many years in a giant chiller. But the trouble with domestic fridges is, even if you can spare the space, you're regularly defrosting it so the temperature does not stay stable. And that makes a difference. A cool spare room where the temperature stays fairly even is much better.
- Keep unopened packets of seed in the same conditions as opened packets – don't do as so many people do and leave them lying around in the greenhouse. They'll be fit for nothing by the time you get around to putting them in.

CONTROLLING SLUGS AND SNAILS ORGANICALLY

Slugs and snails have a taste for tender edible crops, and besides reducing the plants to lace doilies, mollusc-ridden vegetables are not very appetizing. Even if you're prepared to turn a blind eye to slugs and snails in the rest of the garden, the veg patch or salad bed is the one place you need to do something to keep them under control. These days, there is a wide range of organic barriers, traps and deterrents available at garden centres and from specialist organic supply catalogues. Nothing is 100 per cent effective, but none will harm other forms of wildlife.

- **Yucca extract** – Sold as a spray, which you apply to the ground as a barrier that molluscs won't cross. Use it around individual plants, the base of containers and growing bags, or around the edge of entire beds of vegetables.
- **Mineral barriers** – Various makes are available, using granules that slugs and snails hate to cross. They work by absorbing the slime exuded by molluscs, which literally sticks them to the spot and the sun dries them out.
- **Physical barriers** – Spread a 2.5cm- (1in-) wide barrier of really sharp grit around at-risk plants or the edge of vegetable beds to deter slugs and snails.
- **Traps** – There are various manufactured traps that you fill with milk or beer (in taste tests, it's been found that slugs actually prefer lager that's been left to go flat). Alternatively, make your own traps from old saucers filled with the slugs' favourite tipple. Don't sink jam jars of beer into the ground, as they also trap and drown beneficial creatures such as black ground beetles.
- **Copper tape** – Acts like a tiny electric fence fixed around the edge of vegetable beds. Copper rings (right) have the same effect. Molluscs won't cross because the copper houses a natural tiny electrical charge they evidently don't care for. Available from specialist organic gardening catalogues.
- **Biological slug control** – Beneficial nematodes are one of the most effective ways of saving plants from slugs (see General Garden Tasks, p.125), including species that live in the soil such as the keeled slugs that bore into potatoes. Nematodes have little effect on snails.
- **Natural predators** – Hedgehogs, blackbirds, frogs and toads all feed on slugs, and thrushes crack open snail shells on 'anvil' stones in prominent points around their territories. Even foxes will take snails if they're hungry enough – a big snail contains a fair bit of meat.

- Pumpkins, squashes and trailing varieties of courgettes – 2m (6ft) apart; non-trailing varieties 1m (3ft) apart.

Tomatoes

Plant tomatoes in the warmest, sunniest spot, spacing them 45cm (18in) apart. Give each of them a 1.25m (4ft) cane and sink a plastic flowerpot into the soil at the base of each plant to make watering easier.

Outdoor cucumbers

Plant outdoor varieties of cucumber 1m (3ft) apart at the end of the month in rich soil, setting each plant on top of a low mound of soil so that the 'neck' isn't left sitting in a puddle of water, which can easily make it rot. Train the main stem of the plant up a cane or trellis. Water sparingly at first, but once the plant starts to put on a spurt of growth increase the watering and begin 'little and often' liquid feeding – use any good liquid tomato feed diluted down to quarter strength, and give each plant 600ml (1 pint) or so once a week at first, increasing to

Outdoor cucumbers need to be planted on top of a mound of soil with a cane or trellis to grow up.

Transplant leeks to their final growing positions.

To harvest asparagus, cut just beneath the surface of the soil with a sharp knife when the spears are about 15cm (6in) or so high.

twice weekly once the first cucumbers appear. In theory, you need to pick the male flowers off cucumber varieties that are not all-female (male flowers lack the tiny baby cucumber attached behind the yellow petals), although outside you can normally get away without doing this.

TRANSPLANT LEEKS AND BRASSICAS
Leek and brassica plants will be ready for transplanting now. Water them well the day beforehand, then ease them out of the ground with a hand fork, and they are all ready to move. Have the new space prepared ready for them. Drop leek plants into holes made with a dibber, 10cm (4in) deep, and 'puddle' them in with a watering can. Space them 10cm (4in) apart in rows 30cm (12in) apart. Plant brassicas at the appropriate spacing (see April, p.99) and firm them well.

EARTH UP POTATOES
Continue earthing up potatoes (see April, p.100).

PROTECT CARROTS FROM CARROT FLY
Cover your carrots with very fine-mesh insect-proof netting if you didn't sow a carrot-fly-resistant variety (see April, p.103).

HARVEST VEGETABLES
Harvest asparagus, except in the first year (see April, p.102), lettuce, radishes and rocket.

FRUIT

ROUTINE CHORES
Most of the work in the fruit garden this month is leading up to a good crop of fruit. If the weather turns dry, get into the habit of watering any soft fruit bushes with swelling fruit, as a sudden drought can seriously reduce the size of your crop, and at worst make the lot fall off. But the competition is hot – there are other fruit-lovers waiting around every corner to get their teeth into your harvest.

GROWING STRAWBERRIES
Strawberry plants want treating with kid gloves as they approach ripening time.

Prevent rot and grey mould
- Once the green fruits are starting to swell, try to avoid watering strawberry beds; the fruit tends to rot or develop grey mould if it is in contact with damp ground, and also attracts slugs.

- It's also a good idea to slide a strawberry mat around the 'collar' of each plant, or tuck handfuls of straw around them, to cushion them from harm. Lift the trusses of flowers or green fruit carefully, slide the mat or straw under, and then lower the flowers gently back down.

- If you grow your strawberries in containers, you can't afford to stop watering, so just be as careful as you can and make sure the water goes on the compost and not on the fruit. At least in containers there's usually good air circulation around the fruit, which means less risk of grey mould.

Protect strawberries from birds
To save your crop from birds, the trick is to get some netting over the plants *well before* the first fruits ripen. But it's no good just laying the netting straight on top of the plants – birds aren't daft. They soon learn they only need to perch on top and poke their beaks through the mesh. Make yourself a temporary

Slide a mat around the collar of each strawberry plant to protect it from rot and grey mould.

'cage' out of bamboo canes and drape your netting over that, leaving a flap you can peel back to pick the fruit. Birds are good at breaking and entering if you don't close it down again properly afterwards.

• For strawberries grown in containers, push some split canes in around the edge of tubs or hanging baskets and drape your netting over that. If netting will spoil your decorative effect, just take a risk if the containers are close to the house, and hope birds won't spot them until you've had your share of the ripe fruit.

FRUIT TREES
Fruit trees can safely be left to do their own thing this month; it's only newly planted ones that need watering.

Codling moths are a common pest of apples and plums, but not ones that you're likely to see until you sink your teeth into maggoty fruit later on in the summer. You know what they say: there's only one thing worse than biting into an apple and finding a maggot in it, and that's biting into an apple and finding half a maggot in it. Until quite recently, the only way to avoid the problem was to spray the trees several times during the growing season, but now there's a very sneaky organic remedy that just involves hanging traps up in the trees (see box, below).

CODLING MOTH TRAPS
Codling moth traps (right), which are an organic method of protecting apple and plum trees, look like bright yellow or green tents – insects are evidently very attracted to these colours – and inside are cunning sex traps. Each trap comes as a kit. Inside each 'tent' you place a small quantity of pheromone, which lures male codling moths to their doom – once inside they are glued to the spot. With the males out of action, female codling moths remain infertile so they don't lay eggs, so the result is no maggots in your fruit.

For this to work properly, it's essential that you use enough traps – the going rate is one per six trees – and you need to put the traps out as soon as the first males are flying. Fruit-growers will use yellow sticky strips of the sort used as 'flypapers' in the greenhouse to check what is about, but as a rule of thumb, if you put your tent traps out from early this month and leave them out until August, topping them up with a second helping of pheromone about halfway through the codling moth season, you should have good results.

If your neighbours grow fruit, persuade them to use the same technique so that all the males in the area are mopped up. Both apples and plums are affected by codling moth, but by different strains of the moth, so you'll need a different type of pheromone for each trap.

UNDER COVER

A greenhouse needs ventilation as the weather warms up. Open the windows in the morning and close them in the evening.

GREENHOUSE VENTILATION

Ventilate the greenhouse by day and water plants more frequently now the weather is warming up and plants are growing faster. If you don't already have them, automatic ventilator openers are a 'must' for anyone who's out at work all day, or simply doesn't want the bother of opening and closing greenhouse windows morning and evening. These handy gadgets can be fitted to your normal ventilators, and they are on duty constantly; they are 'driven' by pistons of paraffin wax that react to changing temperatures and push the ventilators open as much as necessary.

APPLY SHADING PAINT TO THE GREENHOUSE

It's worth applying shading paint to your greenhouse to help keep temperatures down and prevent seedlings and delicate plants from scorching. Use a proprietary liquid shading paint specially produced for greenhouse use, available in garden centres – it's designed to come off fairly easily at the end of the season, unlike house paint, which you'd find hard to shift from glass. Dilute it according to the manufacturer's instructions and paint it on with a wide decorator's paintbrush or use an old garden spray gun, putting a thin layer all over the outside of the roof.

If your conservatory is in a very sunny spot it's also worth applying to the south side of it, if you can do so without ruining your view of the garden from indoors. Alternatively, invest in external roller blinds, which you can raise and lower according to the weather.

DAMP DOWN REGULARLY

Damping down is an old-fashioned but effective technique for keeping the greenhouse cool in summer; the 'buoyant' atmosphere it creates is also very beneficial for humidity-loving plants, so it's well worth doing if you grow melons, cucumbers, peppers, chillies and aubergines, or fuchsias and other subtropical pot plants. Tomatoes and pelargoniums (geraniums) aren't so keen, and cacti and succulents are positively anti-damping down, so if you grow those don't bother damping down except in the most searing hot conditions.

- Damping down is easy – just spray water from a hose or can on to the greenhouse path and under the staging. It works a bit like putting water onto the hot coals in a sauna, causing moisture to evaporate and circulate around the plants, bathing them in a current of damp air. As a useful bonus, damping down is a brilliant way of deterring red spider mite, since the little brutes hate humid air.

PRICK OUT AND POT ON

Continue to prick out and pot on seedlings, cuttings and young plants (see April, p.107–9). Also, pot on begonias and gloxinias (see April, p.109).

HARDEN OFF PLANTS

Until you're certain the last frost has passed and the nights aren't too cold, continue hardening off bedding plants and frost-tender veg by standing them outside on fine days and returning them to the greenhouse at night (see April, p.108). Once all danger of frost has passed, they're safe to plant out.

TAKE CUTTINGS

You can take cuttings from tender perennials, such as pelargoniums and fuchsias, between now and mid-September (see June, p.171).

SUMMER GREENHOUSE CROPS

As soon as you're able to move all your frost-tender plants outside there's suddenly much more room for growing other things in the greenhouse. If you haven't already planted tomato plants do so now, and by the end of the month you can also plant sweet peppers, chillies, aubergines, cucumbers and melons.

How and where to plant

- If you're planting crops in the border soil, dig out any weeds and fork it over. Work in some chicken manure pellets, if you didn't manure the ground in winter, or a generous sprinkling of general-purpose organic fertilizer.

- Plant all the vegetables mentioned above 75 × 75cm (30 × 30in) apart. It might look like very generous spacing now, but once the plants have reached the greenhouse roof and the leaves reach their full spread, you'll see that they needed every inch of it. Push a strong cane or stake in alongside each plant, and tie the main stem to it. Tall-growing plants, such as tomatoes, cucumbers and melons, need a stake almost as tall as the greenhouse roof, but sweet peppers, chillies and aubergines make shorter, bushier plants, so a 1m (3ft) stake is enough.

Watering

Water new plants in with about 600ml (1 pint) of water, but keep them slightly on the dry side for the first 7–10 days, to encourage the roots to dive down faster. In the case of tomatoes, it pays to keep them a little short of water right to the time the first truss (bunch) of fruits has started to swell up slightly. Cucumber and melon plants are very susceptible to rotting off at the neck if kept too wet in the early stages, so water sparingly until they are 60–90cm (2–3ft) high, after which they are generally safe. On fine days, spray the plants over with plain water from a hose to keep humidity high, as it helps the plants to settle in, and in the case of tomatoes it aids pollen germination, which helps the first fruit set more easily.

Feeding

A fortnight after planting, start feeding all your summer greenhouse crops with liquid tomato feed every 2 weeks.

May is planting time for tomatoes.

Training and trimming

You will need to train and trim your summer greenhouse crops weekly from now on.

- Tomatoes (upright varieties) – Tie the main stem up to a tall cane and tie in new extension growth every week. Nip out all sideshoots, as they waste the energy of the plant. The flowers grow in trusses straight from the main stem of the plant – take care not to remove them by mistake when taking out sideshoots.

- Tomatoes (bush varieties) – Tie the main stem to a short stake. Don't remove sideshoots, as they carry the fruit on bush varieties.

Tie tomato stems to a cane or stake.

Tying sweet peppers to a stake (above left); removing male flowers from a cucumber (above centre); removing sideshoots from tomatoes (above right).

Early pot-grown potatoes will be ready for harvesting now.

● Sweet peppers, chillies and aubergines – Tie the main stem to a short stake. Don't trim plants or remove sideshoots.

● All-female varieties of cucumber – Tie the main stem up a tall cane and tie in extension growth every week. Remove all sideshoots, as cucumbers are produced directly from the main stem. Take care not to remove flowers when taking out sideshoots.

● Melons and non-F1 varieties of cucumber – Tie the main stem to a tall cane, and tie in extension growth every week. Pinch out sideshoots after their second leaf, but as the plants grow taller allow sideshoots to grow higher up the stem and either train them out along netting or let them dangle back down the plant if there's no room.

Melons need pollinating before they set fruit, so if bees don't come into the greenhouse, do it yourself with a soft artist's brush, going around each open flower in turn every day. Cucumbers on the other hand must *not* be pollinated as they would develop hard seeds and a bitter flavour, so remove male flowers by hand. You can tell male and female flowers apart because the female ones grow on the end of a tiny cucumber, whereas male flowers just grow on a thin, short stalk.

HARVEST BABY SPUDS

If you planted early potatoes in pots at the start of the season, you'll be ready for your first taste. There's no need to tip the pots out, just rootle around in the compost near the surface of the containers with your fingers and see what you can find that's big enough to eat, leaving the plants to continue growing and the remaining spuds deeper down to keep swelling. By the time you've had a few handfuls in this way, take the plunge and tip out a complete potful next time round, and with luck it should be well packed with tasty young spuds.

NATURAL PEST SPRAYS

There are several safe sprays you can use to help in the battle against greenhouse and garden pests, without going against your 'green' principles. Don't use them at the same time as biological control insects are in action under glass (see box opposite), as even the safest sprays can't tell friend from foe.

Soft soap – not the same as the bar from your bathroom – is currently approved for use against most common insect pests. For advice and information on other permitted pesticides, check the website of the Pesticide Safety Directorate – www.pesticides.gov.uk.

BIOLOGICAL PEST CONTROL UNDER GLASS

The warm, cosy atmosphere under glass acts like a house party for pests, but there's no need to bring a bottle because organic remedies actually work better. Pests rapidly build up natural resistance to chemicals, so you get much better results from a combination of natural pest-killing products and physical traps, or by introducing beneficial insects as biological control.

Biological control works well under glass, as introduced pests can't easily fly away, and being largely foreign bugs they prefer the warmer conditions under cover. It's also a good way to keep conservatory pests under control because that's about the last place you want pests making a mess of your decor, neither do you want to be spraying smelly chemicals.

Whitefly

Whitefly (below left) look like clouds of low-flying dandruff when you brush affected plants with your hand. You have to look hard to spot them otherwise, because they live in colonies underneath the young leaves near the top of the plant. Besides the adults, which are the flying form, you may spot silver 'scales' stuck to the undersides of the leaves; these are the larval stage, which are particularly difficult to tackle using conventional chemicals.

- You can help to avoid a serious outbreak of whitefly by not growing fuchsias or tomatoes and peppers, as these are their favourite food plants, and by making sure plants are given generous spacing; a congested greenhouse is always a target for pests of all sorts.
- Use yellow sticky traps to keep whitefly numbers below the level where they cause

serious damage; hang them above particularly at-risk plants, and disturb the foliage regularly to make the pests fly up. Don't use yellow sticky traps at the same time as a biological control, as they'll also catch 'good' insects.

- Introduce the parasite encarsia as biological control sometime this month. It arrives as parasitized whitefly scales on small cards – hang these in several places around the greenhouse close to badly affected plants so that emerging encarsia can go straight to work. They lay their eggs in the scales of whitefly – you can tell affected scales, as they turn black instead of white – and instead of a whitefly hatching out, out pops another encarsia.
- Even more efficient is a relative of the ladybird called delphastus, which attacks both adult whitefly and scales, and will wander around the greenhouse much more than encarsia in search of a good feed. Unfortunately, it can't be used on tomatoes.

Red spider mite

Red spider mites are almost invisible to the naked eye, and you'll need to use reading glasses or a magnifying glass to spot them. They look like flocks of animated beige-coloured dust prowling around the growing tips of shoots and the youngest leaves, and all sorts of plants can be affected – they are very fond of cucumber and melon plants, but will attack almost anything. In severe cases, you can see very fine webs near the top of affected plants (below centre), which by then will be looking bleached and unhealthy, with tiny yellowish speckles or yellow or brown leaves.

- Red spider mites like hot, dry conditions, so keeping the greenhouse well ventilated

and regularly damped down (see p.142) will help to deter attacks.

- If opting for biological control, introduce the predatory mite phytoseiulus as soon as the weather is warm enough for them to survive but before the infestation becomes too large for them to cope, i.e. now. And in case you are wondering why red spider mites are called red when they are actually beige, it's because they turn red in winter.

Greenfly

Greenfly (below right) are probably the best-known greenhouse pest. They can affect virtually any plants under glass, where they breed phenomenally quickly due to the constant warmth and huge food supply. Where there are only a few they won't do enough damage to bother about, but get into the habit of checking plants regularly.

- If you see small colonies of greenfly, wipe them off between your fingers.
- If you spot what looks like a dead aphid that has turned to a crisp brownish 'shell' it has been parasitized by a naturally occurring insect called aphidius, so leave it alone and you'll have free biological control – instead of a young whitefly hatching, a new aphidius will emerge. You can buy aphidius to introduce as biological control; if you want to give it a try, now is the time to introduce it.
- The native spider population of the greenhouse will take care of enormous numbers of greenfly, for free, if you don't use chemicals. The tiny money spiders are the best of the lot, but any time you're evicting spiders from inside your house consider re-homing them in the greenhouse.

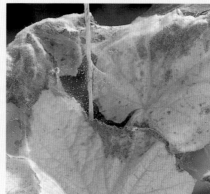

WATER GARDEN

ADD NEW FLOATING PLANTS

Ponds still look quite green this month, owing to myriads of tiny, single-celled algae floating in the water. However, the water eventually settles down once the weather warms up and plants such as waterlilies and water hawthorn start growing vigorously and shading the water. If you don't already grow them, it's worth introducing a plant or two to your pond just for the beneficial effect their big, floating leaves have on stabilizing the water temperature and thus helping to establish a healthy biological balance in the pond.

The aim is to plant enough plants with floating leaves so that by midsummer they cover half to two-thirds of the surface of the water in the pond. It'll take a year or two for the plants to reach their full potential, so don't expect the 'cure' to be 100 per cent effective straight away.

Waterlilies are practical as well as beautiful: they shade the water, which stabilizes the temperature and enables other pond-life to thrive.

Water hawthorn

A wonderful plant for a small pond, the water hawthorn (*Aponogeton distachyos*) can be introduced from April onwards throughout the summer. It grows about 1m (3ft) across, with widely spaced oval leaves and white flowers, whose petals pile up into waxy mounds. It blooms from April to September or later, and the flowers have a noticeable scent of hawthorn – if you can get your nose near enough.

Waterlilies

The best time to put new waterlilies into the pond is from May to the end of June, as they need warmer water in which to establish themselves. Waterlilies come in a huge range of varieties, many of which are far too big for small garden ponds – they were originally bred in the 19th century for lakes at country houses. Choose a variety such as pink *Nymphaea* 'James Brydon' or red *Nymphaea* 'Froebelii' for a small pond.

Other floating water plants

There are other floating water plants available, but it pays to be very choosy. The water soldier (*Stratiotes aloides*) is a reasonable plant for a pond, being both native to Europe and a curiosity (it looks slightly like a semi-submerged pineapple). But it's not that much use to the pond's ecology as it doesn't create much shading.

Several other floaters have much smaller leaves, and since they aren't attached by roots to the bottom of the pond they tend to drift down one end in windy weather, which isn't so helpful. Some are tropical species, which can cause problems – azolla, for example, is

DEALING WITH GREEN GUNGE

If a pond stays seriously green and you feel you really must do something about it, sink a wad of organic barley straw (sold specially for 'clearing' ponds) into the water. If you must use something out of a bottle, go for a biological product. This works by increasing the numbers of naturally occurring beneficial bacteria, which help to keep the biological balance of a mature pond. Quite honestly all you really need to do is give it time and it'll happen all on its own.

HOW TO DIVIDE A WATERLILY

1 Lift the lily's planting basket out of the pond. If it's too far from the edge to reach, it's a case of going paddling. Don't drag a reluctant basket – ease it out with care, as you don't want to risk perforating your liner and making it leak.

2 Tip the plant out and split the fat tubers up, in the same way as you would with a perennial plant in your flower border (see March, pp.64–5). Don't over-divide waterlilies – choose a healthy looking tuber about 22cm (9in) long to replant.

3 Fill the planting basket with fresh pond compost (available in water garden centres) and plant the tuber horizontally, so the roots are buried in the compost but the tuber is on top. Put some gravel or pebbles over the compost to keep the plant in place when it goes back into the water, but make sure the tuber isn't covered.

4 Lower the plant back into the water. The trick is to thread a pair of strong strings through the sides of the basket, one at each edge, so two people can between them lift the basket out over the pond and slowly lower it in. Then one lets go of his or her strings, so they can be pulled out.

---

considered inadvisable to grow in case it survives our increasingly mild winters and escapes into wild waterways, where it is proving a great nuisance. Avoid parrot feather (*Myriophyllum aquaticum*) for the same reason.

DIVIDE OVERGROWN WATERLILIES

Waterlilies are plants that don't like a lot of fuss. They'd really prefer to be left alone, but there comes a time when they're so overgrown that they take up most of the pond, or they stop flowering, or they won't grow, and you have to do something. In a small pond you'll only need to divide waterlilies every 6–7 years (see box above). May is strategically the best time to do this, because the water is warm and they are wanting to grow; if you do it at the wrong time, the fat tubers just rot and you lose the plant.

DEAL WITH UNWELCOME WATERWEEDS

Don't imagine for a minute that putting in a pond means you won't have to do any weeding. 'Good' waterweeds do a great job of oxygenating the water, but they are potentially large spreaders that need regular thinning out, and there are also algae and unwanted water plants that

arrive all on their own, so once the spring flush of growth has started you'll need to stop the pond becoming congested.

Take a look roughly once a month from now on through the summer, and deal with the excess. Any weed that you pull out of the water will be teeming with tiny pond-life, from freshwater shrimps to tadpoles, so I always drape the debris over the edge of the pond for a couple of days, which gives everything a chance to wriggle back into the water. After that, put the lot on the compost heap, where it is a useful supplier of nutrients.

Blanket weed

Blanket weed is different from your usual waterweeds. It starts the season as loose, green, thread-like strands, and soon bulks up to make great floating wads of green cotton wool, which eventually erupt into Martian-style bubbles of gloop on the surface of the water. If blanket weed is a problem, it's usually a sign that there are nutrients in the water that are feeding it – they can come from fertilizers washed into the pond when rain runs off a cultivated garden, or from nitrates in the tap

Remove blanket weed as soon as you can using a long cane.

Right: To get fish used to their new home, lower the plastic bag into the pond and leave it there for an hour or so before opening.

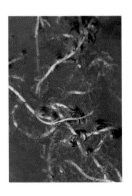

Thin out large clumps of elodea (top) and remove all duckweed (above) from the pond.

water you use to top up the pond – either way, you want blanket weed out.

To remove blanket weed, stick a long cane into the middle of a thick mass, twist it around so it looks like green candyfloss, and pull it out. If you have a big pond, a wire rake pulls more out faster, but take care you don't catch the pond liner and tear it.

Elodea

The commonest oxygenating waterweed species is elodea, which resembles green ropes with short, stubby leaves lined up all along it. If it is overgrown and threatening to choke the pond, this is a good moment to tug out a few handfuls to thin out the biggest clumps. Don't overdo it, because waterweeds are the lungs of the pond and the only hiding places for fish until your waterlilies grow.

Duckweed

A single duckweed plant is a tiny thing consisting of a pair of minute oval leaves joined together in the middle with a frail dangling root. You wouldn't think it would cause much trouble, but there's never just one of them – it's dreadfully invasive, and quickly builds up into dense green mats that totally swamp the pond and kill off everything in it by cutting out the light completely. It's very easy to introduce duckweed accidentally on new plants you put into the pond, so wash them off well first. But birds can drop pieces, so it'll usually find you one way or another. You'll never get rid of it entirely, but keep scooping it out with a shrimping-style net every time you see a decent 'raft' of it at any time in summer.

INTRODUCE NEW FISH

Now that the water has warmed up and the biological activity in the pond is increasing, it's a good time to introduce new fish if you want to – but don't imagine last year's have vanished, if you don't happen to see them. They're probably still shy after spending the winter hiding down in the depths of the pond, and once you start feeding them they'll start coming up to the surface. What's more, they will probably be breeding, so in another few months

you'll start to see small fish you didn't know you had. In a wildlife pond, fish are best avoided, as they'll feed on tadpoles and young newts.

If you have made a new pond over the winter, wait a couple of months for the microscopic water life to appear, and for water plants to establish and spread before introducing your fish. When you buy them from a garden centre or pond specialist, they are handed over in plastic bags that are half full of water and half full of air. The move to a new home is quite stressful for fish, so take pains to do everything as gently as possible to avoid panicking them.

● Keep the bag of fish inside a pot on the way home so the water doesn't slosh about too much, then lower the bag into the pond and leave it to float there for an hour or so. Only then should you undo the neck of the bag, but don't tip the fish out – let them swim out in their own good time, and don't be surprised when they spend the next week or so hiding in the waterweeds instead of coming out. They will appear in time.

FEED FISH

Continue to feed fish if you want to (see April, p.114).

PROJECT Make a herbal hanging basket

If you enjoy cooking it's hard to grow too many herbs in the garden, but they have to be handy; a hanging basket of herbs outside the back door or on the patio wall near the barbecue is ideal. You can stuff it full of all your culinary favourites, and add a few flowers to stop it looking too leafy. They are also handy for Pimms! The end result makes a refreshing change from the usual bedding plants – it's scented, it's useful, and as a bonus it's quite good at fending off flies.

What you need

Large, wire-framed hanging basket

Moss or similar plant-through lining material (see p.132)

Suggested plants (alter to suit your own taste): one each of curled parsley, borage (above left), climbing nasturtium (above centre), basil, Greek oregano or marjoram, variegated pineapple mint, variegated apple mint (above right), leaf coriander, prostrate rosemary, purple sage and a scented-leaved pelargonium such as tangerine-scented 'Prince of Orange', 'Chocolate Peppermint' or lemony *P. crispum* 'Variegatum'

1 Arrange the plants attractively before you start, then fill the basket in the same way as described earlier for planting a wire basket with bedding plants (see p.132).

2 Plant half of the herbs in through the side of the basket and the rest in the top. The variegated mint is quite a weak grower, so it won't take over during a single summer unlike other kinds of mint.

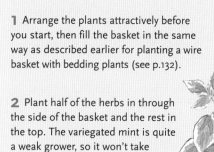

3 Train the climbing nasturtium up the chains of the basket and along the bracket holding it up; you'll need to tie it in place – despite its name, its natural instinct is to trail and not climb.

4 Hang the basket in a warm, sunny, sheltered place, which helps concentrate the scent of the herbs. Water regularly and feed every two weeks with a general-purpose liquid feed, organic if possible. As short-lived annual herbs, such as basil and leaf coriander, come to an end, replace them with new plants.

147

JUNE

June is the start of the blowsy season, when all the big, over-the-top summer flowers make their first appearance. For a couple of months the garden looks like the top of a chocolate box. Roses are right there at the forefront, and if there's one thing they must have to earn a place in my garden, it's scent (see pp.150–1).

The weather is improving in leaps and bounds in June, so if you still have tender plants you felt a tad iffy about planting out in May, or you happen to live fairly well north, then plant them out now. They'll soon catch up so you won't have lost out. There's lots to keep on top of in June, but this is when all the work starts to pay off – perennials and shrubs cover the ground and begin smothering out weeds, the lawn won't be growing quite so fast as the weather gets hotter and drier, and the patio starts to look a lot more colourful. So get the essentials out of the way and then settle into some really constructive gardening – but don't forget to leave time to sit down and enjoy the view.

THE BIG PICTURE roses

Rosa **'Paul's Himalayan Musk'** (above) is a breathtaking rambler. Alright, so it only has one short season of bloom, but when it arrives you will know why you looked forward to it, and that makes it all the more special. Masses of petite, double pompon flowers in the softest blush-pink turn the plant into a cascade of flowers. Allow 8 × 4m (25 × 12ft).

PEAK SEASON June–July.
GROWING CONDITIONS Any soil at the foot of a sunny wall, or, better still, allow it to wander into a tree.

Rosa **'Margaret Merril'** (above) has one of the finest fragrances of any rose, and I'd grow her just for that. But her Floribunda flowers are well above average – big clusters of almost iridescent, pearly, warm white blooms with a hint of a crinkle around the edges. Even though this rose doesn't have the natural disease resistance of some, I'd put her right at the top of my 'A' list; she's well worth the risk. Size 90 × 60cm (3 × 2ft).

PEAK SEASON June–October.
GROWING CONDITIONS Rich, fertile soil in sun.

Rosa **'Alan Titchmarsh'** (above) is a repeat-flowering modern shrub rose with sweetly scented, fully double, peony-shaped flowers of rich pink. (Well, I had to include it, didn't I?) The foliage is disease-resistant and the plant has a rounded habit. Size 1.5 × 1.5m (5 × 5ft).

PEAK SEASON June–October.
GROWING CONDITIONS Rich, fertile soil in full sun.

Rosa 'Marchesa Boccella'
(above) is a wonderful old garden
rose, and the sort of shrub rose
that I love the most. The soft pink
flowers are flattish and fully
double, with the most wonderful
fragrance. They are also produced,
off and on, all through the summer.
The foliage is pretty disease-
resistant, and the bush is relatively
tidy at 1.2 × 0.6m (4 × 2ft).

PEAK SEASON June–September.
GROWING CONDITIONS Rich,
    fertile soil in full sun.

Rosa 'Charles de Mills' (above)
is one of the most spectacular
shrub roses, because its rich
crimson-magenta flowers look as
though they have been sliced off
in the bud, allowing the flower to
open into a spectacular rosette; it
also has good, mid-green foliage.
This is about the last shrub rose
I would want to give up. Size
1.5 × 1m (5 × 3ft).

PEAK SEASON June–July.
GROWING CONDITIONS Rich,
    fertile soil in full sun.

Rosa 'Compassion' (left) is the
sort of climber you'd call a really
sensible choice; reliable
and healthy, with fragrant, peach-
apricot flowers produced in a
series of flushes right through the
summer. Deadhead regularly to
keep the flowers coming. Allow
an area 3 × 2.5m (10 × 8ft).

PEAK SEASON June–September.
GROWING CONDITIONS Rich,
    fertile soil in sun. Grow against
    a wall or through a tree.

Rosa 'Geranium' (above) is one
of the most popular species roses,
grown for its big scarlet-orange
bottle-shaped hips that follow
on from the single red flowers
in early summer. Not as big as
some rose species, 'Geranium'
grows into a loose, arching shape
eventually occupying a space
2.2 × 1.5m (7 × 5ft).

PEAK SEASON May–June
    (flowers), July–November (hips).
GROWING CONDITIONS Any
    reasonable soil in sun.

OLD FAITHFULS

Potentilla fruticosa (above) is a handy shrub for the front of a border; it makes a low mound of ferny foliage studded with wide rosette-shaped flowers, 2.5cm (1in) across, mostly in the yellow-orange-red range, depending on variety. **Potentilla fruticosa 'Abbotswood'** is a popular white, 75 × 75cm (2½ × 2½ft); **'Tangerine'** is a reliable buff-orange at 60 × 60cm (2 × 2ft), and **'Elizabeth'** is a primrose yellow at 1 × 1.5m (3 × 5ft).

PEAK SEASON June–September.
GROWING CONDITIONS Well-drained soil in sun or light shade; red varieties are best in light shade as the flowers fade in sun.

Dianthus 'Doris' (left) is a modern pink that produces its frilly pale pink flowers with cherry 'eyes' constantly all summer – a real trouper. The silvery green clumps of foliage slowly spread to 20 × 30cm (8 × 12in). If you only grow one variety of pink, make it 'Doris'.

PEAK SEASON June–September.
GROWING CONDITIONS Well-drained soil in sun. Good for a rock feature, a gravel garden, and the front of a border.

Philadelphus are popular shrubs, with fragrant white flowers that give them their common name of mock orange. There are quite a few varieties in different sizes, so choose one that's right for your space – this isn't a shrub you can butcher to make it fit a smaller space without sacrificing flowers, although it needs correct pruning to keep it tidy. **Philadelphus 'Belle Etoile'**, 1.5 × 2.5m (5 × 8ft), is single, with reddish staining at the centre of the flowers and a powerful fragrance, while **'Manteau d'Hermine'** is fully double, again with a glorious scent, but very compact at 1 × 1.5m (3 × 5ft). **Philadelphus coronarius 'Variegatus'** (above), 2.5 × 1m (8 × 3ft), is the one to go for if you want a bit of everything, as it has creamy variegated leaves that are almost an exact match for the single flowers.

PEAK SEASON June–July.
GROWING CONDITIONS Any reasonable soil in sun or light shade.

Clematis are real stars of summer, and there's a whole group of large-flowered hybrids that start flowering now and keep going right through until early autumn without a break. They include **'Hagley Hybrid'**, shell pink, 2.5m (8ft), **'Jackmanii'**, purple, 5m (15ft), **'Jackmanii Superba'** (above), rich purple, 3m (10ft) and **'General Sikorski'**, lavender, 3m (10ft).

PEAK SEASON June–September.
GROWING CONDITIONS Fertile soil, with roots in shade (e.g. under bits of paving stone) and tops growing out into good light. Any aspect except north-facing.

Geranium × *riversleaianum* **'Mavis Simpson'** (above) is one of my favourite hardy cranesbills. She smothers herself in soft pink flowers from one end of summer to the other on a knee-high rug of spreading, downy leaves – wonderful ground cover.

Geranium macrorrhizum is one of the best for a small garden, as it spreads its mounds (30 × 120cm/ 1 × 4ft) of aromatic, downy leaves across the ground to create brilliant ground cover, ideal under roses or shrubs. The flowers, carried in early summer, are pale pink in **'Ingwersen's Variety'**, a deeper shade of rosy crimson in **'Bevan's Variety'**, or the usual magenta-pink of the species. I'd give any of them house room for their versatility and interest. The reddish cranesbill seedheads follow the flowers, and in autumn the foliage turns ruddy to brighten the dullest days.

PEAK SEASON June–September.
GROWING CONDITIONS Any reasonable soil in sun or light shade.

Hostas look their very smartest shortly after the new leaves have unfurled themselves fully but before they have time to be jaded by summer heat. Hostas do flower, but the leaves are their main attraction. They are very collectable, and addiction is likely. There are large glaucous species such as **'Sum and Substance'**, gold forms such as **'Piedmont Gold'**, and variegated varieties, for example **'Gold Standard'** (above), gold with a deep green edge, to name but a few. I've always found that **'Frances Williams'**, glaucous green with a butter-yellow edge, is as slug- and snail-resistant as any.

PEAK SEASON June–September.
GROWING CONDITIONS Moist soil with added organic matter in light shade, although sun is fine for all except gold forms as long as the ground does not dry out. Good for ground cover under trees or shrubs and in boggy soil around pond edges. Also brilliant for pots, especially where slugs are a problem in open ground.

Waterlilies are pond essentials. The leaves shade the water and prevent over-heating, as well as providing cover for fish, and the flowers look like floating pompons. When buying a waterlily, make sure it's a suitable size for the area of the pond – some grow far too big. *Nymphaea* 'Rose Arey' (above) is good for a small pond and has bronze-tinged leaves and pale pink flowers with yellow stamens. It covers an area about 1.2m (4ft) square.

PEAK SEASON June–September.
GROWING CONDITIONS Stand the planting basket at a depth where there's 30–45cm (12–18in) of water over the crown.

Bearded irises flower slightly ahead of the main rush of summer perennials and have a short – but glorious – season. Dwarf Bearded varieties (22–30cm/9–12in), Intermediate Bearded varieties (45cm/18in) and Tall Bearded varieties (60–90cm/24–36in) flower in order of height, with the shortest starting in May, so plant several kinds if you're a real iris-fancier or you want longer continuity. Tall Bearded irises are the most popular kind that you'll find in most garden centres in a range of varieties; some have huge flowers with contrasting 'beards' on the lower petals. **'Black Swan'** (above) is such a deep purple it is almost black; and **'Party Dress'** has frilly pink flowers that completely live up to its name. Specialist nurseries stock a staggering selection.

PEAK SEASON June.
GROWING CONDITIONS Sunny, well-drained soil, where the rhizomes are not overshadowed by surrounding plants. Don't plant deeply – the top half of the rhizomes should be visible.

SOMETHING SPECIAL

Convolvulus cneorum (above) belongs to the same family as the dreaded bindweed, but there the resemblance ends. This is a little charmer, with silvery leaves and round, wide white flowers that are pink in bud. It won't creep more than 45cm (18in) in any direction over the summer.

PEAK SEASON June–September.
GROWING CONDITIONS Well-drained soil in a sunny site, on a raised bed or rock garden, or for hanging baskets and other containers. Be prepared for it to be short lived and keep a few rooted cuttings handy as replacements.

Aristolochia macrophylla (above) isn't the sort of thing you'll find easily, and unless you have a mild, sheltered spot it's not worth risking – but if you have, give it a go. It's a sensational climber, with huge heart-shaped leaves and flowers that look like the traps of some exotic carnivorous plant, green with purple blotches. The bent stem and flared 'bowl' of the flower give it the common name of Dutchman's pipe. I wish I could suggest growing it in the conservatory if you don't have the right conditions, but at 6m (20ft) it's too big and grows too fast, so it's outdoors or nothing.

PEAK SEASON June.
GROWING CONDITIONS Fertile soil with plenty of organic matter, in a mild sheltered spot in sun or light shade.

Alstroemeria (above) is a perennial that can be difficult to establish, but plant breeders have now produced good new strains, available in most garden centres. The varieties sold as *Alstroemeria* **Princess lilies** in particular look set to become the new 'old faithfuls', with varieties from 30–90cm (1–3ft) that make them suitable for borders, cut flowers or containers. All are named after royalty and bloom throughout the summer, with big heads of mask-shaped flowers in shades of pink, green and red. Spent flower stems must be tugged out when they are over to keep them flowering.

PEAK SEASON June–September.
GROWING CONDITIONS Fertile, well-drained soil in full sun.

Cytisus battandieri, pineapple broom (above), is the sort of eye-catching wall shrub that makes you determined to grow it. It needs plenty of room – at least 3 × 3m (10 × 10ft) – although an unpruned plant is capable of covering the side of a house. The silky foliage, which looks nothing like that of a conventional broom, and large yellow, pineapple-scented, cockade-shaped flowers make this a real looker.

PEAK SEASON June–July.
GROWING CONDITIONS Sunny wall with well-drained soil.

Primula florindae, giant cowslip (above), is a corker for your bog garden. The nodding yellow 'cowslip' flowers grow in a bunch on top of a 60cm (2ft) stem from a cabbagey-looking rosette of leaves a good 45cm (18in) across. A group of them reflected in water with a foreground of hostas is hard to beat. Also good are the **Harlow Carr hybrids**, candelabra primulas with tiers of flowers that may be yellow, pink, orange or crimson on stems 60cm (2ft) tall.

PEAK SEASON June–July.
GROWING CONDITIONS Fertile, damp to boggy soil in sun.

OTHER PLANTS IN THEIR PRIME IN JUNE

- **Trees** *Crataegus persimilis* 'Prunifolia', *Laburnum*, *Liriodendron tulipifera*, *Styrax japonicus*
- **Shrubs** *Buddleja alternifolia*, *Colutea arborescens*, *Cornus alba*, *Cornus kousa*, *Cornus florida*, *Cotoneaster*, *Deutzia*, *Indigofera heterantha*, *Kolkwitzia amabilis*, *Leycesteria formosa*, *Magnolia sieboldii*, *Nandina domestica*, *Physocarpus*, *Piptanthus laburnifolius*, *Sambucus nigra*, *Spiraea nipponica*, *Stephanandra incisa*, *Syringa*, *Tamarix tetrandra*, *Viburnum lantana*, *Viburnum opulus*, *Viburnum plicatum* 'Mariesii' (see p.119), *Weigela florida*
- **Evergreens** *Buddleja globosa*, *Cistus*, *Coronilla glauca*, *Crinodendron hookerianum* (see p.122), *Daboecia*, *Embothrium lanceolatum*, *Erica tetralix*, *Escallonia*, *Genista hispanica*, *Genista lydia*, *Hebe* (see p.178), *Hypericum calycinum*, *Hypericum* 'Hidcote', *Kalmia latifolia*, *Olearia*, *Phlomis fruticosa*, *Photinia davidiana*, *Prunus laurocerasus*, *Pyracantha*, *Rhododendron* hybrids (see p.118), deciduous rhododendrons (azalea) (see p.119), *Santolina chamaecyparissus*, *Spartium junceum*, *Teucrium fruticans*, *Vinca*
- **Climbers/wall shrubs** *Abutilon vitifolium*, *Clematis* 'Barbara Jackman', *Clematis* 'Bees Jubilee', *Clematis* 'Duchess of Edinburgh', *Clematis* 'Nelly Moser' (see p.119), *Clematis* 'Proteus', *Clematis* 'Vyvyan Pennell', *Clematis* 'Comtesse de Bouchaud', *Clematis* 'Mevrouw le Coultre', *Clematis* 'The President', *Clematis montana*, *Clematis* Viticella cultivars (see pp.180 and 202), *Clianthus puniceus*, *Eccremocarpus scaber*, *Fremontodendron californicum*, *Hydrangea anomala* subsp. *petiolaris*, *Lonicera periclymenum* 'Belgica' (see p.121), *Lonicera* × *brownii*, *Wisteria floribunda* (see p.120), *Wisteria sinensis*
- **Perennials** *Acanthus spinosus*, *Achillea filipendulina*, *Achillea ptarmica*, *Ajuga*, *Alchemilla mollis*, *Anthemis tinctoria*, *Aruncus dioicus*, *Astilbe*, *Astrantia major*, *Campanula lactiflora*, *Campanula glomerata*, *Campanula persicifolia*, *Catananche caerulea*, *Centaurea dealbata*, *Centranthus ruber*, *Corydalis flexuosa* (see p.122), *Crambe cordifolia*, *Delphinium*, *Dictamnus albus*, *Eremurus bungei*, *Erigeron*, *Euphorbia griffithii*, *Euphorbia characias* subsp. *wulfenii* (see p.120), *Geum* 'Mrs. J. Bradshaw' (see p.121), *Geranium endressii*, *Geranium psilostemon*, *Geranium sanguineum*, *Geranium* 'Johnson's Blue', *Geranium* × *oxonianum* 'Wargrave Pink', *Helianthemum*, *Heuchera*, *Incarvillea delavayi* (see p.122), *Iris* (Tall Bearded), *Lamium maculatum*, *Lavatera* × *clementii*, *Leucanthemum maximum*, *Lupinus*, *Lysimachia punctata*, *Nepeta*, *Paeonia lactiflora*, *Papaver orientale*, *Persicaria*, *Polygonatum multiflorum*, *Rheum palmatum*, *Salvia superba*, *Sisyrinchium striatum*, *Stachys byzantina*, *Thalictrum dipterocarpum*, *Tiarella cordifolia*, *Trollius*, *Veronica gentianoides*, *Veronica spicata* subsp. *incana*, *Verbascum*
- **Bulbs** *Allium*, *Anemone* De Caen Group and St Brigid Group, *Camassia*, *Gladiolus*, *Lilium*, *Scilla peruviana*
- **Bedding/patio plants/biennials** *Alyssum*, *Aquilegia*, *Calendula*, *Campanula medium*, *Centaurea cyanus*, *Dianthus barbatus* (see p.120), *Digitalis*, *Eschscholzia*, *Iberis*, *Lathyrus odoratus*, *Limnanthes*, *Linaria*, *Lobelia*, *Lunaria*, *Tropaeolum majus*, *Viola*
- **Rock plants** *Armeria maritima*, *Dianthus*, *Erigeron mucronatus*, *Gentiana acaulis*, *Gentiana verna*, *Geranium cinereum*, *Lewisia cotyledon*, *Lithodora diffusa*, *Penstemon pinifolius*, *Phlox douglasii*, *Rhodohypoxis baurii*, *Sisyrinchium*, *Thymus serpyllum*, *Veronica prostrata*

JUNE at-a-glance checklist

GENERAL GARDEN TASKS (p.157)
✔ Water and deadhead plants regularly.
✔ Remove perennial weeds.

LAWNS (p.157)
✔ Mow regularly.
✔ Feed the grass with a liquid lawn feed if it needs a quick green-up.
✔ Water a new lawn.

TREES, SHRUBS AND CLIMBERS (p.158)
✔ Propagate shrubs and roses by taking softwood cuttings.
✔ Remove suckers from roses.
✔ Keep on top of training climbing and rambling roses.
✔ Layer clematis.
✔ Prune *Clematis montana* if necessary.
✔ Pinch dead flowerheads carefully from rhododendrons.
✔ Continue to clip privet and other fast-growing hedges.

FLOWERS (p.161)
✔ Dig up tulip and hyacinth bulbs when the foliage dies off, and store dry bulbs in a cool, dark shed ready to replant in autumn.
✔ Tidy up perennials after flowering.
✔ Plant out summer bedding plants, and lilies and cannas that were potted up earlier in the season.
✔ Sow biennials, fast-growing annuals for autumn colour, and flowers for cutting and drying in drills outdoors.
✔ Sow winter and early spring bedding plants in pots or trays under glass.
✔ Take cuttings from short-lived perennials (e.g. pinks and perennial wallflowers) and rock plants (e.g. aubretia, rosette-forming plants and miniature shrubs and other bushy rock plants).

PATIOS AND CONTAINERS (p.165)
✔ Bring out planted containers and hanging baskets from under glass if you haven't already, and plant up any new ones now that the danger of frost has passed.
✔ Water and feed containers and hanging baskets, and keep newly planted trees, shrubs, perennials and rock plants watered in dry spells while they get established.
✔ Deadhead flowers.

VEGETABLES AND HERBS (p.166)
✔ Sow lettuce, rocket, spring onion, radish, oriental leaves including pak choi and Chinese cabbage, maincrop carrots, peas, swedes, witloof chicory, endive, calabrese, sweetcorn, French and runner beans, courgettes, squashes and pumpkins.
✔ Continue planting greenhouse-grown frost-tender vegetables outside.
✔ Transplant leek and brassica seedlings.
✔ Harvest lettuce, calabrese, rocket, radishes, spring onions, gooseberries, early potatoes, overwintering onions, last of the asparagus.

FRUIT (p.168)
✔ Keep all fruit trees and bushes well watered in dry spells.
✔ Thin heavy crops of plums, apples and pears.
✔ Prune fan-trained apple or pear trees if necessary.
✔ Harvest rhubarb and strawberries.

UNDER COVER (p.170)
✔ Damp down the greenhouse regularly and apply a second coat of shading paint if necessary.
✔ Water and feed plants regularly.
✔ Continue to pot up rooted cuttings and pot on young plants and seedlings.
✔ Sow cineraria and calceolaria for Christmas-flowering pot plants.
✔ Take cuttings from tender perennials (e.g. fuchsias and pelargoniums).
✔ Plant new crops.
✔ Keep tying in and pinching out sideshoots of tomato plants, and feed once a week.
✔ Continue pollinating melons and remove male flowers from cucumbers.

WATER GARDEN (p.172)
✔ Continue removing unwanted weeds.
✔ Introduce new fish.

Watch out for
● Lily beetle.
● Blackspot, powdery mildew and rust on roses.
● Blackfly on broad beans.
● Bud blast on rhododendrons.
● Anthills and nests building up in the lawn, in pots, rock features, containers, paths and the patio.

Get ahead
● Protect developing soft fruit from birds with netting *before* the fruit starts to ripen, or it will be too late.
● Propagate short-lived perennials such as pinks, border carnations and perennial wallflowers when they are only 2–3 years old to ensure you have new plants before the current ones are finished.

Last chance
● Harvest asparagus before the middle of the month.
● Plant peppers, cucumbers, tomatoes, melons and aubergines in the greenhouse or in tubs on the patio.

GENERAL GARDEN TASKS

SUMMER PROPAGATION

You *can't* call yourself a real gardener unless you grow at least a few of your own plants from scratch. At this time of year you don't need a greenhouse, cold frame or heated propagator – summer propagation is plant-raising as nature intended. By sowing seed or taking cuttings now, you can save money by growing plants you'd otherwise have to buy later. It's a good way of producing plants to stock up a stall for a fund-raising event, and it's always handy to have a few 'spares' in case of disaster, or just to share with family and friends.

BORDER MAINTENANCE

Fill in gaps in borders with bedding plants. Water the plants thoroughly in dry spells and deadhead regularly. Keep on top of perennial weeds such as bindweed; annual weeds become less of a problem in borders and the vegetable patch now they're being shaded out by cultivated plants.

LAWNS

MOW REGULARLY

Lawns are usually growing fast and furious by June, as long as we have the occasional shower of rain, so mow the lawn regularly every week and trim the edges (see March, p.57). If there isn't much rain, and a long, hot, dry summer seems to be on the cards, play it safe and hoist the blades of your mower up a couple of notches so you aren't cutting it so closely – it'll stay a good deal greener during a drought.

QUICK LAWN GREEN-UP

If you want to give the grass a quick boost, then a dose of liquid or soluble feed, applied through a watering can or a hose-end dilutor, pays off within days. It's fine for a quick green-up because the nutrients are already in 'drinkable' form that is easily taken in by grass roots. However, it doesn't have the same long-lasting effects that are provided by a granular feed or, better still, a slow-release feed, both of which are best applied in April or May. Don't risk using any kind of feed, even a liquid one, if the grass is suffering from drought – it won't help at all and in severe cases it can even scorch the grass.

WATER A NEW LAWN

If you have a new lawn that you've made this spring from seed or turf, and the weather turns very dry, then you'll need to water it if you possibly can. Give it a good soaking once a week during long, dry spells instead of damping it over little and often – stand an old tin can on the grass so you can see how much you've put on, and keep the sprinkler on until there's a good 2.5cm (1in) in the can. But don't waste water on established lawns, which can take care of themselves.

A liquid lawn feed in early summer will quickly green up your lawn.

Using a sprinkler
Before using a sprinkler, do check with your water supply company, as you'll probably need to buy a licence.

Left: Gaps in the border can be filled with colourful bedding plants, such as cannas, now the weather is warmer.

TREES, SHRUBS AND CLIMBERS

PROPAGATE SHRUBS

Summer is the perfect time for propagating any of the easier shrubs from softwood cuttings. You can root them in the open ground in a spare bit of land down the garden, using home-made lemonade bottle cloches. Use this technique for shrubs such as cornus, berberis, deutzia, hebe, potentilla, forsythia, philadelphus, hydrangea, ribes and weigela. Start propagating them as soon as this year's soft young shoots have grown big enough to use as cuttings – to around 10–15cm (4–6in) – which, depending on how good the weather is, will be any time in June or July. By the autumn, the new plants will be well rooted and ready for potting, but leave them where they are until then – don't rush it.

PROPAGATE ROSES

When you buy roses from a garden centre or nursery, they've been grafted on to the roots of another species of rose. It doesn't make much difference to us gardeners; if anything it's a pain because rose rootstocks are well known for producing lots of suckers. No, the main reason is to make life easier for the nurserymen, who find it most convenient to produce roses on a 'factory farming' system. By growing whole fields full of roses on the same rootstocks, they are able to have hundreds of different varieties, all the same size and ready to sell at the same time, and process them mechanically – almost like harvesting a field of corn.

But it's not often realized that roses *will* grow on their own roots. The big difference is that when they do, you see more of their individual peculiarities in terms of shapes, sizes and habits of growth. Strong-growing varieties grow taller, and weak varieties weaker. One or two develop strange wandering tendencies, more like raspberry canes than bush roses, but with most varieties you'd never know the difference, so if you want to share roses with a friend, taking cuttings is the best way to do it.

HOW TO TAKE SOFTWOOD CUTTINGS FROM SHRUBS

1 Snip soft shoot tips off the parent plant, and remove the lower leaves. Make a clean cut across the base of the stem with a sharp knife, just below a node (the joint where a leaf joins the stem). If the remaining leaves are very large, cut them in half to reduce water loss. The cutting should be 8–10cm (3–4in) long when prepared.

2 Dip the base of the cuttings in rooting powder, and dib them into well-prepared ground about 15cm (6in) apart. It's as well to take a few more than you really need as they won't all root.

3 Water them in, then cover each cutting with a mini-cloche made by cutting a plastic soft drinks bottle in half. Use the top half as your cloche, with the cap screwed on to start with, so that humidity builds up underneath.

4 After 2 or 3 weeks you can remove the cap to let in some fresh air as the cuttings start to take root. Another 4 weeks later, and you can ventilate more by removing the bottle for a few hours every day, replacing it overnight. The idea is to gradually acclimatize the cuttings to the outside air.

HOW TO TAKE ROSE CUTTINGS

1 Take rose cuttings as for shrubs (see opposite) except cut the shoots when they are a bit bigger, about 15–20cm (6–8in) long. Nip the growing tip out of the shoot before you get it to root, because the tips of rose cuttings are very soft and likely to develop fungal disease, which then kills the lot off.

2 You can root rose cuttings in the ground, as for shrubs, or push half a dozen cuttings in around the edge of a 20cm (8in) pot filled with seed compost, and cover the top with a large, loose polythene bag after watering them in. Keep the cuttings in good light but out of direct sunlight, and water again as needed to stop the compost drying out.

3 By autumn you'll have well-rooted cuttings ready to pot individually. Don't be tempted to plant rooted cuttings straight out into the garden beds. Grow them on in pots until they are roughly as big as the plant you'd buy in the shops – otherwise they'll just get swallowed up by bigger plants, weeds and pests, trodden on, or broken off. It's a tough life out there.

Tie in new shoots of climbing and rambling roses to keep them secure.

ROSE DISEASES

Whatever kind of roses you grow, they'll be flowering their hearts out in June. It's the height of the flowering season, but it's also the time rose diseases start to show up.

Blackspot is usually the one you see first. It looks just like ink spots on the leaves, which in a bad attack can spread until entire leaves look like they've been hit by the black death. Then they drop off. Powdery mildew and rust may start to appear later this month, or not until later in the summer depending on the weather, but as a general rule they'll be more prevalent if the weather is hot and dry, as the plants are put under more stress.

You can spray, of course, but if you want perfect roses you need to keep at it, every fortnight, right through the summer from start to finish. Quite honestly though, ask yourself if it's worth it. Nowadays, modern roses are bred for natural disease-resistance, and even though they aren't totally immune, you can leave them to cope. If your roses are generally prone to problems, I'd be tempted to bin them and buy some new disease-resistant ones.

REMOVE SUCKERS FROM ROSES

Don't just snip suckers off at ground level, or they'll grow back stronger than ever; instead, trace each one back to its origins – dig down with a small hand fork until you find the point where the sucker grows out from a root, and then tear it out. It's far less likely to grow back. If you have an old rose bush that's surrounded by suckers with very few stems growing from the original plant, then frankly it's probably better to dig the whole thing out and replace it.

TRAIN ROSES

Keep on top of training climbing and rambling roses. Tie in new shoots regularly during the growing season so they don't hang down. Where you want to train a young plant to cover a wall or arch, choose strong, well-placed stems arising from close to the base of the plant, spread them out so they cover the area, and tie them firmly to their supports using proper plastic plant ties instead of string, so they won't give way unexpectedly after a few years.

Above: Cover a layered clematis shoot with a stone to anchor it (top) and remove faded camellia blooms (above).

Below: Herbaceous borders are at their peak.

LAYER CLEMATIS

Clematis are among the most popular of garden plants, but growing them from cuttings is a job for a nurseryman or a real enthusiast with all the gear – they aren't easy. At home, if you want to grow your own, the answer is to layer them. Follow the instructions for layering a shrub (see March, p.61), and then cover the layered section with a tile or a handful of pebbles to keep it cool and shady if there aren't any surrounding plants to do the job for you. Since clematis have longer, springier stems that bend down more easily than shrub stems, you won't need as much to hold them in place.

After layering, leave it a year, watering in dry spells. At the end of that time you should find the layered piece of stem is quite a bit longer, and has a good set of roots. Take your secateurs and sever the umbilical cord joining it to the parent plant, and there you are – a brand new clematis, for nothing.

Unless it's a good size and you delay digging it up until spring or autumn, don't plant the new clematis straight in the garden. Pot it first, push a cane into the pot to train it up, and wait until it has grown a good rootball before planting it out – that'll improve its chances of survival no end.

MOVING HOUSE

When you're moving house, you can't just strip the garden and take it with you. Plants are regarded like the fixtures and fittings indoors. When you have a few treasured plants of sentimental value, let the vendor know they are not included in the sale, or remove them well before putting the house on the market, and fill the space with something else so there isn't a gap in the garden. But as a general rule, if you want to take plants then it's far better to root cuttings (see pp.158, 159 and 171), or layer more difficult-to-root plants, such as clematis and rhododendrons, so the parent plant is left behind (see left). Young plants also 'move' much better, and it's less bother than digging up mature plants.

DEADHEAD CAMELLIAS

Remove faded flowers from camellias.

PRUNE *CLEMATIS MONTANA*

Clematis montana needs pruning only when it is very overgrown and out of control. When this is the case, cut it back severely after it's finished flowering; you'll sacrifice flowers for a year or two, but the plant will soon recover.

DEADHEAD RHODODENDRONS

Pinch out dead flowerheads carefully without damaging the shoots. Watch out for bud blast, which you can identify by blackish flower buds that didn't open and are now covered with 'whiskers'; snap these off and destroy them.

PLANT CONTAINER-GROWN TREES, SHRUBS AND ROSES

The whole ideal of growing trees, shrubs and roses in containers is to make it possible to plant them virtually all the year round, even during the summer when they are in full flower. But if the weather is hot and the soil is dry, be prepared for the fact you'll need to keep them watered for the rest of this season. If it looks like being a scorching summer, you might think about putting off any further planting until the autumn.

CLIP HEDGES

Continue to clip privet and other fast-growing hedges such as *Lonicera nitida* (see May, pp.127–8).

FLOWERS

HARVEST AND STORE SPRING BULBS
Paradoxically, the flowers that are most on people's minds at the start of summer are spring bulbs. Some can be left in the ground, but others are best dug up and stored under cover for the summer.

Bulbs to leave
Naturalized daffodils, snowdrops, bluebells and squills are perfectly happy to be left in the ground all year round. Once the foliage dies down they stay safe underground, and they'll prefer to be in dry ground during the summer while they are dormant. If you have these bulbs in the lawn, wild garden or shrub border, you can safely forget about them.

Bulbs to move
Some bulbs are better dug up, dried off and stored after flowering (see below). In these cases, dig the bulbs up once they are dormant, dry them off and store them in a cool, airy shed for the summer. Spread them out in shallow trays or hang them up in an old vegetable net, so there's plenty of air circulation.

- Tulips and hyacinths are very rarely happy to be left in the ground. They hale from hot, dry places, such as Iran and Turkey, where the ground dries out so they have a good summer 'baking'. Over here, if they aren't dry enough when dormant they rot, or they are tunnelled by boring larvae, which lets bacteria in with the same result. So play safe, and dig them up once the flowers are over and the leaves have died off, and store them in the shed. If you're adamant that tulips should be left to flower in the garden year after year, then plant them to a depth of 22cm (9in), which makes them more reliably perennial.

- It's no good thinking you can leave spring bulbs in ground where you want to plant summer bedding, or even between conifers or rhododendrons, which you may need to water in a dry spell – the bulbs won't like being wet when they should be dry, and rotting is the usual outcome.

- The other spring bulbs you really must dig up, dry off and store are any that you've grown in containers as spring bedding. You'll need the container for something else virtually as soon as the flowers are over. In this case, don't wait for the leaves to die down – dig them up and replant them temporarily in a spare patch of ground down the garden until they're fully dormant, then dig them up again, twist off the dead foliage and store them as usual. They'll stay in store happily until autumn, when it's time to replant them.

TIDY UP PERENNIALS AFTER FLOWERING
- Cut back and divide spring-flowering perennials if you didn't last month (see May, p.129).

- Remove old flower stems of hellebores. Collect and sow hellebore seeds as you go.

- Cut back oriental poppies once they've flowered.

- Once the flowers of *Euphorbia characias* subsp. *wulfenii* are completely over, you need to cut the old flowered stems right back close to the ground, to prevent the clumps from getting congested with dead stems. Leave the young stems, that is those without a dead flowerhead at the tip, since those are the ones that'll carry next year's flowers. Take great care in pruning this plant, since the sap tends to squirt out, and it's nasty stuff you don't want getting on your skin, and especially not in your eyes.

PLANT OUT SUMMER BEDDING PLANTS
Continue planting out summer bedding plants and water regularly.

PLANT OUT CANNAS AND LILIES
Bulbs of cannas and lilies that were potted up earlier in the season can be planted out now.

Hellebores start turning brown and unsightly by the summer, so remove faded flowers and save seeds.

Dealing with naturalized bulb foliage
As long as the required 6 weeks have gone by since the bulbs finished flowering, you can now chop down bulb foliage or run the mower over areas of lawn with bulbs naturalized in them without causing problems.

SOW BIENNIALS

Biennials are flowers that grow one year and flower the next. They include foxgloves (*Digitalis*), Canterbury bells (*Campanula medium*), evening primrose (*Oenothera biennis*), sweet Williams (*Dianthus barbatus*), *Campanula pyramidalis*, *Verbena bonariensis* and honesty (*Lunaria annua*), and although they are often thought of as 'old fashioned', they are very useful for filling all sorts of gaps in any garden. A lot of them flower in that awkward 'pause' between the last of the spring flowers and the first of the summer ones, and several are brilliant for cutting.

- Sow biennials now in a vacant row in the vegetable patch, or make a small nursery bed for them down the garden. Prepare the ground and sow the seed in shallow drills, sprinkling them as thinly as possible – it's just like sowing veg (see March, p.68).

Many biennials, like these sweet williams, are at their best in early summer.

- When the seedlings come up, thin them out to about 8–10cm (3–4in) apart. Keep them watered and weeded, and watch out for the usual summer plague of slugs and snails (see May, pp. 125 and 137). Treat the young plants to an occasional dose of dilute liquid tomato feed, say every 2–3 weeks.

- By late summer or early autumn they'll be ready to transplant to their flowering positions. You'll have all the plants you can use for the price of a packet of seeds and it's not as if it's hard work – a few hours is all it takes.

SOW LATE SUMMER BEDDING FOR AUTUMN COLOUR

Now that the seasons have altered, summer often goes on longer and the first proper frost may not happen until as late as mid-November, so you can easily be left with a long gap in your flowering schedule at the end of the season. That's why it's often worth sowing some hardy or half-hardy annual seeds early this month, to flower from August onwards. Good, fast-growing annuals include clarkia, limnanthes, candytuft and calendula. It's especially worthwhile if you take your summer holidays in August, as it means you come home to a new batch of bedding just coming into flower, ready to give your jaded borders a new lease of life – you could have another 2 months of colour to come.

- Sow late annuals in the same way as biennials (see above), in a spare patch of ground down the garden, and thin them out and feed them as for biennials. They grow much faster than early, indoor-sown ones. When they're big enough, dig them up and move them to their flowering positions; apart from watering, they are no trouble in the meantime.

SOW FLOWERS FOR CUTTING OR DRYING

If you want flowers for cutting, such as ostrich-plume asters (*Callistephus chinensis*), or everlasting flowers such as helichrysum (*Bracteantha*) or helipterum (*Rhodanthe*) for drying, then now is a good time to sow them outdoors. Given our current longer summers, you can produce a useful crop without a greenhouse or heated propagator.

- Sow the seed in rows wherever you have a patch of well-prepared ground to spare, in the vegetable garden or a proper 'cutting garden'. Thin them out and leave them to grow and flower where they are – they'll grow much faster if you don't transplant them at all. Prepare the ground and sow seed thinly *in situ*, as if you were planting veg (see March, p.68). Thin out to 10 or 15cm (4 or 6in), depending on the growth habit of the individual type of plant; some are bushier and others more upright. Keep them weeded and watered as for veg, then pick when at the appropriate stage for drying.

- When it comes to harvesting, they won't be as early as flowers sown under glass in spring and planted out in May, but this way you avoid most of the work and instead of picking in fits and starts all summer, you'll be able to do a few bulk swoops towards the end of the season – great if you want to do your dried flower harvest all at once, or if you are growing for a special event in late summer.

SOW WINTER AND SPRING BEDDING
Winter and early spring bedding also need sowing now.

Wallflowers
Wallflowers (*Erysimum cheiri*) are particularly easy to raise as they are actually biennials, so just treat them in the same way as the summer-flowering sort (see p.164). Thin the seedlings out to 8–10cm (3–4in) apart, and by transplanting time in autumn they will make good bushy plants – any that look a bit spindly or tall and skinny need their growing tips nipped out to make them branch.

Sowing bedding in pots
Most plants used as winter and spring bedding need sowing in pots, since their seeds are either very small or very expensive; by giving

them a touch more individual care you can really make every seed count. This group includes double forms of *Bellis perennis* daisies, Brompton stocks (*Matthiola incana*), polyanthus, coloured primroses, winter-flowering pansies and ornamental cabbages and kales.

- To sow winter and spring bedding seed in pots, follow the instructions given in March (p.73), but instead of putting the pots in a heated propagator, stand them in a shady cold frame, on a shelf in the porch, in the carport or on a windowsill in the shed – somewhere safe, and as long as there's light but not direct sunlight. The greenhouse or conservatory are going to be a bit too hot for them right now. Once the plants are big enough to stand up for themselves, the pots can be placed out in a semi-shady spot in the garden, but again watch out for slugs and snails; it's always small seedlings they go for first.

SOW SEED OF HARDY HERBACEOUS PERENNIALS
At this time of year, it's usually most convenient to sow perennials outside in a seedbed (see March, p.62–3). Alternatively, if you want, hardy perennials can be sown in pots now, then pricked out into pots and raised in a cold frame or on a sand bed, although it makes extra work that you can usually do without once the summer is under way, and it's not really necessary to go to so much trouble in summer.

TAKE CUTTINGS FROM SHORT-LIVED PERENNIALS
Some perennial plants are notoriously short lived, particularly pinks, border carnations and wallflowers. These need propagating every few years so you have a supply of young plants to replace the old ones before they give up the ghost.

Seeds of winter bedding plants can be germinated on a shelf in the garden shed.

HOW TO PROPAGATE PINKS

1 Tug out as many pink pipings as you need – they are normally 8–12cm (3–5in) long, depending on the vigour of the variety (see box below).

2 Pull the leaves from the bottom half or two-thirds of the cutting, then dib five or six cuttings in around the edge of a 10cm (4in) pot filled with seed compost mixed with a little silver sand to improve the drainage.

3 After watering the cuttings in, stand the pot on a shady windowsill indoors, or in a porch or sunroom, and keep an eye on them. Water them just enough to stop the compost from drying out.

4 After about 8 weeks they should be rooted well enough to pot individually. When you pot them, nip out the growing tip at the end of each shoot to encourage the young plants to start branching, or they can become straggly.

Knives for cuttings
When taking cuttings, a sharp penknife kept specially for the job or a craft knife with a disposable blade are ideal.

Pinks and border carnations

Left to their own devices, most pinks are only at their peak for about 3–4 years. Once the original plants become very woody, with little or no new growth and not many flowers, they simply 'fade away', and by that time you've left it too late to take cuttings. The trick is to propagate them before you really need to. Cuttings root best from parent plants that are 2–3 years old, while they are still producing plenty of strong young shoots.

Wallflowers

Perennial wallflowers, such as *Erysimum* 'Bowles Mauve' and the double wallflowers *Erysimum cheiri* 'Bloody Warrior' and *Erysimum cheiri* 'Harpur Crewe', for instance, need propagating every 2–3 years. They root easily enough from softwood cuttings, as for pelargoniums and fuchsias (see pp.170 and 171), taken now.

TAKE CUTTINGS FROM ROCK PLANTS

Now that the majority of rock plants have finished flowering, they will be starting to produce stocky new shoots that make perfect propagation material. Even though adult rock plants like sunny, well-drained conditions, cuttings root best in slightly shadier and more humid conditions. Avoid watering them more than you have to – ideally the compost should stay just moist, no more. At this time of year, cuttings of most rock plants will be rooted and ready for potting after 8 weeks or so, but wait until you see them start to grow.

● In the case of aubrieta, clip the plants over lightly to tidy them up once the flowers are over, and about 6 weeks later you'll find masses of fresh, new, non-flowered shoots about 2.5–4cm (1–1½in) long. Snip off as many as you need, remove the leaves from the

---

PINK PIPINGS
Pinks are some of the easiest plants to grow but they do tend to become tired quite quickly. , like all the rest, is best renewed from pipings every two or three years, so that plants are always youthful and vigorous.

bottom half of the shoot, and dib each cutting to half its depth into a pot of seed compost.

● For miniature shrubs and other bushy rock plants, cut off new, non-flowered shoots about 2.5–4cm (1–1½in) long (no clipping is necessary). Prepare the cuttings and root them in the same way as for aubrieta, but add about 25 per cent silver sand or potting grit to the seed compost to open up the texture and improve drainage.

● With rosette-forming plants, such as saxifrages, sempervivums and sedums, use as cuttings non-flowered rosettes that appear naturally around the collars of plants. Remove a few lower leaves and push several in around the edge of a pot of gritty compost to take root. In some cases, you'll find rosettes have already formed small roots of their own, so just ease them carefully out of the soil. They're what we call 'Irishman's cuttings', which means cuttings that are already semi-rooted. They can be potted individually in small pots, but since they don't have a lot of root it pays to treat them like normal cuttings until they have formed a good potful.

PATIOS AND CONTAINERS

BRING OUT CONTAINERS AND HANGING BASKETS

If you planted up your containers and hanging baskets early and kept them under glass to protect the plants from frost, and if you didn't bring them out in May, you can bring them out now.

PLANT UP CONTAINERS AND HANGING BASKETS

If you didn't plant up half-hardy annuals and tender perennials last month, you can plant them up now that the danger of frost has passed.

CONTAINER AFTERCARE

The big job from now through the summer is keeping on top of watering and feeding, but it pays to keep pace with the weather. It's worth looking after containers, because regular care keeps the same set of plants looking superb right up until the first frosts, which these days may not be until October or November. I call that darn good value.

Pelargoniums and argyranthemums can flower from one end of summer to the other in patio containers.

When to water and feed

When containers are first planted and the summer hasn't really got going, you'll probably only need to water every 2 or 3 days. In fact, overwatering can be a problem when the weather is dull and plants aren't growing very much – but check anyway. Do the finger test – prod, and if the compost feels like a well-wrung-out flannel it's fine; if it feels at all dusty then it needs watering. You won't need to start feeding containers for 4 weeks after they are planted up; there are enough nutrients in the compost to last until then.

Towards the end of June, as the weather warms up and the plants are growing faster and filling the containers, they'll start to need more 'life support'. You may need to water every day, and liquid feed every week or two, depending on the weather.

Right: Keep on top of hoeing in the vegetable garden.

Deadhead flowers

Once the first flush of flowers comes to an end you'll also need to start deadheading. Get into the habit of giving containers a good going-over at least once a week. By preventing the plants from setting seed you encourage them to try harder, which means they keep producing new buds and more flowers. Don't just tug off the actual heads, because that leaves a sea of stalks that doesn't look very attractive; instead, nip off the flower complete with its stem, as close as you can to where it joins the main plant.

Herbs make practical as well as ornamental container plants.

PLANT HERBS IN CONTAINERS

Now the last frost is well past, it's safe to plant cold-sensitive herbs such as basil outside; they make good plants for containers and many people prefer a hanging basket or tub of mixed herbs outside the back door to a container of bedding plants. You can have the best of both worlds by putting edible flowers, such as heartsease or borage, into an 'edible' container with a few favourite herbs and some decorative cut-and-come again lettuce such as 'Red Salad Bowl'.

VEGETABLES AND HERBS

KEEP UP WITH THE VEGETABLE PATCH

As you use early crops, spaces start appearing in the vegetable patch. Don't leave the ground empty for long. Each time you finish a row of lettuce or radishes, clear out all the old roots and leaves, sprinkle a handful of organic general fertilizer along each metre (3ft) of row and work it in, then sow or plant your next crop. Keep watering young vegetables and hoe regularly.

SOW VEGETABLES

All the usual salads and mainstream summer roots can still be sown now: lettuce, rocket, spring onion, radish, maincrop carrots, peas and swedes, and you can also still sow witloof chicory, as well as endive and hearting varieties of chicory, such as radicchio, and calabrese. (For further information on sowing and thinning, see April, pp.97–9.)

Oriental leaves

The big new addition to the veg-sowing list for this month are oriental leaves. They include Chinese cabbage, pak choi and unusual leaf crops such as red mustard – if you sow them too soon you are just asking for them to bolt, but now and July are perfect.

A few varieties, such as mizuna and mibuna, are non-hearting types that keep growing well into the winter if you cover them with cloches once the weather turns colder; and if you're looking for something a bit different, particularly if you are a fan of salads or stir-fries, then it's well worth giving them a go.

● Sow the seed thinly in rows, and when the seedlings are 2.5cm (1in) or so high start thinning them out – the thinnings are brilliant for adding to salads, so don't let them go to waste. As the crops grow, continue thinning them out in easy stages, until they end up about 15–20cm (6–8in) apart, depending on the ultimate size of the variety. They'll be ready to use in August or September.

PLANT OUT AND DIRECT-SOW FROST-TENDER VEGETABLES

Plant out frost-tender vegetables, including outdoor tomatoes and cucumbers, if you haven't already done so. You can also sow seeds of the others – sweetcorn, French and runner beans, courgettes, squashes and pumpkins – straight into the ground (see May, pp.135–8).

HARVEST YOUR HOME-GROWN VEG

The great thing about having your own vegetable plot is that the harvest festival continues all summer long, and each month

that goes by adds to the list of fresh home-grown food you can pick and put on your table. This month you can harvest early potatoes, overwintering onions and the last of the asparagus, as well as lettuce, calabrese, rocket, radishes, spring onions, peas and globe artichokes at the end of the month.

Early potatoes

Your first new potatoes are the big treat this month, but how do you tell when they are ready to eat without digging the whole plant up to take a look? Easy – cheat. Rummage around in the soil with your fingers. You'll soon be able to feel the fledgling spuds. If they are anything from pigeon's-egg size upwards, winkle out the biggest to eat now and leave the rest where they are to keep growing. It's amazing how quickly new potatoes start to 'bulk up', and after a few weeks of pinching the odd few spuds you can dig up a plant at a time. Work a fork well down under the plant to 'lift' it, complete with roots and spuds, and then forage gently around in the soil so you don't leave half the crop behind. When you reach the end of the row, re-use the space to grow something else ASAP.

Harvesting 'Lollo Rossa' – an ornamental lettuce with frilly, red-tinged leaves.

Some early potatoes will be ready for harvesting now.

Overwintering onions can be harvested now.

Overwintering onions

Overwintering onions will be ready for using this month. These are the onions that were planted last autumn (see September, p.233), which have grown slowly right through the winter and are now smallish but perfectly acceptable early-season onions. Don't wait for the leaves to turn yellow, because these aren't the sort of onions you can keep. No, overwintering onions are specially designed to fill the gap between the last of the stored onions and the first of the new maincrop batch. So any time you need an onion, just raid your veg patch, taking them fresh from the ground starting with the biggest first. Aim to clear the last of them no later than the middle of August, when your main crop of onions is ready. The sooner they are out, the sooner you can use the space for something else.

Asparagus

This is your last chance to harvest asparagus. Picking should stop in the middle of June. Asparagus is a perennial plant that relies on its leaves to make carbohydrate, which is stored in its thick, fleshy roots to see it through winter and fuel next year's crop, so if you don't leave the 'fern' to grow from now until the end of the summer, you've shot yourself in the foot. Meanwhile, sprinkle a few handfuls of general-purpose organic fertilizer along each side of the rows to give the plants a boost.

PROTECT YOUNG BRASSICAS AGAINST BIRDS

Protect newly planted brassicas from pigeons, if they are troublesome in your area, by putting a framework of canes around the plants and draping strawberry or fruit-cage type netting over the top. If you do a good job of it, leaving no gaps, it'll also keep out cabbage white butterflies so you'll also save yourself a lot of caterpillar-picking later.

Right: Thin out the fruits on apple trees now so that they are spaced 10cm (4in) apart.

FRUIT

TREE MAINTENANCE

Keep all fruit trees and bushes well watered in dry spells to prevent the developing fruit being shed prematurely. Continue rubbing out unwanted shoots on wall-trained fruit (see April, p.106).

PLUMS, APPLES AND PEARS

- Thin heavy crops of plums early in the month to prevent branches breaking. After the June drop (when small fruits fall naturally to thin the crop), thin again in July if it seems necessary. This is a good technique to stop Victoria plums from falling into the common habit of carrying very heavy crops one year and nothing the next.

- After the June drop, thin out apples and pears if they have set very heavy crops. With cordon, espalier or step-over trees reduce the fruit to no more than one per 10cm (4in) of branch.

- Put up pheromone traps to protect plums and apples against codling moth if not done before (see May, p.139).

• If fan-trained apple or pear trees have been neglected, now is the time to prune them. Don't try to over-complicate the issue, simply cut out any bushy stems sticking out from the framework of branches towards the path, taking care to avoid those parts of the branch structure carrying fruit.

PICK STRAWBERRIES

Strawberries are a real treat this month; it's a fair bet that the early ones that were brought on in the greenhouse or under cloches will be ready in time for Wimbledon Week, with the outdoor crop following on a week or two after that, depending on the weather.

When you pick strawberries, don't just pull the fruit off their stalks leaving the calyxes attached to the plants – that leaves tiny traces of fruit behind, which attracts grey mould that spreads to the remaining fruit. Nip off strawberries complete with a short stalk. And you'll find the fruit stays fresher if you keep it in the fridge for a day or two before you eat it.

In the event of a rainy spell around strawberry-picking time, keep a close watch for grey mould, and pick any affected fruit before it spreads to the others. It can wipe out a whole year's work if you let it.

HARVEST RHUBARB

Continue pulling sticks of rhubarb until the end of the month, then let the plants grow naturally to recover their strength.

PROTECT REDCURRANTS

Birds love redcurrants and will go for them more so than any other fruit except strawberries, so drape the plants with bird netting as soon as the first fruits start to show the first hint of colour.

• Use a heavy-duty natural fibre netting or high-tech cellulose threads, which look like white synthetic 'blanket weed', which you open out to cover fruit bushes in a bird-proof 'spider's web' (available from specialist organic gardening catalogues). Don't use thin plastic netting, which often traps birds by the legs, making them an easy meal for a passing predator.

• If you don't mind the idea of birds taking part of your crop, then hang up some old CDs, tin cans or strips of tin foil, which flash and bang in the sun and wind, and will frighten birds off – until they get used to them. Personally, I'm quite prepared to share, for the fun of watching the birds' antics.

EARLY GOOSEBERRIES

Gooseberries are still small, green and under-ripe, so birds won't bother about them, yet. But if you want an early gooseberry pie you can thin the crop out now and cook the small fruit you remove, with plenty of sugar – they'll taste quite sharp. This is a particularly good idea if you grow dessert gooseberries such as the popular red variety 'Whinham's Industry'. The idea here is to thin the crop so that you have fewer but fatter gooseberries, which you leave hanging on the bush to ripen fully and eat raw as fresh fruit towards the end of July. If you've never thought about dessert gooseberries, they are well worth it – they are a real dual-purpose fruit so you get two bites of the cherry, if you see what I mean.

A fruit cage is the only reliable method of protecting currant bushes and raspberries from birds.

Washing strawberries
Don't wash strawberries unless you have to. They taste much better eaten as nature intended, straight from the plant. To stop the fruit being splashed with mud, and prevent grey mould, put down strawberry mats or lay straw under developing trusses of fruit (see May, p.138).

UNDER COVER

GREENHOUSE MAINTENANCE
Damp the greenhouse down regularly, and apply a second coat of shading paint if it is very hot (see May, p.140).

PLANT AFTERCARE
Water and feed plants regularly (see p.141).

POTTING UP AND POTTING ON
Continue to pot up rooted cuttings (see April, p.109) and pot on any remaining young plants and seedlings (see April, p.109).

SOW WINTER AND EARLY SPRING BEDDING PLANTS
Winter and early spring bedding plants may be sown in pots or trays under glass (see Flowers, p.161).

Sprinkle water over the greenhouse floor to reduce the temperature and increase humidity.

SOW CINERARIA AND CALCEOLARIA
Now is the time to sow cineraria and calceolaria for Christmas-flowering pot plants. They aren't the easiest things to grow, as you have to be unbelievably accurate over watering – not enough and the plants keel over; too much and they wither away. But if you get it right you'll feel justifiably pleased with yourself.

● Sow the seeds very thinly on the surface of a fine layer of horticultural vermiculite sprinkled over a potful of seed compost, and keep in a cool place out of bright light, such as a shady spare bedroom indoors; the greenhouse and most windowsills are far too hot and bright. When the seedlings are big enough, prick them out into individual pots and grow them on in a cool, shady sand bed, protecting them from pests, particularly slugs and snails. If all goes well, pot them on into 12cm (5in) pots when they fill the originals with roots later in the summer, usually around September.

TAKE CUTTINGS FROM TENDER PERENNIALS
Pelargoniums, fuchsias and all sorts of half-hardy plants root very easily from cuttings taken any time between May and mid-September, but if you want spare plants to give away to visitors, it's a good idea to have some on the go now – most kinds take about 6 weeks to root and another 2–4 weeks to turn into a young plant similar to the sort you'd buy at a garden centre.

If you've never tried rooting cuttings before, pelargoniums and fuchsias are very good plants to cut your teeth on, because they root easily and grow fast. Once you have learnt the technique on these (see box opposite), you can apply it to anything else that can be rooted from softwood cuttings. I always think of them as the perfect plant propagator's apprenticeship.

TAKE CUTTINGS FROM SHORT-LIVED PERENNIALS AND ROCK PLANTS
Propagate short-lived perennials and rock plants by taking cuttings (see Flowers, p.161).

WATERING POT PLANTS

I'm a great believer in giving pot plants individual attention but it does take time, and if you have a struggle to keep up with watering in summer, then it may be worth putting in capillary matting or an irrigation system. If you're going to put in an irrigation system, I'd suggest you put it in at the start of the summer so you have time to sort out any little teething troubles before it's too late.

Capillary matting

Hot weather means pot plants need a lot more watering, and if hand watering takes too long then it's often helpful to lay capillary matting – a fibrous water-holding 'blanket' – all over the staging, and stand the plants on that. As long as you start the ball rolling by watering the plants well first, all you need to do from then on is to damp over the matting every morning with a watering can or hose, and plants can draw up what they need.

If you use capillary matting, you'll still need to apply liquid feed to each pot through a can – if you simply let it soak into the matting it encourages algae to grow, and in no time your pristine sheet of matting is a sea of heaving green gunge.

Irrigation system

There are various types of irrigation system, but the one that works best in the greenhouse consists of a main 'feeder' pipe that connects to your garden hose, from which small-bore tubes lead off to dripper nozzles, which you station alongside individual plants in the greenhouse border or stick on spikes in pots. You can also set them up so as to keep capillary matting damp. It's very easy to connect the entire system to a timer attached to your outdoor tap and set the lot to turn itself on and off automatically, which is great if you're going away for a few days and don't want to bother a neighbour.

However, don't think you can just set the greenhouse to 'automatic pilot' and forget about it – you'll still need to feed plants by hand, and you do need to cast an eye around regularly to check that everything is working, because you sometimes find a nozzle blocks or a pipe kinks or something springs a leak. But if you are really pushed, it can make the difference between being able to cope and letting plants die.

HOW TO TAKE SOFTWOOD CUTTINGS FROM TENDER PERENNIALS, E.G. PELARGONIUMS AND FUCHSIAS

1 Select a strong, healthy shoot, about 8–10cm (3–4in) long for pelargoniums and 2.5–5cm (1–2in) for fuchsias. Snip the shoot cleanly from the parent plant with a sharp knife, then remove the lower leaves. Cut off the base of the stem cleanly immediately below the lowest leaf joint.

2 Dip the end of the cutting in rooting powder, which contains fungicide to help prevent rot and plant hormones to encourage roots to form quickly.

3 Tap the surplus rooting powder off, then with a pencil or dibber, insert the cutting into a pot of seed compost, to about half its length. If you have several cuttings of the same variety, dib five in around the edge of a 10cm (4in) pot. Water them in well, and label with the name of the variety.

4 Fuchsias and other thin-leaved plants need humidity, so slip the pot inside a large, loose plastic bag. Naturally drought-tolerant plants, such as pelargoniums, prefer to be left in the open air to root. Stand the pots in a shady place with a constant temperature, e.g. a north-facing windowsill indoors. Check cuttings after 6–8 weeks; when rooted, pot up each one individually (see April, p.109).

PLANT NEW CROPS

There's still time to plant summer greenhouse crops such as peppers, cucumbers, tomatoes, melons and aubergines, and in a cold northern area June is actually the best time to put them in if you don't have heating, as the weather is warmer. But I wouldn't want to leave it later than the middle of the month, otherwise you may be pushing your luck to ripen tomatoes and melons by the end of the summer, and slow-growing peppers and aubergines may not have enough growing time to produce a worthwhile crop.

CARING FOR CROPS

Greenhouse crops planted in May will be growing away well by now, and need regular attention. Feed everything with organic liquid tomato feed once a week, and water regularly – increase the frequency as the weather warms up and the plants grow larger, as they'll need it.

- Keep tying in the new growth of tomato plants to upright canes, and pinching out sideshoots before they get out of control (see May, p.141).

- Continue pollinating melons to ensure the fruit sets, but prevent cucumbers from being pollinated by removing the male flowers, or they'll develop hard seeds inside and taste bitter (see May, p.142).

Tomatoes are often easier to water if a plastic flower pot is sunk into the earth alongside them – then the water and feed can go straight to the roots instead of running off the surface.

A pond has a soothing effect on a garden and provides another habitat, where you can enjoy watching fish and other wildlife.

WATER GARDEN

ENJOY THE POND

June is very much the time to keep a watching brief on ponds. No, it's not a case of looking out for likely jobs to do – it's the season for sitting and enjoying the sheer tranquillity of water. It's what ponds are for. So sit back and study the wildlife, the fish, and the pattern made by the fountain spraying onto the water's surface.

POND MAINTENANCE

Continue removing blanket weed and duckweed, and thinning excess oxygenators (see May, pp.145–6).

INTRODUCE NEW FISH

If you want to put some new fish into the pond, now is a good time to do it as the risk from herons is at an all-time low in summer, and fish 'move' best once the water temperature has risen and the pond ecology has had a chance to sort itself out. You can introduce both large fish and also the small ones, 2.5cm (1in) or so long, which don't have a good survival rate if you try and shift them too early in the season while the water is still cold. For details on introducing new fish to a pond, see May, p.146.

PROJECT Glamorize the garden

When you have been to all the trouble to create a good-looking garden, you need an excuse to show it off once in a while. Have a few friends round for a sit-down dinner on the patio. These days it's increasingly popular to hold full-blown family birthday celebrations in the garden in summer, with a mini-marquee and all the trimmings.

The great thing is to have the garden looking its very best for the occasion, which means starting work well in advance.

As early as possible:
- Plant shortly-to-flower bedding to fill gaps in beds and borders, plant some extra-special containers for key places round the house and garden.
- If your event is this month, your newly planted summer bedding plants may not be at their best in time, so plant tubs and hanging baskets early and bring them on under glass, or make use of pot chrysanths, spider plant, kangaroo vine and other tough indoor plants for spectacular instant outdoor containers.
- Plan a few special attractions, like scented corners or containers planted in the theme of the occasion, such as yellow flowers for a golden wedding.

Four weeks from the off:
- Feed the lawn, assuming conditions are suitable.
- Take out weeds by hand, or use a combined weed and feed treatment if you aren't 100 per cent organic. Water well two days later if it hasn't rained.
- Keep on top of mowing and hedge cutting.

A few days beforehand:
- For an evening party use marker lights to edge paths and steps for safety and to illuminate the outline of the garden.
- Use spotlights to light up focal points or special features of the garden.
- Light up garden seats, the gazebo, and the area where you'll be serving food and drink and sitting to eat. Remember to test all new lights thoroughly.

At the last minute:
- Mow and edge the lawn.
- Give hedges a final trim.
- Pressure wash paving and patio and arrange containers attractively.
- Give beds and containers a last tidy up.
- Weed paths and rake gravel to remove footprints.

Have fun!

Afterwards the thing that will have suffered most is the lawn, so after clearing up:
- Spike well-trodden areas of the lawn well with a fork to aerate the soil.
- If the weather is on the dry side give it a good watering if you can, subject to hosepipe regulations, but if the ground is reasonably moist apply a weak liquid feed.
- Try to keep off it as much as you can for a few weeks – with care it'll soon be back on its feet.

JULY

July is peak flowering time for most gardens. The garden is a paintbox of summer perennials, bedding plants are blooming fit to bust, and containers and hanging baskets are in full swing, so nothing else poses serious competition in the looks department. If you don't have a good show of flowers now, you're not trying. Annuals and perennials are out in force before summer heat and drought blunt the show, and the kitchen garden is reaching a crescendo of salads and summer vegetables. But over the horizon, the summer holidays are looming.

When you're preparing to leave your garden for a week or two, don't forget security. It's a good idea not to put containers of plants in the front garden – if they die when you're away, it will be obvious that you're not there to look after them, but it's just as obvious if they suddenly vanish to the back of the house. Make sure the lawn is cut and the beds weeded before you leave, pack all your garden tools and ladders away in the shed or garage, then lock the door. And lock your side gate if you have one.

THE BIG PICTURE flowers

Agapanthus (above) have an exotic, sunny look, with large, loose balls of blue or white blooms perched on strong, straight stems above strappy foliage. The huge African agapanthus that you see in the Channel Islands is a tad too tender to do well in the UK, although people *will* bring it back from their holidays, but there are a good many modern varieties that flower well here, even in an average summer. Some are quite compact, such as *Agapanthus* 'Lilliput', deep blue, 38 × 45cm (15 × 18in), which makes them good for growing in containers as well as planting out in borders.

PEAK SEASON July–September.
GROWING CONDITIONS Fertile, well-drained soil in a sunny, sheltered spot, or grow in large containers and move under cover for winter.

Lilium regale, the regal lily (above), is probably the best known of a large and lovely group of summer-flowering bulbs, many of which are strongly scented – this species is particularly heady of perfume. The large white, flared-trumpet flowers have yellow throats inside and maroonish stripes on the outside; they grow at the top of tall stems, which give them a natural leg-up in a busy border. Best grown in clumps (allow 10 × 45cm/4 × 18in) among shrubs or perennials, but like most lilies it's a bit fussy about its growing conditions.

PEAK SEASON July–August.
GROWING CONDITIONS Well-drained, fertile soil containing lots of organic matter, but not too chalky, in a sunny spot with roots shaded by surrounding plants.

Crocosmias, which we used to call montbretias many years ago, are clump-forming herbaceous perennials with long, grassy leaves and twin rows of tubular buds that open out into sprays of (usually) orange flowers. *Crocosmia* 'Lucifer' (above), 1.2 × 1m (4 × 3ft) is the tallest grower and the one you'll see on sale everywhere, with deep paprika-red flowers. 'Solfatare' has pale yellow flowers and is not far behind in the popularity stakes, but if you want to be cool go for the more unusual 'Emily McKenzie', whose flowers are orange with brownish throats, or 'Star of the East', which has huge, pale-curry-coloured flowers that open into wide-faced stars. 'Jackanapes' is a curiosity with alternate red and yellow petals, and 'Golden Fleece' is a lovely late-flowering yellow that keeps going long after the early varieties have faded. All these grow about 60cm (2ft) high in clumps that soon reach 45cm (18in) across.

PEAK SEASON July–August.
GROWING CONDITIONS Fertile, well-drained soil in sun with some shelter.

Penstemons (above) have spikes of colourful trumpet-shaped flowers that keep going all summer. They may look like old-fashioned cottage-garden flowers but they are great for mixing with grasses or exotic foliage plants, and are very easy-going. 'Blackbird' has deep purple flowers; 'Sour Grapes' is an unusual combination of blue, purple and grey, and 'Firebird' is startling scarlet. 'Andenken an Friedrich Hahn' (syn. *Penstemon* 'Garnet') is a rich wine red and stunning among frothy grasses. No garden should be without it. Hybrids like these grow about 60 × 45cm (24 × 18in). They are hardier than is often thought, but even so a lot of people like to keep cuttings under cover in winter as insurance, just in case a bad winter kills the original plants.

PEAK SEASON July–October.
GROWING CONDITIONS Well-drained, fertile soil in a sunny spot.

Lavenders are equally at home in an old-fashioned cottage garden, in a formal herb garden or a modern flowerbed. Short, dumpy kinds, such as *Lavandula angustifolia* 'Hidcote', violet flowers, 45 × 30cm (18 × 12in), make first-class dwarf flowering hedges for edging paths or borders, filling the whole garden with a hefty scent of the furniture polish your mum used to use. Small varieties of lavender will grow in pots if you are very careful about watering, because if they dry out badly just once they are impossible to resuscitate. Lavender flowers are good for cutting or drying; sachets of dried lavender heads tucked in drawers make a good grandmother's remedy against clothes' moths, which are making a comeback now that natural fibres are back in fashion. Both flowers and leaves of French lavender (*Lavandula stoechas* cultivars, above, 60 × 30cm/ 24 × 12in, whose flowers are topped with coloured 'wings') can be used as culinary herbs for a taste of Provence, although they don't have as much scent as other lavenders.

PEAK SEASON July–August.
GROWING CONDITIONS Well-drained, sunny spot with some shelter.

Fuchsias (above) are classics for containers – very reliable and long-flowering, with an enormous range of varieties with ballet-skirt or drop-earring shapes in endless colour combinations. There are upright varieties that grow naturally bushy, and trailing varieties that are best for hanging baskets. Patio plant specialists usually stock hundreds of different kinds, which you can often buy cheaply as rooted cuttings. The very large-flowered kinds, such as the **California Dreamers Series** often have flowers that are a bit frail for conditions outside – they do better in the warmth and shelter of a carport, greenhouse or porch.

PEAK SEASON July–October.
GROWING CONDITIONS Good, moist potting compost, in a sheltered situation shaded from strong midday sun, or in light shade.

Continental cascade pelargoniums (above) are improved versions of the old ivy-leaved pelargoniums, available in a wide range of colours. The petals are narrow but each plant carries so many flowers that it's almost impossible to see the leaves when they're planted in a windowbox or hanging basket. Famous for growing on Swiss chalets in holiday posters, they are one of the very best choices of summer bedding for containers in a hot, sunny spot where plants run the occasional risk of drying out.

PEAK SEASON July–October.
GROWING CONDITIONS Good soil-based potting compost, in a sunny place.

Cleome hassleriana (**syn.** *Cleome spinosa*), spider flower (above), is a most unusual half-hardy annual – once seen, never forgotten. The very upright 1m (3ft) stems are topped with a loose mound of pink, white or mauve flowers with long, spidery stamens sticking out all round. It goes well with other tall annuals, such as cosmos, and it's good for planting in natural-looking clumps in gaps in a border. One to get the neighbours talking.

PEAK SEASON July–October.
GROWING CONDITIONS Fertile, well-drained soil in a sunny, sheltered spot.

OLD FAITHFULS

Petunias (*Calibrachoa* – above) are firm favourites for hanging baskets, with large, flared saucers or frilly double rosette flowers. The **Surfinia Series** are very reliable, even in a slightly iffy summer, and they also have a surprisingly strong scent, although you'll only notice it when they are grown under cover or in a very sheltered corner. In a more exposed place, choose one of the small-flowered strains such as **Million Bells Series**, which stand up to the weather better. A good strain of petunia like these will keep flowering right through until the autumn, if you keep them well fed and watered and regularly deadheaded.

PEAK SEASON July–October.
GROWING CONDITIONS Moist potting compost, in a sheltered place shaded from strong midday sun. Also good in light shade under a gazebo or similar structure.

Passiflora caerulea, passionflower (above), is the ideal summer climber for a sunny wall – it'll cover an area up to 2.5 × 5m (8 × 15ft). It flowers for months, with large blue and white rosettes that are often followed by yellow egg-shaped fruits, which you can eat if you really must, but most people don't bother as they aren't a patch on proper passionfruit. The plant holds itself on to trellis by means of tendrils, so there's no need to keep it tied up, and although it is rumoured to be rather tender it's usually only the top that dies back in a hard winter, leaving the roots to produce new flowering stems the following year. In a mild winter it stays put and even retains its leaves.

PEAK SEASON July–October (flowers), September–November (fruit).
GROWING CONDITIONS Fertile, well-drained soil in full sun.

Hebe, or shrubby veronicas as they were once called, are summer-flowering shrubs with fluffy 'bottle-brush' flowers. The smaller species generally have rounded leaves and rounded heads of flower – they include the deservedly popular *Hebe* 'Autumn Glory', which grows 75 × 90cm (2½ × 3ft) and has purple-blue flowers from June to November, and the very dull but widely grown *Hebe pinguifolia* 'Pagei', about the same size but with grey leaves and white flowers. The larger species are much showier, with narrow leaves and long spikes of wispier flowers – they include *Hebe* 'Great Orme', which grows 1.2 × 1.2m (4 × 4ft) with 15cm (6in) pink bottle-brushes from July to October and 'Watson's Pink' (above), which grows to 1m (3ft) high, with pink flowers fading to white in June and July. Hebes are often thought to be unreliably hardy, but as a general rule the smaller the leaves the tougher the plant. When grown by the seaside they are capable of withstanding much windier conditions than they put up with inland.

PEAK SEASON July–October.
GROWING CONDITIONS Not too fertile, well-drained soil in sun.

Buddleja davidii is the butterfly bush, which is smothered in colourful fluttering insects most of the time the long ice-cream-cone-shaped heads of flower are in bloom. Most varieties make big shrubs 2.5 × 1.8m (8 × 6ft) or more; 'Black Knight' (above) is the old favourite, with deep purple flowers; 'Royal Red' has dark mauve flowers; 'Harlequin' has mauve flowers and variegated leaves; 'Nanho Blue' is good for a smaller garden, as it grows about 60cm (2ft) less all round than other varieties, and *Buddleja* 'Lochinch' is useful in that it flowers rather later than the rest, producing its pale violet flower spikes in late summer and autumn. Buddleias need hard annual pruning or they soon look straggly and grow half as big again.

PEAK SEASON July–September.
GROWING CONDITIONS Well-drained soil in sun.

SOMETHING SPECIAL

Hydrangeas come in two sorts, the familiar mop-heads or Hortensias, with an entire dome of flowers forming the head, and Lacecaps (above), with a ring of flowers around the edge and sterile florets in the centre. *Hydrangea macrophylla* 'Mariesii Perfecta' (syn. *H.m.* Blue Wave') is a reliable blue that changes to a good pink when grown on alkaline soil. *Hydrangea macrophylla* 'King George' has red flowers that fade to cherry with green highlights. Hydrangea flowers are good for cutting, but will dry attractively on the plant and persist until the papery petals are blown away in autumn gales. Expect plants to make 1.2 × 1.2m (4 × 4ft).

PEAK SEASON July–September.
GROWING CONDITIONS Moist, fertile soil containing plenty of organic matter in sun or light shade. Red varieties need alkaline soil and blue varieties need acid to keep their colour; on the wrong type of soil some varieties will change colour completely, while others simply turn a muddy in-between mauve. White hydrangeas aren't fussy but are best on neutral soil. Grow blue hydrangeas in tubs of ericaceous compost to keep them blue if you have the wrong soil.

Ceanothus, Californian lilacs (above), are some of the most glamorous shrubs you can grow, with their big heads of fluffy blue flowers. They really do come from California, so they need planting in conditions as close to Californian as you can manage. Evergreen varieties mostly flower earlier in the season, but deciduous kinds flower from now until autumn. The best of the lot is *Ceanothus × delileanus* 'Gloire de Versailles', 1.8 × 1.8m (6 × 6ft), a deciduous type with enormous heads of powdery blue flowers, exactly the same shade as a summer sky when the sun shines. With this on your patio, you could almost be in Hollywood.

PEAK SEASON July–October.
GROWING CONDITIONS Well-drained, sunny but sheltered spot; train flat against a south-facing wall if in any doubt.

Solanum crispum 'Glasnevin', the Chilean potato vine (above), fools a lot of people. Its bunches of small, pointed, lilac and yellow flowers look exactly as if an errant potato plant has suddenly decided to shin up your wall. Although it belongs to the same family, there aren't any tasty tubers buried underground (well, someone *always* asks). The leaves look nothing like spud foliage, and the stems belong to quite a large scrambling plant, 5 × 5m (15 × 15ft). This species is the hardiest of the potato vines. The white-flowered *Solanum laxum* 'Album' (syn. *S. jasminoides* 'Album') looks terribly classy, but can't be relied on to make it through winter unless you have a very favoured spot.

PEAK SEASON July–September.
GROWING CONDITIONS Well-drained soil against a sunny wall.

OTHER PLANTS IN THEIR PRIME IN JULY

- **Trees** *Aesculus indica, Catalpa bignonioides, Eucryphia*
- **Shrubs** *Abelia chinensis, Aesculus parviflora, Colutea arborescens, Cornus florida, Cornus kousa, Cytisus, Deutzia, Fuchsia* (hardy), *Indigofera heterantha, Leycesteria formosa, Philadelphus* (see p.152), *Phygelius, Potentilla fruticosa* (see p.152), *Rosa* (see pp.150–1), *Spiraea japonica* 'Anthony Waterer'
- **Evergreens** *Ceanothus* 'Autumnal Blue', *Cistus, Daboecia, Desfontainea spinosa, Erica cinerea, Escallonia, Gaultheria procumbens, Hypericum calycinum, Hypericum* 'Hidcote', *Phlomis fruticosa, Prunus laurocerasus, Santolina chamaecyparissus, Spartium junceum, Teucrium fruticans, Vinca, Yucca filamentosa*
- **Climbers/wall shrubs** *Abutilon vitifolium, Actinidia deliciosa, Berberidopsis corallina, Eccremocarpus scaber, Clematis* 'Comtesse de Bouchaud', *Clematis* 'General Sikorski' (see p.152), *Clematis* 'Hagley Hybrid' (see p.152), *Clematis* 'Jackmanii' (see p.152), *Clematis* 'Mevrouw le Coultre', *Clematis* Texensis Group, *Clematis* 'The President', *Clematis* 'Ville de Lyon', *Clematis* Viticella Group (see pp.180 and 202), *Cytisus battandieri* (see p.154), *Fallopia baldschuanica, Fremontodendron californicum, Jasminum officinale, Hydrangea anomola* subsp. *petiolaris, Lonicera periclymenum* 'Belgica' (see p.121), *Lonicera periclymenum* 'Serotina', *Magnolia grandiflora*
- **Perennials** *Acanthus spinosus, Achillea filipendulina, Alchemilla mollis, Alstroemeria* (see p.154), *Anemone, Aruncus dioicus, Astilbe, Astrantia major, Campanula latifolia, Campanula lactiflora, Catananche caerulea, Centaurea dealbata, Centranthus ruber, Chrysanthemum maximum, Crambe cordifolia, Delphinium, Dianthus, Dicentra, Dictamnus albus, Echinops ritro, Erigeron, Eryngium, Euphorbia characias* subsp. *wulfenii, Geranium endressii, Geranium* 'Johnson's Blue', *Geranium × oxonianum* 'Wargrave Pink', *Geranium sanguineum, Geum* 'Mrs. J. Bradshaw' (see p.121), *Gypsophila paniculata, Helenium, Helianthus* (see p.202), *Hemerocallis, Heuchera, Iberis sempervirens, Kniphofia, Lavatera × clementii, Liatris, Ligularia, Lysimachia nummularia, Lysimachia punctata, Lythrum, Monarda, Nepeta, Paeonia, Persicaria affinis* (see p.200), *Phlox paniculata* (see p.200), *Platycodon grandiflorus, Potentilla, Primula florindae* (see p.155), *Prunella, Rheum palmatum, Rudbeckia, Salvia × superba, Scabiosa, × Solidaster, Stachys byzantina, Stipa* (see p.221), *Thalictrum dipterocarpum, Tiarella cordifolia, Verbascum, Veronica gentianoides, Veronica spicata* subsp. *incana*
- **Bulbs** *Allium, Begonia, Cardiocrinum giganteum, Dahlia* (see p.201), *Galtonia, Gladiolus, Lilium*
- **Bedding/patio plants** All summer bedding (hardy annuals and half-hardy annuals) and patio plants
- **Rock plants** *Acaena, Anacyclus pyrethrum* var. *depressus, Aster alpinus, Campanula, Convolvulus cneorum* (see p.154), *Dianthus, Dodecatheon meadia, Erigeron mucronatus, Gypsophila repens, Leontopodium alpinum, Lithodora diffusa, Mazus reptans, Penstemon pinifolius, Rhodohypoxis baurii, Sempervivum, Sisyrinchium, Thymus serpyllum, Veronica prostrata*

Trachelospermum asiaticum, star jasmine, is another slightly tender climber. Its special feature is a strong jasmine scent. The flowers are clusters of large, cream, single stars, which look good against the oval evergreen leaves. Grow it over an arch or pergola (it will eventually cover an area 5 × 5m/15 × 15ft) or on a wall around your patio doors, where you'll appreciate the scent most. The cream- and green-leaved *Trachelospermum jasminoides* (above) looks more spectacular but doesn't flower so freely or grow so vigorously, and it's a lot less hardy. My advice, if you fall for the variegated version, is to grow it in a large, wire-framed hanging basket, tying the stems around the outside so it makes a perfect sphere, and keep it in the conservatory in winter.

PEAK SEASON July–August.
GROWING CONDITIONS Fertile, well-drained, lime-free soil, in a sunny, sheltered spot.

***Clematis* 'Etoile Rose'** (above) is a beautiful Viticella clematis, with split-bell-shaped flowers of deep rose, edged with lighter pink. It is perfect for training up and over evergreen shrubs, where it will brighten their countenance in summer and can be cut to the ground in winter to reveal the evergreen's glory.

PEAK SEASON June–September.
GROWING CONDITIONS Cool, moist but well-drained soil (even over chalk) with its head in full sun.

JULY at-a-glance checklist

Romneya coulteri, the tree poppy (above), is a shrub that behaves like a herbaceous perennial, as it dies down in a cold winter. The attractive, glaucous-grey-green foliage makes you wonder if it's a peony when it appears in spring, but when the flowers appear in midsummer they open out into huge white, crinkly 'poppies' with a mass of golden stamens in the middle of each. Spectacular – but you need the right spot. Reaches 1.5 × 1m (5 × 3ft).

PEAK SEASON July–September.
GROWING CONDITIONS Very well-drained, sandy-ish soil, in sun with some shelter. When you find the right spot it will romp away; if you don't it will sulk.

GENERAL GARDEN TASKS (P.182)
✔ Prepare the garden if you are going away in the summer – water well, set up an automatic watering system, pick fruit and veg, feed greenhouse plants.

LAWNS (P.183)
✔ Raise the cutting height of the lawn mower blades during hot, dry spells when the grass is under stress to keep it green without watering.
✔ Avoid watering the lawn, except a new lawn in very long, dry spells.

TREES, SHRUBS AND CLIMBERS (P.184)
✔ Prune and deadhead roses.
✔ Prune philadelphus and wisteria.
✔ Clip privet and other fast-growing hedges such as *Lonicera nitida*.
✔ Continue taking softwood cuttings of shrubs.
✔ Take internodal cuttings of clematis.
✔ Cut lavender for drying.

FLOWERS (P.187)
✔ Deadhead bedding plants, perennials and roses, and cut out flowered stems of perennials such as lupins and delphiniums as they go over.
✔ Divide old clumps of bearded irises and replant.
✔ Cut and dry everlasting flowers.
✔ Feed herbaceous perennials.
✔ Save seeds from alpines, perennials and hardy cyclamen.
✔ Plant autumn-flowering bulbs.
✔ Deadhead, feed and water annuals and tender perennials regularly.
✔ Disbud tuberous begonias.

PATIOS AND CONTAINERS (P.189)
✔ Water, feed and deadhead container plants regularly.

VEGETABLES AND HERBS (P.190)
✔ Sow maincrop carrots, early peas, spring cabbage, kohl rabi, turnips, lettuce, radishes, endive, chicory, oriental leaves including Chinese cabbage and pak choi, winter radishes and spring cabbages.
✔ Keep vegetables well watered in dry spells.
✔ Harvest vegetables as soon as they are ready, although root crops can stay in the ground.

✔ 'Stop' outdoor tomatoes.
✔ Cut and dry or freeze herbs.

FRUIT (P.192)
✔ Tidy strawberry beds and grow spare strawberry plants from runners.
✔ Harvest raspberries, redcurrants, blackcurrants and gooseberries.
✔ Thin out fruit.

UNDER COVER (P.194)
✔ Keep on top of ventilating, watering and feeding, and apply another layer of shading paint if weather is very hot.
✔ Thin out seedlings of biennials and prick out winter/spring bedding and seedlings of plants sown earlier for winter-flowering pot plants.
✔ Train a standard fuchsia.
✔ Repot cyclamen corms saved from last winter and water very lightly to start back into growth.
✔ Water and feed greenhouse plants more often now the weather is hotter and the containers are filling with roots.
✔ Pick summer greenhouse crops regularly.

WATER GARDEN (P.196)
✔ Provide more oxygen if necessary by thinning waterweeds or running a fountain.
✔ Top up the pond when the water level drops due to evaporation in hot weather.
✔ Divide water irises.

Watch out for
● Containers drying out.
● Cabbage white butterflies laying eggs on brassica plants.
● Potato blight on potatoes and tomatoes.

Get ahead
● Order spring-flowering bulbs from mail-order magazines.

Last chance
● Plant out bargain-basement bedding plants early in the month. Garden centres will often be selling them off cheaply now.

GENERAL GARDEN TASKS

WATCH OUT FOR PESTS AND DISEASES

Keep on top of pests and diseases – with warm, wet weather these can multiply dramatically (see May, pp.125, 133–4 and 142–3).

GET ORGANIZED FOR YOUR SUMMER HOLIDAYS

A holiday lasting 2 or 3 weeks is a long time for the garden to get by without you, but you can minimize the effect of your annual exodus on the garden with a bit of advance preparation. Naturally, it's best if you can call on some help to take over essentials such as watering, but even if you can't there's still lots you can do now to avoid coming home to an abandoned garden (see box below).

If you're lucky enough to have a 'treasure' who regularly cuts your grass and tidies your borders, the obvious solution is to ask them to put in a few extra hours while you're away, and water your containers, vegetables, greenhouse and houseplants, as well as carry out their usual routine. It'll cost you, but it's worth it for the peace of mind.

Otherwise, cultivate a kind gardening friend or neighbour. There's a limit to what you can ask them to do, so leave having cut the lawn and got weeding bang up to date. Make things as easy for them to manage as possible – it's amazing the way simple jobs take twice as long when you do them in someone else's garden – so leave the hose out, lift down any hanging baskets that are out of reach, and group far-flung containers together to make them quicker to whip round. And don't forget to show your appreciation. The golden rules are – *always* let them use any fruit or veg that are ready while you are away, *always* bring them back a present, and *always* return the favour when they take their own holidays.

THE HOME-ALONE GARDEN

Leaving the garden to cope on its own doesn't have to be too much of a problem if you're organized about it, and put in a spot of last-minute effort before going away.

Lawns

Don't do anything that will encourage the grass to grow fast while you're away, so give summer feeding and watering a miss, and teach it to struggle.

Beds and borders

As long as all the exposed soil was well mulched in spring and you don't get plants used to regular watering, well-established shrubs and perennials won't suffer when you go away for a few weeks. The things that won't be happy if we don't have any rain are annual bedding plants, but you can reduce the risk by watering them very well just before you go.

Containers

These are the big problem, as they normally last only a few days at most without watering. The best solution if are going away in summer, is to have an automatic watering system that drips water to each tub, trough or hanging basket individually (see June, p.171). If you have no irrigation, then move all your containers to a cool, shady spot, stand them in saucers and give them a long drink before you go, or make your own emergency watering system (see Project, p.197).

Fruit and veg

Fruit isn't a problem if you holiday in August, since the soft fruit will have been picked before you go, and apples and pears, etc. won't be ready until after you get back. If you holiday in July, then encourage friends and neighbours to pick and enjoy your soft fruits while you're away. With veg, water everything very well before you go and hope for the best. Pick as much as you can a day or two before you go, and what you can't use, freeze or give away. It does pay to plan your veg patch with the holiday season in mind, so you stop sowing or planting fast-growing crops, such as lettuce, 8 weeks before you go away. Then there's nothing to ruin while you aren't there.

Greenhouse plants

When you know you always go away in summer, don't risk growing summer crops such as tomatoes, peppers and aubergines in pots or growing bags. Grow them in the greenhouse border soil, where they have a huge root-run, with lots of organic matter. Give them a good feed and really soak the ground well with water before you go, and leave the ventilators and door open if you can, as it helps to keep the temperature down so plants don't use so much water.

Greenhouse pot plants are the things that will really suffer if you can't get someone to take over the watering while you are away, so all you can do is to take them outside and stand them in a cool, shady spot, plunged to their rims in damp soil. If you are a greenhouse enthusiast my advice is to either phone a friend, put in a good reliable automatic watering system (see June, p.171 and Project, p.197) or take your holidays when your plants don't need much attention.

Houseplants

Indoor pot plants are no problem if all you have are a few huge specimens in big pots. As long as they're standing in a shady room and they are well watered before you go, they should be perfectly happy left for 2 weeks. Smaller pots will hold out best if they are well watered just before you go, then placed on an old, wet bath towel or a well-soaked piece of capillary matting, laid in the bottom of the kitchen sink or bath.

LAWNS

RESIST WATERING THE LAWN

Summery July weather always used to see gardeners reaching for the lawn sprinklers, but years of hosepipe bans and metering have broken us of the habit, which is all to the good because it really was a terrible waste of water in most cases. Oh, I know if you have a real 'show garden' you like to have a nice green lawn to set off your flowers, but it's as well to be a bit more public-spirited these days, and in any case most lawns are very long-suffering and can easily survive a dry summer. There's a big hidden benefit – grass stops growing when it's short of water, so it doesn't want mowing so much. The worst that will happen is the lawn turns a bit brown; but it's not dead, just resting – and it soon greens up again once it starts raining in autumn.

CONTINUE TO MOW

The best way to keep your lawn green in a hot, dry summer is by not cutting it too short, which is why I'm always banging on about raising the blades of your mower in dry spells. Lift the cutting blades up 1cm (½in) and you'll quickly see the difference. But don't stop cutting the grass entirely, as it looks scruffy, and some of the grasses will run to seed and weeds will run riot – they can keep growing long after the grass stops. No, cut it every couple of weeks, whatever happens. Every time you mow, trim the edges to keep the grass looking neat.

NEW LAWNS

- If you made a new lawn in spring, water if you really must, but only in long, dry spells; hopefully new lawns are starting to stand on their own feet by now.

- If you're planning to make a new lawn in autumn, and have a major perennial weed problem, start digging the area over now, removing weeds and levelling, as it's going to take time to clear (see September, pp.226–7).

CLOVER AND TREFOIL LAWNS

The crafty way to keep a lawn green without watering, even in a dry summer, is to cheat and mix grass with clover, which stays green and keeps growing even in hot, dry weather. It also fixes nitrogen from the air in its roots and slowly releases it into the soil, which feeds the grass and acts like free slow-release fertilizer. Most people don't need to introduce clover, as it turns up on its own as a lawn weed. Stopping the use of lawn weedkiller will encourage its growth, but it still takes time to spread throughout a whole lawn, and for the best effect you need to have your clover distributed evenly through the grass.

If you want to go for a more wildflower look, all sorts of creeping trefoils can be used, which have small yellow 'clover' flowers. They also fix nitrogen and stay green in hot weather, but for some people trefoils are a weed too far.

A lawn containing clover and/or trefoils can be cut as short as usual for a more traditional effect, but leaving it slightly longer in summer pays bigger dividends, as it stays a lot greener and feels cooler underfoot. The one drawback, if you leave it long enough to flower, is that it attracts bees in droves, so watch out if you have small children running around barefoot.

How to create a clover or trefoil lawn

- If you plan on sowing a new lawn in September or April, the easy way to incorporate clover is to mix white clover seed in with the grass seed. Some suppliers sell Kentish white clover especially for lawns, but any white clover seed will do. You can buy trefoil seeds from wildflower specialists.
- If you have an established lawn, you can add clover plants or trefoils, if you can find them, in the same way as you'd introduce any wildflower species, by planting pot-grown plants into the turf in spring or autumn. If you can't find pot-grown plants for sale, sow your own this autumn or next spring to plant later.

A well-grown lawn with crisply defined edges will always show off border plants well.

TREES, SHRUBS AND CLIMBERS

PRUNE AND DEADHEAD ROSES

Prune old-fashioned roses, shrub roses, and climbers and ramblers after flowering if necessary (see box below). Also, deadhead all kinds of roses after flowering, except for those species grown for their hips. Don't just snip off the dead heads – follow the stem back for 8–10cm (3–4in) and cut it off just above a healthy leaf. If there's a young sideshoot appearing lower down the stem, prune just above that, and you'll have your next flower all the faster. When you cut roses to put in a vase you're actually doing the same job, but just a bit earlier than usual and with a longer stem.

FEED ROSES

As soon as the June flush of flowers is over, all roses will be ready for a feed – it gives the plants a boost and helps to bring on the next batch of flowers. Use a general-purpose feed, or a special rose food that is high in potash and magnesium. If your roses are growing in a mixed border, feed the whole area, as the other plants will appreciate it too, but sprinkle the feed carefully between the plants. Don't leave fertilizer granules resting on plant leaves or lodged in the crowns, as they can 'scorch'; wash them off with the hose. In any case, it's a good idea to water fertilizer in, so it's dissolved in the soil moisture. Plants can only 'drink' – they can't cope with solid food.

PRUNE ROSES

A lot of climbers and ramblers, old-fashioned roses and shrub roses only produce one flush of flowers each year, which comes to an end sometime during July (the precise timing can vary from year to year with the weather). Prune these after they have completely finished their year's blooming.

Some varieties from these same groups of roses 'repeat-flower' in early and late summer, and there are others that flower almost continuously from June until October, so they need deadheading normally after each flush of flowers is over, and then pruning immediately after the full display is over. As a rule of thumb, all you do to them then is what amounts to long deadheading. This automatically leaves the plant looking tidier, but none of them are chopped down hard in the way you'd do modern roses, which aren't pruned until spring (see March, pp.59–60).

Climbers and ramblers

With climbers and ramblers, the actual amount you remove depends on the vigour of the individual variety. A big, strong-growing rambler that makes a lot of long growth each season will need quite long pieces cut out, leaving the main framework of the plant intact; with vigorous climbers, take the flowering stems back to within 15cm (6in) or so of the main framework of the plant. Smaller, slower-growing varieties of both may only need 15cm (6in) of growth removed, and some can be left unpruned if the plants look tidy. There's no need to try to prune climbing or rambler roses that are growing up through trees. (See also p.60.)

Old-fashioned roses

Tall, straggly varieties of old-fashioned roses can also be cut back quite hard after they finish flowering – up to half their height if need be. Naturally neat, compact varieties won't need much more than taking off the dead head with 15cm (6in) of stem to keep them looking tidy.

Species and shrub roses

If you grow varieties of species and shrub roses that are only grown for their flowers then these can be pruned in the same way as old-fashioned roses, but whatever you do *don't* prune those varieties (such as *Rosa rugosa* and *Rosa* 'Geranium') that are grown for their cheery autumn and winter hips, or you won't have any. If they need tidying up, trim them lightly after the hips have dropped off, in late winter or as late as mid-March.

Modern bush roses

Modern bush roses, the sort we always used to call hybrid teas and floribundas, are not pruned in summer at all – it's all done in March (see p.59) – but you will need to deadhead them regularly. They'll keep flowering from June to the first frost, but what's not generally realized is that the flowers don't follow on from each other flat-out, they actually appear in a series of distinct flushes. The June flush is by far the biggest, but the same bushes then repeat-flower regularly through the season until stopped by a combination of low light and low temperatures, in late autumn.

To keep them flowering as continuously as possible, you need to go round deadheading at the end of each flush of flowers. It's the same basic principal as deadheading bedding plants or perennial flowers – the faster you take off the old flowered stems, the faster the plant can make the new growth that carries the next crop of flower buds.

PRUNE PHILADELPHUS

There are plenty of shrubs that you never need go near with the secateurs, but philadelphus is not one of them. It is one of the few shrubs (along with forsythia, wisteria, winter jasmine and roses) that really does need pruning every year once it's well established, otherwise it grows big and straggly and what flowers there are will just be lost in the foliage. A properly pruned shrub, on the other hand, looks much more compact and will be studded with flowers in midsummer. When the last flowers are over, it's time for its annual tidy-up.

● Follow the flowering stems right back until you find a sideshoot that doesn't have the remains of dead flowers at its tip, and cut just above it. Treat each flowered shoot in the same way, and by the time you've finished the shrub will look neater and tidier and will be about two-thirds the size. It might look drastic, but it needs doing.

● If yours is a fairly mature shrub, with lots of congested old woody stems in the centre, choose one or two older stems to cut out completely, so that you slowly rejuvenate the shrub over several years. Don't try and restore a geriatric philadelphus all at once, or it just sends up thickets of long, whippy, non-flowering shoots, which makes things worse than ever.

● After pruning, feed and water. It's not essential, but it helps to encourage new shoots.

PRUNE WISTERIA

If you never prune anything else at all in the garden, the one thing you can't afford to leave running riot is wisteria. At best, you'll never see any flowers as they are lost in the over-growth, and at worst it'll rip your drainpipes down and bury your house under a jungle.

Wisteria trained against a wall

The trick with training wisteria against a wall is to start as you mean to go on.

● When you first plant wisteria, train a framework of main stems out along horizontal wires until it has covered as much wall as you are prepared to allow it.

● Each July, take your stepladder out and cut all the long, whippy tendrils back to 15cm (6in) long. This stops the plant running wild, and makes it build up lots of short, flowering spurs, forcing it to have fewer leaves and more flowers. At the same time, cut the main stems back to the limit of their patch to stop them trying to grow out of bounds. If it makes a lot of new growth later in the season, cut it all back again in midwinter (see January, p.20).

Training wisteria as a standard

When you don't have room to let a wisteria climb over a wall, the alternative is to train it as a standard. Incredibly for such a huge plant, it makes a very successful small flowering tree, with attractive spiralling stems and masses of flowers, although it can be a tricky business making sure it doesn't slump as it becomes heavier. You can plant it in the ground, or in a large tub on the patio.

● The technique of training a standard wisteria is almost identical to training a standard fuchsia (see Under Cover, p.194). Plant it, let it twine itself up a strong stake, tie it in at regular intervals, say every 10–15cm (4–6 in), and when it reaches the top keep 'stopping' the new shoots until it forms a dense head. Once formed, a standard wisteria will need pruning each year about now. It's the same idea as before, but much quicker and easier to get at. Just cut back all the tendrilly new growth to 15cm (6in).

CLIP HEDGES

Continue to clip privet and other fast-growing hedges such as *Lonicera nitida* (see May, pp.127–8).

TAKE SOFTWOOD CUTTINGS FROM SHRUBS

If you didn't take softwood cuttings in June, you can still do so now (see June, p.158).

The no-prune wisteria
If you don't want to prune a wisteria at all, plant it up against a very large tree and let it go. A 'loose' wisteria can make 18m (6oft) or more. It'll take a few years to flower, and your best view will be from an upstairs window because all the flowers will be around the outside of the canopy, but in the right spot it can look wonderful. Just don't try it in a tiny garden.

Tie in long and questing stems of wisteria if you need them to cover more of the wall. Otherwise cut them back to 15cm (6in).

HOW TO PROPAGATE A CLEMATIS

1 Cut off about 60cm (2ft) of stem from the tip of a young clematis shoot and, keeping it with the tip uppermost, start snipping off cuttings from the bottom of the shoot. Each cutting needs to be 8–10cm (3–4in) long, each with one pair of leaves at the very top, with 2.5cm (1in) or so of bare stem at the base. Use only the bottom 30cm (12in) of your piece of stem and discard the top 30cm (12in), as the material at the tip of the shoot will be too soft.

2 Fill a pot with seed compost and dib your three or four cuttings in around the side, so the bare stem is buried and the leaves are left sticking out at the top. Water, then stand the pot inside a large, loose plastic bag or clingfilm, which traps humidity around the cuttings and acts like a small-scale greenhouse. Keep them in a cool place out of direct sun.

3 The cuttings can take months to root, so keep an eye on them regularly and water just enough to stop the compost drying out. You'll know they're rooted when you can see new shoots starting to grow, so pot them all up individually at that time (see April, p.109). They'll need potting on several times until they are about as big as the clematis plants you buy at the garden centre before they can be planted out in the garden.

Lavender is ideal for drying, so cut the flowers now and enjoy them in the months ahead. (See also p.188.)

PROPAGATE CLEMATIS

Clematis can be grown from cuttings, but they aren't the easiest kind to root, so it pays to take more than you need. Clematis are propagated by what's called 'internodal cuttings', so called because instead of cutting immediately below a node, or leaf joint, as you do with softwood cuttings, these are cut between two nodes.

● If this method sounds like too much trouble, the alternative is to try layering instead (see June, p.160).

CUT LAVENDER FOR DRYING

Cut flowers of English lavenders (the French type flower slightly earlier but don't have anywhere like as much scent) with long stalks and hang bunches upside down in a cool airy place out of sunlight to dry. You can use them as they are as dried flowers to put in a vase, or separate the flowers to use as potpourri or for filling scented sachets.

FLOWERS

GARDEN GROOMING

What makes midsummer such an exciting time of year in the garden is the way that new flowers are coming out every day. The evening tour of the grounds is something I particularly look forward to. But as fast as new plants are starting their annual flush of flower, earlier ones are going over, so it's worth doing a spot of grooming as you go.

Cut back lupins and delphiniums

Big, glamorous spikes of lupins and delphiniums look enormously spectacular while they're at their best, but as soon as they're over the dead or dying flower stems look really tatty, so the border is better off without them. If you remove them as soon as it needs doing, there's a sporting chance that – given a halfway decent summer – the plants will go on to produce a few late flowers.

- Follow the dead flower stem right back down into the crown of the plant, and cut if off just above the basal cluster of leaves. If there's a sideshoot part of the way down the main stem that still has flowers or buds to come, simply snip just above the junction with it.

- When you've cut back the whole plant, sprinkle a handful of general-purpose organic fertilizer around the plant and water it well in – this improves its chances of flowering again the same season.

Deadhead other perennials

- Early perennials, such as pulmonaria and brunnera, will be well over and their foliage starting to look tired. They may also have a touch of powdery mildew, a fungal disease that looks as if someone has dusted the plants with talcum powder, which is common in hot, dry weather. Now's a good moment to give them a haircut. Chop all the foliage off close to the ground with the secateurs and clear it away. Give the plants a feed and water well – soon they'll produce a new burst of clean, healthy foliage to set off later summer flowers.

- You can do the same with herbaceous peonies and oriental poppies, which flowered in May/June, if their foliage looks a bit grim by now. As these are big, bushy plants,

Remove delphinium stalks as soon as they've finished flowering, and with luck you may have some new flowers later in the season.

HOW TO DIVIDE AND REPLANT IRISES

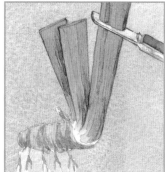

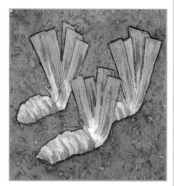

1 Use a garden fork to ease the plant out of the ground, taking care not to skewer the rhizomes. Pull the clump apart with your fingers. Throw away all the oldest bits from the middle of the plant and divide up the healthy young material, which has all the leaves, from around the edge of the clump.

2 Take a sharp knife and cut the leaves down by half their length, so the new plants don't lose too much water before they can re-root – it is the middle of summer, after all. Work a little well-rotted organic matter and some general fertilizer into the soil.

3 Plant two or three of the new divisions back into the original gap. Plant them so the rhizomes lie horizontally along the ground, with only the roots and lower half buried – the top half needs to be exposed to the sun, otherwise the plants will grow leaves but not flowers.

Hanging flowers to dry

Flowers with stiff stems and tiny flowers, such as statice and gypsophila, can be dried upright by standing the bunches in empty containers. Flowers with weak necks and heavy heads, such as helichrysum, need to be hung upside down in small bunches.

Hang flowers for drying upside down, in bunches, in a dark, well-ventilated place such as a shed.

cutting them back is going to leave a big gap in your border, so have a few pots of lilies or alstroemeria handy, to stand in the space.

DIVIDE AND REPLANT BEARDED IRISES

Bearded irises will have finished flowering about 6 weeks ago, and that's the perfect time to divide up tired old clumps. You can always tell when they're ready for dividing, because the plants die out in the middle, leaving a hollow circle of rhizomes surrounded by a ring of sword-shaped leaves. Bearded irises can be 'difficult' unless they are planted just right (see illustration, p.187). The ideal situation is well-drained soil, where the plants are in sun all day long, so not over-shadowed by other plants. If bearded irises won't flower, the problem is nearly always that they've been planted too deeply.

CUT AND DRY EVERLASTING FLOWERS

All sorts of summer annuals and perennials make good cut flowers, but everlasting flowers – which include statice, helichrysum, gypsophila and rhodanthe – are the dual-purpose kind that you can use fresh, or dried to keep all-year-round.

Cutting flowers for drying

When you want everlasting flowers for drying, cut them at a slightly earlier stage than for fresh flowers, as they carry on opening while they are drying. If you leave them too late, they'll have 'blown' – they'll already be shedding petals by the time they've dried out. Pick everlasting flowers early in the morning when they're at their freshest, remove any foliage from the stems, then divide them up into small bunches.

Drying flowers

Choose an airy shed or a spare room indoors with a good current of air passing through to dry flowers. They need to be out of sunlight, so they don't fade – a dark place is best for flowers drying upside down, otherwise the flowerheads bend towards the light. It's difficult to say how long it will take flowers to dry, as it varies from plant to plant and according to outdoor weather conditions. As a general rule, wait until flowers feel almost crunchy before using them or storing them in a cupboard for winter.

Drying seedpods

Seedpods, such as nigella (love-in-a-mist), *Scabiosa prolifera* and poppies, are much easier to deal with than flowers, as you don't pick them until the petals have fallen and the seedpods are fairly firm anyway. De-leaf the stems as before, and stand the stems upright in empty jars out of sunlight in a cool, airy place. They'll turn to natural beige and browny shades as they dry, but some people like to colour them with spray paint or silver or gold glitter to turn them into decorations for Christmas or other special occasions.

FEED HERBACEOUS PERENNIALS

Give herbaceous perennials, particularly late-flowering kinds, e.g. Michaelmas daisies, phlox and Japanese anemones, a feed by sprinkling general-purpose organic fertilizer carefully between the plants and water it well in.

SAVE SEEDS

Save seeds from alpines, perennials and hardy cyclamen as they are about to ripen, for sowing later (see August, pp.209–10).

PLANT AUTUMN-FLOWERING BULBS

Plant autumn-flowering bulbs, such as colchicum, as soon as they become available, usually around the end of the month (see August, p.210). Keep an eye on your local nursery or garden centre so you get the cream of the crop.

MAINTAIN ANNUALS AND TENDER PERENNIALS

Deadhead, feed and water annuals and tender perennials regularly.

DISBUD TUBEROUS BEGONIAS

If you want superb tuberous begonias that look like show-winners, here's a tip. As soon as the flower buds are big enough to see what's what, look at each side of them and you'll see a pair of much smaller 'budlets', which only ever develop into small single flowers. Rub those two carefully out while they are tiny, and you'll have a much bigger and better show from the double central flower, and a better chance of a rosette at the show!

PATIOS AND CONTAINERS

PEAK SEASON CONTAINER CARE

If your patio tubs, troughs and hanging baskets don't look stunning this month, you've picked the wrong hobby. Summer bedding plants should be at their absolute peak. The big trick is to keep them looking that way, which means stepping up the watering, feeding and deadheading. Now that the containers are packed tight with roots, it's amazing how much more water they need, and hot, dry weather doesn't help – if you add a light breeze to the equation, the rate of drying out almost doubles.

Watering

You don't need to bother testing the compost with a finger by now – you can tell by the weather and the size of the plants when they need daily watering. But even once-daily may not be enough for small containers that are well filled with flowers if the weather is unusually warm or breezy. In those conditions, play safe and water morning and evening – you can hardly overdo it, as any surplus water will simply drain away.

If you're worried about being able to keep on top of watering, just for the hottest summer months, it's permissible to stand pots in plant saucers and fill them up with water before you go to work – that acts as a reservoir they can draw on during the day. Don't risk it in a 'typical' dull British summer.

Feeding

Any summer bedding and tender perennials in containers will need serious feeding from now onwards. They'll have used up most of the nutrients in their potting compost by now, and since they are in full growth, flowering their socks off, and the container is fast filling up, they need a boost. You can use any of the special feeds for containers, but when you have lots of other plants to feed as well, and you only want to buy one product that does for everything, you can't go wrong with a liquid tomato feed, which provides the high potash levels that all flowering (and fruiting) plants need.

- Dilute the feed down to half the usual strength recommended for tomatoes, and use it on all your containers once a fortnight, building up to once a week as the summer progresses and containers become more packed with plants. Use as much of the diluted feed as you'd normally use plain water, i.e. as much as it takes to thoroughly damp the compost throughout the container.

All flowering and fruiting plants in containers will need frequent feeding now with a high-potash liquid fertilizer.

There's no need to colour scheme every planting. Bright mixed summer bedding can be very jolly.

Deadheading

The secret of keeping container plants flowering and looking their best all the time is to deadhead them, little and often.

Deadhead your pelargoniums frequently to encourage continuous flowering.

- Go over the plants every day or two – once a week at the absolute outside – nipping off dead and dying flowers between your fingers. If the stems are too tough or wiry for fingernails to cope, use a small pair of snips or scissors. Most flowers, for example petunias, have quite short stems so you only need to remove the flower itself, but if you have plants with long-stemmed flowers it's worth removing the entire stem as well, so plants aren't left looking like a sea of spikes.

DEALING WITH DRIED-OUT CONTAINERS

In hot weather, the biggest risk is that containers dry right out. When compost becomes bone dry, it shrinks away from the sides of the container, so that next time you water the liquid runs straight out without soaking in. You think you've done the watering, and can't understand why all your plants start wilting like crazy. When that happens, you need to act fast, or within a few days they'll be past saving.

- With large containers, drip water slowly into the middle – at first it'll just make a puddle on the surface, but once it starts to soak in you can pour slightly faster as the compost absorbs the water. Keep adding more, slowly, until the compost is completely rehydrated, and water normally from then on.
- With small pots, the simple answer is to stand them in a bucket of water for a few hours, then when they've soaked up as much water as they can just lift them out and they'll be right as rain. That's also the best way to deal with hanging baskets that have dried out badly, particularly the sort with open, wire-mesh sides, which are notoriously difficult to re-wet when they dry out. Lift them down, give them a thorough soak in a big bowl of water, and water regularly from then on.
- If plants have wilted badly in a dried-out container, you'll put them back on their feet faster if you take off all the dead heads and wide-open flowers, and in severe cases trim back over-long or out of shape stems, to reduce water loss while they recover. Don't be tempted to help them along by liquid feeding; it can just overload them when they're already badly stressed. Wait until they've perked up and are clearly growing happily again.

VEGETABLES AND HERBS

CLEAR THE GROUND

As you use early crops, clear the ground, sprinkle organic fertilizer and fork it over, so you can re-use the space as quickly as possible. Keep down weeds by hoeing regularly between rows.

SOW VEGETABLES

Vegetables to sow now include maincrop carrots, lettuce, spring cabbage, kohl rabi, turnips, endive, chicory, oriental leaves including Chinese cabbage, pak choi and winter radishes; if you want garden peas in late summer/early autumn, sow an early variety this month as they mature faster than maincrop kinds, so they'll be ready in time.

WATER THE VEGETABLE PATCH

Vegetables and salads grow fast and furious in summer's warmth, but water is the limiting factor – it's vital to keep crops well watered at all times. Stop-go growth is guaranteed to make just about any veg tough and tasteless, while even a hint of stress sends susceptible types running to seed prematurely.

- Most at risk are cauliflowers, celery and celeriac, but lettuce, onions, Chinese cabbage, beetroot and radishes will soon follow suit if conditions become remotely stressful, and frankly it's a waste of time sowing spinach in summer as it bolts almost straight away, even if you can keep it watered – the weather is just too hot. Beans will be tough and stringy if they go thirsty.

- Watch out for runner beans that won't set – water them generously and spray the foliage with plain water from the hose as humidity helps.

KEEP UP WITH PRODUCTION

When you're used to shopping at the greengrocer's, a veg patch in peak production can often catch you out. When everything is coming on thick and fast, the big problem is trying to eat what's ready before it goes over. The last thing you want, after you've just spent months looking after growing crops, is anything going to waste. And since the great veg explosion coincides with holiday time that's not easy. Root crops, such as carrots and potatoes, are no trouble, because if you leave them in the ground they just keep growing bigger, but other vegetables can spoil if left for too long.

- Harvest radish, overwintered onions, calabrese, spring onions, rocket, courgettes, French and runner beans, garlic, baby beetroots, turnips and globe artichokes (see April, p.102).

- If you don't pick courgettes or French and runner beans daily they grow so fast that they'll spoil, and if you leave tough old beans or swelling marrows on the plants it stops the next batch of tender baby veg developing until you've cleared the backlog. With these, what you can't use the same day can at least go into the freezer.

- Some crops don't 'stand' for very long once they're ready to use, so summer cabbage, cauliflowers and particularly lettuce want

using as soon as they're ready. The way to avoid having a glut of these is to start using them as soon as possible. Don't wait until the whole row is ready, start cutting the first ones as soon as they're fit to use, even if small.

- Learn to plant less of each kind of veg – with experience you learn how much of a kind to plant at a time.

WATCH OUT FOR PESTS

- Cabbage white butterflies lay eggs on brassica plants – remove patches of eggs from the undersides of the leaves or remove caterpillars while tiny, before they wreck your vegetables.

- Any rain in July invariably triggers an outbreak of potato blight, so if the weather is wet spray maincrop potatoes and outdoor tomatoes with Bordeaux mixture at 2-weekly intervals from now until mid-August to prevent an attack wiping out your plants. Blight spreads like wildfire unless it's treated quickly. Foliage of affected plants looks as if it has been burnt – it turns black and dies off within a few days. Tomatoes develop brown,

Pick off caterpillars as soon as you see them.

PRESERVING HERBS

Herbs are available in large quantities this month, and if you want to preserve some to use in winter, the time to do it is before they start flowering, otherwise the leaves lose a lot of their flavour and the stems become distinctly tough and woody. Cut clean, healthy sprigs, and rinse them in cold water to dislodge dust and insects.

- To make herb-flavoured oils, place a few good-looking sprigs of herbs in a jar of good olive oil, and leave for a few weeks in a cool cupboard.
- To dry herbs, shake the water off them and hang small bunches up in a warm, airy place out of sunlight, or pop them on a baking tray for half an hour in a warm oven. Crumble them on to a sheet of paper, pick out the twiggy bits, and store the dry, leafy herbs in clean, dry glass jars

out of sunlight. That way, they'll stay green instead of fading to an unappetizing shade of khaki.

- To freeze herbs, chop them up finely and put a teaspoonful of each into the squares of an ice-cube tray. Top them up with water, and put in the freezer. Once frozen hard you can tip out the herb-cubes into plastic bags and label them – you'll never know which is which later otherwise. One deep-frozen herb-cube looks very like another.
- To make mint jelly, use your favourite recipe for apple jelly but add lots of chopped mint. Try using eau de cologne mint instead of the usual garden mint; it smells as good as it tastes. You can adapt the same recipe to make other herb jellies – sage jelly and thyme jelly are worth a stab and go well with pork as well as lamb.

Once broad bean plants are 60cm (2ft) high, cut out the shoot tip so that it is not colonized by blackfly.

withered-looking blotches that rapidly spread until the whole fruit turns black and drops off. Remove foliage from affected potatoes; the tubers may escape the disease, since they're underground, but I'd be inclined to use them as soon as possible – don't try to store them. Don't put affected tomatoes, potatoes or foliage on the compost heap.

PLANT OUT WINTER BRASSICAS AND CALABRESE

Finish planting out winter brassicas sown in April and May, and plant out the calabrese plants raised last month.

SOW SPRING CABBAGES

Make two sowings of spring cabbage, in mid- and late July if you live in the north, or late July and mid-August if you live further south, and you'll have some tight, tasty hearts to look forward to when there's not much in the veg patch next spring. Oh, I know cabbage brings to mind school dinners when you'd rather be thinking of tucking into something far more glamorous – but when you grow your own, the flavour and freshness is right up there in the luxury league.

'STOP' OUTDOOR TOMATOES

'Stop' outdoor tomatoes by nipping out the very top of each plant; use your finger and thumb like pincers to remove the very tip of the stem. Cordon tomatoes – the ones that grow on a thick single stem – are easy, as there is only one stem to 'stop', but if you grow bush tomatoes, which have lots of stems, it's worth stopping the end of each.

'Stopping' – as the name suggests – stops the stems growing any longer, and instead diverts all the plants' resources into swelling and ripening the remaining fruit, so you don't end the season with bucketsful of green tomatoes. In the north of the country, stop outdoor tomatoes at the end of July, but down south you can leave it as late as mid-August.

FRUIT

REJUVENATE STRAWBERRY PLANTS

Don't just forget about your strawberry bed when you've picked all the fruit. It needs clearing up ready for next year. Most people don't bother, but it makes more of a difference than you realize. When you grow your strawberry plants in pots, hanging baskets or those special jars that are like a series of holes arranged vertically, you can't chop the lot back in one fell swoop. The only way is to do it the hard way with scissors, but when it's only a few plants it won't take long.

- Gather up all the straw to put on your compost heap, or if you used re-usable strawberry mats, take them up, clean them and put them away to use another year.

- Take the shears or a rotary line trimmer and give the whole bed a haircut, chopping all the plants down about 5cm (2in) from the ground. You could mess about for hours, snipping away at the plants one at a time, but there's no need. This is much quicker.

- Rake off all the rubbish. You'll also be getting rid of any potential disease organisms and a lot of pests such as snails, besides removing unwanted runners before they have the chance to root.

- Finish off by putting some fertilizer down. Sprinkle a handful of organic rose or tomato fertilizer over each square metre (yard) – don't worry about getting it over what's left of the plants, because the next job is to wash it in with the hose, and give the bed a thoroughly good soaking. It looks dreadful when you've finished, but don't let that worry you – within a few weeks you'll see lots of new growth, and the plants will be completely rejuvenated.

GROW NEW STRAWBERRY PLANTS FROM RUNNERS

Strawberry plants have a relatively short life. After 3 or 4 years the old ones are worn out and need replacing, and although you can buy plants in autumn or next spring, it's very easy to raise your own. When you go to tidy up your old plants, identify one or two really strong, healthy productive ones at the end of a row and instead of cutting them back, leave them alone so they grow some strong, healthy runners to use as new plants later (see box right). By the autumn, you'll have some nice young strawberry plants with a good set of roots growing well in pots, and that's the time to sever the umbilical cords and collect up your crop of young plants. You can either plant them as a new row in your strawberry bed to replace the old plants that you've ditched, or keep them under cover for the winter and use them to plant a new container next spring.

HARVEST FRUIT

Harvest raspberries, redcurrants, blackcurrants and gooseberries.

PROTECT RIPENING FRUIT

Where pratical, drape peach, cherry, plum and nectarine trees with old net curtains or fruit netting to protect them from birds. Where they are grown against a wall, the easy way is to fix a timber batten along the top of the wall above the tree and use it to secure a 'curtain' of netting that can be rolled down into place whenever it's needed for protection from birds, or from frost in early spring. Wasps shouldn't be a problem if you keep ripe fruit picked regularly, clear away windfalls, and prevent birds pecking the fruit – wasps attack fruit that's already damaged.

THIN OUT FRUIT

Thin heavy crops of fruit on apples, pears and plums to prevent branches breaking (see June, p.168).

HOW TO PROPAGATE STRAWBERRY PLANTS FROM RUNNERS

1 Fill half a dozen small pots with seed compost and sink them into the ground all around your 'parent plants'.

2 Make some small 'hairpins' out of thin wire, and peg the tiny plants that grow at the end of the runners down into them. Replant them when they are sufficiently established.

You can harvest blackcurrants individually from the bush, or cut off a whole stem and pick the fruit off indoors.

UNDER COVER

GREENHOUSE PLANT CARE

Keep on top of ventilating, watering and feeding, and apply another coat of shading if the weather is very hot.

THINNING AND PRICKING OUT SEEDLINGS

Thin out seedlings of biennials, and prick out winter/spring bedding and seedlings of plants sown earlier for winter-flowering pot plants (see April, pp.107–8).

CONTINUE TAKING SOFTWOOD CUTTINGS

Continue taking softwood cuttings of pelargoniums, fuchsias and other half-hardy perennials.

TRAIN A STANDARD FUCHSIA

It takes a year or more to train a really good standard fuchsia (see box below), but you'll have a reasonable specimen by the end of the summer.

FLORISTS' CYCLAMEN

Last Christmas's cyclamen plants will have spent early summer as dormant tubers, but right now they are poised to start growing again.

- Cyclamen plants that were put outdoors in the shade for the summer will often start growing gently all on their own if there's been the odd shower of rain to 'wake them up'. Watch out for slugs and snails, which have a nasty habit of appearing as soon as there's anything tender, green and leafy on the horizon. Repot them now if they need it, but otherwise pots of cyclamen will be quite happy left outdoors until September.

- Dormant cyclamen that have been kept in the greenhouse won't experience nature's natural early morning call, so give them a light spray of water to start the ball rolling. Repeat this once a week for 2–3 weeks, then repot each plant into a very slightly larger pot with some fresh John Innes potting compost. Once they start growing some new leaves, begin watering cyclamen very gently indeed to start with, and in 6 or 8 weeks you'll have a good potful of foliage with the first flower buds forming. Keep them in a cool, shady spot under the staging until autumn, as they hate bright sun or a lot of heat.

Hot chilli peppers
If you want really hot peppers, wait for them to ripen completely and don't over-water the plants, to concentrate the flavour. The strongest flavour is in the seeds, so take them out before using the chillies if you don't want to explode.

HOW TO TRAIN A STANDARD FUCHSIA

1 Choose a strong, straight, rooted cutting that has not had its growing tip nipped out to make it branch. Pot it and train it up a split cane, tying the new growth in every few inches with raffia or soft twine to keep the stem straight.

2 When the plant fills its pot with roots, repot it into a 12 or 15cm (5 or 6in) pot and replace the split cane with a 60cm (2ft) bamboo cane.

3 Remove any sideshoots that appear from the stem until the plant reaches the top of the cane, then remove the growing tip of the plant and allow sideshoots to grow from the top 15cm (6in) of stem.

4 When these sideshoots reach 5cm (2in) long, nip the very ends out to encourage them to branch, and continue doing this with the subsequent sideshoots to form a dense, bushy 'head' to the plant.

GREENHOUSE CROP CARE

Step up watering and feeding all greenhouse crops (using high-potash tomato feed) and continue tying in new growth and removing sideshoots from tomatoes.

PICK SUMMER CROPS

For the next couple of months, walking into the greenhouse is like going into a high-class greengrocery department. But when you've never grown greenhouse crops before, how do you tell when they are ready to pick?

Tomatoes

Tomatoes taste best when you leave them on the plant until they turn completely red-ripe so they develop their full flavour, but once they reach that stage pick them within a few days, before they go soft. People who grow tomatoes for the first time are often amazed at how much more flavour their own tomatoes have than the ones you buy in the shops. That's because most 'bought' tomatoes are picked while they are hard and green so they travel well instead of arriving squashed.

Peppers

Peppers are ready to eat as soon as they are approaching fist-sized. The longer you leave them, the thicker the walls become and the more the flavour develops. If you leave them long enough they'll change colour. I know a lot of people think red and green peppers are different varieties, but in fact all peppers start out a greenish shade and it's not until they ripen that they turn red – or with some varieties it's yellow, purple, orange or brown – just give them time. If you pick your peppers green, you'll pick lots per plant, as new peppers are produced right through the summer, since the plant wants a chance to set seed. But if you prefer red peppers you won't have half so many as the plant won't produce new fruit while the first lot are still ripening. It's just nature's way.

Chilli peppers are fiery, hot, long, narrow, pointed peppers. Leaving them to ripen allows the colour to change from green to orange then red, and the longer you leave them the hotter the flavour becomes.

Aubergines

Aubergines, like sweet peppers, can be used as soon as they are about fist-sized. The larger you leave them to grow, the fewer fruit each plant produces and the more chance there is that hard seeds will have formed inside the flesh – so picking them small is the answer.

Cucumbers

Cucumbers grow quickly: they only need to reach their full length and then swell out all the way along, and they're ready to pick. It's not a good idea to leave them on the plant after that, as they become bloated and coarse-textured, and the plant won't produce more cucumbers until the mature ones have been cut. If you can't use a cucumber that is ready straight away, keep it in the fridge, not on the plant.

Watch out for cucumbers that develop a swollen bulge at one end, because they usually have a bitter taste and hard seeds in the centre, which happens when they have been pollinated (see box below).

Melons

Melons, unlike cucumbers, have to be pollinated to set fruit, and it takes quite a while for the fruit to swell up to full size and even longer for them to ripen, so they won't be ready until later in the summer. There's no mistaking a ripe melon; it makes itself known by the haunting scent wafting through the greenhouse, so just follow your nose. If you gently press the tip of the melon with your thumbs, either side of the scar where the flower fell off, it will give very slightly to confirm it's ripe and ready to eat. If in doubt, wait another day or two before cutting the fruit from the stem. Give it a couple of hours in the fridge to chill before tucking in – a really ripe melon is one of life's great culinary experiences.

Pick cucumbers frequently; if left on the plant for too long they will deteriorate.

Prevent pollination
If you start to find cucumbers with a swollen bulge at one end, fix net curtains over the greenhouse ventilators to stop bees pollinating the plants. It can happen even to all-female varieties of cucumbers if there are melons growing within range, which is why it's not recommended to grow the two together in the same greenhouse.

WATER GARDEN

Right: Dividing irises can be hard work, as they have extremely tough roots.

BEAT SUMMER POND PROBLEMS

By now the pond should be looking a picture, with waterlilies and marginal aquatics nicely in flower, and floating leaves covering at least half of the water, creating a cool, safe environment for fish. But hot weather can be a problem for ponds.

Provide more oxygen

If you see fish gasping for air it's a sign that the water is short of oxygen. That could be because you have too many fish for the size of the pond, or it may mean that waterweeds are badly overgrown and are using up all the oxygen at night – they only make it during the day when the sunlight is on their leaves.

- If you can see waterweeds pushing up above the surface, or you can feel thickets of the stuff everywhere when you put your hand in, it's a fair bet it wants thinning out anyway, so pull some of it out. Drape it over the side of the pond for a few days so that any water life can escape, then put it on the compost heap – it makes a good natural 'starter'.

- Running a fountain is good for the whole pond ecosystem in summer, as the moving water dissolves oxygen and returns it to the water as it falls back into the pond.

Keep the pond topped up

The other common summer problem with ponds is evaporation. Hot, sunny weather, especially when coupled with a light breeze, can cause the water level in the pond to drop alarmingly. A lot of people think the pond must have sprung a leak, but a leak loses water at the same rate all year round – if it varies according to the weather, evaporation is to blame.

- All you can do is top the pond up regularly with the hose. If you find you're adding a lot of tap water, then it's worth visiting your local pond centre and buying a treatment that neutralizes the chlorine and lime in the

water – in large quantities it can affect the balance of the pond, but a little now and again won't hurt. And it beats leaving pond life high and dry.

DIVIDE WATER IRISES

If you have overgrown water irises growing around the side of the pond, this is the time to divide them. If you do it in spring along with other marginal plants you won't have any flowers this year, which is why it's best to wait until a few weeks after flowering finishes – the same as for herbaceous irises in your perennial border.

- Divide water irises in exactly the same way as other marginal plants (see April, p.113). It's hard-going, since they make great thick tussocks that are very difficult to get out of their baskets, let alone split apart. With a very overgrown plant, you may need to cut away the old basket, then slice through the plant with a sharp spade.

SOLAR FOUNTAINS

You don't have to lay on an electricity supply especially for a pond fountain – solar fountains are available now at quite a reasonable price and you just put them straight into the pond. Some types have a solar panel built in, so the unit floats freely in the pond, and others have a rectangular panel that you need to put in a sunny position, from which a wire runs to the pump on the floor of the pond. The latter are more powerful, but you do have to hide all the gubbins.

PROJECT Make an emergency watering system

When you can't make other provisions for looking after plants, rather than leave them untended, knock together an emergency watering system to use on the patio, in the greenhouse, or around the garden. You can use this system to water plants growing in the ground or in growing bags, by tucking the end of the wick into the soil or compost near the plants, as long as the bucket is raised up enough for its base to be at least a few inches above the level of the plant roots.

What you need

A bucket

Greenhouse staging, chair, or stack of bricks

Plants in pots

Old cotton towelling or sheets, capillary matting or similar water absorbent fabric cut into long strips about 10cm (4in) wide

2 Water the plants very well first. Soak the towelling fabric or sheets in water to act as 'wicks', then tuck one end of a damp wick firmly into the compost in the pot and drape the other end into the bucket of water, making sure it is long enough to reach right down to the bottom of the bucket.

3 You can add liquid feed to the water if you want to, since it's only a temporary set-up and there is nothing to block up.

4 Very soon, water will start to soak slowly down the wick and into the pot, keeping the compost moist. The rate the bucket empties will depend on the number of plants it is catering for and what the weather is like – it lasts longest in the shade.

1 Fill the bucket with water and stand it up on a stool, old wooden chair, greenhouse staging or stack of bricks – whatever is handy – with the pots of plants around the base.

AUGUST

When the going gets tough, the tough get going ... and that's exactly what happens to your summer flowers. Once the weather turns hot and sunny, a lot of the 'regulars' come to an early end, especially if they're a tad short of water at the roots – and you don't need me to remind you that August is the season of holidays and hosepipe bans. But by bulking up your borders with late starters that stand the heat, you can see your garden safely through the difficult season and make a smooth transition into autumn.

August is the culmination of months of effort; what's more, dry weather means there's little or no lawn mowing to do, and weeding and hedge-clipping are at a seasonal ebb, so you can sit back and enjoy the garden. Make the most of the summery weather – spend more time with your flowers, be creative with home-grown herbs and salads, and stoke up the barbecue. Look out for butterflies and other sorts of mini-wildlife – even humming-bird hawk moths in a hot summer. And if you fancy a change of scene, it's a great time to go garden visiting.

THE BIG PICTURE summer stayers

Phlox paniculata, border phlox (above), doesn't start flowering until summer is well under way, and looks its most luxuriant just when a lot of perennials are coming to an end. There are plenty of varieties: **'Starfire'** has scarlet flowers, **'Balmoral'** is a bright lipstick-pink, and **'Harlequin'** has purple flowers with variegated foliage; they make durable clumps approximately 90 × 45cm (36 × 18in).

PEAK SEASON Late July–September.
GROWING CONDITIONS Well-drained soil with plenty of organic matter, in sun or light shade.

Fuchsia **'Riccartonii'** (above) is one of the really tough, tried and tested hardy fuchsias, making a modest bush about 90 × 60cm (3 × 2ft). The flowers are unusually slim and elegant, with very long stamens hanging down like ballet dancers' legs, well below the purple and red 'skirts' of the flowers. In a cold area the stems are usually killed off down to ground level in winter, but in a mild spot the woody framework of branches persists and produces a slightly larger bush; in the West Country, they are even grown as hedges.

PEAK SEASON Late July–October.
GROWING CONDITIONS Any well-drained soil in sun or light shade.

Japanese anemones look like rows of faces peering over a fence. The stems are tall and straight, with large, round, flat flowers arranged loosely at the top, but they all face the same way – towards the light – so it's no good planting them where they'll turn their backs on you. Several varieties are available with pink or white flowers and of various heights. *Anemone hupehensis* **'Hadspen Abundance'** (above) has single, deep mauve-pink flowers with paler edges, 90 × 45cm (36 × 18in); *Anemone × hybrida* **'Honorine Jobert'** has single white flowers, 1.2 × 1m (4 × 3ft); and **'September Charm'** has very large, single, pale pink flowers, 90 × 45cm (36 × 18in).

PEAK SEASON Late July–October.
GROWING CONDITIONS Any well-drained soil in sun or light shade. They can take a year or two to settle in. Be patient.

Persicaria affinis, the ornamental knotweed (above), is very jolly, with pink poker flowers standing up straight above a mass of ground-covering foliage, which takes on autumn tints towards the end of the season. **'Darjeeling Red'** is a knockout, with large 'dock' leaves and bright pink and red pokers, 30 × 60cm (1 × 2ft). **'Donald Lowndes'** is similar but with smaller leaves and more of a pink and mauve colour scheme.

PEAK SEASON Late July–September.
GROWING CONDITIONS Ordinary soil beefed up with plenty of organic matter, in sun or light shade.

OLD FAITHFULS

Sedum spectabile, the ice plant, is well known for its drought tolerance and late summer flowers that attract butterflies and bees. **Sedum 'Herbstfreude'** (**syn. S. 'Autumn Joy'**) is the standard late-flowering variety, with flat, wide heads of russety salmon-pink. Even though the flowers don't open properly until September, the flat green heads of buds add architectural interest to the border. Other varieties start sooner – there's **Sedum spectabile 'Iceberg'** (above), with white flowers, and **'Brilliant'**, which is more of a deep shocking pink. **Sedum telephium** subsp. **maximum 'Atropurpureum'** is a not dissimilar-looking plant that is well worth growing for its purple foliage and sprays of pink flowers.

PEAK SEASON August–October.
GROWING CONDITIONS Well-drained soil and a sunny spot.

Phygelius capensis, Cape figwort, is a very exotic-looking plant that's become much better known over the last few years. The flowers look like bunches of bright orange-red tubes growing in large, loose-tiered arrangements held up over the 2m × 60cm (6 × 2ft) plants. Although people often think of it as a herbaceous perennial, phygelius is actually a shrub with tender stems that often dies down to ground level in winter, in the same way as hardy fuchsias. **Phygelius × rectus 'Salmon Leap'** has orange flowers, **'Moonraker'** is yellow and **Phygelius aequalis 'Sani Pass'** (**syn. 'Sensation'** – above) has cerise pink/rich violet flowers. These all grow to about 90 × 60cm (3 × 2ft).

PEAK SEASON Late July–October.
GROWING CONDITIONS Well-drained soil with some organic matter, in sun or light shade. In cold areas it's best grown against a sunny wall for shelter.

Perovskia 'Blue Spire' (above) is like a cross between a sage bush and a bunch of pipe-cleaners. The sage-scented leaves are much spikier in shape than those of sage, but you'll hardly see them because the whole shrub is a mass of many-branched silvery stems outlined in tiny lavender balls of flower, so all you see from a distance is a lilac haze. A plant at its peak stands 1 × 1m (3 × 3ft), but the stems tend to flop, so it's not the sort of thing to plant along the edge of a big border or path, unless it's supported by other plants. Needs annual pruning and twiggy pea stick supports to keep it tidy. **'Little Spire'** is more compact and self supporting.

PEAK SEASON August–October.
GROWING CONDITIONS Well-drained soil in sun.

Dahlias (above) are the classic late summer flower, growing from tubers that aren't entirely hardy, so in most of the country they are lifted and stored for the winter and replanted each year (see November, p.281). Tall border dahlias are often grown at country houses in formal beds of their own, but in 'normal' gardens you can plant them in mixed borders or with exotic plants for a subtropical look. Flowers come in various shapes and sizes, from large Decoratives, which are dinner-plate sized, through spiky 'Cactus' flowers to tiny tight Pompons, in just about every colour except blue, green and black. Plant a few in the veg patch to provide flowers for cutting.

PEAK SEASON Late July–October.
GROWING CONDITIONS Rich, moist, fertile soil with plenty of organic matter, in sun.

Hibiscus syriacus, hardy hibiscus (above), look exotic but they are brilliant late season shrubs that are easy to grow. The foliage and flowers look just like the tropical hibiscuses that we grow as indoor plants, but make taller plants (2 × 1m/6 × 3ft) and with a different colour range. '**Blue Bird**' (**syn.** '**Oiseau Bleu**') has large, deep lavender-blue flowers with purple 'eyes' in the centre; '**Woodbridge**' is mauve-pink with a deep mauve eye; and '**Red Heart**' is white with a red eye. They make neat, upright shrubs that are slow to come into leaf and are slow-growing, but they are no trouble at all. A real joy.

PEAK SEASON August–October.
GROWING CONDITIONS Well-drained soil in a sunny spot.

Phormium tenax is New Zealand flax (above), star of I hate to think how many episodes of *Ground Force*. I chose it for its contemporary architectural shape and year-round evergreen effect. There are plenty of varieties, with long, strap-shaped leaves in green, bronze or beetroot-red, sometimes with yellow, red, orange or pink stripes – sometimes all at once – making clumps 1.2 × 1.2m (4 × 4ft). *Phormium* '**Maori Sunrise**' has a concoction of colours that you normally only see in a drink with an umbrella floating in it – apricot, pink and bronze; *Phormium tenax* '**Variegatum**' has bold green and cream bands; *Phormium* '**Dazzler**' has burgundy foliage with broad pink stripes rather like pyjamas. Dwarfer kinds, for example '**Bronze Baby**', are good for pots. Although foliage is the main attraction, when grown in the ground and given a few years to mature, you'll often find phormiums producing a tall, very exotic flower spike – clusters of miniature velvety antlers mounted on top of a stiff, upright stem – around July/August.

PEAK SEASON All year round (plant), August–November (flower).
GROWING CONDITIONS Well-drained soil in sun.

Helianthus, sunflowers (above), are some of the easiest of annuals for children to grow, and right now they'll have reached their maximum height and will be in full flower. Giant sunflowers can reach 38cm (15in), because they only produce a single stem with one whopping great head at the top, but nowadays there are also branching varieties that can be used as cut flowers, and very dwarf sunflowers that are good for pots on the patio. Shorter varieties tend to flower first as they have less growing to do. When sunflowers are over, leave the seedheads standing until midwinter, as many of them are packed with free birdseed.

PEAK SEASON July–September.
GROWING CONDITIONS Fertile, well-drained soil in sun.

Clematis **Viticella cultivars** start to flower late in the season, when a lot of the large-flowered hybrids are either taking a brief breather or running out of steam altogether. The flowers are the same shape as the most popular clematis – like big floral plates – but a couple of sizes smaller. They also have a huge advantage over large-flowered hybrids, as they don't seem to be affected by clematis wilt, and pruning is very simple – you can do it if you want, otherwise don't bother. *Clematis* '**Polish Spirit**' (above) has flowers the colour of methylated spirit, '**Minuet**' has small mauve flowers edged in white, '**Alba Luxurians**' has greeny-white flowers, and '**Purpurea Plena Elegans**' has extraordinary double rosette flowers in a dusky light reddish purple. All grow to about 3m (10ft).

PEAK SEASON Mid-July–September.
GROWING CONDITIONS Fertile, moist soil, any aspect except north, with roots growing in shade and stems growing out into sun; it also looks good growing loose through trees or large shrubs.

SOMETHING SPECIAL

Tamarix pentandra (above) is the seaside staple you see everywhere along the South coast – a really tough and wiry shrubby tree that stands everything from salt spray and sandstorms to the odd passing tornado, despite growing in ground that's little more nutritious than sand and pebbles. In late summer and autumn it erupts into a froth of tiny pink flowers that outline the fox-coloured stems. Also invaluable for windswept spots inland, or anywhere you want to create an artificial seaside-style garden.

PEAK SEASON August–
   September.
GROWING CONDITIONS Well-
   drained soil in sun.

Crinum × powellii (above) is a summer-flowering bulb that could have been designed for exotic gardens. It has a huge bulb with a long, tapering swan-neck that needs to be left above the ground when it's planted in spring, and by late summer you'll have a flowering stem several feet high topped by large, slightly fragrant, pale pink, lily-like flowers. Plants grow 1.2 × 0.7m (4 × 2½ft) with strap-shaped leaves. Most impressive planted in a clump among exotic foliage plants.

PEAK SEASON August–
   September.
GROWING CONDITIONS Very
   well-drained soil, but with
   plenty of organic matter, in a
   very sheltered, sunny, south-
   facing site in a mild area. Don't
   disturb once established, and
   protect bulbs in winter, as
   they're not very hardy.

Campsis × tagliabuana **'Madame Galen'**, trumpet vine (above), is one of the most spectacular flowering climbers you could choose, with large bunches of vivid flame-red and sunset-orange flowers at the tips of the stems. The plant is perfectly hardy but only flowers in a hot, sunny site – the stems need a lot of sun to ripen them enough to promote flowering – but in the right spot the display is staggering. You might almost be out in the West Indies.

PEAK SEASON August–
   September.
GROWING CONDITIONS Fertile
   soil on a sunny, south-facing
   wall in a reasonably mild area.

Salvias are usually thought of as lurid-red bedding plants, but shrubby salvias (above) are a different group of late-flowering plants. They are relatively new to a lot of gardeners, but now that longer autumns give us time to enjoy the flowers, we are starting to see much more of them. You'll need to go to a specialist nursery or plant fair to find them, but it's well worth the effort. *Salvia uliginosa* grows tall, 1.5 × 0.6m (5 × 2ft), with branching spikes studded with enchanting sky-blue, speedwell-like flowers – unusually for this group it needs soil that stays moist. *Salvia microphylla* grows 60 × 90cm (2 × 3ft) and has smallish green leaves and bright carmine flowers that stud the entire bush; *Salvia confertiflora*, 1.2 × 1m (4 × 3ft), has spikes of red fluffy 'pipe-cleaners' standing up from the plant, which has large, sage-like leaves that smell of under-done steak when touched. I grow all of these in a sunny border and they are wonderfully rewarding.

PEAK SEASON July–the first hard frost.

GROWING CONDITIONS Well-drained soil with plenty of organic matter in sun; borderline hardy. Cuttings root easily, so keep some in a frost-free greenhouse in winter as insurance.

OTHER PLANTS IN THEIR PRIME IN AUGUST

- **Trees** *Eucryphia, Koelruteria paniculata, Sophora japonica*
- **Shrubs** *Abelia chinensis, Aesculus parviflora, Aralia elata, Buddleja davidii* (see p.178), *Ceanothus × delileanus* 'Gloire de Versailles' (see p.179), *Ceratostigma willmottianum, Clerodendrum trichotomum, Colutea arborescens, Hydrangea arborescens, Hydrangea macrophylla* (see p.179), *Hydrangea paniculata, Hydrangea quercifolia, Hydrangea villosa, Indigofera heterantha, Leycesteria formosa, Potentilla fruticosa* (see p.152), *Rosa* (see pp.150–1), *Romneya coulteri* (see p.181), *Spiraea × japonica* 'Anthony Waterer'
- **Evergreens** *Calluna, Ceanothus* 'Autumnal Blue', *Cistus, Daboecia, Desfontainea spinosa, Erica cinerea, Erica tetralix, Erica vagans, Erica vulgaris, Escallonia, Eucryphia × nymansensis, Gaultheria procumbens, Genista aetnensis, Hebe* (see p.178), *Hypericum calycinum, Hypericum* 'Hidcote', *Itea illicifolia, Lavandula × intermedia, Lavandula stoechas* (see p.177), *Magnolia grandiflora, Myrtus communis, Olearia, Santolina chamaecyparissus, Spartium junceum, Tamarix pentandra, Teucrium fruticans, Vinca, Yucca filamentosa*
- **Climbers/wall shrubs** *Actinidia deliciosa, Clematis* 'Comtesse de Bouchaud', *Clematis* 'General Sikorski' (see p.152), *Clematis* 'Hagley Hybrid' (see p.152), *Clematis* 'Jackmanii' (see p.152), *Clematis* 'Mevrouw le Coultre', *Clematis tangutica* (see p.221), *Clematis* Texensis cultivars, *Clematis* 'The President', *Clematis tibetana* subsp. *vernayi* (see p.221), *Clematis* 'Ville de Lyon', *Eccremocarpus scaber, Fallopia baldschuanica, Fremontodendron californicum, Jasminum officinale, Lonicera × brownii, Lonicera periclymenum* 'Serotina', *Magnolia grandiflora, Passiflora caerulea* (see p.178), *Solanum crispum* 'Glasnevin' (see p.179), *Trachelospermum asiaticum* (see p.180)
- **Perennials** *Achillea filipendulina, Agapanthus* (see p.176), *Alstroemeria* (see p.154), *Anthemis, Aster amellus, Aster × frikartii, Astilbe, Astrantia major, Campanula lactiflora, Catananche caerulea, Ceratostigma plumbaginoides, Centaurea dealbata, Centranthus ruber, Clematis heracleifolia, Crocosmia* (see p.176), *Dianthus, Dictamnus fraxinella, Echinops ritro, Eryngium, Geum* 'Mrs. J. Bradshaw' (see p.121), *Gypsophila paniculata, Helenium, Hemerocallis, Heuchera, Lavatera clementii, Leucanthemum maximum, Liatris, Ligularia, Limonium latifolium, Lychnis chalcedonica, Lysimachia, Lythrum, Monarda, Nepeta, Penstemon* (see p.176), *Platycodon grandiflorus, Prunella, Rudbeckia, Salvia × superba, Scabiosa, × Solidaster, Stipa* (see p.221), *Thalictrum dipterocarpum, Veronica spicata* subsp. *incana, Zauschneria californica* (see p.222)
- **Bulbs** *Begonia, Canna, Cardiocrinum, Eucomis, Galtonia, Lilium regale* (see p.176), *Tigridia*
- **Bedding** All summer bedding (hardy annuals, half-hardy annuals) and patio plants
- **Rock plants** *Acaena, Anacyclus pyrethrum* var. *depressus, Campanula, Convolvulus cneorum* (see p.154), *Cyananthus, Dianthus plumarius, Geranium cinereum, Gypsophila repens, Lithodora diffusa, Mazus reptans, Penstemon pinifolius, Rhodohypoxis baurii, Silene uniflora, Thymus lanuginosus*

AUGUST at-a-glance checklist

GENERAL GARDEN TASKS (p.206)
- ✔ Water and feed plants frequently, particularly those in containers outdoors, greenhouse pot plants, and the veg patch, as well as any shrubs or perennials planted this summer.
- ✔ Weed the borders regularly.
- ✔ Deadhead annuals, roses and other flowering plants, and cut back perennials after flowering.
- ✔ Apply vine-weevil control to plants in containers outside and under cover, in greenhouse borders, and around plants at risk in the garden.

LAWN (p.206)
- ✔ Mow regularly, but don't water or feed.

TREES, SHRUBS AND CLIMBERS (p.207)
- ✔ Feed camellias and rhododendrons and water well.
- ✔ Trim pyracantha.
- ✔ When the flowers are over, clip dwarf hedges of lavender, rosemary and santolina.
- ✔ Clip beech, hornbeam, Leyland or thuja hedges late this month or early next month.
- ✔ Take semi-ripe and heel cuttings of woody herbs, shrubs and roses, and propagate clematis and rhododendrons by layering.

FLOWERS (p.209)
- ✔ Cut and dry everlasting flowers.
- ✔ Save seed from rock plants, trees and shrubs, hardy annual flowers, perennials and bulbs.
- ✔ Pot up self-sown seedlings.
- ✔ Plant autumn-flowering bulbs.
- ✔ Divide bearded irises.
- ✔ Take cuttings of alpines.

PATIOS AND CONTAINERS (p.211)
- ✔ Keep on top of watering, feeding and deadheading containers, which is needed more than ever this month.

VEGETABLES AND HERBS (p.212)
- ✔ Harvest French and runner beans, lettuce, beetroot, turnips, courgettes, onions, pencil leeks, marrows, calabrese, summer squashes, second early potatoes, the first outdoor tomatoes and globe artichokes.
- ✔ Sow early carrots, peas, turnips, lettuce, baby spinach leaves, spring cabbages, oriental leaves including pak choi and Chinese cabbage.
- ✔ 'Stop' outdoor tomatoes.
- ✔ Cut and dry or freeze herbs.
- ✔ Take cuttings from herbs.

FRUIT (p.213)
- ✔ Prune gooseberries, redcurrant and blackcurrant bushes and summer fruiting raspberry canes now that all the fruit has been picked. Also, summer-prune cordon-trained apple trees and fan-trained fruit trees.
- ✔ Harvest blackberries, loganberries, peaches, nectarines, apricots, the last of the summer raspberries and early varieties of eating apples.
- ✔ Cut strawberry runners from the parent plant.

UNDER COVER (p.215)
- ✔ Ventilate the greenhouse and damp down regularly in hot weather.
- ✔ Take softwood cuttings of pelargoniums, fuchsias, and other frost-tender plants to overwinter, late this month.
- ✔ Sow winter- and spring-flowering pot plants for the greenhouse or conservatory.
- ✔ Plant specially prepared bulbs, such as hyacinths, for forcing, if you want them to flower in time for Christmas.
- ✔ Increase feeding of tomatoes, continue pinching out sideshoots, and remove lower leaves that turn yellow.
- ✔ Harvest greenhouse tomatoes, peppers, aubergines, cucumbers and melons.

WATER GARDEN (p.216)
- ✔ Clear out yellowed or decomposing water lily leaves from the pond; thin out excess older leaves if the plants are overgrown and covering the pond completely.
- ✔ Thin out excess oxygenating waterweeds.
- ✔ Top up water levels if necessary.

Watch out for
- Symptoms of drought.
- Powdery mildew, particularly on roses and honeysuckle.
- Caterpillars on cabbages, calabrese, cauliflower, sprouts and other brassicas.
- Blight on potatoes and tomatoes.
- Slugs and snails.

Get ahead
- Prepare ground for a new lawn, so it's ready for sowing in September.
- Stake tall brassicas to prevent them being flattened later by strong winds.

Last chance
- Finish summer-pruning of wisteria.
- Finish dividing bearded irises.

GENERAL GARDEN TASKS

REGULAR MAINTENANCE TASKS

The following need to be carried out regularly throughout August:

- Look for symptoms of drought in containers, vegetables, potted plants under glass, shrubs or perennials planted this summer. Look out for slugs and other pests and diseases (see May, pp.125, 133–4 and 142–3).

- Deadhead annuals, roses and shrubs, and continue cutting back perennials.

- Water and feed regularly, and continue to weed borders.

APPLY VINE-WEEVIL CONTROL

Apply a second dose of vine-weevil control to containers, greenhouse pot plants and greenhouse border soil, and around at-risk plants in the garden (see May, pp.125 and 134).

LAWNS

DON'T WATER OR FEED

This is a difficult time for lawns, but if yours is looking a tad jaded, bear with it. Don't be tempted to start watering for a quick fix – it's just a waste – and don't be tempted to feed, because far from having the desired effect, it'll just make it go brown even faster than ever. In 6 weeks or so a few decent rains will have put grass back on its feet again.

MOW REGULARLY

Continue to mow the lawn regularly as long as it continues to grow. If you've been away and the lawn is overgrown, see box below.

PREPARE FOR A NEW LAWN

If you're planning to make a new lawn in autumn, you could start digging the area over now, as it's going to take time to clear, particularly if you have lots of perennial weeds (see September, pp.226–7).

POST-HOLIDAY STRATEGY

August is one of the quietest months in the garden, but if your patch has been doing its own thing while you've been away on holiday, it will be ready for a little TLC when you get back. My advice is don't 'leave it for another day' – catch up as fast as possible, and get back to your usual routine while there's still time to enjoy the last of the summer. When you arrive home, have a quick check round, and do any urgently needed watering straight away.

Lawn

The lawn is the first thing to tackle. If by some miracle we've had rain while you've been away, you may come home to grass that looks like a hayfield. In this case, don't try and cut it short all in one go – you'll just be cutting into thick brown stems, which leaves the grass looking like a sea of stubble. No, do it in easy stages. Raise the blades of the mower as high as possible and just top it lightly first time round, then lower the blades a notch each time you cut it again until it

arrives back to its usual level – this 'teaches' the grass to grow leafy again.

Even if the weather has been dry and the grass hasn't grown much, lawn weeds will have done so. A quick once-over with the mower decapitates them and evens out any patches of lush or coarse faster grasses. Your lawn edges have probably gone to pot while you've been away, so whip around them with long-handled edging shears, neatening them up again. Once the lawn is in hand, the whole garden looks instantly better.

Beds and borders

Have a good look around your borders. Overgrown weeds that are threatening to shed seeds need dealing with promptly, even if you only pick off the flowering heads for now. But go around the whole garden ASAP, bringing all the weeding and deadheading up to date, because now they are in flowering mode, weeds will pull out all the stops to shed seeds – and at this time of year it won't take them long.

Patios and containers

If containers have suffered badly and don't look as if they're worth saving, take an executive decision – tip them out and start again. If you holidayed early you may find a few very late bargains in the summer bedding department at nurseries or garden centres, but frankly I'd be inclined to steal a march on the neighbours and skip straight on to the autumn and winter planting schemes. It'll be much better value in the long run.

Greenhouse

Give everything a good feed and water regularly; go around picking ripe crops, tidying up plants, and clearing up as necessary.

Veg patch

Give everything a good watering if the ground is dry, collect any crops that need picking, and find time to clear vacant rows and refill them with autumn/winter crops as soon as possible.

TREES, SHRUBS AND CLIMBERS

FEED CAMELLIAS AND RHODODENDRONS

Feed camellias and rhododendrons with high-potash tomato feed, and keep them well watered this month, as it will help them flower better next year; this is when they are initiating their flower buds.

DEADHEAD ROSES

Continue to deadhead roses (see July, p.184).

TRIM PYRACANTHA

Pyracantha berries have swelled and will start ripening any minute now. The only trouble is that the plant will have grown a lot since the berries 'set', so your autumn and winter display is already vanishing underneath a mass of this year's new growth.

Now is exactly the right moment to go around with the secateurs and cut back all the new growth just beyond the berries to expose them. Besides making a much better show, this also tidies up the shape of the plant and stops it growing big and scruffy. It's a good idea to do it to the usual shrubby pyracantha in the border, but when you have a trained one growing flat against a wall it's essential, otherwise it'll soon bush out and block the path.

PRUNE WISTERIA

Complete summer pruning of wisteria (see July, p.185).

CLIP LAVENDERS AND DWARF HERBAL HEDGES

If you have formal beds or paths edged with dwarf herb hedges of lavender, santolina or rosemary, then now's the time to give them a trim. The timing is just right to clear off the dead flowerheads and re-shape the plants. They'll be able to make a bit of re-growth before winter so they look neat but natural rather than surgically precise. If you have the same plants growing informally around the garden, it's not a bad idea to give them a haircut too as they tend to grow very leggy otherwise.

- Clip the plants back just beyond the base of the old flower stems. Use shears or single-handed sheep shears, whichever you prefer. As long as you do this every year from the time you plant them, they'll never look straggly.

- Don't leave lavenders until spring, as you sometimes see suggested, because if you clip or prune them then they don't flower well during the summer, and the soft growth that results is very much at the mercy of the spring weather. And it's not a good idea to prune any of these plants back hard, so you are cutting into old, thick, woody stems. Herb experts seem to get away with it, but for most of us it's a recipe for disaster – the plant usually turns up its toes.

CLIP HEDGES

Give beech, hornbeam, Leyland or thuja hedges a second trim late this month or early next month (see May, pp.127–8).

Dahlias and cannas give any border a tropical touch.

This is the ideal time to remove old lavender flowers and trim and reshape the plants.

HOW TO TAKE SEMI-RIPE CUTTINGS

1 Select shoots that are young and vigorous and firm to the touch and cut them off with secateurs. Choose slightly longer shoots than you'd use for softwood cuttings, say 15–20cm (6–8in). Ideally, choose non-flowering shoots, but remove any buds or flowers if you can't find any propagating material without them.

2 Trim the base of the cuttings below a leaf joint. Choose a point where there is about 5–10mm ($^1/_4$–$^1/_2$in) of darker, woodier-looking stem at the very base. The prepared cutting will be 10–15cm (4–6in) long. Remove lower leaves and thorns from prickly plants. Insert the cuttings 8cm (3in) apart in trays of cuttings compost. Water in and stand them in a cold frame.

Layering rhododendrons in pots

If you don't have acid soil, which means you have to grow rhododendrons in tubs, you can still try your hand at layering by parking a spare container of ericaceous compost alongside the first and layering a suitable shoot into that.

TAKE SEMI-RIPE CUTTINGS

All sorts of plants can be grown from semi-ripe cuttings taken now and during the first half of September – woody herbs, most of the shrubs that can be grown from softwood cuttings in June and July, roses and lavender. But don't panic, you won't have to learn yet another new technique. Semi-ripe cuttings are almost the same as softwood cuttings, but because the summer is 2 months further on, the new shoots that have appeared this year by now have started turning very slightly woody at the base – so cuttings made from them are what are known as 'semi-ripe'. They take longer to root than softwood cuttings, so they are made a bit longer – bigger cuttings have more 'reserves' with which to survive – and the slightly woody end means they are less likely to rot. Most cuttings can be potted up or planted out in May. Some may take longer and will have to wait until autumn.

TAKE HEEL CUTTINGS

Some plants make very dense, branching growth and you may not be able to find semi-ripe cuttings as long as 15–20cm (6–8in). Also, with fast-rooting plants such as lavender, and woody herbs such as rosemary and ornamental sages, you can get away with shorter cuttings of 10–15cm (4–6in) long. Where longer shoots are not easy to find, what you can do is make heel cuttings. These are just semi-ripe cuttings that have been made by tearing suitable sideshoots away from a main stem, leaving a 'heel' of bark attached to the base of each. Remove the shoot tip as before, but to trim the base simply take a sharp knife and trim away the tail end of the heel.

PROPAGATE CLEMATIS

Propagate clematis by layering (see June, p.160).

LAYER RHODODENDRONS

Rhododendrons (including azaleas) are very difficult to root from cuttings – nurserymen have special equipment or they'll graft them, which is why plants are expensive to buy. But you can sometimes raise a rhododendron or two at home by layering a shoot from a plant you already have growing in the garden.

- To layer, follow instructions on layering a shrub (see March, p.61), burying a 30cm (12in) section and making sure the same length is showing above the ground.

- After about 18 months you should see the young plant starting to grow from the end of the buried shoot, and when it looks to be doing well, dig it up and sever the 'umbilical cord' linking it to the mother plant. Try to do this in April, or wait until September, when evergreens transplant best anyway.

DEAL WITH MILDEW

Powdery mildew starts to rear its ugly head in late summer, and some plants are more prone to it than others – roses and honeysuckles are particularly at risk. Affected plants look as if they've been liberally dusted with talcum powder. Powdery mildew is always worse where plants are under stress, so you tend to find it affecting roses in beds where the soil has dried out badly.

- Spraying with fungicide is the obvious knee-jerk reaction – look for one of the organic types based on sulphur if possible – but it's also a good idea to improve the conditions that are creating the stress. Soak the ground well with water and follow up with a high-potash feed; mulch generously now, and repeat the following spring.

- In the case of roses, if mildew is a regular occurrence, as well as feeding, watering and mulching, try working a little sulphur into the ground – products are available specially by post or at garden centres – or consider replacing regular offenders with more disease- resistant varieties. This seems to me to be infinitely preferable to waltzing around with a sprayer every couple of weeks.

- Instead of growing a honeysuckle in a tub, as some people do, choose something more suitable – clematis are a much better choice of climber for containers. Honeysuckles do much better in the ground; even so, if they are planted up against a wall the foundations soak up a lot of the moisture so they still need regular watering in dry weather.

FLOWERS

CUT AND DRY EVERLASTING FLOWERS

Continue to cut and dry everlasting flowers (see July, p.188).

SAVE YOUR OWN SEEDS

As you go around the garden tweaking and titivating, watch out for flowers that have finished their annual growth cycle – especially those from which you want to save seed. If you belong to one of the specialist societies that runs its own seed-exchange scheme, or you feel like starting a seed swap at your own gardening group, then it's worth having something to donate. Even if you don't, saving seed from your own 'special' plants is a good insurance policy. So what's it worth saving seeds from?

Hardy annuals

A lot of hardy annuals shed their own seed naturally, so you often find self-sown plants popping up in places you may or may not want them. If you like to be a bit more organized about it, go around snipping off not-quite-ripe seedheads into a paper bag, write the name on

Collect up seeds from poppies before they self-sow and use them elsewhere in the garden.

Don't forget to enjoy your garden this month – the reward for all your work.

the front, and hang the bag up in a cool, dark, airy place to finish drying. I know you can buy packets of hardy annuals easily enough in the shops, but there's something very earthy about saving seeds from your own garden. Besides saving yourself a few bob, you can select your favourite colours and gradually produce your own strain. Good things to save include sweet peas, nasturtium, nigella, eschscholzia and other types of poppies.

Rock plants, bulbs and perennials

Unusual species of rock plants, bulbs and perennials are most in demand by seed-exchange schemes, but unless they are pure species and not named varieties they won't usually come true from seed. Collect the semi-ripe seedheads in paper bags as before, then hang them up in a dark, airy place – with a lot of species the seedpods will open, naturally releasing the seed into the bottom of the bag, where they can be collected up easily. Otherwise, you need to open the seedheads individually to extract the seeds, and pick out the bits of 'chaff' and debris to clean up the sample.

Plant colchicums as soon as they are on sale in nurseries and garden centres.

POT UP SELF-SOWN SEEDLINGS

With a lot of early-flowering garden plants it'll be too late to save seeds, but as you work around borders, look out for self-sown seedlings. This is the time of year you'll often find quite large colonies of plants, such as

hellebores, that are well worth saving. It's often difficult to put a name to very small seedlings, but once they have their first true leaves you can easily recognize them as small replicas of a nearby plant, so don't be over-scrupulous with the weeding. Self-sown seedlings can often be a good way to increase your stock for free, without all the bother of taking cuttings or sowing seed. By this time next year they'll be fair-sized plants, fit to plant out in the garden, and you'll have some useful swaps to trade with gardening friends.

- Go round digging up seedlings and potting them up – in the case of plants that don't like being moved as adults, such as hellebores, moving seedlings is the best way to start a new clump. Label the pots.

- Treat newly potted seedlings like unrooted cuttings until they've found their feet and are growing well. Put them in a shady cold frame, under the staging in a cool part of the greenhouse, on a shelf in the carport or even a shady windowsill indoors to grow on, where you can keep an eye on them.

PLANT AUTUMN-FLOWERING BULBS

When people think of bulbs, they usually automatically think of spring-flowering bulbs, such as daffodils and tulips. But, there are summer-flowering bulbs and also autumn-flowering kinds. The last group include autumn crocuses, colchicums and sternbergias, all of which appear in garden centres early this month. Because they flower in autumn, you have only a few weeks to get them planted before they start to flower, so buy them early and put them in straight away.

They all need well-drained soil in sun, although colchicums are also happy in light, dappled shade in the gaps between shrubs. Dry colchicum bulbs will also flower if they are placed on a windowsill indoors – with no compost and no water. They are a curiosity grown like this, but plant them out in the garden straight after the flowers are over.

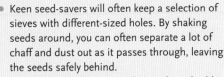

SEPARATING AND STORING SEED
- Keen seed-savers will often keep a selection of sieves with different-sized holes. By shaking seeds around, you can often separate a lot of chaff and dust out as it passes through, leaving the seeds safely behind.
- Another good wheeze is to lay seeds and rubbish on a flat surface and breathe very gently over the top – the heavier seeds stay put, while dust and lightweight bits of chaff blow away.
- Cleaned samples of seed are best stored in small paper envelopes inside screw-top, airtight jars somewhere dark in a room where the temperature stays steady. For best results, drop in a sachet of silica gel crystals. To re-use the sachets, dry them off in a warm oven to remove any residual moisture.

PLANT SPRING-FLOWERING BULBS

Plant narcissi and daffs between late August and late September.

DIVIDE BEARDED IRISES

Complete the division of bearded irises (see July, pp.187–8).

TAKE CUTTINGS OF ALPINES

To propagate alpines, you'll be taking very small semi-ripe or heel cuttings (see Trees, Shrubs and Climbers, p.207), depending on the growth habit of the individual type of plant. In some cases, e.g. sempervivums and saxifrages, all you'll be able to do is detach individual rosettes and remove the very lowest leaves to reveal a small length of stem. Insert the cuttings into a free-draining mixture of seed compost mixed with about 10 per cent sharp sand, water them in, and leave them to root in a cool shady place. Water sparingly and pot the plants individually when they are well rooted.

PATIOS AND CONTAINERS

KEEP CONTAINERS GOING

Now that tubs and hanging baskets are at their peak, the containers are packed solid with roots, so it's more essential than ever to keep plants frequently fed and watered.

- If the weather is really hot, give them an extra watering once the sun goes off them in the evening, so they have all night to soak up a good, long drink.

- To keep up the nutrients, change to quarter-strength liquid tomato feed at every watering if you find it easier to remember than feeding 'properly' once a week. All being well, you should be able to keep containers going for another month or two yet – but it becomes more of a struggle.

- Like any pot-bound plants, container plants out on your patio are desperately trying to set seed and die. Hot, dry weather will only be encouraging this, so don't give them any opportunity – double your vigilance on the deadheading. It's a pain, I know, and it's now you'll really be starting to wonder if you haven't made up a few more containers than you can really cope with – but stick with it. It would be a shame to spoil it all now for want of a little attention.

- Remember to feed and water permanent plants in tubs, such as shrubs and small trees.

POST-HOLIDAY PROBLEMS

If you've been away and your pots have dried out (see General Garden Tasks, p.206), consider setting up an irrigation system for next year (see June, p.171, and July Project, p.197).

Left: By late summer, your hanging baskets will need frequent watering and feeding, particularly in hot weather.

VEGETABLES AND HERBS

PICK YOUR CROPS

It's home-grown veg harvest time – this is a good month for inviting friends around, as there's so much that needs to be eaten. The following are ready for harvesting: French and runner beans, lettuce, beetroot, turnips, courgettes, onions, garlic, pencil leeks, marrows, calabrese, summer squashes, second early potatoes, outdoor tomatoes, and globe artichokes (see April, p.102).

LATE-SUMMER SOWINGS

The end of the summer is in sight, so as rows fall vacant, refill them with sowings of fast-growing varieties that will be ready to use quickly. In practice, that means sowing early varieties of carrots, peas and turnips as, odd though it sounds, they are the quickest to mature. If you have cloches or horticultural fleece, then you can deploy them in another month or 6 weeks, when the nights start getting cold, and they'll extend your cropping season well into autumn. Meanwhile, there is still time to sow lettuce, baby spinach leaves for salads, and you may want to sow a last few spring cabbages. In a good summer or a mild area, it's also worth sowing Chinese cabbage and pak choi.

CROP CARE

● One of your top priorities this month is keeping on top of the watering. You will also need to weed around recently sown crops, although most of the veg garden will be fairly thickly covered with crops so weeding is minimal in August.

● Thinking ahead, it's worth hammering stakes in alongside tall brassica plants, such as Brussels sprouts, sprouting broccoli and black Tuscany kale ('Nero di Toscana'), since strong winds can flatten top-heavy plants, which puts paid to your delicious, fresh midwinter veg.

● Take precautions against carrot fly by using insect-proof netting (see April, p.103).

OUTDOOR TOMATOES

'Stop' outdoor tomatoes if not done last month (see July, p.192).

CUT AND DRY OR FREEZE HERBS

Continue to cut and dry or freeze herbs (see July, p.191).

TAKE CUTTINGS FROM HERBS

Take semi-ripe cuttings from shrubby herbs such as bay, rosemary, sage and hyssop (see Trees, Shrubs and Climbers, p.207).

Home-grown peas are among the greatest delights of the vegetable garden.

Luscious-leaved chard makes a great foil for late summer flowers.

FRUIT

PRUNE FRUIT TREES AND BUSHES

Summer pruning is a job your grandfather probably did very little of, because fashions have changed and these days we tend to grow more compact trained fruit trees such as espaliers and cordons. It's these that need summer pruning, as well as soft fruit shortly after you've finished picking.

Pruning is the one job most new gardeners find terrifying. Oh, I know it always sounds complicated, but really there's nothing to worry about once you get started, and if you make the odd slip with the secateurs it's not the end of the world. The great thing about plants is they soon grow missing bits back again.

Summer-fruiting raspberries

Raspberries are even easier to prune than bush fruit. The normal summer-fruiting kind grow on a 2-year cycle – the canes grow one summer, then fruit the next. To prune raspberries, see the bow below.

Gooseberries and redcurrants

Gooseberry and redcurrant bushes are dead easy:

- Just cut back all the sideshoots by one-third. Do that whether your plants are allowed to grow naturally as bushes, or trained as cordons on a fence or against a wall.

- Both gooseberries and redcurrant plants are always grown on a leg – that is a short 'trunk', maybe 15–20cm (6–8in) high, between the ground and the place where the first branches spread out. Legs should be clean-shaven, so if there are any sideshoots growing out of yours, now's the time to whip them off while you have the secateurs handy.

- If you have a major structural rejuvenation in mind for old plants, that's a job to leave for the winter, when the plants lose their leaves and become dormant (see January, p.24).

Blackcurrants

Blackcurrants aren't difficult either. Don't try and prune them in the same way as gooseberries and redcurrants – they have a completely different style of growth. They should grow bushy right from the base.

- A lot of people nowadays prune their blackcurrants at the same time as they pick them, by cutting whole fruiting stems and

---

HOW TO PRUNE SUMMER-FRUITING RASPBERRIES

1 Cut all the old fruited canes down to 2.5cm (1in) above ground level. They're easy to spot, as the tops have a cluster of short sideshoots still bearing the brown calyces showing where you picked the fruit.

2 Tie in all the new unfruited canes that have grown up over this summer to a 'fence' of horizontal wires, spacing them out about 15cm (6in) apart.

3 If your raspberries have grown a tremendous crop of new canes, simply weed out the ones that have come up in the path instead of along your row, and thin out the rest, leaving the strongest canes 15cm (6in) apart.

4 If the rows haven't produced enough new canes to tie them 15cm (6in) apart, carefully dig up any that are growing in the path and transplant them into the row to fill it out.

bringing them into the kitchen to strip the fruit off in comfort, at a table.

- If you can't bring yourself to do that, then wait until after the fruit has been picked and then simply cut out two or three of the older stems close to the ground. This encourages new shoots to spring up from low down the plant. This way you're constantly replacing the older unproductive stems with new, high-yielding younger ones, so the plants don't grow geriatric.

Compact apple trees

Cordon apples are easier to prune than a traditional standard tree, because at least you can reach everything while you're standing on the ground. A cordon-trained tree consists of a trunk, from which twiggy clusters of short shoots or 'spurs' grow, and it's these that carry the fruit. Cordon trees can be upright, or planted on a 45-degree slope against a fence or horizontal wires.

- During the summer, long straight shoots grow out of the spurs, and these need cutting back now to about one leaf from the point where they leave a spur. Cut off any new shoot growing straight out of the tree trunk to leave it 10cm (4in) long, so it starts to form a new spur, which in turn will carry more fruit in future.

- Cut the growing tip of the trunk (or leader, in proper gardening parlance) off at a convenient height, which is usually as much as you can comfortably reach, i.e. about 2m (6ft) from the ground. That stops the tree growing any taller.

- If you have an espalier-trained tree, regard it as an upright trunk with several pairs of horizontal cordon trees growing out of it, and prune each branch as if it were a cordon apple tree in its own right.

You will need to prune compact apple trees this month for greater fruit yield next season.

WHAT NOT TO PRUNE

Although it sounds like open season on fruit pruning, there are some plants that you really mustn't chop about right now:

- Don't prune figs and grapevines, as they bleed badly if the stems are cut in summer; you can only cut them when they are safely dormant in midwinter (see January, pp.23–4).
- Don't prune autumn-fruiting raspberries, because you are only just starting to pick the fruit late this month; wait until late winter (see February, p.41).
- Don't prune standard apples and pears yet – instead, do this in midwinter (see January, p.23).
- It is best to keep the pruning of standard cherries and plums to the minimum, but if you must do it, carry it out in spring (see April, p.106), just after they've started growing, to avoid diseases that otherwise enter the plants through open wounds in winter.

Fan-trained fruit trees

Fan-trained fruit trees, such as peaches, nectarines, plums and cherries, can be dreadfully complicated if you want to prune them 'properly', but all you really have to do is keep each tree growing flat against the wall and shaped like the spokes of a fan.

- Tie in all the new shoots you can to the trellis or whatever support system the tree is growing against, and pinch out the growing tips of new sideshoots that are growing away from the wall. You can also 'stop' any shoots that you don't want to grow any longer by pinching out the growing tips.

PICK FRUIT

Harvest blackberries, loganberries, tayberries, peaches, nectarines, apricots, the first of the early varieties of eating apples (use them straight from the tree as they don't keep), and the last of the summer raspberries.

CUT STRAWBERRY RUNNERS

Late this month or next month, cut strawberry runners that were pegged down last month from the parent plant, to plant out or pot up to be forced inside during the winter for early fruit in spring (see October, p.257).

UNDER COVER

GREENHOUSE TASKS

Keep greenhouse crops fed, watered and ventilated, and damp down regularly in hot weather to keep them cool.

TAKE LATE CUTTINGS

In another 6–8 weeks, the first frost could kill off frost-tender plants such as pelargoniums and fuchsias. In the past, people used to bring them under cover for winter protection, but these days most of us find it more convenient to take cuttings.

Softwood cuttings, rooted now or early next month, can be left in small pots or trays until potting time in April, so they take up much less greenhouse space than great big, tatty old plants that have been dug up and repotted. What's more, autumn-rooted cuttings make much better plants next summer, as they are only youngsters. By then, the old plants, if you've kept them, are tough and woody, and they never flower half as well as youngsters.

Pelargoniums and fuchsias aren't the only things you can propagate now as a means of hanging on to your stock through the winter. Any other tender perennials can be treated the same way – they include all the popular patio and container plants such as verbena, argyranthemum, *Helichrysum petiolare*, penstemons and shrubby salvias.

- Take softwood cuttings in exactly the same way as you did in summer (see June, p.171), but instead of potting them as soon as they are rooted, leave them where they are until next spring.

GROW WINTER AND SPRING FLOWERS

If you're planning to heat the greenhouse or conservatory in winter, it's worth growing some flowering pot plants to cheer up the 'off' season. You can also take them indoors for temporary winter colour.

Hyacinths for Christmas

It seems premature to start thinking about Christmas already, but if you want forced hyacinths on time, you need to keep a watch on the garden centres now, because the new season's bulbs will be arriving some time this month, and the first things on your shopping list should be specially prepared hyacinths. Hyacinth bulbs that are described as 'specially prepared for Christmas' will cost you a bob or two more than the normal kind, but they've undergone heat treatment to fool them into flowering early, hence the extra cost. Normal, untreated hyacinths – and indeed other spring bulbs such as daffs – can also be forced using the same basic method, but they very often don't appear in the shops quite so early (look out for them in September) and they won't flower in time for Christmas. The best you can expect is that they'll bloom a few weeks earlier than if you planted them outdoors.

If you don't get the hyacinth bulbs planted by the middle of September at the absolute latest, you can't guarantee having them in

HOW TO PLANT HYACINTH BULBS INDOORS FOR CHRISTMAS

1 Plant each specially prepared, Christmas-flowering hyacinth bulb in its own individual pot, about 1cm ('/₂in) wider and 2.5cm (1in) deeper than the bulb. Plant in potting compost, so their noses are just showing above the surface. Water lightly and stand in a cool, dark place, e.g. a cupboard under the stairs or the garage. Check regularly and water if the compost starts to dry out. Protect from mice.

2 When the flowers start to open, select all the plants with flowers at exactly the same stage and plunge them, pots and all, up to their rims in a large container filled with moss for a professional-looking display, and bring them into the house. People will wonder how on earth you managed to get all your bulbs to reach exactly the same size and stage of maturity on the same day!

Young cineraria plants can be potted up now and kept under glass for winter flowers.

flower for 25 December, and frankly I'd feel a lot happier about putting them in before the end of August to be sure of the timing. Don't rush to bring them into the living room – it's important to give bulbs time to take root. If you bring them in too soon, you just end up with a lot of leaves and flowers with very short stems.

Cineraria, calceolaria and column stocks

Pot up any young plants of cineraria, calceolaria and column stocks you sowed in June. Cineraria and calceolaria may, with luck, be flowering in time for Christmas, or shortly afterwards, and column stocks make scented pot plants for early spring; if you grow a row or two in the greenhouse border, you can cut them to put in a vase indoors.

Florists' cyclamen

Florists' cyclamen are more of a long-term project. Sow seeds now to have plants coming into flower in time for Christmas next year. Soak the seeds in tepid water for 12 hours, then mix them with damp sand and keep them in a cool place out of the sun until you see the first signs of germination. When that happens, spread them out – sand and all – over the top of a tray of seed compost, keep them at about 10°C (50°F) through the winter (the propagator is ideal) and make sure they don't dry out. Keep the tiny plants growing steadily right through the summer if you can, and pot them up when they're big enough to handle.

Schizanthus and salpiglossis

Poor man's orchid (schizanthus) and salpiglossis are particularly spectacular. Sow them now, prick out the seedlings when they're big enough, one each per 8cm (3in) pot or a group of five in a 12–15cm (5–6in) pot, and grow them steadily in a frost-free greenhouse through the winter. Water carefully to avoid problems with mildew and you should have a good show of annual pot plants flowering in spring.

Narcissus

Narcissus varieties such as *Narcissus papyraceus* and *Narcissus* 'Grand Soleil d'Or' are fragrant, small-flowered narcissi with clusters of blooms on tall stems. They can be planted in three layers in a 20cm (8in) pot of multipurpose compost to bring early flowers into your house. They tend to shoot up earlier than hyacinths, sometimes taking only a couple of months to flower, and will fill your rooms with a delicious scent. Plant late September to mid-October for flowering over the Christmas season.

TOMATOES

Tomato plants are growing at their maximum rate, so you need to do the following:

- Increase feeding (using a high-potash tomato feed) and watering to keep pace.

- Continue pinching out sideshoots of cordon kinds (see July, p.195).

- If you see any old leaves at the bottom of the plant starting to turn yellow, snap them off cleanly where they join the main stem, as the plant has finished with them – if left, they'll only provide a starting place for fungal disease. De-leafing also lets more light and air circulate between the plants. But don't remove healthy green leaves, as the plant needs them for photosynthesis; contrary to popular belief, removing them doesn't speed up ripening.

PICK CROPS

Harvest greenhouse tomatoes, peppers, aubergines, cucumbers and cantaloupe melons (see July, p.195).

WATER GARDEN

CLEAR THE POND

Clear out yellowed or decomposing water lily leaves from the pond, thin out excess older leaves if the plants are overgrown and covering the pond completely, and thin out excess oxygenating waterweed. Remove blanket weed (see May, pp.145–6).

TOP UP WATER LEVELS

Keep ponds and water features topped up with water.

PROJECT Drying and processing chillies

Growing your own chillies is amazingly productive, in fact a single plant carries more chillies than most people could use in a couple of years. Very mild chillies can be stuffed with cream cheese and eaten just as they are, but anything hotter needs preserving for later.

What you need

Red, ripe chillies

Large darning needle

Strong thread (button thread or fine nylon line)

2 Take a large darning needle and some strong thread – button thread or fine nylon line is perfect. Thread the needle and push it through the neck of each chilli in turn, so you make a complete string of chillies.

3 Hang the chilli string up in an airy place out of the sun to dry – in Continental countries you often see chillies festooned around the balcony of town houses, or under the pergola of country villas.

1 Pick red, ripe chillies, wash if need be, and check them over – it's only worth using those that are in perfect condition.

SQUIRREL DETERRENT
If you have any slightly rough or damaged chillies, or simply more than you can use yourself, dry and grind them up – seeds and all. Save the powder in a dry tin, and mix a tablespoonful to a pound of birdseed, so that when you put it out on your bird table in winter the squirrels don't pinch it. Birds either don't mind or don't notice chilli, but squirrels can't stand it.

4 When they are completely dry, hang the string up in your kitchen (avoiding anywhere sunny or humid) and pull off chillies as you want to use them.

5 You can also grind them up to make paprika or hot chilli powder, depending on the strength of the particular variety you've grown. The idea is to crush them to powder in a pestle and mortar, or you can use a herb mill or small blender. For the hottest chilli powder, grind up seeds and all.

6 For a milder version, de-seed the chillies first. Wash your hands well before touching your eyes, as fresh chilli powder will sting badly – it's evil stuff.

SEPTEMBER

With the summer holidays over, it's back to work, and the same is true in the garden. There's a wistful air about it, as you resume regular jobs and take up the cudgels to keep the summer garden going for as long as possible, although the nip in the air at night reminds you that autumn is in the offing.

Not so long ago, September was the end of the season – time to put the garden to bed and brace yourself for the first frost – but not any more. Mild autumns have elongated the gardening season, so now it's worth growing plants that until lately we rarely risked growing – the kind that 'peak' late. They'll slot into summer borders to give you another month or two of colour and interest. If you've taken the plunge and planted an area of flowering prairie, you'll find it's approaching its absolute best right now, as the seedheads of ornamental grasses will coincide with your late perennials.

THE BIG PICTURE late perennials and grasses

Liriope muscari (above) revels in the curious common name of lilyturf – why, I couldn't say. It looks nothing like lilies or turf – if anything, it puts you in mind of an evergreen grape hyacinth that grows in slowly spreading colonies. It has narrow, strap-shaped evergreen leaves and spikes of knobbly lilac-purple flowers. This is another of those plants that should be grown more often; it's great ground cover under shrubs, and quite jolly in a prairie.

PEAK SEASON September– November.
GROWING CONDITIONS Lime-free soil in sun or light shade.

Kniphophias, or red-hot pokers, mostly flower in summer, but when the mainstream species are over the late starters are just approaching their prime. *Kniphofia triangularis* (syn. *Kniphofia galpinii*) is not your regular border version by any means; it has the botanical air you'd expect of a wild species. Clumps grow roughly 90 × 45cm (36 × 18in), the leaves are narrow and grass-like, and the 'pokers' are loose spikes of brilliant red tubes – a good choice for a prairie. *Kniphofia* 'Samuel's Sensation' is a traditional type, 1.5 × 1.2m (5 × 4ft), with two-tone red and yellow pokers. But red-hot pokers don't have to be red: 'Little Maid' (above) has narrow, cream and ivory-white pokers on small grassy-leaved plants, 60 × 45cm (24 × 18in), and 'Percy's Pride', 90 × 60cm (36 × 24in), has green and yellow pokers that look almost lime green from a distance. All the varieties mentioned lose their leaves in winter, which is not the case with all red-hot pokers.

PEAK SEASON September– November.
GROWING CONDITIONS Well-drained soil in sun.

Solidago, goldenrod, is good in late borders and wonderful for prairies – it's the way it grows naturally in the wild. Its varieties are mostly rather upright plants with yellow plumes of flower. 'Golden Wings' is the giant of the family and can reach 1.5 × 1m (5 × 3ft); 'Queenie' (syn. *Solidago* 'Golden Thumb') is the exact opposite at 30 × 30cm (1 × 1ft); for something really different, look out for 'Crown of Rays' and *Solidago rugosa* 'Fireworks' (above), which have flowers that grow horizontally on their stalks. All goldenrods are good for cutting, but the unusual orientation of these two make them particular favourites. For a frothier effect, choose × *Solidaster luteus*, a cross between a solidago and an aster, 90 × 30cm (3 × 1ft), with sprays of tiny, pale yellow daisy flowers and a longer flowering season than most of its cousins; again, it's good for cutting.

PEAK SEASON September– October (solidaster July–September).
GROWING CONDITIONS Any soil except poorly drained, in sun or light shade.

Actaea matsumurae 'White Pearl', bugbane (previously known as cimicifuga), grows 1.1m × 60cm (3½ × 2ft), with spikes of fluffy white flowers that make it look a lot like a late delphinium, except that while real delphiniums are martyrs to every pest going, bugbane fights back with its own built-in insect repellent; if only more plants would take this enlightened view. *Actaea simplex* Atropurpurea Group (above), 60cm × 1.2m (24in × 4ft), has fluffy pinkish white flowers in September and October.

PEAK SEASON September– October.
GROWING CONDITIONS Reasonably well-drained soil containing plenty of organic matter, in light shade. Great between shrubs or in woodland gardens.

OLD FAITHFULS

Perennial grasses of the sort grown for their shaggy flowers and seedheads look increasingly good as the summer moves on, but they are at their best in autumn. *Stipa tenuissima* makes a modest 60 × 30cm (2 × 1ft) clump of dense, feathery plumes that ripple in the breeze. Its big brother, *Stipa gigantea*, is totally different – a neat tussock of evergreen leaves about 60 × 60cm (2 × 2ft), with 1.5–2m (5–6ft) long stems of golden oats that glitter in the sun, forming a large, airy spray overhead. The overall effect is light and hazy, so you can plant this in front of other things without blocking your view. *Pennisetum villosum* (above) has spectacular seedheads, resembling big furry tails on sticks. The plants grow into clumps 60 × 60cm (2 × 2ft), and aren't totally hardy, so they need winter protection in a cold area. *Deschampsia cespitosa* is an evergreen tussock of fine, arching foliage, with a sheaf of slender flowering stems that slowly dry out over the summer and change colour depending on variety.

PEAK SEASON July–November.
GROWING CONDITIONS
  Reasonably fertile soil (lime-free for deschampias) with some organic matter, in sun.

Aster novae-belgii, Michaelmas daisies, are autumn classics, but they are right so-and-sos for powdery mildew, which makes the plants look as if they're covered with talcum powder. Avoid this by growing other species instead. *Aster amellus* varieties have similar daisy-like flowers – 'King George', 45 × 30cm (18 × 12in), has lavender-blue flowers; 'Veilchenkönigin' (above), 45 × 45cm (18 × 18in) has violet-purple flowers; 'Brilliant', 75 × 45cm (30 × 18in), is pink, and being shorter than the 'real thing' you don't usually have to stake them. *Aster pilosus* var. *pringlei* 'Monte Cassino', 75 × 30cm (30 × 12in), has a froth of tiny white flowers, good for flower arranging. There are also *Aster ericoides* cultivars, such as 'Brimstone' (pale yellow) and 'Pink Cloud', growing 90 × 30cm (3 × 1ft), and a good many varieties of *Aster novae-angliae*, New England asters, in the same size range as Michaelmas daisies. 'Harrington's Pink' is popular, a good pink with lots of petals, growing 120 × 45cm (48 × 18in).

PEAK SEASON September–November.
GROWING CONDITIONS Well-drained soil with plenty of organic matter, in sun.

Clematis tibetana **subsp. vernayi** and *Clematis tangutica* are both grown with only half a mind to the flowers – their great assets are big, fluffy seedheads that are seen at their best in the autumn. Flowers and seedheads overlap for a while, doubling the display. Both will grow to 5–6m (15–20ft). *Clematis* 'Bill MacKenzie' (above), a hybrid of *C. tangutica*, has deep, golden yellow lantern flowers.

PEAK SEASON July–October (flowers), September–November (seedheads).
GROWING CONDITIONS Deep, fertile soil, any aspect but north, growing where roots are shaded but stems grow out into good light.

Physalis alkekengi **var. franchetii**, Chinese lantern (above), is great fun. A herbaceous perennial, it has uninspiring small, cream-coloured, bell-shaped flowers that you hardly notice in summer, followed by papery 5cm (2in) lanterns that slowly turn from green to beige and finally a luminous orange-red in autumn. Flower arrangers often cut the stems at that stage to dry out for winter decorations. Plants grow 60 × 90cm (2 × 3ft) but spread by suckers and can roam further if not curbed.

PEAK SEASON September–October.
GROWING CONDITIONS Any reasonable garden soil, in sun or light shade.

SOMETHING SPECIAL

Schizostylis coccinea looks like clumps of rather refined, pint-sized gladioli. '**Major**' (above) is the one you mostly see, with 5cm (2in) diameter coppery-red flowers; '**Sunrise**' is more of a warm salmon shade, and '**Mrs Hegarty**' has clear pale pink flowers that go on for weeks after 'Major' comes to an end; '**Jennifer**' is especially robust, at around 60cm (2ft) high, and her flowers are clear soft pink. Clumps spread slowly to 45 × 45cm (18 × 18in). Every garden should have one.

PEAK SEASON September–November.

GROWING CONDITIONS Moist but not boggy fertile soil, in sun or light shade.

Cyclamen hederifolium (above) is the autumn-flowering hardy cyclamen, whose flowers open before the leaves appear. The leaves are relatively large for a hardy cyclamen, and ivy-shaped, mostly with grey dots and splashes or heavy marbling, which makes a Persian carpet effect when the plants are massed together. Individual plants are only 10 × 10cm (4 × 4in) high. Just as a bonus, the leaves last all winter.

PEAK SEASON September–November.

GROWING CONDITIONS Well-drained soil with lots of humus, in light shade.

***Callicarpa bodinieri* var. *giraldii* 'Profusion'**, beauty berry (above), is a shrub you don't often see, and I can never understand why. Now, I know it sits there doing nothing very much for three-quarters of the year, but just when you need something new to grab your interest, there it is, on cue, with its autumn pyrotechnic display. The leaves turn vivid oranges and reds, coinciding with clusters of small, violet-purple berries, which then remain on the bare twigs until Christmas. Not a colour you often find in the late garden.

PEAK SEASON September–December.

GROWING CONDITIONS Not fussy – any soil except badly drained soil, in sun or light shade.

Zauschneria californica, Californian fuchsia, often causes confusion in nurseries because it isn't a fuchsia at all, and to be honest the flowers are only a tiny bit fuchsia-like. They are long, tubular, and a soft shade of orange, set against delicate, feathery, sage-green foliage. You might find the plain species or its cultivar '**Dublin**' (syn. '**Glasnevin**' – above) – they look very similar. Plants grow 30 × 30cm (1 × 1ft), and may die down to ground level in winter, but they spread gently from underground stems and pop up generally just where you want them. Slightly tender.

PEAK SEASON August–October.

GROWING CONDITIONS Very well-drained, gravelly soil in sun. Best in a raised bed, large alpine sink or rock feature.

Tricyrtis formosana (above) suffers from a very unfortunate common name – toad lily. Anything less like a toad would be hard to find. It's actually a very beautiful plant, something like a tiny tiger lily but with mauve and white spotted flowers instead of the usual loud orange and black colour scheme. It's not the easiest plant to accommodate; it wants woodland conditions, and slugs will divert miles from their route especially to eat it. But it's worth any amount of trouble. It's a little gem.

PEAK SEASON September–
   October.
GROWING CONDITIONS Well-
   drained, lime-free soil with lots
   of organic matter, in light
   shade.

OTHER PLANTS IN THEIR PRIME IN SEPTEMBER

- **Trees** *Sophora japonica*
- **Shrubs** *Abelia chinensis, Aralia elata, Buddleja davidii* (see p.178), *Caryopteris × clandonensis, Ceanothus × delileanus* 'Gloire de Versailles' (see p.179), *Ceratostigma willmottianum, Colutea arborescens, Fuchsia* (hardy), *Hibiscus syriacus* (see p.202), *Hydrangea arborescens, Hydrangea macrophylla* (see p.179), *Hydrangea paniculata, Hydrangea villosa, Indigofera heterantha, Perovskia* (see p.201), *Potentilla fruticosa* (see p.152), *Phygelius* (see p.201), *Rosa* (see pp.150–1), *Romneya* (see p.181), *Spiraea × japonica* 'Anthony Waterer'
- **Evergreens** *Calluna, Ceanothus* 'Autumnal Blue', *Cistus, Daboecia, Erica cinerea, Erica tetralix, Erica vagans, Erica vulgaris, Escallonia, Hebe* (see p.178), *Hypericum calycinum, Hypericum* 'Hidcote', *Myrtus communis, Olearia × haastii, Osmanthus heterophyllus, Spartium junceum, Tamarix pentandra* (see p.203), *Vinca*
- **Berries/fruits** *Chaenomeles, Clerodendrum trichotomum, Cydonia oblonga, Leycesteria formosa, Malus* (see p.244), *Nandina domestica, Passiflora caerulea* (see p.178), *Photinia davidiana, Rosa* 'Geranium', *Rosa rugosa, Sorbus*
- **Climbers/wall shrubs** *Campsis, Clematis* 'Barbara Jackman', *Clematis* 'Bees Jubilee', *Clematis* 'Comtesse de Bouchaud', *Clematis* 'Duchess of Edinburgh', *Clematis* 'General Sikorski' (see p.152), *Clematis* 'Hagley Hybrid' (see p.152), *Clematis* 'Jackmanii' (see p.152), *Clematis* 'Mevrouw le Coultre', *Clematis* 'Nelly Moser' (see p.119), *Clematis* 'Proteus', *Clematis* Texensis cultivars, *Clematis* 'The President', *Clematis* 'Ville de Lyon', *Clematis* Viticella cultivars (see pp.180 and 202), *Clematis* 'Vyvyan Pennell', *Eccremocarpus scaber, Fallopia baldschuanicum, Fremontodendron californicum, Jasminum officinale, Lonicera × brownii, Lonicera periclymenum* 'Serotina', *Passiflora caerulea* (see p.178), *Solanum crispum* 'Glasnevin' (see p.179), *Magnolia grandiflora*
- **Perennials** *Actaea, Agapanthus* (see p.176), *Alstroemeria* (see p.154), *Anaphalis triplinervis, Anemone hupehensis* (see p.200), *Anemone × hybrida* (see p.200), *Aster amellus, Aster ericoides, Aster × frikartii, Aster novae-angliae, Aster pilosus* var. *pringlei, Centaurea dealbata, Centranthus ruber, Ceratostigma plumbaginoides, Clematis heracleifolia, Chrysanthemum rubellum, Cortaderia selloana, Dianthus, Eryngium, Helenium, Helianthus* (see p.202), *Hemerocallis, Heuchera, Ligularia, Monarda, Nepeta, Penstemon* (see p.176), *Persicaria affinis* (see p.200), *Phlox paniculata* (see p.200), *Rudbeckia, Salvia × superba, Scabiosa, Sedum* (see p.201)
- **Bulbs** *Amaryllis belladonna* (see p.246), *Canna, Crinum × powellii* (see p.203), *Colchicum* (see p.245), *Crocus speciosus, Dahlia* (see p.201), *Galtonia, Gladiolus callianthus, Gladiolus murielae, Nerine bowdenii* (see p.246), *Sternbergia lutea, Tigridia*
- **Bedding** Summer bedding (half-hardy annuals) and patio plants
- **Rock plants** *Acaena, Campanula, Convolvulus cneorum, Dianthus plumarius, Erigeron mucronatus, Lithodora diffusa, Silene uniflora*

SEPTEMBER at-a-glance checklist

GENERAL GARDEN TASKS (p.225)
✔ Keep watering and deadheading.
✔ Cut out flowered stems of perennial plants to keep borders tidy as later flowers take over.
✔ Get the compost going – autumn clearing generates a lot of waste for the compost heap.

LAWNS (p.225)
✔ Once the dry weather comes to an end, scarify and spike the lawn and apply autumn lawn feed; add top-dressing, particularly if you garden on clay, chalk or sandy soil.
✔ Repair broken lawn edges and attend to bald patches, broken lawn edges, bumps and hollows.
✔ Make new lawns from seed around the middle of the month, but delay laying turf until October or November.

TREES, SHRUBS AND CLIMBERS (p.228)
✔ Plant and move conifers and evergreens.
✔ Deadhead roses.
✔ Clip hornbeam, beech, Leyland cypress and thuja hedges before the middle of the month, if you haven't already done so.

✔ Cut slow-growing yew and box hedges now if you only want to do the job once each year.
✔ Give fast-growing privet and *Lonicera nitida* hedges their final cut of the season.

FLOWERS (p.229)
✔ Plant spring bulbs, although tulips and hyacinths are best left for another month or two.
✔ Replace summer bedding as it comes to an end with plants for winter and spring, and keep newly planted bedding watered.
✔ Deadhead and protect dahlias.
✔ Support tall flowers.
✔ Collect seed from perennials and alpines.

PATIOS AND CONTAINERS (p.231)
✔ Plant winter bedding and spring bulbs in containers.
✔ Stop feeding permanent plants growing in containers.
✔ Move tender plants under cover in cold areas.

VEGETABLES AND HERBS (p.233)
✔ Cover late crops of salads, courgettes and carrots, etc. with cloches or horticultural fleece and leave nets over brassicas.
✔ Sow overwintering onions as well as quick crops, such as baby spinach, for salad leaves.
✔ Plant spring cabbage plants.
✔ Harvest marrows, courgettes, sweetcorn, French and runner beans, lettuce, rocket, spring onions, Chinese leaves, oriental radishes, autumn cauliflower, cabbages, pencil leeks, maincrop potatoes, onions, shallots, garlic, and the last of the globe artichokes.
✔ Leave tomatoes on the plants until the weather turns, then bring them indoors to ripen.
✔ Cut down asparagus foliage once it has turned yellow or buff (it may occur next month).
✔ Pot up herbs such as chives, mint, basil, coriander and parsley.

FRUIT (p.235)
✔ Pick blackberries, the first of the autumn-fruiting raspberries, early varieties of apples, and later varieties as they ripen, and the first Conference pears towards the end of the month.
✔ Prune cane fruits.

UNDER COVER (p.236)
✔ Reduce the watering and feeding of all greenhouse plants.
✔ Bring in tender plants to overwinter in cold areas.
✔ Plant early spring bulbs in pots.
✔ Sow hardy annuals for early spring flowers in an unheated greenhouse or conservatory.
✔ Stop feeding and reduce the watering of tomatoes, peppers, aubergines, cucumbers and melons. At the end of the month, as crops come to an end, pull out the plants to make room for overwintering tender perennials and exotics.

WATER GARDEN (p.238)
✔ Continue to feed fish until the weather breaks.
✔ Give a final light thinning-out of oxygenating plants, but only if necessary.

Watch out for
● Vine weevil under glass; the main attack comes in April or May, but if you've had problems before keep an eye out for a second batch now.
● Pigeons eating your brassicas.
● Earwigs in dahlias.

Get ahead
● Spring-clean the greenhouse if summer crops, such as tomatoes, have already come to an end; prepare the border soil and sow winter salads.

Last chance
● The middle of September is the absolute latest you can plant Christmas hyacinth bulbs in order to ensure they're in flower for 25 December.

GENERAL GARDEN TASKS

REGULAR MAINTENANCE TASKS

Keep on top of watering, deadheading, cutting back and general tidying around the garden. Continue looking out for pests and diseases (see May, pp.125, 133–4 and 142–3).

SORT OUT THE COMPOST

Buy or make a compost bin or heap and start recycling all your autumn garden waste. You'll be certain of having a home-grown supply of organic compost to use for mulching the garden in spring (see October, p.249).

LAWNS

REJUVENATE THE LAWN

Grass takes a terrible battering and the smaller the garden the more intensively it gets bashed and trampled. When you have children and pets it's used more like an all-weather sportsground-cum-outdoor-leisure-centre, but you still want it to look like the living room carpet.

An annual spring feed is fine for the average lawn (see April, p.88), but a heavily used, small family lawn needs extra help to stop it deteriorating into a sea of mud. Some serious maintenance is called for in autumn (see box below).

FITNESS TRAINING FOR LAWNS

To rejuvenate a neglected lawn, follow the full programme, and to keep a hard-used lawn fighting-fit repeat it every year. It's good exercise too, so if you're not used to hard manual work, divide the job up into several easy stages – it does wonders for the waistline.

Step 1: Mow the grass
Mow the lawn as usual, using the grass box to collect the clippings.

Step 2: Rake out moss and weeds
Rake hard to scratch out moss and 'thatch' – the accumulation of dead grass and old creeping stems that makes a mature lawn feel springy. Raking also lifts up creeping grasses and mats of trefoil that usually pass straight under the mower. If you only have a small lawn, you can rake it by hand with a long, flexible, wire-toothed rake; otherwise buy or hire a powered lawn raker. Don't worry if enormous quantities of rubbish come out of the lawn. If it hasn't been done for years, the lawn can look quite patchy afterwards. It will soon recover.

Step 3: Mow again
Mow the lawn again, but at right angles to how you did it last time, so instead of cutting the grass from the top of the garden to the bottom, you work from side to side. This way you'll chop off all the creeping grasses and weeds raised by raking. The compost heap will be filling up fast.

Step 4: Spike the lawn
It's worth spiking any lawn every 3 or 4 years if you want to keep it in tip-top condition, but a family lawn that really gets badly trodden down needs doing every year, otherwise the turf gets so hard-packed that water can't run away properly. Bad surface drainage encourages moss and discourages grass. In serious cases, you end up with a lawn that's full of liverwort and slimy patches of algae in a wet winter, which makes it slippery to walk on, and more muck than ever comes indoors.

Spiking sorts all that out, by making air holes in the turf and alleviating compaction. You can rent or buy various devices to make the job easier, but again if you only have a small area to do it's often as easy to do it by hand. Using an ordinary garden fork, stab it down 8–10cm (3–4in) deep every 10–15cm (4–6in) all over the grass. If you can't do the lot, at least give the places that get the most wear a good going-over.

Step 5: Feed the grass
It's no good thinking you can use up your spare spring lawn feed or left-over general garden fertilizer. No, in autumn a lawn needs a special low-nitrogen feed. 'More expense' you're probably thinking, but there's a good reason. A proper autumn formula lawn feed toughens the grass up, ready for winter, instead of making it grow fast as a spring lawn feed would do – with cold weather coming up, this would just knock it for six.

Step 6: Top-dress the lawn
Top-dressing is the icing on the cake for a true lawn-lover, but it's worth doing if you garden on lousy clay, chalk or sandy soil, since it is the only way you can beef up the soil once it's covered with turf. Top-dressing works rather like mulching a flowerbed, but there's less of it. You can only put on a very thin layer of material at a time – if you bury the grass you'll kill it.

The idea is to sprinkle a 5mm ($^1/_4$in) layer of very fine material over the grass from a shovel, and then work it in with a stiffish yard broom or besom so that most of it disappears. Some goes down the holes you made when you spiked the lawn, and some is dragged down by worms.

The material you use for top-dressing depends very much on the state of the soil. If you have light, sandy soil, then use sifted topsoil or bags of ready-made, compost-style turf dressing to add some body. On heavy clay soil, a dressing of gritty horticultural sand improves the surface drainage and aeration, besides making the surface firmer in wet weather. For normal soil, a mixture of topsoil, compost and sand is best – keen gardeners usually mix up their own in a barrow and then sprinkle it on through one of those big round garden riddles, the sort that looks like a huge flat sieve without a handle.

Most years, you should be able to start autumn maintenance any time this month, but after a long, hot, dry summer wait until there's been enough rain to soak the ground well so the grass is growing again. You can leave the job until October if need be.

CARRY OUT LAWN REPAIRS

While you're in the mood for lawns, this is a good time to do any running repairs to bald patches, broken edges, or bumps and hollows. But unless you want a lawn that looks like a bowling green, there's no need to be too obsessive – these days the natural look is in vogue, and a few dips and slopes add to the character.

Bald patches

These are easily fixed by scuffing up the soil with the prongs of a fork, sprinkling some grass seed thinly over the top, then roughly covering it with seed compost and keeping it watered. But if you want instant results, just dig out a square in the problem area and patch it with pieces of turf; 30cm (1ft) squares are the easiest to manage and fine for filling small gaps. You can often cut some from elsewhere in the garden, if you want to enlarge a border or make a new bed. Cut turves out with a sharp spade, 4cm (1½in) deep, and then slide the blade underneath to ensure they have a flat level base that lies in place in your prepared patch. The other alternative is to buy a few strips of turf; garden centres often keep a pile of it handy now and in spring for this sort of job.

To repair a broken lawn edge, cut away the piece of turf, turn it around and reseed the bare patch.

Bumps

Whatever you do, don't just ram bumps with the mower. That just slices off the top like a boiled egg, and leaves an incurably bald patch, which is scalped again each time you cut the grass. And don't borrow a garden roller to squash the bump flat – that just compacts the ground so badly that grass can't grow. No, the only solution is to do the job properly. Fetch a spade and skim off the turf. Level the bump, leaving a square of soil with a firm, flat base about 2.5cm (1in) below grass level, then fit the turf back in place.

Hollows

These are no problem if they aren't too deep. Just top-dress the sunken areas four or five times each year between spring and autumn, using the same technique described for lawns earlier (see box, p.225). True, you can only apply about 5mm (¼in) of top-dressing each time, but by keeping at it regularly you'll slowly level the turf off – and without needing major earth-works.

With a bigger hollow, the temptation is always just to whack more turf over the top of what's there to bring the level flush with the surrounding grass. Don't do it. New turf can't root easily into the top of existing grass. Instead, spike the grass that's already there well, then fill up the hollow with topsoil, firm and level the surface, and reseed it or lay turf over that.

Broken lawn edges

If you have a broken edge where the lawn meets a bed or border, remove the square of turf containing the broken edge, lift it out, turn it around and put it back so there is now a firm, straight edge to the lawn, with the broken bit making a hole in the grass. Fill the hole with topsoil, firm it down so it doesn't sink later, and sprinkle some seed over the top. It's a good idea to mark the spot with a couple of canes to stop people walking on your newly sown seed, and you'll have to mow around it for a while, but by next spring you won't see the join.

CREATE A NEW LAWN

Whether you're going to sow seed or splash out on an instant lawn from turf, good soil preparation is the key (see opposite). As September is traditionally the start of the season for making new lawns, push ahead with the soil preparation as soon as you can, then it's all ready for sowing seed later this month or sometime next, or for laying turf in October or November. If we've had a long, hot, dry summer, then the soil will be far too hard to 'work'. Wait until the rain has come and the ground is soft enough to dig, so the clods smash up nicely.

Sowing lawn seed

When you're making a new lawn from seed, you'll be pleased to know that the soil preparation is nine-tenths of the work. The rest is a push-over. Once you've sown the lawn, it doesn't look very promising to start with, but it grows slowly over the winter and by spring it'll be a proper lawn.

- Buy enough seed for the area you want to cover – personally, I'd ignore the old advice to use 50g (2oz) per square metre (yard) and opt for half that amount. It establishes just as fast, but you won't have anything like the trouble with fungal disease, since the grass seedlings won't be so overcrowded. Weigh out 25g (1oz), tip it into a plastic cup and mark the side to use as a measure.

- Sow all the seed (see box, p.228), then go over the area with a rake to mix the seed roughly into the surface of the soil. Don't worry about burying it all.

- With any luck, you've chosen a day for sowing when it's going to rain, but if nothing has happened 48 hours later, then it's probably worth turning the sprinkler on. Give it a fair

ORGANIC MATTER

When creating a new lawn you need to add organic matter. Whatever you can get most of will do fine. It might be matured manure from your local riding stables, council compost from the nearest recycling scheme, or a little something you've knocked up at home in your own bins. If your soil is really poor and thin, you might do better to buy in some serious topsoil – it's cheaper by the lorry load than buying bags from a garden centre.

old soaking, and unless the weather turns really dry that's probably all it will need.

- Within a few weeks you should start to see a haze of green forming over the ground, which slowly develops into a thin rash of grass. It's perfectly natural to find lots of weeds coming up, but bear with it, because once you start mowing the grass they'll disappear all on their own. They aren't 'proper' lawn weeds, they're the same sort that come up uninvited in your borders – and mowing acts like hoeing. Once you start cutting the new lawn regularly next spring, the regular beheading soon kills them off.

HOW TO PREPARE SOIL FOR A LAWN

1 Start by clearing the ground of any weeds, stones and rubbish. Unless your soil is in good shape, you'll need to lay in sensible quantities of organic matter to improve it (see box above). Spread it evenly all over the ground and dig it in. Break down lumps of hard soil by bashing them with the back of a fork.

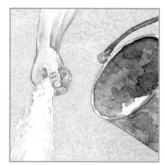

2 While the ground is still only rough-dug, sprinkle on some general fertilizer at about half the usual rate, or use a proper pre-seeding lawn fertilizer. Give the patch a good going-over with a rake, to work in the fertilizer and smooth out the soil, and take out any big stones and bits of root you turn up.

3 Firming comes next. Don't use a roller, feet are best – but be methodical. Start at one end of the patch, and trample the soil in a straight line across the end of the plot, then turn around and trample your way back. Keep doing that until you've covered the whole area in footprints.

4 Rake over your footprints, leaving the ground firm and level, with a surface like fine cake-crumbs. Fill any hollows and leave the ground flat. Remove any more lumps, roots or debris and rake over the marks. You may need to do this two or three times. Keep off the lawn until you are ready to start sowing seed or laying turf.

In autumn, the garden palette starts changing to more sultry tones – rich reds, golden yellows, deep oranges, and mellow purples and blues.

● Keep off the lawn until spring, apart from giving it a light trim once it's grown 5cm (2in) high.

SEED-SOWING TIPS

When sowing lawn seed, it pays to practise your sowing technique so the grass comes up evenly, not in great tussocks with bald patches in between them. Weigh out 25g (1oz) of grass seed – it's roughly a handful – and sprinkle it as evenly as you can over a couple of sheets of newspaper laid out to make 1 square metre (yard). Now remember what that looked like, and go out and do the same thing for real, sprinkling the seed thinly and evenly over the whole of your patch. Still not confident about getting it right? You could always mark the plot roughly into square metres (yards) by laying down strings, or marking the area out with the tip of a cane. Another good tip is to divide the total amount of seed in half and sow one lot right to left and the other lot up and down the patch.

TREES, SHRUBS AND CLIMBERS

PLANT AND MOVE EVERGREEN SHRUBS AND CONIFERS

September is a good time to plant or move evergreen shrubs and conifers, if you weren't able to do it in April. It's probably the very best time if you garden on very light soil that dries out badly in summer, but on heavy soil that's wet in winter I'd wait until April.

Follow the same technique described in spring (see April, pp.89–90), but with one proviso. Autumn and winter are notorious for gales, so you'll need to protect newly planted evergreens from cold, drying winds. Evergreens have a nasty habit of going brown if the foliage becomes desiccated, and conifers are the worst of the lot. It's bad enough when the new and expensive plant ends up looking piebald for a while, but in a bad case the whole thing turns brown and that often kills it completely.

Unless you have a naturally well-sheltered spot, surround newly planted evergreens and conifers with a screen of hessian sacking, or some other small-mesh fabric, tacked to a ring of poles for the entire first winter. Once they're well established there shouldn't be a problem – if there is, then you've chosen the wrong spot and I'd try something deciduous there instead.

DEADHEAD ROSES

Continue deadheading roses as the flowers fade, and prune repeat- or continuous-flowering old-fashioned shrub and species roses (other than those grown for hips) when the last flush of flowers is finished (see July, p.184).

CLIP HEDGES

● Clip hornbeam, beech, Leyland cypress and thuja hedges before mid-September if you haven't done so already (see May, pp.127–8).

● Cut slow-growing yew and box hedges now if you only want to do the job once each year, and give fast-growing privet and *Lonicera nitida* hedges their final cut of the season (see May, pp.127–8).

FLOWERS

PLANT BIENNIALS, AND WINTER AND SPRING BEDDING

Clear summer bedding plants from beds and borders as the plants reach the end of the road later this month. Fork over the areas, working in some well-rotted organic matter, and then transplant summer-sown biennials, or winter and spring bedding, including polyanthus divisions, into the gaps. Keep them all well watered while they find their feet.

If you didn't grow your own, you'll find wallflowers on sale now, either pot-grown or in bundles – they are a speciality of old-fashioned greengrocers. Untie the bundles and stand the plants in a bucket of water overnight for a good, reviving soak before planting them out. There will be plenty of winter-flowering pansies and ornamental cabbages and kales on sale at the garden centres. You might find a few biennials as well, but normally you have to grow your own, and the majority of spring bedding plants aren't usually sold until next spring, when they're starting to flower.

A lot of people like to keep early spring bedding under cover for the winter and only plant it outside once the weather is on the mend in February or March. Coloured primroses are the most delicate members of the spring bedding 'family', and to see them at their best they need keeping in a cold or frost-free greenhouse or conservatory until conditions are relatively kind. They also make brilliant early-flowering pot plants for greenhouses, conservatories and porches.

PLANT SPRING BULBS

The big job to do this month is organize your spring bulb displays for next year. Buy early, while there's still the full range in the shops to choose from – popular varieties disappear like snow off a ditch.

In general, you get what you pay for; the bigger, more expensive bulbs will produce more flowers, and really small, cheap bulbs can prove to be a false economy, as they may not be big enough to flower. Choose plump, firm bulbs, with no visible signs of cuts or bruising. Damaged bulbs aren't worth having, but don't worry about small green sprouts showing at the very tips of bulbs, especially if you don't buy them until a bit later in the season. Give any that have long, spindly shoots a miss though.

How to plant bulbs

Most bulbs can be planted straight away, but leave tulips and hyacinths until October or November – they're late starters, and are safer in paper bags kept cool and dry indoors than in damp ground outside, where they might rot before they have a chance to take root.

- The important thing when planting bulbs is to bury them deeply enough. As a rough and ready rule, aim to plant any bulb three times its own depth, measured from top-to-bottom.

- You can take out individual planting holes with a trowel, but if you have lots to do, it's much easier if you use a proper bulb-planting tool. The one with a metal 'ring' at its tip never seems to dig deeply enough on all but the lightest soil (and shallow-planted bulbs are notorious for not flowering in succeeding years), but the one that is like a set of shark's jaws on a handle is much better, as it can be forced deeper into the soil. You open the 'jaws', push them into the ground, and close them to grab a 'mouthful' of soil; then lift the planter out, drop a bulb down the hole and open the jaws over the top to make it spit the soil out again to plug the gap. Job done, and good fun for younger members of the family.

- If you garden on heavy soil, such as clay, it's well worth dropping a handful of coarse, gritty sand into the bottom of the hole, as this improves the drainage in the crucial rooting zone.

- To plant bulbs in pots, see Under Cover, p.236.

MOWING AROUND BULBS IN LAWNS
It's quite safe to carry on mowing the grass as usual until mid-November or so. After that, mow around the area. The last cut is important though, as it ensures that the grass is still fairly short at bulb-flowering time, so the heads show up well above the grass instead of being hidden in it. Remember that the bulb foliage will have to be left intact for 6 weeks after flowering.

Plant spring-flowering bulbs for a spectacular display next year.

Earwig traps

If earwigs are nibbling the petals of your dahlias, stuff balls of screwed up newspaper into flowerpots stuck upside down on the tops of canes, and pushed in between the flowers; at daylight, the little dears will crawl inside to hide, so you can remove them every morning. But don't destroy them – tip them out down the garden, because for the rest of the year they clear up useful amounts of greenfly.

Planting bulbs beneath shrubs and trees

Nowadays, most bulbs are grown in random groups, or drifts, between shrubs in mixed borders so they look as natural as possible. Instead of being dug up and replanted each year, 'naturalized' bulbs are left permanently in place to spread, and they are only dug up when they are clearly over-crowded.

● When you want to plant bulbs this way, between shrubs or under trees, it's not possible to prepare the ground as well as usual, but dig out any weeds, loosen the soil and work some general organic fertilizer into the area.

● Instead of worrying about 'proper' spacing, scatter handfuls of bulbs around and plant them where they fall – this is the best way to achieve a natural-looking effect. The thing to avoid at all costs is any bulbs that end up in a straight line – even when it's accidental, they always draw your eye straight to them once they're in flower. Curves are best.

Naturalizing bulbs in lawns

Another very good-looking way to grow bulbs is by naturalizing them in the lawn. Daffs and crocuses are the most popular and generally most reliable kinds to use in this way, although squills are good in a slightly shady situation under trees, snakeshead fritillary is good in damp ground, and waterlily tulips will often thrive in a sunny spot with light, well-drained soil. They make much more of a show when they are grouped in definite 'drifts', perhaps following the natural contours of uneven ground, or as a carpet under trees, and it also makes them much easier to mow around.

Rockery bulbs

Some dwarf spring bulbs need exceptionally good drainage, so they're regarded as rockery species. These include the tiny wild narcissi, such as *Narcissus asturiensis*, most fritillaries, *Iris danfordiae*, *Iris reticulata*, ipheions, and botanical tulips, all of which are safest either planted in pots of gritty compost (see Under Cover, p.236) or naturalized in a rock feature or scree bed.

● Where miniature bulbs are planted in a rockery or scree, the ground should already be quite well drained enough for them. Just choose a sheltered, sunny spot, add a light dusting of general organic fertilizer, and make sure they're planted at their correct depth. It's usual to naturalize them in small groups and leave them alone from then on.

DEADHEAD AND PROTECT DAHLIAS

Deadhead dahlias regularly so that new flowers continue to be produced right up until the last possible moment – they should keep going right up to the first serious frost, which may not be for 6–8 weeks yet. Also, be on the look-out for earwigs (see tip box above).

SUPPORT TALL FLOWERS

Support tall-growing clumps of perennial asters, including Michaelmas daisies, which are starting to flop now the flowers are out and making the stems top-heavy.

COLLECT SEED

Keep collecting seed from perennials, alpines, etc. and watch out for any tree and shrub seeds you might want to save (see August, p.209–10).

HOW TO NATURALIZE BULBS IN LAWNS

1 If you're planting bulbs in grass, it's much easier if you strip the turf off first, otherwise you have a tough layer to cut through with your trowel or bulb planter. This also gives you the chance to improve the soil, so work in some well-rotted organic matter, grit if you think it's needed, and some fertilizer.

2 To make the bulbs look as if they appeared naturally, drop handfuls and plant them where they fall, the same as for naturalizing them in borders. Once they're all in, firm the ground, rake it level, then just unroll the turf back over the top.

PATIOS AND CONTAINERS

PLANT WINTER BEDDING IN CONTAINERS

It's a sad fact that the longer you keep your ageing summer bedding plants, the harder they are to keep going. By now, containers are desperately pot-bound and more prone than ever to drying out or starving, and the plants are trying harder than ever to set seed. It only takes a few chilly evenings for them to stop trying, and then it's time to call it a day. Tip them out, and move straight on to your next scheme – the sooner the better really. There's only a limited sales 'window' for autumn and winter bedding, so buy early and beat the rush. Years ago it wasn't worth growing winter bedding, since a long freezing spell put paid to the lot, but milder winters and tougher varieties make them very well worth growing now, and they're ideal for containers in sheltered spots that receive even weak winter sun.

Flowers for winter bedding

Winter-flowering pansies are the most popular bedding plants of all, as they flower from now right through to May or June, pausing only to gather their strength in the coldest spells. Ornamental cabbages only start to change colour once the night temperature drops below 10°C (50°F), so don't expect them to show their normal cream, mauve or purple centres

any earlier than this – garden centres don't usually put them on sale until their colour changes. New improved strains of wallflower, such as 'Aida', are good value, as they flower in autumn and again in spring. When it comes to polyanthus and double daisies, you have the option of leaving them under cover and planting them out in spring (see March, p.66), since you usually lose a few in winter.

PLANT SPRING BULBS IN CONTAINERS

Spring bulbs make dazzling displays in containers, and although you could wait until next year and buy potted bulbs already in flower, it's a lot cheaper – and much more satisfying – to grow your own right from the start.

Suitable bulbs for spring containers

Daffodils, crocuses, anemones, scillas and grape hyacinths all need putting in now. It's as well to leave tulips and hyacinths for another month or two, as they won't start forming roots until then anyway, but if you really want to plant them now, do so – but keep the containers as dry as possible in the meantime.

Choose reasonably compact varieties of daffs; the tall kinds would be too top-heavy for containers. Dwarf varieties, such as *Narcissus* 'Jetfire', 'Tete-à-tete' and 'Jenny' (see March, p.48), are particularly attractive in pots and tubs. You can plant a tub all with the same variety, or mix several different kinds of bulbs

Hanging baskets planted up with winter-flowering pansies can do well in sheltered spots.

WINTER PLANTING TIPS

Plant up winter containers in exactly the same way as summer tubs and hanging baskets (see May, p.131–2), with a few small differences. You need to use more plants, and make better provision for drainage, as the weather is wetter in winter.

- Don't mix water-retaining gel crystals into the compost; instead, add up to 10 per cent perlite or grit to your usual compost to improve drainage.
- Don't use water-holding liners for hanging baskets; instead, use synthetic moss, which looks like fine green threads, as it makes for much better drainage.
- Winter bedding plants won't have time to grow much after they're planted, so put plenty of them in and don't be afraid to pack them close

together – you need to, to make a good show. This isn't a case where less is more – less just looks penny-pinching.
- Don't just park your finished pot out in the middle of your patio. Stand winter containers in a sheltered spot close to a wall, so they're sheltered from cold and rain as much as possible. Alternatively, keep containers planted with spring bulbs and early bedding under a carport or in a porch or cold greenhouse during the worst of the winter weather. Check that pots are not standing in places where puddles gather when it rains hard, or under leaky gutters, where the plants will be flooded. Stand tubs and alpine sink gardens up on bricks or pot feet so that surplus water drains out quicker.

HOW TO PLANT DAFFODIL BULBS IN LAYERS

1 Plant the first layer 2.5cm (1in) or so from the base of the container, pushing each bulb down firmly as if you were screwing in a lightbulb, so its base makes firm contact with the compost. Put as many bulbs in as will fit without quite touching each other.

2 Put enough compost over the top to barely hide the tips.

3 Plant a second layer over the top of the compost, and add a third layer if space permits.

4 In a good-sized tub, you can finish off by planting violets or primroses over the top for a truly 'layered' effect later. It'll look doubly or trebly spectacular when it bursts into bloom next spring.

together. If you're going to do that, it looks most spectacular if you choose varieties that all flower at the same time, otherwise your second 'flush' of flower coincides with a lot of lanky foliage and dead heads, which doesn't look too clever.

Planting spring bulbs

When you start filling the containers, put plenty of drainage material in the bottom, as bulbs can rot if they're waterlogged. Use any good brand of potting compost – not bulb fibre – and add 10 per cent grit or perlite to improve drainage. Plant as many bulbs as you can, for the very best show, but make sure they aren't quite touching each other or the sides of the container. With a really big, deep tub, make full use of the space by planting two or even three layers of bulbs (see box above).

STOP FEEDING

Stop feeding permanent plants growing in containers, for example shrubs and trees.

MOVE TENDER PLANTS UNDER COVER

Gardeners in colder areas, such as the north or very exposed or high-altitude regions, may need to start worrying about the onset of the first frosts and shift pots of tender perennials, for example fuchsias and pelargoniums, under cover. But most of us have another few weeks before we need to think about that, so in the meantime make the most of them.

EVERGREENS FOR WINTER CONTAINERS

Small evergreens can also be valuable in winter containers; plant them as foliage to make a few winter-flowering plants go further, or use them on their own in a cold or windy spot, where flowering plants wouldn't stay the course. You can leave them in containers for the winter and plant them out in the garden in spring.

- Good plants include ivies, santolina, euonymus, evergreen sedges and grasses, and small pots of shrubs such as evergreen cotoneaster, choisya, clipped box and conifers, but see what else your local garden centre has to offer.
- If you don't want to bother replanting bedding every season, you could also plant suitable evergreens, such as phormiums, for growing in all-year-round containers (see March, p.67).

VEGETABLES AND HERBS

PROTECT CROPS

All should be well under control in the veg patch this month; there's still plenty to pick and eat, but things are growing markedly more slowly now, and by the end of the month cool nights will mean that it's worth covering late crops of salads, courgettes, carrots and the like with cloches or horticultural fleece so they keep growing. Don't be tempted to take the nets off brassica plants if you live in an area with a pigeon problem, since they'll be even keener than ever to fly down for a feed from now through the winter.

WHAT TO SOW

There's not much in the way of mainline veg you can sow now with any real hope of harvesting them this year, but quick crops, such as baby spinach leaves and corn salad, are worth sowing if you can cover them later. There are also several varieties of overwintering lettuce you can sow now, but it has to be said they are nowhere near as reliable as summer lettuce because so much can go wrong with them, from pests and pigeons to bad weather and rotting roots. If I have a greenhouse, frankly I'd far rather sow winter lettuce and other out-of-season crops in the soil border under glass.

Overwintering onions

The one thing you really must grow is overwintering onions. You can either sow them now, in vacant rows in the veg plot, and thin them out or transplant them in October; or if you can't be bothered messing about with seeds and seedlings, wait until next month and buy overwintering onion sets (see October, p.257) – whichever you feel happiest with.

What's so special about overwintering onions? They fill space in the veg patch that would normally just be left empty for the winter, and vacate it again next May and June, in good time to plant summer crops in the space. There's no need to wait until the onions are 'ready' – you can pull the odd one when you need it, as soon as the bulbs are big enough to use – and leave the rest to keep growing. In fact, that's the best way to use them, because they don't store well. Overwintering onions won't grow huge, but they are well worth having, and you'll be using them when onions are none too special in the shops, because it's after the end of the season for stored maincrop onions. Don't go mad and fill the garden with them though; one packet of seeds or bag of sets is enough.

- Prepare the ground as usual before sowing onion seeds (see March, pp.68–9), and sow them thinly in drills about 1cm (½in) deep in rows 15–20cm (6–8in) apart – just enough room to run a hoe through – then thin them out to 10cm (4in) apart.

WHAT TO PLANT

Do plant some spring cabbage plants – even if you aren't a great cabbage fan. Home-grown spring cabbage, raised organically and eaten within hours of coming in from the garden, tastes like a different vegetable entirely from the stuff you buy in the shops. I've known confirmed cabbage-haters lap it up and come back for second helpings.

HARVEST VEG

Now is the time to harvest marrows, courgettes, sweetcorn, French and runner beans, lettuce, rocket, spring onions, Chinese leaves, oriental radishes, autumn cauliflower, cabbages, pencil leeks, and any remaining onions and shallots for storing. Also, harvest the last of the globe artichokes, and begin lifting root vegetables and maincrop potatoes at the end of the month.

Onions and shallots

Some crops need a little preparation for harvesting. Bend the leaves of onions and shallots over at the neck early this month if they haven't done it for themselves, and once the leaves turn brown, pull the plants up but leave the bulbs on the ground to continue drying off. After 7–10 days, lay them in trays,

Harvest runner beans regularly so they are always tender.

or bundle them into nets to hang up in the shed, where they'll keep best in the light, unless you fancy turning them into French-style plaits to hang up on the kitchen wall. They are quite easy to make (see box below).

Tomatoes

Leave the last tomatoes on the plants until very cold nights mean you can't take the risk any longer, then pick them and bring them indoors to ripen; in southern gardens, that won't be until next month.

CUT DOWN ASPARAGUS FOLIAGE

When asparagus foliage has turned yellow or buff, and there's no more life left in it, which in some gardens won't be until next month, mulch the soil with 2.5–5cm (1–2in) of well-rotted manure to 'tuck the bed up' for winter.

FRENCH ONION STRINGS

You can make strings of shallots or garlic in exactly the same way as onions (see below). If you're hanging them in the kitchen for decoration, keep them in an airy place, as a lot of humidity or steam from cookers and washing machines is likely to shorten their shelf-life.

HAVE FRESH HERBS FOR WINTER USE

Keep yourself in fresh herbs through the winter, without having to buy them from the supermarket.

Mint

Dig up a few roots of mint, curl them around the sides of a 12cm (5in) pot half-filled with potting compost, and cover them with another 2.5–5cm (1–2in) of compost. On a windowsill indoors they'll soon sprout, and will then keep growing throughout the winter.

Chives

Dig up and divide a plant of chives, cutting the tops down to within 2.5cm (1in) of the top of the roots, and pot up one of the best pieces to grow indoors. Again, it will soon be sprouting again and you'll have new growth to cut when you need it.

Basil, coriander and parsley

It's also worth sowing some pots of basil, leaf coriander and parsley; they'll germinate quickly indoors, and you can start snipping at the young plants as soon as they're big enough. If you re-sow each time half the old potful has been used, you'll always keep yourself supplied.

HOW TO MAKE FRENCH ONION STRINGS

1 When you harvest the onions, retain as much of the old straw-like foliage as possible, rather than twisting off the tops. Starting off with three onions with good long, strong, dead leaves, straightened out, begin to plait the foliage together.

2 If there isn't much foliage, or if it's not very strong, you can reinforce it by plaiting hairy hessian twine or hanks of raffia in with it for a stronger finish.

3 Each time you add 2.5cm (1in) or so to the plait, add the next onion and amalgamate its foliage with that of the lowest onion of the bunch, and keep plaiting, adding some more strands of raffia when needed to keep the plait an even thickness.

4 Make the rope anything from 30–90cm (1–3ft) long, depending on how many onions you have. For an authentic French-look onion string, make two identical ropes of onions, and wire them together at the top so you can sling the result over a nail or hook in your wall.

FRUIT

PICK FRUIT AS IT RIPENS

- Leave blackberries to turn a deep, velvety black before picking them, and gently ease the berry off the plant, leaving the hard central 'core' behind.

- Watch out for the first autumn-fruiting raspberries sometime this month; it's likely to be closer to the end than the beginning. You can usually get away without netting them, since for some reason birds don't seem to have latched on to the existence of late raspberries yet and – so far at least – they largely leave them alone.

- Pick early varieties of apples and eat them straight off the tree, even a few days in the fruit bowl is enough to put them past their best. Don't even think about storing them. Gather the biggest and most undamaged windfall apples – both cookers and eaters – as soon as possible after they fall and use them for cooking, after removing the bruised bits. Leave any you don't want on the lawn for the birds.

- You might find the odd 'Conference' pear just about ready at the end of the month – look out for those whose skins are turning a more yellowy khaki shade, when the rest are the usual unripe greeny brown. Pick the ripening fruit and give them a few days in the fruit bowl indoors to reach their peak, or stew them.

PRUNE CANE FRUITS

Loganberries and tayberries ripen slightly ahead of their relatives, blackberries, so the canes will be ready for pruning sooner. Blackberries can continue fruiting well into September, but they all need pruning in the same way once you've picked the crop. The technique sounds simple, and it is, provided you've trained your plants properly (see right). A properly trained blackberry, or blackberry relative, will give a prodigious crop, and the prickly stems give you a good boundary that shelters the garden from the worst of the wind, as well as repelling livestock, vandals and intruders. It's worth putting the effort in.

Training and pruning cane fruits

Blackberries and their relatives work on the same 2-year cycle as raspberries – the canes that grow this year fruit next year and are then cut right out. However, instead of growing upright like raspberries, the other cane fruits are naturally more undisciplined and can make 6m (20ft) long sprawling 'tentacles', which are much more difficult to deal with.

A completely untrained blackberry, loganberry or any other member of the family is frankly a menace, as you can't get at it to sort it out properly. If you've inherited a neglected one, the best thing to do is chop the lot down to the ground now and start again, training next year's canes out to one side. You'll miss a year's fruiting, but that's better than getting into an even worse mess.

As soon as apples will part easily from the tree they are ready to be harvested.

HOW TO TRAIN AND PRUNE CANE FRUITS

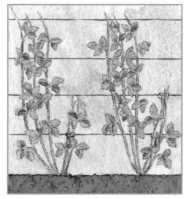

1 If you want an easy life, it pays to keep the 2 years' canes separate. When you first plant your blackberry, tayberry or loganberry, train all the canes out vertically along a fence or row of posts and wires, to one side of the plant. Those canes will carry next year's fruit. The new batch of canes that grow next year won't fruit until the year after that, so train them out in the opposite direction to avoid confusion.

2 Pruning is then dead easy: as soon as you've picked all the fruit each autumn, cut off all the fruited canes to about 15cm (16in) from the ground.

UNDER COVER

REDUCE WATERING AND FEEDING

Towards the end of the month, gradually reduce the feeding and watering of all greenhouse plants as their growth slows down now that the nights are getting cooler.

REMOVE SHADING AND VENTILATION

Towards the end of the month, if light levels are low, you could wash off the shading paint from the outside of the glass – but most people simply leave it until their big greenhouse 'spring-clean' later in the autumn (see October, p.258), when the greenhouse has largely been cleared of crops.

BRING IN TENDER PLANTS TO OVERWINTER

Towards the end of the month in colder areas you could bring tender plants under glass. In the south there are still several weeks of the season left yet, so you may want to wait longer.

PLANT BULBS TO FLOWER AT CHRISTMAS

Mid-September is the very last date for planting specially prepared bulbs if you want them to flower in time for Christmas (see August, pp.215–16). But if you've bought some and forgotten about them – it happens all the time – don't bin them. Plant them anyway, using the same technique, and all that will happen is they'll flower a bit later, in January or even February, when, let's face it, you'll still be very pleased to see them.

PLANT EARLY SPRING BULBS IN POTS

Spring bulbs make a stunning display in the greenhouse or conservatory, whether it's completely unheated or you keep it frost-free. They flower several weeks earlier than bulbs outdoors when there's not a lot of colour under glass, besides giving you something to tinker with in the winter when little else is growing. The big benefit of having them under cover, apart from earliness, is that as they are up on the greenhouse staging where you can see them, they won't be bashed about by bad weather – and you can enjoy them in comfort yourself.

- Choose compact varieties – dwarf daffs, crocuses, scillas and anemones are fine. You can also use dwarf tulips and normal unprepared hyacinths, but they are best not planted for another 6 weeks or so (see October, pp.260–1). Buy the biggest and best bulbs you can find, as they'll have more flowers than little economy jobs, which may not actually be big enough to flower at all.

- Plant the bulbs in pots of your usual potting compost, and stand them in a cool, dark place to start with. Once the nights turn cold naturally from about the end of October onwards, you might just as well have them in the greenhouse where you can keep an eye on them.

- Watch out for mice, slugs and snails, and water as sparingly as you can get away with – overwatering will just make the bulbs rot. As the shoots grow, later in the winter, turn the pots around occasionally so the plants don't all lean over one way.

Plant rockery bulbs in pots

Suitable species include ipheions, *Iris reticulata*, *Iris danfordiae*, dwarf fritillaries (known to enthusiasts as 'frits') and other little treasures.

- Put plenty of drainage material, such as crocks or a handful of gravel, into the bottom of clay flowerpots, roughly half-fill the pots with the home-made bulb potting compost (see box opposite), and plant your bulbs close together but not quite touching. Don't mix different kinds together; keep each pot for a single variety. Cover them with more 'dirty grit', and top the pot off with 1cm (½in) of clean grit.

- Keep the pots in a cold frame, porch, or unheated greenhouse, where they'll be protected from rain and safe from mice and other pests.

Rockery bulbs require excellent drainage; put gravel or crocks into the pots before planting, use gritty compost, and then top with clean grit.

> **ROCKERY BULB POTTING COMPOST**
> To grow rockery bulbs in pots, you need to make up your own bulb-potting compost. Make up a mixture that alpine addicts refer to half-jokingly as 'dirty grit' – which is roughly equal parts of John Innes potting compost and coarse potting grit (a special lime-free sand for horticultural purposes that you'll find on sale in bags in a garden centre).

- When the rock plants flower, you can arrange them along the top of a low wall or up the edge of a flight of steps to make a spring display, or maybe put them on a table on the patio; they're also just the job for filling the shelves of your auricula theatre early in the season (see April Project, p.115).

POT ON CALCEOLARIAS AND CINERARIAS

When the calceolarias and cinerarias that were planted around June fill their original pots with roots, pot them on into 12cm (5in) pots, if you didn't do this in August.

SOW OUT-OF-SEASON HARDY ANNUALS

Quite a few hardy annuals make superb late winter and early spring flowering pot plants for the greenhouse or conservatory, and unlike a lot of fancier plants they'll be quite happy whether you have any heating on or not. Good kinds to grow this way include compact varieties of calendula marigold, candytuft, and non-trailing varieties of nasturtium. It's also worth trying unusual hardy annuals that you might not have grown outdoors, such as mignonette (*Reseda odorata*), which was once grown on cottage windowsills in the days before central heating. The plants grow into a pagoda-like shape studded with heavily scented, red-fringed green flowers. If you want something really easy and unusual, try violet cress (*Ionopsidium acaule*), which makes tiny mounds of violet flowers and is a little gem for winter or early spring.

- Sow the seeds in trays or pots as usual (see March, pp.73–4), and keep them in a cool, shady spot while they germinate.

- Prick them out into individual 10cm (4in) pots when they're big enough to handle (see April, pp.107–8). They don't need feeding, as there's enough nutrient in the compost and too much only makes them soft and less keen to flower. If you're growing violet cress, don't bother pricking the seedlings out, just transfer small clumps of seedlings into 8cm (3in) pots. The plants flower within weeks, while they're mere mounds a few centimetres across.

- As winter draws on, reduce watering to a minimum without letting plants wilt, but protect them from slugs and snails, and ventilate as much as possible to avoid humidity, which just encourages fungal disease.

RIPENING THE LAST OF THE SUMMER CROPS

Summer crops, such as tomatoes, cucumbers, peppers and aubergines, will continue fruiting until the nights turn cold, when everything slows down. Some people pull the plants out around the middle of the month so there's room to bring tender plants inside for winter protection, but if you don't need the space for anything else, gardeners in the milder counties can often keep greenhouse crops going well into October. Either way, the trick is to avoid being left with a load of half-grown produce that you can't use for anything. You can be very crafty about it.

Tomatoes

- About 6 weeks before you want to pull the plants out, stop feeding them and cut back drastically on watering. It's a sneaky way of tricking the plant's biological clock into panic mode, telling it to work fast if it wants to set seed, so all the full-sized fruit ripens in double-quick time. As belt and braces, nip the top out of each plant, and continue removing sideshoots so that all the energy is diverted into swelling the remaining fruit.

- Extra warmth always comes in handy for ripening late fruits, so reduce the ventilation from now on, except on really hot, sunny days, and snap the leaves off the lower half of the plants to let more light and air through to the fruit.

Pick tomatoes as soon as they are ripe.

- A fortnight before you want to pull the plants out, stop watering altogether and keep the ventilators shut.

- When you can't delay any longer, pick off all the full-sized green fruits – anything smaller will never ripen, but is fine for making chutney – and lay them out on a shelf indoors, in a not-too-warm place out of sunlight. Most of them should ripen naturally over the next 2 or 3 weeks. They won't ripen faster on a sunny windowsill – rather the reverse, they just shrivel up.

Cucumbers and melons

- Coax the last late cucumbers to swell by taking out the tops of the plants and nipping off the tips of sideshoots a couple of weeks before you plan to pull the plants out. Cucumber plants are badly affected by powdery mildew as autumn approaches, so pick off leaves that look as if they've been dusted with dirty talc.

- Melons behave much the same, but because it takes so much longer for a melon to ripen, frankly you won't have any more fruit once those that were swelling up in August have ripened. Finish what's there now, and then pull the plants out. Half-grown fruit will never make it.

Peppers and aubergines

Peppers and aubergines are also quite temperature-sensitive, and without extra heat at night it's highly unlikely any more flowers will set fruit from now on, so just concentrate on pushing along those that have already set and are starting to swell. The good thing about both crops is that undersized fruits are perfectly useable – but once the evenings turn cold there won't be any more.

- Cut down watering and feeding slightly for 2–3 weeks before you want to pull the plants out, and shut the greenhouse down earlier in the afternoon to trap the heat inside. Keep the ventilators shut altogether on dull days.

You can tell when a melon is ripe because it starts to release that unmistakeable 'melony' aroma.

Right: The pond continues to give great pleasure with little input required this month, so make the most of it!

SOW WINTER SALADS AND PARSLEY

Prepare the border soil and sow winter salads, such as baby spinach leaves, overwintering spring onions (which are the same as normal spring onions, but just special varieties that are robust enough to 'stand' through the winter), corn salad and winter lettuce. Also, sow parsley in a pot for a winter crop.

WATER GARDEN

EASY DOES IT

This is your last chance this year to enjoy the pond at its peak, so don't hold back. There's very little to do except sit back and enjoy it. If you feed your fish, you can continue to do so until the weather starts to 'break', although this may not be until late next month in a lot of the country. There's no need to start cutting back waterside plants until the foliage begins to 'go over'. If oxygenating plants are getting out of control, you can give them a last light thinning out, but go easy because they won't make much more growth this year and you need to leave plenty to provide fish and water wildlife with cover and oxygen over the winter. Green blanket weed can still be pulled out (see May, pp145–6).

PROJECT Plant stepping stones in the lawn

It's hard to keep a lawn looking good all year round, especially in a small garden, when you have no choice but to walk on it all the time. Whether you're working on your beds and borders, wandering around enjoying the flowers, or going down to the shed to feed the rabbit, you can't help wearing 'tracks', especially in winter when the ground is soft.

What you need is a hard surface to walk on, but there's no need to put in a solid path. Instead, sink some stepping stones into the surface. They are easy to put in, and they stay firm, but are very versatile – if you have a change of plan in years to come, you can always lift them out again and plug the gaps with turf. It doesn't take long to do, once you get started, and well-placed stepping stones add character to the garden as well as being practical.

What you need

Paving slabs

Sharp spade

Sharp sand

1 Work out where you need to walk, and lay a series of round or hexagonal paving slabs on the lawn, spaced a comfortable walking pace apart. They can run in a straight line in a fairly formal space, or you can make them follow the outline of a major border, or skirt around the contours of sloping ground. Check how they look from an upstairs window.

2 When you're happy with the layout, use the slabs as a guide and cut around each one with a sharp spade.

3 Set the slab aside and work the spade under the cut-out shape to remove the piece of turf. Enlarge the hole slightly so that it is 1cm (^{1}/$_2$in) deeper than the paving slab, but leave a firm, flat base.

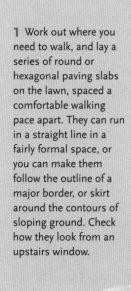

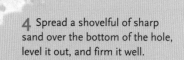

4 Spread a shovelful of sharp sand over the bottom of the hole, level it out, and firm it well.

5 Replace the paving slab. It should sit fractionally below the level of the turf, so that when you cut the grass the mower passes cleanly over the top.

239

OCTOBER

Now, I know a lot of people will be thinking, 'oh autumn', and shut the shed door until spring, but the year isn't over yet. One big benefit of the shifting seasons is that autumn is no longer just a temporary blip separating summer from winter – instead, October is the start of a brand new season with a pattern all of its own. We'll still have the usual mists and mellow fruitfulness, naturally, but there's also a rich tapestry of autumn colours and late flowers to look forward to, when the low, slanting orange sun of an Indian summer is punctuated by refreshing evenings with a nip in the air.

October signals the biggest quick-change act in the gardening year – when the leaves start to 'turn' and the landscape catches fire. You don't need a garden the size of a country park to see the benefit, but don't rely on leaf colour entirely – berries and fruits also contribute to the great autumn colour-up.

THE BIG PICTURE autumn colour

Liquidambar styraciflua, sweet gum (above), has maple-shaped leaves and is totally over the top when it comes to hot autumn colours. The tree makes a cone shape, 15 × 10m (50 × 30ft), so needs plenty of space. It is magic, but ideally choose it at this time of year so that you can check on the brightness of its colour – some seedlings can be muddy of tone.

PEAK SEASON
October–November.
GROWING CONDITIONS Any garden soil except chalky or boggy, in sun or light shade.

Acer japonicum varieties are the ideal alternative if you can't meet the rather fussy growing requirements of *Acer palmatum* cultivars. *Acer japonicum* 'Aconitifolium' (left) is one of the very first acers to 'turn' in autumn, and it has brilliant red leaves resembling frilly edged horse chestnuts. *Acer japonicum* 'Vitifolium' has red vine-like leaves. Both grow approximately 5 × 5m (15 × 15ft) and are stunning.

PEAK SEASON
October–November.
GROWING CONDITIONS Any reasonable soil that's not boggy in sun or light shade.

Japanese maples are what autumn is all about, as they change from the green of summer to flaming autumnal red. *Acer palmatum* 'Ôsakazuki' is the one that does it best, with classic maple-shaped leaves that change through every shade of orange and red before falling. It starts off as a chunky shrub and eventually becomes a medium-sized, dome-shaped tree 5 × 5m (15 × 15ft). *Acer palmatum* Dissectum Viride Group (above) has elegant, deeply divided green leaves that turn shades of orange and yellow in autumn, making a 2 × 2.5m (6 × 8ft) mound. *Acer palmatum* 'Sango-kaku', 5 × 4m (15 × 12ft), has maple leaves that turn bright gold in autumn, with red young twigs that then provide winter interest after the leaves have fallen.

PEAK SEASON
October–November.
GROWING CONDITIONS Fertile, ideally lime-free soil with plenty of organic matter, in a very sheltered site in light shade.

OLD FAITHFULS

Cercidiphyllum japonicum, katsura tree (above), grows too big for small gardens, but if you have room for just one large tree this is a good one. The leaves are large and kidney-shaped, turning through every shade of yellow, pink, orange and red as autumn progresses, coupled with the unique scent of toffee apples – a real talking point in any garden. It eventually makes a tree, 18 × 8m (60 × 25ft), but takes a heck of a long time getting there. It can also be grown as a multi-stemmed tree, which makes it shorter but wider. There's also a relatively compact variety, **Cercidiphyllum magnificum**, which grows about half the usual size, but you'll only find it at a specialist nursery.

PEAK SEASON
   October–November (but the leaves are also pretty and purplish when they unfurl in spring).
GROWING CONDITIONS Fertile, well-drained and preferably lime-free soil with plenty of organic matter, in a sheltered spot in sun or very light shade. Terrific for a woodland garden.

Parthenocissus quinquefolia, Virginia creeper (above), has fantastic red autumn colour but the sheer size is too much for most people. It's great if you have a big tree you can send it up, or a long tunnel or pergola for it to cover, but be very cautious about letting it loose over your house, as the 'suction pads' it uses to hold on can damage mortar and brickwork. I'd much prefer to use it to disguise an old outbuilding or large eyesore, such as a gasometer. It's also good grown horizontally, as ground cover over a bank or in a wild garden.

PEAK SEASON
   October–November.
GROWING CONDITIONS Fertile soil, but not badly drained, in sun or light shade.

Euonymus, spindle bush varieties, in its deciduous form has staggering autumn colour. Though not much seen in 'polite' gardens, they are very good for the back of a country garden border and wonderful for wild or woodland-inspired gardens. As shrubs go, they aren't small, but they stand pruning – or you can grow them as small trees, which allows you to plant other things underneath. **Euonymus europaeus 'Red Cascade'** (above) is probably the best known, with oval leaves that turn crimson in autumn and fall to reveal dangling bunches of strange, lobed red fruits. **Euonymus latifolius** is similar but has locket-shaped red fruits 2.5cm (1in) across. **Euonymus alatus**, the wild spindle tree, also has vivid red autumn colour, but its great claims to fame are the peculiar corky flanges running along the trunk and branches, which are most visible in winter after all the leaves have dropped. This is really one for the wild garden. All three will grow roughly 2.5 × 2.5m (8 × 8ft).

PEAK SEASON
   October–November.
GROWING CONDITIONS Tolerate most soils except badly drained soil, and prefer sun or light shade.

SOMETHING SPECIAL

Pyracanthas (above) are famously prickly evergreen shrubs with red, orange or yellow berries that last late into winter. They can be grown as freestanding shrubs, or trained out flat against a wall. Birds mostly leave pyracanthas until after they've eaten other berries, so the plants usually stay colourful until Christmas or later. *Pyracantha* 'Mohave' has red berries, 'Orange Glow' is one of the best for orange berries, and the fruits of 'Soleil d'Or' are golden yellow. Plants will grow to 2.5 × 2.5m (8 × 8ft) or more against a wall, and they look superb trained as espaliers if you've time left after stuffing your mushroom.

PEAK SEASON October–January.
GROWING CONDITIONS Not
  fussy about soil in sun or light
  shade.

Crab apples are some of the best trees for small gardens, with something to offer for much of the year (see also April, p.80). Birds are very fond of the smaller crab apples, and some are clearly tastier than others, so if you want to encourage airborne visitors I would recommend *Malus × zumi* 'Golden Hornet', but for a long-lasting display of fruit grow *M. × robusta* 'Red Sentinel' (above), whose bounty often stays on the tree as late as March. For crab apple jelly, there's only one choice – *M.* 'John Downie' – which has large peach and scarlet, flask-shaped fruit. If massive crops of ornamental fruit are your top priority, go for *M. × scheideckeri* 'Red Jade'. Crab apples are available growing on dwarfing rootstocks, so now you can specify a tree that stays small – say 3 × 2.5m (10 × 8ft) – although most existing crab apples will grow rather bigger, around 5 × 4m (15 × 12ft).

PEAK SEASON (fruit)
  September–December.
GROWING CONDITIONS
  Reasonably well-drained,
  fertile soil in sun.

Crataegus crus-galli, cockspur thorn, is an under-rated tree, 8 × 8m (25 × 25ft), which has creamy blossom typical of hawthorns in spring, very good autumn colour, and a fine crop of large red berries that last well into winter. *Crataegus persimilis* 'Prunifolia' (above) is similar, with unusually large red berries, much loved by blackbirds who can *only just* manage to swallow them. If you have a windy spot or heavy clay soil, these are trees you can always rely on.

PEAK SEASON
  October–December.
GROWING CONDITIONS Not
  fussy about soil in sun or light
  shade.

Rosa 'Fru Dagmar Hastrup'
(above) is a particularly tough
Rugosa rose, growing roughly
1.2 × 1.5m (4 × 5ft). It tolerates
frankly pretty dreadful growing
conditions but still comes up
trumps. The single, pale pink
flowers in summer coincide with
large, tomato-shaped hips, which
ripen in sequence until late
autumn or early winter, by which
time the birds will have scoffed
the lot. The leaves are large and
distinctively leathery-textured.
It is one of the best plants for
flowering hedges in exposed
gardens, and a great bird-puller.

PEAK SEASON July–December.
GROWING CONDITIONS Can be
    tricky on limey soil. Likes plenty
    of sun.

Colchicum is often called autumn
crocus or meadow saffron. The
bulbs only appear on sale in late
summer, and need planting straight
away, as they start flowering within
a few weeks. Each one produces
several clusters of violet, crocus-
like blooms, with the leaves
following later – hence the other
common name of 'naked ladies'.
Colchicum 'Waterlily' (above) is
the most glamorous cultivar, with
large double flowers, 20 × 10cm
(8 × 4in), although they do tend to
topple; **Colchicum byzantinum**
(**syn.** **C. autumnale 'Major'**) is
smaller and stronger and has many
more flowers, 12 × 8cm (5 × 3in);
Colchicum 'The Giant' is similar
but with bigger flowers, 20 × 10cm
(8 × 4in), but not as many of them.
Just as a novelty, you can sit a bare
colchicum bulb on a windowsill
indoors to watch it flower, then
plant it outside later.

PEAK SEASON
    September–November.
GROWING CONDITIONS Well-
    drained soil containing plenty
    of organic matter, in sun or
    light shade.

Mespilus germanica, medlar
(above), has large, pale pink 'pear
blossom' in spring, followed by
golden autumn leaf colour and
strange fruit that looks as if it's
been carved out of wood and
hangs on the trees long after the
leaves have dropped. Enthusiasts
'blet' medlars, picking them in
mid- to late October, and allowing
them to mature until they soften
and turn dark brown but don't
quite rot, when they are ready to
eat. But even if you just regard it
as an ornamental curio, the
medlar makes a most attractive
small garden tree.

PEAK SEASON
    October–December.
GROWING CONDITIONS Any
    reasonably well-drained soil in
    sun or light shade.

Amaryllis belladonna (above) is sometimes called belladonna lily or amaryllis. (It's not the same as the indoor bulb, hippeastrum, which is sometimes rather confusingly called amaryllis). The real amaryllis behaves in very much the same way as nerine by flowering before its leaves appear, with 60cm (2ft) stems of mauve, lily-like flowers. Quite glamorous.

PEAK SEASON
September–October.
GROWING CONDITIONS Hot, dry, sunny spot with very well-drained soil, ideally at the foot of a south-facing wall. Dislikes being disturbed.

Nerine bowdenii (above) also flowers ahead of its leaves. The 45cm (18in) stems are topped with large, curly petalled, bright pink, funnel-shaped flowers, and the strap-shaped leaves usually start to appear as they're going over. The bulbs only do well in a situation where they'll get a good 'baking' in summer when they're dormant, and they don't like other plants shading their bit of soil. Find a spot for them in a sunny border against the house wall, and they'll wow you each autumn.

PEAK SEASON
September–October.
GROWING CONDITIONS Hot, dry and very sunny spot with well-drained soil, ideally at the foot of a south-facing wall. Do not disturb.

OTHER PLANTS IN THEIR PRIME IN OCTOBER
- **Trees** *Arbutus × andrachnoides*
- **Shrubs** *Abelia chinensis, Caryopteris × clandonensis, Ceanothus × delileanus* 'Gloire de Versailles' (see p.179), *Ceratostigma willmottianum, Fuchsia* (hardy), *Hebe* (see p.178), *Hibiscus syriacus* (see p.202), *Perovskia* (see p.201), *Phygelius* (see p.201), *Rosa* (see pp.150–1)
- **Evergreens** *Calluna, Elaeagnus pungens, Hypericum calycinum, Hypericum* 'Hidcote', *Osmanthus heterophyllus*
- **Berries/fruits** *Callicarpa bodinieri* var. *giraldii* 'Profusion' (see p.222), *Chaenomeles, Clerodendrum trichotomum, Cotoneaster, Crataegus crus-galli, Crataugus persimilis* 'Prunifolia', *Cydonia oblonga, Leycesteria formosa, Myrtus communis, Nandina domestica, Passiflora caerulea* (see p.178), *Pernettya, Photinia davidiana, Physalis alkekengi* var. *franchetii* (see p.221), *Rosa rugosa, Rosa* 'Geranium', *Sorbus, Symphoricarpos, Viburnum opulus*
- **Climbers** *Clematis tangutica* (see p.221), *Clematis* Texensis cultivars, *Clematis tibetana* subsp. *vernayi* (see p.221), *Clematis* 'Ville de Lyon', *Eccremocarpus scaber, Fallopia baldschuanica, Passiflora caerulea* (see p.178)
- **Perennials** *Actaea, Anemone hupehensis* (see p.200), *Anemone × hybrida* (see p.200), *Aster ericoides, Aster novae-angliae, Aster novi-belgii* (see p.221), *Aster pilosus* var. *pringlei, Ceratostigma plumbaginoides, Chrysanthemum rubellum, Clematis heracleifolia, Cortaderia selloana, Kniphofia* (see p.220), *Lavatera × clementii, Liriope muscari* (see p.220), *Penstemon* (see p.176), *Sedum* (see p.201), *Saxifraga fortunei, Schizostylis, Solidago* (see p.220), *Stipa* (see p.221), *Tricyrtis formosana* (see p.223)
- **Bulbs** *Crocus speciosus, Cyclamen hederifolium* (see p.222), *Dahlia* (see p.201), *Sternbergia lutea*
- **Bedding** Some summer bedding – *Amaranthus, Arctotis, Cleome, Cosmos, Dahlia* (see p.201), *Fuchsia* (see p.177), *Gazania, Impatiens, Nicotiana, Pelargonium, Petunia* (see p.178), *Rudbeckia, Salvia* (see p.204), *Tagetes, Tropaeolum majus* (nasturtium) and shrubby *Salvia* spp until first frost/bad weather. Winter bedding – ornamental cabbages and kales, winter-flowering pansies
- **Rock plants** *Dianthus plumarius, Gentiana sino-ornata, Persicaria vacciniifolia, Silene uniflora, Zauschneria californica* (see p.222)

OCTOBER at-a-glance checklist

GENERAL GARDEN TASKS (p.248)
✔ Tidy borders lightly, clearing weeds and cutting down flower stems.
✔ Compost all green rubbish generated by clearing the garden. Don't put woody material or the roots of perennial weeds on the compost heap unless they are first put through a shredder.

LAWNS (p.250)
✔ Make a new lawn by laying turf.
✔ Reduce mowing, and clear piles of dead leaves from the lawn to stop the grass turning yellow.
✔ Carry out autumn lawn care if you haven't done it yet.

TREES, SHRUBS AND CLIMBERS (p.252)
✔ Plant container-grown trees, shrubs, climbers and roses.
✔ Plant bare-root plants towards the end of the month, provided the ground is ready and once the leaves have fallen off.
✔ Check tree ties in windy weather.
✔ Cut back tall shrubs, e.g. lavatera and *Buddleja davidii*, if necessary.
✔ Prune late-flowering climbing roses and repeat-flowering old-fashioned roses.

✔ Towards the end of the month take hardwood cuttings of roses.
✔ Pot up cuttings taken in summer.
✔ Trim privet hedges.

FLOWERS (p.253)
✔ Remove fallen leaves from the crowns of plants to prevent rotting.
✔ Continue replacing summer bedding with winter and spring bedding as the flowers come to an end.
✔ Lift tender perennials and tender bulbs and bring indoors.
✔ Continue planting spring bulbs.

PATIOS AND CONTAINERS (p.254)
✔ Plant winter and spring bedding and spring bulbs in containers.
✔ Containers will need occasional watering but aim to keep the compost just moist rather than wet.

VEGETABLES AND HERBS (p.255)
✔ Gather to store or use fresh: sprouts, leeks, autumn cauliflowers, maincrop potatoes, Jerusalem artichokes, carrots, parsnips, pumpkins and winter squashes.
✔ Protect salads and late root crops with horticultural fleece to extend the growing season.
✔ Once the veg patch is cleared, carry out winter digging.
✔ Cut down asparagus foliage.
✔ Plant spring cabbage and overwintering onion sets. Also plant garlic towards the end of the month or next month.
✔ Remove yellowing leaves from winter brassicas.
✔ Dig up witloof chicory and start forcing if required.
✔ Pot up herbs for winter use.

FRUIT (p.257)
✔ Create new strawberry beds and plant young plants raised from this year's runners.
✔ Pick apples and pears for storing mid-month.
✔ Prepare for new fruit trees and plant if conditions allow.
✔ Prune blackberries and hybrid berry fruits.

UNDER COVER (p.258)
✔ Have a good clear out of the greenhouse, and prepare for cold weather.
✔ Bring frost-tender plants inside for the winter.
✔ Reduce the amount of water given to greenhouse plants as the nights get colder and the growth rate slows down.
✔ Sow early annuals.
✔ Plant tulips, hyacinths and narcissus in containers.
✔ Sow winter lettuce, corn salad, baby spinach leaves, overwintering spring onions, early carrots, and mange-tout peas in the soil border to have out-of-season crops.

WATER GARDEN (p.262)
✔ Have a pond clear-out: cut down the dead and dying leaves of marginal plants, remove floating water plants, scoop out excess sludge from the bottom of the pond, and cover the pond with netting.

Watch out for
● First frosts – make sure tender plants are safely inside the greenhouse.
● Toadstools and fairy rings in the lawn – brush them off with a broom.

Get ahead
● Sow early annuals, e.g. sweet peas, in an unheated greenhouse or cold frame if you want early flowers next year – otherwise, wait and sow them in spring when there's less risk of losses.
● If you garden in a wet area or on clay soil, get ahead with winter digging.

Last chance
● Dry seedheads early this month, before they deteriorate.
● Sow a new lawn if you haven't yet, before the new grass gets hit by hard frosts.

GENERAL GARDEN TASKS

TIDY UP THE BORDERS

Tidy borders lightly; cut down dead flower stems (except those that have seedheads that the birds will appreciate feeding from), and clear weeds. Don't do a total 'spring-clean' though, as spiders and other beneficial creatures need a certain amount of winter 'cover'.

DRY SEEDHEADS

Dry the seedheads of teasel, honesty and annual flowers grown especially for winter flower arranging. Do the job early this month, before they deteriorate.

DIG EMPTY AREAS OF SOIL

Dig or fork over any patches of vacant ground as they are freed up around the garden, so they're ready for replanting, or simply to keep the ground weed-free.

TIDY ROCK GARDENS AND RAISED BEDS

Clear dead leaves and weeds away from rock plants and other tiny plants that are easily smothered.

KEEP PLANTS SAFE

Before the first frost make sure all tender plants are safely inside the greenhouse.

FEED THE BIRDS

Traditionally, gardeners start feeding birds in October and continue throughout winter until about March. However, wildlife experts now recommend that we feed the birds all year round, owing to a shortage of suitable facilities in wild habitats. Put out clean water every few days, and make sure water is available when puddles, bird baths and other water sources freeze over on cold winter mornings.

Make sure that there is always plenty of food put out for birds. Berrying trees and shrubs will also attract birds to the garden.

Compost takes about 3–6 months to mature, so it is useful to have several bins for organic matter at various stages of decomposition.

MAKING COMPOST

If there's ever a 'best' time to start a compost heap autumn is it, because that's when the garden is generating rubbish from just about every department. There are all the pensioned-off bedding plants from your flower garden and summer containers, retired tomato plants from the greenhouse, cast-off crop debris from the veg patch, and perennial stems from the herbaceous border, not to mention thatch and moss raked out of the lawn, and all that nourishing stuff you've baled out of the pond.

One way or another we're talking about quite a lot of rubbish. But left to its own devices, garden refuse has a nasty habit of turning slimy and smelly and attracting flies, or merely mummifying instead of turning into compost, so instead of just piling it up and hoping for the best, it pays to do it properly. Here's how:

Compost ingredients

You need three things to make a heap work – bulky natural ingredients, beneficial bacteria, and moisture. When all three are present, it can't help but rot.

- The main bulk of the heap comes from garden rubbish. You can add anything of a vegetable nature – annual weeds, fallen leaves, lawn mowings, soft hedge clippings, kitchen peelings and teabags – but nothing with woody stems, perennial roots, seedheads or plant diseases. You can also use any natural materials, such as unprinted paper, cotton or woollen fabric, but tear them up a bit first.
- Beneficial bacteria, which help to activate the heap, come from animal manures, sludge and waterweeds out of your pond, and garden soil. Add a shovelful especially, or just leave some on the roots of weeds. Otherwise, use a compost starter out of a packet or bottle.
- For moisture, use a hose to damp compost ingredients as you add them to your heap, and cover it over to keep the damp in.

Composting methods

The bin method

If you have a small garden, don't bother trying to make a compost heap – you won't have enough rubbish. Unless it's at least 1.2 × 1.2 × 1.2m (4 × 4 × 4ft), it won't heat up enough to 'work' properly, so instead use a compost bin, which looks like a bottomless plastic dustbin. The sides and lid of the bin trap the heat inside, which means the contents heat up quickly and 'cook' efficiently so the compost is ready in a few months. It's effortless – or very nearly so. Have a second bin, so you have somewhere to put the next batch of garden rubbish while the first bin is rotting down. Remember, the cardinal rules are that the material should be mixed, moistened and firmed.

- Stand your bin directly on to the soil, so that red manure worms can find their way in – they help 'digest' the contents fast once it's partly decomposed.
- Start piling a good mixture of ingredients in – don't use too much of one material, and mix different things together. Damp the ingredients if they're dry, add a sprinkling of soil to encourage bacteria, and firm each layer as you go.
- When the bin is full, cap it with about 5cm (2in) of soil. After 3 months in summer, or 6 months in winter, your compost will be ready to use.

Compost heaps

By starting a heap in autumn you'll be certain of having a home-grown supply of organic compost to use for mulching the garden in spring, when the timing is perfect to start a new compost heap to take your summer supply of rubbish. It's the ultimate in recycling. Compost heaps can be a tad trickier than bins, and the big drawback of a traditional compost heap is that only the inside 'cooks' properly; the outside just acts as insulation.

- If you're the type to do a huge clear-up that produces an enormous quantity of rubbish all at once, mix all the ingredients together first, then pile them up in a large heap, watering it as you go, and then cover the lot with a tarpaulin or piece of old carpet to keep the heat and moisture in. Come back in 6 months' time, and with luck all but the very outside layer will be ready to use.
- If you accumulate rubbish bit by bit over the season, mark out a space 1.2m (4ft) square. Spread your first layer of rubbish out to cover it, water and firm it down, then sprinkle a thin layer of soil over the top. Add each new layer of material neatly, to keep the shape of the heap, giving it a firm edge that won't collapse, and firming and watering each new addition. When you reach 1.2m (4ft) high, cover it with a final layer of soil and leave it to rot.
- After 3 months (summer) or 6 months (winter), fork the undecomposed material from the top and sides of your original heap and use it to start a second compost heap alongside the first.

Uncompostable rubbish

What happens to all the stuff you can't put on the compost heap? These days it can be quite a problem, because bonfires are very much frowned upon. Even if you don't have neighbours to be annoyed by the smoke, it is not the thing these days to create air pollution, and sending rubbish to landfill sites isn't very much better when you're trying to be 'green'.

- Plastic fertilizer and compost bags often come in handy for storing garden gear in the shed, or for shifting weeds or taking unavoidable rubbish to the tip, so re-use any you can.
- Diseased plant material, roots of perennial weeds, and weeds with seedheads are best laid out on a patch of vacant land or concrete path to dry in the sun, then 'flash' them with a flame gun or one of those electric weed guns that look like a very hot hairdryer, to kill everything off. Stack them at the bottom of a compost heap, where they'll cook thoroughly, or if you feel nervous about that, pile them into large plastic sacks, damp them and add a handful of compost activator, then tie the tops and stack them well out of the way for a year. At the end of that time they should have broken down completely.
- Woody material, such as prunings and thick plant stems, can often be used as plant supports around the garden, otherwise cut it up small or put it through a shredder and mix with leafy ingredients to put on the compost heap. Alternatively, pile woody stems in a heap of their own in a damp corner and leave them to rot down. As they do, they will provide a good habitat for beetles and other garden fauna.
- Any green waste that you don't have room to compost at home can be taken to a council recycling scheme. They'll do the composting for you, then sell you back the finished product. Well, it's a fair exchange.

LAWNS

SOWING AND MOWING A NEW LAWN

If the weather wasn't suitable for sowing grass seed last month, you can still do it this month – but as ever, you're very dependent on how the weather behaves. There's no point pushing ahead if the ground is bone dry – wait until we have good growing conditions – but don't leave it too late, as you don't want new grass being caught up with hard frosts too soon. Don't rush to cut autumn-sown grass; the most you'll probably be able to do this year is give it a first light topping or two with shears (see March, p.56) and wait to start proper mowing next spring, when it's well rooted in.

LAY TURF

When you want an instant lawn and don't mind paying for the privilege, turf is the answer. October and November are the very best months for laying turf, although in a mild winter, if the soil stays in a workable state, you could lay it right through the winter and as late as March.

Rolls of turf should not be left stacked for more than two days or they will turn yellow.

Various grades of turf are available; the cheapest stuff often contains a fair proportion of weeds and bare patches, as it has usually been cut from pasture or parkland, where livestock have had a go at it. Cultivated turf is the 'Axminster' of the species, and you can pay about as much for it as good-quality carpet. With turf, you definitely get what you pay for.

Laying turf takes a lot more effort than sowing grass seed, even if soil preparation is the same (see September, p.227). Have the ground prepared well in advance, and arrange for the turf to be delivered when you want it, because turf arrives as grassy 'Swiss rolls' that 'go off' after a few days if they are left rolled up, as light can't reach the leaves. If you can't use the turf straight away, there's nothing for it except to unroll it and lay it out flat, temporarily. While you lay the turves (see box below), don't, whatever you do, walk on the prepared soil, or the turf will end up being uneven, after you've been to so much trouble to make the ground firm and flat.

HOW TO LAY TURF

1 Start at one end of the area, where there is a long, straight edge, and lay a row of turves along it.

2 Place planks over the turf you've just laid, and use those to walk on while you lay the next row of turves alongside them. Make sure the turves fit snugly up against each other, and stagger them so the cracks don't run continuously across the grass; lay them in the same sort of pattern you see with bricks in a wall.

3 As you lay each turf, firm it down with the back of a rake, or lay a thick plank over it and thump this with the head of a sledgehammer held upright in a butter-churning motion. Don't belt seven bells out of it – just give it a smart tap at 30cm (12in) intervals along the plank to bond the turf with the soil.

4 When you reach the edge of a flowerbed, lay the turf over the edge and trim it to shape with an old carving knife, following the curve. If you've pressed your turves up close together as you work, you shouldn't see any gaps when you've finished laying the lawn, but if there are any simply go round filling them with soil, and they'll soon disappear.

TOADSTOOLS

It's toadstool time. All sorts of alarming outcrops pop up in autumn – mostly in lawns – but it's really nothing to worry about. When the weather is warm and moist, and there's organic matter in the ground, fungi can appear almost overnight. They aren't doing any harm, and the sort that grow in lawns are unlikely to be poisonous, but even so, parents of the sort of small children who put everything into their mouths may prefer not to have any toadstools around.

The good news is most toadstools are only here temporarily in the autumn if the weather agrees with them, and they vanish as soon as there's a proper frost. Until then, if you don't like the look of them, the easy answer is simply to cut the grass more often and just let the mower chop them up, or else sweep them off with a besom. Good autumn lawn care helps too, because regularly removing thatch from the lawn removes the organic matter that toadstools live on.

Fairy rings

The sort of toadstools that lawn-lovers worry about are the kind that make 'fairy rings'. The slowly widening circle of small, honey-coloured 'mushrooms' will be present for much of the year. They die down in very cold or wet weather, but in a hot, dry summer they just sit there looking shrivelled.

The problem with fairy rings is not so much the toadstools themselves, it's their effect on the grass. In the middle of the ring the grass looks stunted and yellow, due to a combination of starvation and drought. It's all down to the fungus's thread-like underground mycelium, which take all the nitrogen out of the ground, and their sheer mass virtually makes the ground waterproof so rain can't soak in. In contrast, just outside the circle of mushrooms is a band of bright lush green grass, where the mycelium breaks down organic matter in the soil and releases nitrogen, which gives the grass a temporary boost.

What to do about fairy rings

Gardening lore is rife with old wives' tales for things you can water on fairy rings, but they really have very little effect, and are technically illegal when they have not been approved by the ministry for use against mushrooms. Oh yes, it's good to know that the long arm of the law even reaches fairy rings.

The only worthwhile method is digging them out, and even then the experts are a bit iffy about whether it works, but give it a go if you like. Remove the soil from a fairy ring 45cm (18in) deep and for 15cm (6in) beyond the outer extent of the mushrooms, to be sure of removing all the mycelium. Then refill the hole with new topsoil and re-seed or turf the area, and dispose of the infected soil.

It's probably worth doing in your posh lawn, but in a naturalistic-style garden a fairy ring looks quite charming. Put a standing stone or a chunk of fallen log in the middle to use as a seat, and turn it into a feature. It'll save you an awful lot of work, and just think of the kudos to be had from owning the sort of wild feature that money can't buy.

New turf aftercare

As long as the ground is moist, and it rains within a couple of days of laying the turf, a new lawn shouldn't need watering. If conditions turn dry though, put the sprinkler on for a couple of hours and give it a really good soaking – don't half do the job. Rainfall is a good reason for doing your turfing now; if you wait until spring, the odds are you will need to do a lot of watering, since April showers are a thing of the past – nowadays it is often one of the driest months of the year.

New turf takes a few weeks to take root, and until it does, *keep off it*. It's very easy to check progress. Simply lift a corner of a turf here and there – if it peels up, leave it a bit longer, but if it has a firm grip on the ground you can let the kids out to play on it. Once it has rooted itself down all over, you can start mowing it, and using it as if it had been there for years.

REDUCE MOWING

Mowing is usually reduced now, as dictated by the weather – anything from once a fortnight to once a month now.

LAWN MAINTENANCE

If you had a long, hot summer, or didn't get around to concentrating on autumn lawn care in September, do so now (see September, p.225).

REMOVE LEAVES

Clear piles of dead leaves from the lawn to stop the grass turning yellow, and use leaves to make leafmould (see November, p.275).

Make sure newly laid turf does not have a chance to dry out before it roots into the soil.

TREES, SHRUBS AND CLIMBERS

This is a great time to plant container-grown shrubs and roses.

PLANT CONTAINER-GROWN WOODY PLANTS

Although you can plant container-grown trees, shrubs, woody climbers and roses virtually all year round, and many people prefer to plant them in spring (see March, pp.57–9), in general autumn is the very best time of all. Woody plants 'take' particularly well now, because the ground is in perfect condition – still warm from the summer, but moist right through, thanks to seasonal rainfall. There's plenty of worm activity, and soil bacteria are having a final fling.

Trees and shrubs are in just the right state as well, with roots raring to go but no new top-growth to lose water through transpiration. If you take the opportunity to plant now, they will be thoroughly well established by the time next summer brings the next batch of difficult growing conditions. Instead of having to worry about watering, you can leave autumn-planted subjects to look after themselves.

When to delay planting

The time I would advise delaying planting until spring is for anyone who gardens on low-lying ground or heavy clay soil that stays very wet in winter, in which case newly planted roots simply 'drown', so you're better off waiting until spring, even if it means you may need to keep new plants watered for much of the summer.

When planting in autumn, stick to planting hardy, woody plants. Small, hardy plants, such as alpines and herbaceous flowers, are better planted in spring or summer for the simple reason that it's not so easy to tell if they're alive at this time of year, when they've died down. You don't want to end up buying 'dead pots' – very exasperating. In any case, soft plants such as these 'take' better when planted at the start of the growing season rather than at the end of it.

PLANT BARE-ROOT PLANTS

If suitable plants are available, and the ground is ready, you can start planting bare-root woody plants as soon as the leaves have dropped off (see November, p.276).

CHECK TREE TIES

After a spell of windy weather, it's worth going around the garden to check that plants haven't been blown over, tree ties snapped or stakes shifted. Tree ties need checking every year and loosened as the girth of the trunk expands, so they don't cut in and throttle the plant or cut it in half. It only takes a few minutes, but a little attention to detail can save you a packet on replacement plants.

SOIL PREPARATION BEFORE PLANTING

In the days before container-grown plants, gardeners were advised to 'spend as much on the hole as the plant', and while you don't need to go quite that far now – the price of plants has rocketed, after all – good soil preparation is worth doing. It makes an incredible difference to the speed at which new plants 'take off', and they'll grow ten times better afterwards. Yes, really. It also avoids those sudden deaths that are all too common when people just 'bung 'em in any old how'. It's plain daft to risk a twenty-quid plant for want of a barrowload of muck and a few minutes' work to plant it properly. To recap, dig a large planting hole, several times the size of the roots of your plant. Work plenty of well-rotted organic matter into the bottom of the hole, and also into the soil you removed from the hole. Back-fill around the roots with a mixture of soil and organic matter.

What about fertilizer?

Some people swear by bonemeal when they are autumn planting. The theory is it helps a new plant establish itself by providing phosphates for the roots, but in practice bonemeal takes ages to break down before it's available to plants. It's more for the benefit of the gardener, who likes to feel sanctimonious, than for the plants. There's certainly no point in using a quick-acting general-purpose fertilizer in the autumn, as plants can't make use of it, and by the spring – when they can – it'll have been washed away by the rain. Frankly, I wouldn't bother with fertilizer at all until next spring, when your usual feed and mulch routine will supply all the plants will need.

TIDY LARGE SHRUBS

Cut back tall shrubs, such as lavatera and *Buddleja davidii*, just enough to tidy them.

PRUNE ROSES

Prune late-flowering climbing roses, and cut back repeat-flowering old-fashioned roses after they finish blooming (see July, p.184).

PICK OFF DISEASED ROSE LEAVES

Pick off any rose leaves that are badly disfigured by blackspot, and collect up fallen leaves from under roses. Consider replacing badly affected plants with disease-resistant varieties.

START TO TAKE ROSE CUTTINGS

Towards the end of the month you can begin to take hardwood cuttings of roses (see November, p.279). They root best now.

POT UP CUTTINGS TAKEN IN SUMMER

Dig up and pot up the shrub cuttings taken this summer and rooted into the garden soil. Nip out the very tips to encourage branching and keep them in a cold frame or greenhouse through the winter. If cuttings haven't made new growth, they are probably not yet well rooted. Keep them weeded and leave them until the spring.

TRIM PRIVET HEDGES

Give privet hedges their last cut of the season.

FLOWERS

WHAT TO DO WITH PERENNIALS

Years ago, it was traditional to give perennial borders a thorough clear-out in the autumn, but nowadays we're more likely to leave the job until spring. It's not that we're all a lot lazier or untidier than our parents. No, longer autumns make it worthwhile growing lots of later-flowering perennials; the craze for grasses means we also have seedheads that look good well into winter, and today's gardens are 'greener', with more emphasis on encouraging wildlife, so a big autumn blitz really isn't an option.

- Just tidy away the worst of the rubbish, leaving seedheads for birds to feed on, and hollow stems for spiders and various beneficial insects to overwinter in. Don't worry about gathering up fallen leaves from beds and borders, because the worms will drag them down into the ground, where they break down and improve the soil. And in a wild garden, or around the back of the shed, a pile of leaves makes good winter quarters for your resident hedgehog. So keep your tidying to a minimum, and do most of it in spring. Only where leaves sit in the crowns of plants need they be removed to prevent rotting.

Don't be too hasty when it comes to cutting down perennials and grasses. Many of them are very attractive as they fade.

PLANT WINTER AND SPRING BEDDING

You can continue replacing summer bedding with winter and spring bedding until the end of the month (see September, p.229).

POT UP TENDER PERENNIALS

Before there's a risk of frost, pot up any tender perennials, such as pelargoniums and half-hardy fuchsias, and move them back indoors or into the greenhouse (see Under Cover, p.260).

LIFT TENDER BULBS

Lift and store tender summer-flowering bulbs and cannas. Lift gladioli when the foliage is dying down but before frost can kill off the corms; in mild areas, you can often get away with leaving them outside all year round if the ground is well drained. Leave dahlia tubers in the ground until the foliage has been blackened by frost (see November, p.281).

PLANT SPRING BULBS

There's still time to plant the spring bulbs you didn't plant last month (see September, pp.229–30). Also, now is the time to plant hyacinths and tulips, although you can plant them next month too. Find a sheltered, sunny spot with well-drained soil; put a handful of grit into the bottom of the planting hole as belt and braces, if drainage is less than perfect (as a rough guide, ask yourself if puddles hang about for more than a few hours after rain in winter). If the soil is very heavy, it's better to plant tulips in containers (see Under Cover, p.260).

PLANT LILY BULBS

Plant or divide and move lily bulbs. Lily bulbs don't like drying out, so replant them again straight away, and don't try to store them.

Plant out winter-flowering pansies and other spring bedding plants.

Right: Heathers that flower in winter can be packed into containers to brighten up a patio or doorstep.

PATIOS AND CONTAINERS

REPLACE SUMMER BEDDING

Continue replacing summer bedding and patio plants with winter and spring bedding (see September, p.231).

SPRING BULB REMINDER

If you haven't got around to planting your spring bulbs just yet, don't worry – there's still time yet. The thing to avoid doing at all costs is putting them in a safe place, and forgetting all about them until February or so. You'd be amazed at how often people ask me if they can still plant their bulbs when that happens, which is often not all that long before they should be flowering. The answer is that you can plant them in late winter or spring, but don't expect miracles – it'll take them a year or two to recover and resume normal service. Daffs really do prefer earlier planting (see September, pp.231–2), but hyacinths and tulips are happier planted now or even next month. If you still have other bulbs waiting to go in, don't hang about – get them planted.

PLANT UP CONTAINERS

Plant some evergreens and shrubs in containers for winter colour (see December, p.298).

VEGETABLES AND HERBS

HARVEST VEG

There's no risk of running out of veg this month, which is good news for your greengrocery bills. The big job that wants doing this month is harvesting veg that you'll store for winter use. There's a fine dividing line between leaving crops outside as long as possible to finish ripening completely, and leaving them out too long so they're ruined by cold and wet, so keep an eye on the weather. If it looks like a rainy spell is due, bring your vegetable harvest forward slightly. And if the autumn turns out to be damp, your best bet is to lay crops out one row deep in stacking trays and move them into a shed to dry, bringing them outside on fine days, and then back to the shed at other times to continue drying – plenty of air circulation between trays will be vital.

Late-sown summer crops

If you still have late-sown summer crops, such as peas, Chinese cabbage, pak choi, lettuce, and carrots in the ground, cover them with horticultural fleece now, as the extra warmth will keep them growing a little longer yet. Unless the weather turns very bad, you could still be picking them early next month, given a bit of protection.

Sprouts and leeks

The very first of your winter crops of sprouts and leeks will be ready to start using sometime this month. Make sure you use the early varieties first, as they won't stay in good condition once the weather deteriorates. Late-standing varieties will continue bulking up all the time 'good growing weather' continues, but they are the only ones that are capable of standing up to cold and icy weather after Christmas. That's why it's worth labelling veg crops – 'early' and 'late' varieties don't look all that different at this stage.

Autumn cauliflowers

Pick autumn cauliflowers as soon as they form a good-sized head, because they soon 'blow' if you leave them too long. If you have too many to use at once, break them down into individual florets, blanch them briefly in boiling water, then freeze them.

Onions, shallots or garlic

Harvested onions, shallots and garlic should be kept in a cool, bright, dry place to prevent them sprouting.

Potatoes

Maincrop potatoes are best left in the ground as long as possible, even if the foliage is yellowing, until you are forced to dig them up owing to imminent frosts or very wet weather. If we have a lot of rain after a hot, dry summer, semi-dormant spuds can often start growing again. If that happens they won't 'keep', and if it's really wet you can expect an invasion of slugs and other pests that will bore into underground tubers and set them rotting. If weather is wet and frosts are imminent, whip them out quick.

Keep on top of harvesting vegetables this month.

Dig up your maincrop potatoes now; they can be spoiled by cold, wet weather.

Pumpkins benefit from late harvesting, so they can ripen fully, but remove them quickly if weather is damp or frosty.

● Lay the potatoes out in shallow trays to dry, then store them in thick paper sacks, the sort potatoes are sent to greengrocers in, or better still use hessian sacks that you can still sometimes buy from pet shops or seed firms. Remember that the way to stop potatoes sprouting is to keep them in the dark; with onions the reverse is true – they need to be stored in good light.

● The only exception to October harvesting is the 'Pink Fir Apple' potato, which can keep growing until mid-November. As long as the soil stays in a suitable state, i.e. not too wet, and while there's no threat of a proper frost, leave that variety in the ground until then for the biggest crop, and to allow the tubers to ripen off properly so they store well.

Jerusalem artichokes

Jerusalem artichokes also want lifting before the weather turns wet. Cut the top of the plants off to clear the decks of the mass of 2m (6ft) tall stems while you're digging up the tubers; rub the soil off (it's never a good idea to wash root veg as they store better slightly 'dirty'); then dry the tubers off thoroughly before storing them in trays.

Carrots and parsnips

Carrots and parsnips are much better left in the ground and dug up fresh when you want them, as the soil keeps them in much better condition. If you have claggy clay soil, or it's a wet autumn, they'll try very hard to rot once conditions turn cold, so if you haven't used them by the middle of November I'd dig them up and store them (see November, p.283).

Pumpkins and squashes

The crop that really makes you feel that it's harvest festival time are pumpkins, a group that includes the real show-bench giants, as well as winter squashes, vegetable spaghetti, and the ornamental gourds used for flower arranging. Wait as late as you dare before you cut them, as the longer you leave them the more they'll continue ripening, which means they store better, but watch the weather. A proper frost or seriously damp weather will wreck your crop, so get them under cover fast.

● Cut pumpkins and squashes with about 2.5cm (1in) of stem, wipe the dirt off and leave them outside so the skins dry in the sun. They'll keep until about Christmas in a frost-free shed if you protect them from mice and damp, although they store much better in a covered porch or a cool room indoors, where they make good autumn decorations.

AUTUMN CLEARANCE

As soon as the soil is cleared of summer crops, dig it over and work in garden compost or other well-rotted organic matter. If you garden in a wet area or on clay soil, get ahead with your winter digging as early as possible (see November, p.272), as unsuitable soil conditions mean you may not have another chance until late spring.

CUT DOWN ASPARAGUS FOLIAGE

If you haven't yet cut down your asparagus foliage, do so now (see September, p.234).

OVERWINTERING ONIONS

Fill any vacant rows in the vegetable plot, after preparing the ground, with overwintering onions (see September, p.233). Transplant overwintering onion seedlings if you sowed your own last month, but what most people find easiest is simply planting overwintering onion sets. Plant them like spring-grown onion sets (see p.69) in prepared soil, leaving enough room to run a hoe through between the rows later; about 15cm (6in) apart in each direction is fine.

PLANT SPRING CABBAGE

If there are spaces in your vegetable plot, fill them with spring cabbage plants (see September, p.233).

PLANT GARLIC

Plant garlic late this month or next month (see November, p.283).

WINTER BRASSICA CARE

Remove yellowing leaves from Brussels sprouts and other winter brassicas.

FORCE WITLOOF CHICORY

If you grew witloof chicory this summer, now is the time to dig up the roots, twist the stems off the tops, and clean off the worst of the soil. Store them in trays in the shed. You can start forcing a few roots at a time any time from now, through winter (when people are often glad of any fresh food from the garden) and up until early spring (see January, p.26).

POT UP HERBS

Continue to pot up herbs for winter use (see September, p.234).

FRUIT

PLANT STRAWBERRIES

If you want to plant a new strawberry patch, now is the very best time to do so. If you have an existing strawberry bed, it's a good idea to take out the oldest row of plants and replace them with new ones, as after 3 or 4 years strawberry plants are getting a bit long in the tooth.

If you grew your own plants from runners this summer (see July, p.193), they'll be just right for planting now. If you didn't order plants through the post, and you can't find any at garden centres, you'll just have to wait until April. It's not the end of the world, but by planting them now, young plants have longer to establish, which means they'll give a bigger crop in their first summer. A new strawberry bed, or a new row in an old strawberry bed, needs good soil preparation.

● Clear out the old plants and any weeds, and fork in as much well-rotted organic matter as you can spare. Plant them 30cm (12in) apart in rows, leaving 45cm (18in) between rows so you have room to walk between them for weeding. Set them in place firmly, making sure the crown of each plant is slightly above soil level so they aren't smothered. Water in, and keep plants weeded. Wait until spring to feed them.

STORE APPLES AND PEARS

Some varieties of apples and pears are ready for eating early, straight off the tree, and they don't keep. Other varieties do store well, but they need watching carefully. Mid-October is about as long as they can safely be left hanging on the trees before you really need to pick them, but leave them until then if you possibly can, so they ripen properly. If the evening weather forecast mentions gales or storms, it's best to go out and pick them ASAP. Windfalls will be bruised, so these are the fruits to use straight away, or prepare for cooking and pop in the freezer – they'll just rot otherwise. Any you don't want, leave on the lawn for the birds – blackbirds, redwings and fieldfares go mad over them.

Pick and store apples and pears, taking care not to bruise them.

As long as the weather is reasonably mild, many vegetable crops will be perfectly happy outdoors.

- For storing, only perfect, unblemished fruit will do. Pick the lot carefully by hand, and check each one over before putting it in store.

- Clean, dry fruit will keep in the salad compartment in the bottom of your fridge for about 4–6 weeks. Place the rest inside wooden boxes or large polythene bags, with a few air holes punched in them, and store them in a cool, airy shed or outbuilding, where they'll be safe from frost, mice and damp. Okay, conditions won't be as good as you'd find in an old-fashioned fruit store, but how many of us have one? With luck, apples and pears in the shed should keep for 6 weeks or more, and even perhaps up to Christmas.

- Keep checking stored fruits every week, and use them as fast as you can; it only takes one apple to go bad and it'll rot the rest if it's not spotted in time.

PREPARE FOR NEW FRUIT TREES
Order new fruit trees and bushes, prepare the ground for planting, and plant if soil conditions are right (see November, p.284).

PRUNE BLACKBERRIES AND HYBRID BERRY FRUITS
After harvesting, prune blackberries and hybrid berry fruits (see September, p.235).

UNDER COVER

CLEAR OUT THE GREENHOUSE
Once the last of the summer crops has been picked, the greenhouse needs a good clean-out, ready for winter. Choose a fine day for the job and dig out your oldest clothes, because you're going to get dirty and wet. You'll need a bucket of warm water and a stiff brush, some greenhouse disinfectant and a sulphur candle from your local garden centre or hardware shop.

- Start by pulling out all your old tomato plants, and anything else that's been growing in the soil borders.

- Clear out all the dirty pots, used seedtrays and other junk you've poked underneath the staging, waiting for the day you have time to sort them out – today's the day. Empty the greenhouse completely, and stand all the pot plants outside on the lawn for now.

- Wash down the inside of the glass with greenhouse disinfectant, taking care to scrub the glazing bars up in the roof and gaps where panes of glass overlap, as these are the places where a lot of muck gathers and pests, such as red spider mite, go to hibernate as the days shorten. Scrub down the staging and paving slabs with more disinfectant solution, then rinse everything off with plenty of clean water.

- If you have a heated propagating case, empty it, wash and rinse it well inside and out.

- Clean the outside of the glass, washing off any remaining summer shading paint.

- For a final thorough fumigation, close the ventilators and stand a sulphur candle in the middle of the floor. Light it, and retreat fast, closing the greenhouse door behind you so the smoke can't escape. Wait until the smoke has subsided and the fumes have completely dispersed – several hours later – before opening up the house and starting to move the plants back inside.

HEATING THE GREENHOUSE

If you intend heating the greenhouse in winter, do the following:

- Pin up bubble-wrap insulation in the roof to cut down heat loss, but leave the ventilators free so there's still a chance to provide some fresh air on warm days.

- From about mid-October on, or shortly before your first anticipated frost, plug your heater in, and set the thermostat to an economical 3–4°C (38–40°F), so that it comes on automatically on cold nights to stop the temperature falling below freezing. A 2kw heater is adequate for keeping an average 2.5 × 2m (8 × 6ft) greenhouse frost-free. Stand it roughly in the middle of the floor, so that the heat can circulate easily, but raise it up on a few paving slabs so that the fan isn't ingesting dirt and dust, which shortens the life of the motor.

- It pays to invest in a maximum/minimum thermometer so you can check that the heating has been working properly while you weren't there watching it.

ROUTINE CHECKS ON THE GREENHOUSE

Whatever you grow, it's a good habit to check the greenhouse at least once a week, even in the depths of winter, but in autumn and spring I'd suggest dropping in every day or two. Don't think of it as a chore – a greenhouse makes a great bolt-hole any time you fancy a quiet half hour, and there's always something that needs doing. Keeping your treasures alive and happy through the winter is a real test of the gardener's art. Come spring, you'll feel really chuffed when everything has pulled through.

- Check your thermometer regularly. If the minimum temperature has dropped below 3–4°C (38–40°F) overnight, you may need to turn the thermostat on the heater up a tad. If the temperature is rising above 27°C (80°F) by day, ventilate more, as there'll be greater risk of fungal diseases, which can make plants rot. Each time you check the thermometer, remember to re-set it so you always read off the latest results.

- Pick plants over regularly to remove dead or diseased leaves, plus the last of the flowers as they go over – they are the first places grey mould and rot start up. While you're at it, look plants over for any pests, such as slugs or snails, and send them packing.

- Water as little as possible – just enough to stop plants shrivelling or shedding leaves when they shouldn't. Do the job in the morning on a fine day, when you can leave the ventilators open for a while afterwards. Avoid humidity building up at all costs, as it leads to a lot of fungal disease and rotting plants.

PROTECT FROST-TENDER PLANTS

Having some heating in your greenhouse or conservatory opens up your gardening horizons enormously. When you can keep frost-tender plants through the winter, instead of spending a fortune replacing them every year, it becomes much more practical to assemble a good collection of all the different summer bulbs and corms, exotic plants and half-hardy

Cost-cutting tip
If you only have a few plants to keep through the winter, it isn't worth heating the whole greenhouse especially. If there isn't room for them on a windowsill indoors, or in a corner of the conservatory, then simply screen off part of the greenhouse with polythene and just heat that. Alternatively, root as many plants as you can fit into a heated propagator placed on the staging.

Left: Bubble wrap provides excellent insulation for the inside of the greenhouse.

Before overwintering half-hardy perennials, such as pelargoniums, cut back the stems by about half.

perennials, so you can afford to be quite creative with them in the garden in summer, as well as making big flowering displays under glass.

Now that there's a good chance of 'proper' frosts clobbering the garden, tender plants should all be moved safely back under cover. Although they aren't growing actively, you can't afford to forget about them – they still need looking after, but winter storage is very different from summer growing.

Corms and tubers

- Potted plants with underground corms, tubers or rhizomes, such as begonias, gloxinias, zantedeschias, cannas and hedychiums, should have their watering gradually reduced so they are allowed to die down gradually from mid-September onwards. When the foliage is completely brown, cut it off just above the top of the pot, but leave the plants in their pots.

- Begonias, gloxinias and zantedeschias store best bone-dry in a spare room indoors, where it's warmer. If you're bringing clumps of cannas or hedychiums in from the garden, dig them up and fit them into pots only slighter bigger than their ball of roots, and fill the gap with potting compost. Cannas and hedychiums are happy in the greenhouse, placed under the staging, and will need very light occasional watering, just enough to stop the rhizomes shrivelling.

Half-hardy perennials

- Half-hardy perennials, including fuchsias, pelargoniums, and tender varieties of shrubby salvias, need cutting back to around half their height – around 15cm (6in). That way, they take up less room, and it also removes a lot of leafy growth that would otherwise go mouldy in winter.

- If the plants are already growing in pots, just clean them up and stand them close together on the staging; but if they've been growing out in the garden, dig them up, remove most of the soil from the roots, and pot them up.

- Fuchsias lose their leaves entirely and spend winter as bare 'sticks', which don't want more than the very lightest occasional watering, but pelargoniums and other half-hardy perennials need a little water to stop them from withering.

Tender exotics

- Pots of large conservatory plants and shrubby exotics (e.g. citrus, palms, bananas and oleander) that are placed outside on the patio, or used in trendy exotic beds for the summer, just need to be moved back under cover. Clean the pots up and evict any snails

---

PLANT TULIPS IN PANS

Tulips don't do terribly well on heavy soil, and if that's what you have, it's better to grow them in clay pans (a 'pan' is the name for a shallow flower pot) filled with potting compost, one variety per pan. The dwarfer varieties, such as waterlily tulips and small botanical varieties, are often grown this way, but I also plant the taller and more spectacular varieties, for example parrot tulips and the wasp-waisted lily-flowered tulips, this way too.

The great thing about growing tulips in pots or pans is that they're much safer from all the things that tend to nobble tulips in the open ground – soil pests, mice and a wide range of rots. And since pans are portable, you can keep them under cover until the last minute and then choose a suitable spot where the flowers won't be badly bashed about by spring weather.

- Plant pans of tulip bulbs in the same way as any spring bulbs in containers (see September, p.236), stand them in a cold frame or in an unheated greenhouse until they're just coming into flower, then arrange them to taste. I like mine clustered in groups on the terrace, or to brighten dreary corners.
- After the flowers are over, feed the bulbs with liquid tomato feed to plump them up, and gradually reduce the watering until 10–12 weeks later, when the bulbs are dormant again. Shake the soil off and store the larger bulbs in the shed to grow again next year.

or other pests. They'll need watering sparingly through the winter, again giving them just enough so that they don't dry out completely.

● Bougainvillea can grow quite big and is best grown in a large pot on a section of trellis or similar support, and pruned back roughly to a convenient size when you bring it inside for the winter. It likes to spend winter almost entirely bone dry.

● Cacti and other succulents need a good, bright situation close to the glass, so they can benefit from weak winter sun. Cacti and stone plants (lithops) like to be kept bone dry in winter, but the other succulents like very light watering – just enough to stop them from shrivelling.

SOW EARLY ANNUALS

In the South of France, gardeners habitually sow their hardy annuals out of doors in autumn to have early spring flowers, but it's debatable whether the seasons have advanced enough for us to get away with it here yet. Oh, I know you often find self-sown hardy nasturtiums popping up about now, but they nearly always vanish again during the winter. Some people may like to take the risk, but for everyone else I'd suggest sowing some in an unheated or frost-free greenhouse now, and keeping the plants under cover so you have good-sized plants to put out in spring for early flowers (for details on sowing seed in pots, see March, pp.73–4).

Particularly worthwhile sowing now are sweet peas, cerinthe, eschscholzia, poppies, phacelia, pansies and violas, cornflowers, echium, clarkia, nigella, annual gypsophila, plus any of the hardy annuals suggested for sowing last month to produce early pot plants under glass (see September, p.237) – sowing them now gives you young plants to set out next spring.

PLANT HYACINTHS IN POTS

You can also plant ordinary garden hyacinths (i.e. not the more expensive ones that have been specially prepared for forcing, which have very early flowers) in pots and treat them in

exactly the same way as tulips (see box opposite). Keep them in the greenhouse or cold frame, and they'll still flower a few weeks earlier than bulbs planted outdoors, so you can bring them indoors or use them for brightening up the conservatory or a shelf in the porch, or plunge them into patio containers.

PLANT NARCISSUS

Plant narcissus in pots up to mid-October for flowering over the Christmas period (see August, p.216).

GROW VEG FOR WINTER OR EARLY SPRING

Once the greenhouse has had its annual 'spring clean', you can use the soil border for growing a few winter salads or early spring veg. Sow rows of winter lettuce (choose a variety described on the back of the packet as 'suitable for winter sowing under glass'), corn salad (alias lamb's lettuce), baby spinach leaves (look out for a variety described as 'suitable for autumn sowing' on the packet), overwintering spring onions, and early varieties of carrot or mange-tout peas. It doesn't matter if the greenhouse isn't heated in the winter, but if it's kept frost-free, the crops will be slightly earlier. If the space is otherwise going to be left empty, you might just as well use it for something useful.

STRAWBERRIES IN POTS

If you want to plant strawberries in pots or hanging baskets, frankly I'd much rather wait until April so they won't have to face a winter outdoors until they're well established; in pots, the roots aren't as well insulated as when they're growing in the ground (see April, p.105). Move existing strawberry pots and baskets close to a wall for shelter over the winter, and in case of severe freezing spells later, lag them with bubble wrap or put them temporarily into a shed or greenhouse so the compost doesn't freeze solid.

Bring tender pot plants back into the greenhouse in early October at the latest.

WATER GARDEN

CLEAR OUT THE POND

After months of needing little more than occasional 'water weeding', the pond will be ready for its annual autumn once-over. The main reason for sorting the pond out at the end of the season, instead of leaving it until spring, is to keep the water as clean as possible. Any organic waste that gets into the pond now rots down and fouls the water, using up oxygen that hibernating fish, frogs and other water life need, besides adding to the layer of sludge in the bottom.

Cut down and clear plants

Start by cutting down all your marginal plants to 5cm (2in) above water level, now the flowers are finished and the leaves are dying off naturally. Fish out any tender free-floating plants, such as water lettuce and water hyacinth, as they don't survive winter in the open, and pull out any yellow, dead or dying water-lily leaves within reach.

Large ponds
If you have a pond that's too big to de-sludge, remove dying leaves from, or cover with a net, don't worry. The bigger the pond, the more beneficial bacteria, sludge-feeding plants and plant-eating fish you'll have, so a large pond or lake pretty well takes care of itself.

Cleaning the water garden in autumn is vital for pond-life.

Clear out sludge

Once you've cleared the decks a bit, if yours is a small pond it's worth clearing out some of the sediment from the bottom. It can build up fast, and if you leave it for several years you can find your pond has vanished and all you have left is a bog garden.

You might wonder how so much sludge appeared in your pond in the first place. It's a natural accumulation of decaying water-plant leaves, fish and snail manure, dead algae, plus any odd bits of soil, grass clippings and leaves that fell in the pond when you were gardening nearby – it all adds up. The resulting sludge is fine in small quantities – after all, it's what your water plants root into and feed off – but more than 2.5–5cm (1–2in) is too much of a good thing. There's no need to empty the pond; just use an old flowerpot to scoop out as much as you can reach when you kneel on the edge. Don't stand in it, or you'll almost certainly start a leak. Put the sludge on the compost heap, or straight onto your veg patch: it's rich stuff that's too good to waste.

Remove the pump

If you normally have a fountain or waterfall running in the summer, you can either lift the pump out of the water, clean it out, dry it and put it away in a warm, dry place for the winter, or else leave it where it is and keep it running in all but the coldest weather.

Cover the pond with netting

Tidy up the patch of garden all around the edge of the pond, and stretch a net over the surface of the water. The main reason for this is to keep falling leaves out of the pond in autumn, but it will also stop herons making a meal of your fish.

REDUCE FEEDING OF FISH

Stop feeding fish, if you've been doing so during the summer.

PROJECT Growing mushrooms

Years ago there was a brief craze for growing mushrooms in the lawn by inoculating it with mushroom spawn in the autumn. Unfortunately, it rarely worked, and very few people produced any mushrooms that way. What's much more successful is growing mushrooms indoors. Although they were traditionally grown in the cellar, or in the cupboard under the stairs, mushrooms thrive in the steady temperature of a centrally heated house in winter. Contrary to popular belief, they don't have to be kept in the dark – mushrooms make novel pot plants for a living room. It's nothing new – the Victorians used to do it.

Mushrooms are quite fascinating to watch. They only take about 4 weeks to start appearing and they keep cropping for 6 weeks or more. You'll pick lots from a very small space, and children are spellbound at the way the white caps seem to appear, as if by magic, from nothing but 'dirt'. Mushroom spawn isn't easy to get hold of these days, but you'll sometimes find it in some of the larger garden centres, either as part of a mushroom kit, or occasionally by mail order from seed catalogues.

MUSHROOM-GROWING FROM SCRATCH

If you want to grow your own mushrooms completely from scratch, you have to start by making mushroom compost. It's only worth doing if you do it on quite a large scale, since it takes a large volume of horse manure to heat up enough. Make friends with your local riding stables.

What you need

Horse manure

Thermometer

Mushroom spawn

Sterilized soil

1 Stack a cubic metre (yard) of fresh strawy horse manure, moisten with water until damp, and cover it with polythene or old carpet so it heats up quickly. Check the temperature in the centre with a soil thermometer – it should shoot up to over 38°C (100°F). When the temperature starts to drop, turn the heap so that the sides are in the middle and the manure in the centre is now on the edges and it should soon heat up again.

2 This time, wait until the temperature drops to below 21°C (70°F), then spread the stuff out in trays 15–20cm (6–8in) deep (for bulk production) or in decorative containers about 30cm (1ft) long × 15cm (6in) wide, and 'seed' it with grains of mushroom spawn, according to the instructions on the packet.

MUSHROOM KITS

A mushroom kit will come complete with everything you need. Some are supplied with a solid block of mushroom compost, to which you introduce the spawn and 'casing' material provided (the soil that is used to cover the compost). The block of compost is encased in a plastic bag, so find a suitable-sized container to stand it inside, and follow the instructions provided.

Some mushroom kits are supplied as loose compost and spawn, and it's much easier to be creative with these. Tip the compost into a decorative bowl, or the sort of pot-plant container that doesn't have drainage holes in the bottom, and again follow the directions provided.

I'd suggest starting the kit off in a cupboard and bringing it out when the first mushrooms start to appear, since it takes about 4 weeks, and a pot of bare compost doesn't look quite so fascinating. You can keep picking them for 6 weeks or more. There's no smell or anything unpleasant. Once mushrooms start popping up, stand the container on a table or a shady windowsill well away from a radiator.

Cut them as small 'button mushrooms', or wait another couple of days until they open wider as 'flats', which some cooks claim have more flavour. Either way, there's a knack to picking mushrooms. Cut through the stem cleanly, just below the surface of the compost, then use some of the casing material (the compost) to fill the hole where the mushroom came out. If you don't do that, an alien fungus gets in and turns the hole mouldy, and kills off all the mushrooms growing around it.

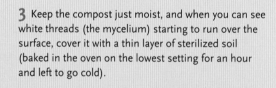

3 Keep the compost just moist, and when you can see white threads (the mycelium) starting to run over the surface, cover it with a thin layer of sterilized soil (baked in the oven on the lowest setting for an hour and left to go cold).

4 With luck, 4 weeks later you'll have mushrooms. Pick them as before (see above), and after your time is up, and no new mushrooms are emerging, use the spent mushroom compost on the garden.

NOVEMBER

November is the beginning of a new gardening year, as it's the start of the bare-root planting season, when deciduous shrubs and trees can be planted or dug up and moved while dormant with little check to their systems. At one time, it was the only season when trees and shrubs could be planted, but since the advent of container-growing they can now be moved at any time of year and the season has mercifully expanded.

Once the autumn leaves have fallen, evergreens really come into their own. They give the garden year-round backbone and some are very striking, in shades of gold, reds, bronze or blues, as well as in plain green or with various variegated patterns; many have incredible leaf shapes and feathery or brocade-like textures. A great number are well worth growing for their attractive flowers at various times of year, but one of their greatest advantages is that they make a superb backdrop for winter attractions such as seasonal flowers, frosty grasses, late berries, craggy tree trunks and coloured stems of shrubs.

THE BIG PICTURE evergreens

Arbutus unedo, the strawberry tree (above), makes a compact, slow-growing, fairly upright shrub or small tree, 8 × 8m (25 × 25ft) in time, with reddish brown bark, which in late autumn bursts into flower and fruit simultaneously. This apparently impossible trick is quite easily explained when you realize the clusters of white, bell-shaped flowers are 12 months removed from the fruit – the fruits you can see ripening now are actually from last year's flowers. The 'strawberries' don't look like strawberries at all – if anything, they look more like small lychees – and although they aren't harmful, they aren't worth eating either.

PEAK SEASON November–December.

GROWING CONDITIONS Not fussy, provided ground is not boggy; happy in sun or light shade, and puts up with polluted town-centre gardens.

Fatsia japonica, false castor oil plant (above), is one of those architectural-looking evergreens that could almost be living sculpture. A potentially large shrub, 3 × 4m (10 × 12ft), it's fairly slow-growing and can be kept smaller by pruning without much trouble; it's also good for training out over a wall. The huge, hand-shaped leaves can be 30cm (12in) across or more on large specimens and are favourites with flower arrangers. In late autumn the leaves are joined by rounded clusters of large, fluffy, cream-coloured flowers, followed by black berries very similar to those of ivy.

PEAK SEASON November–December.

GROWING CONDITIONS Not fussy, but best in light shade.

Elaeagnus × ebbingei (above) has silvered-bronze foliage with a slight texture of suede, caused by tiny hairs all over the surface of the leaves and young stems. It's as tough as old boots, ideal for an exposed or seaside garden. Just as you're taking it for granted, it surprises you in November by breaking out into a rash of almost invisible small, greenish-white, bell-shaped flowers tucked well away inside the wall of foliage, from which their haunting, disembodied scent leaks out. It grows 3 × 2.5m (10 × 8ft), but can be kept a bit smaller by pruning. Makes a good windbreak. If you want a more varied look, go for *Eleagnus × ebbingei* 'Gilt Edge', which has an irregular rim of gold around the leaves.

PEAK SEASON November.

GROWING CONDITIONS Any soil, except boggy, in sun or light shade.

OLD FAITHFULS

Iris foetidissima (above) is not the familiar 'flag' iris. It's an evergreen species, whose bright green, dagger-shaped leaves add variety to a winter border, not least because they are punctuated by the seedheads, which split open in late autumn to show off rows of bright red seeds. They always remind me of gaping mouths filled with bloodstained teeth, but maybe I've just watched one Hammer horror film too many. The plant rejoices in the common name of stinking gladwyn or roast-beef plant, because the foliage has a strange, meaty smell when bruised. The flowers, in early summer, are nothing to write home about – a washed out pale blue-grey – but the variety *I.f. var. citrina* has prettier, pale yellow flowers. Self-seeds slightly.

PEAK SEASON November–January.
GROWING CONDITIONS Not fussy, including solid clay and poor, dry soil under big trees, in sun or shade.

Prunus × subhirtella **'Autumnalis'** (above) is the tree to grow for cherry blossom in winter, when the blossom is outlined against a tracery of bare branches. It's an absolute delight. The flowers are small, double, somewhere between off-white and pale magnolia, and the tree makes an elegant shape that reaches roughly 6 × 3m (20 × 10ft). There are varieties with pinker flowers, such as **'Autumnalis Rosea'** (my all-time favourite) and an attractive weeping version, **'Pendula Rosea Plena'**, at 6 × 6m (20 × 20ft); plain 'Autumnalis' has the most prolific display of winter blossom.

PEAK SEASON November–March.
GROWING CONDITIONS
Reasonably well-drained, fertile soil in sun.

Erica carnea varieties, or winter-flowering heathers, are plants that many people fight shy of. Yes, I know they were massively overdone years ago, when heather and conifer gardens were all the rage with people who didn't want to do any gardening. But winter heathers keep flowering even when things turn cold, and they're happy in windy places where other flowers don't stand a chance, so in those situations don't knock them. Closely planted, they make a good ground-covering carpet (each plant grows to about 38 × 38cm/ 15 × 15in), but they are also at home planted temporarily in winter tubs or – amazingly – in hanging baskets. Good varieties include **'Springwood White'**, **'Springwood Pink'** (above), **'King George'** (an old mauve-pink variety but with one of the longest flowering seasons of all), and **'Vivellii'** (bronze-tinted foliage and purple flowers).

PEAK SEASON November–March.
GROWING CONDITIONS Well-drained soil with plenty of organic matter, in full sun. Acid soil is not essential for cultivars of *Erica carnea*, but avoid really chalky ground.

Viburnum rhytidophyllum
(above) is a large, dome-shaped
evergreen, 4 × 4m (12 × 12ft),
with long, oval, dark green
leathery leaves backed with what
looks like cream suede.
It is tough, and good at screening
off eyesores in the town or
country, but in winter
it has large, flat heads of pale
brown, suede-effect buds that
stand out well against the foliage.
They open in spring into almost
elder-like white flowers. A good
shrub for growing clematis
through, as the flowers contrast so
well with the foliage.

PEAK SEASON November–March.
GROWING CONDITIONS Not
  fussy as long as the soil isn't
  badly drained, and prefers a
  position in sun or light shade.

Viburnum davidii (above) is
a small evergreen viburnum,
1 × 1.5m (3 × 5ft), with strongly
ribbed oval foliage, and bunches
of upstanding berries in an eye-
catching shade of turquoise that
last late into winter. The only
slight drawback – and the reason
why you don't see it all that
often – is that male and female
flowers appear on separate plants,
so you need one of each to do the
biz. Local authorities often plant
it in groups, with one male and
up to six females. Lucky chap.

PEAK SEASON November–
  January.
GROWING CONDITIONS
  Reasonably well-drained soil
  with some organic matter, in
  sun or light shade.

Viburnum* × *bodnantense
'Dawn' (above) is the first of
three viburnums that are great
garden plants at this time of year.
It is deciduous, grows to about
3 × 2m (10 × 6ft), and from late
autumn until early spring its bare
branches are decorated with tiny
bunches of rosy-pink-budded
flowers that fade to white as they
open. Cut a few sprigs for the
house and savour their sweet
scent. It can be set back a bit by
frost, but will usually recover to
flower over a long period.

PEAK SEASON November–March.
GROWING CONDITIONS Any
  reasonably well-drained soil in
  sun or dappled shade.

SOMETHING SPECIAL

Winter-flowering pansies (*Viola × wittrockiana* cultivars – above) are some of the most reliable out-of-season bedding plants you can find, good for gaps in sheltered borders and for planting in winter containers with evergreens. The **Universal Series**, in particular, is well known for flowering through all but the very worst weather (size 15 × 8cm/ 6 × 3in), although if the ground is frozen for long you'll lose the lot. Milder winters mean that we can now risk winter bedding schemes we'd never have bothered with years ago.

PEAK SEASON November–May.
GROWING CONDITIONS Well-
   drained soil with some organic
   matter, in a sheltered spot in
   sun or light shade.

Potted topiary (above) is a good winter standby, for perking up the patio or front doorstep, or plugging a gap down the garden. Box is one of the very best subjects for training, as it is slow-growing, shade-tolerant, and trims easily into simple shapes such as domes, but you can be more adventurous and go for spires and spirals, or even peacocks, chickens or teddy bears. You can also buy them ready-trained in various sizes – all it takes is money.

PEAK SEASON All year round.
GROWING CONDITIONS Soil-
   based potting compost, kept
   moist but not waterlogged,
   in sun or shade.

Ornamental cabbages (above) must be the unlikeliest bedding plants ever, but they are surprisingly glamorous – mauve, pink or cream hearts with green frills around the edge, like giant rosettes, 30 × 20cm (12 × 8in). **Ornamental kales** come in similar colour schemes but with longer, shaggier leaves. They both sit there looking colourful all winter, and only start to run to seed in early spring – nature's way of reminding you it's time to plant your spring bedding. And before you ask, yes, you can eat ornamental cabbages if you really want to, but the whole idea is to look at them. If you want cabbage to eat frankly I'd settle for a 'January King'.

PEAK SEASON November–March.
GROWING CONDITIONS
   Reasonably well-drained soil or
   containers, in sun or light
   shade.

OTHER PLANTS IN THEIR PRIME IN NOVEMBER

- **Trees** *Arbutus × andrachnoides*
- **Shrubs** *Fuchsia* (hardy), *Viburnum farreri*
- **Evergreens** *Mahonia japonica*
- **Berries/fruits** *Callicarpa bodinieri* var. *giraldii* 'Profusion' (see p.222), *Chaenomeles, Cotoneaster, Crataegus* (see p.244), *Euonymus europaeus* (see p.243), *Malus* (see p.244), *Mespilus germanica* (see p.245), *Myrtus communis, Nandina domestica, Passiflora caerulea* (see p.178), *Pernettya, Photinia davidiana, Pyracantha* (see p.244), *Rosa* 'Geranium', *Rosa rugosa, Symphoricarpos*
- **Climbers/wall shrubs** *Clematis tangutica* (see p.221), *Clematis tibetana* subsp. *vernayi* (see p.221), *Jasminum nudiflorum* (see p.12)
- **Perennials** *Aster ericoides, Aster novae-angliae, Aster novi-belgii* (see p.221), *Aster pilosus* var. *pringlei, Cortaderia selloana, Kniphofia* (see p.220), *Liriope muscari* (see p.220), *Saxifraga fortunei, Schizostylis, Stipa* (see p.221)
- **Bulbs** *Colchicum* (see p.245), *Crocus cancellatus, Crocus longiflorus, Cyclamen hederifolium* (see p.222)
- **Bedding** *Viola* cultivars
- **Rock plants** *Gentiana sino-ornata, Persicaria vacciniifolia*

Gaultheria procumbens, checkerberry or wintergreen (above), is a gem for winter containers, and teams well with winter heathers and skimmias. It's also good for ground cover under shrubs if your garden has acid soil. A low, spreading evergreen, 15 × 60cm (6 × 24in), it has neat, oval, dark green leaves and bright red berries that are reminiscent of gobstoppers. The clusters of small white, bell-shaped flowers earlier in the season are nothing special.

PEAK SEASON November–March.
GROWING CONDITIONS Lime-free soil in shade.

Skimmia is an invaluable small evergreen shrub for winter interest. Several kinds are well worth growing, but some of the best varieties are unisex, so it takes two to berry. *Skimmia japonica* 'Veitchii' is a female form, grown for its big red berries; *Skimmia japonica* 'Rubella' (above) is all-male, and produces pyramidal heads of pale pink buds that open out to white flowers in spring. I'd grow the two in the same hole, as they go together perfectly – both reach roughly 60 × 60cm (2 × 2ft).

PEAK SEASON November–March.
GROWING CONDITIONS Well-drained, lime-free soil with some organic matter, in light shade.

***Clematis cirrhosa* 'Freckles'** (above) is an evergreen clematis, and not as fragile as it's often made out to be. Quite a big, strong climber, this plant is ideal for growing through a deciduous tree. The flowers appear in all except truly abysmal weather right through winter, but don't go thinking of your conventional clematis flowers – these are cream cups, dappled with lots of tiny, brick-red spots that always remind me of an exotic bird's egg.

PEAK SEASON November–March.
GROWING CONDITIONS Fertile soil, growing where its roots are in shade and stems climb out into sun for at least part of the day.

NOVEMBER at-a-glance checklist

GENERAL GARDEN TASKS (p.272)
✔ Carry out winter digging or forking over.
✔ Winterize the garden – check the whole garden over for anything that's likely to be at risk from cold, wind or waterlogging.

LAWNS (p.274)
✔ Keep off the lawn if possible, or protect it with a temporary path and sprinkle with sand if it's slippery.
✔ Continue cutting the grass all the time it keeps growing, but raise the blades.
✔ Collect up dead leaves from the lawn and make leafmould and potting compost.
✔ Lay turf if you didn't last month.
✔ Dig over areas for new lawns.

TREES, SHRUBS AND CLIMBERS (p.276)
✔ Plant and move bare-root trees, shrubs, roses and hedging.
✔ Stake newly planted trees.
✔ Look after newly planted trees and shrubs.
✔ Renovate old trees, shrubs and climbers.
✔ After leaf fall, take hardwood cuttings of easy shrubs, roses and soft fruit bushes.
✔ Sow seed of hardy shrubs and trees.

FLOWERS (p.281)
✔ Continue planting tulips and hyacinths.
✔ Divide fibrous-rooted perennials.
✔ Dig up dahlia tubers once the plants start to die off after the first hard frost.
✔ Plant lily bulbs.
✔ Protect young and slightly tender plants from cold and wet.
✔ Remove dead leaves from tops of plants.

PATIOS AND CONTAINERS (p.282)
✔ Protect container plants from wind, persistent rain and continuous cold weather.

VEGETABLES AND HERBS (p.283)
✔ Plant garlic.
✔ Continue forcing witloof chicory.
✔ Continue to harvest leeks and Brussels sprouts. By the middle of the month, if you haven't used your carrots and parsnips yet, dig them up and store them in the fridge or shed.

FRUIT (p.284)
✔ Continue planting fruit trees.
✔ Plant summer-fruiting raspberry canes.
✔ Check fruit in store for bruising or other damage.

UNDER COVER (p.284)
✔ Ventilate the greenhouse well on sunny days, reduce watering to a bare minimum, and continue regular dead leaf picking.
✔ Check bulbs being forced for early flowering weekly, and move them indoors when the buds show the first hint of colour.
✔ Sow hardy plants from seed.
✔ Create winter displays under glass.
✔ Check stored fruit, vegetables, and bulbs and corms for signs of rotting – use affected vegetables straight away.
✔ Grow windowsill salads and herbs.

WATER GARDEN (p.286)
✔ Do your autumn clear-out if you didn't last month.
✔ Clean the pool filters and check all cables for pumps and lights if leaving them in the pond.

Watch out for
● Snails congregating in crevices around the garden to hibernate.
● Mice in sheds and greenhouses, especially where there are stored fruit, vegetables or dahlia tubers.
● Pigeons pinching your winter greens.
● Squirrels digging up your bulbs.
● Windy weather disturbing tree stakes and ties, and ties chafing the bark.

Get ahead
● Think about any garden designing, alterations or construction you'd like to do over the winter, while there's not much routine gardening to do; start planning, collect catalogues and order materials.
● Give the lawn mower a maintenance check now or over the winter.
● Dig over the vegetable patch while the ground is workable.
● Start winter pruning.
● Mulch fruit trees.

Last chance
● Plant daffodils, narcissus bulbs and crocus corms as soon as possible. You're late!

GENERAL GARDEN TASKS

WINTER DIGGING AND FORKING OVER

Winter digging is one of those seasonal must-dos, but there's no need to half kill yourself. Oh, I know there are still those who think we should all be out double digging, but it's just not necessary, unless you've set your heart on making a name for yourself on the summer produce show circuit. Giant vegetables appreciate a good, rich, deep bed, but for everyday gardening you can afford to go easy.

When to dig and when to fork over

It's only ground that is actually bare in winter that needs proper winter digging, and that usually means annual flowerbeds and veg gardens (see box below). Ground that has already been well cultivated in the past won't need more than a light turning over with a fork (see box opposite). If you have some spare garden compost or well-rotted manure, spread it over the ground first so it automatically gets turned in as you work.

On thin soil overlying chalk, like mine, or on heavy clay soil, forking over is about as much as you ever need to do, because if you try digging chalky soil or heavy clay deeply all you do is bring infertile subsoil to the surface, which is no good for plants. On soils like these, concentrate on adding organic matter regularly and building up a good layer of topsoil. That's also the best way to go about improving shallow soil underneath big trees, where there are lots of roots near the surface.

When to postpone winter digging

If you have a wet, clay soil, leave it well alone, and don't attempt to dig it now. If it looks like Plasticene, the clods turned over by your spade will set like concrete in summer, and you can never smash them up to make decent soil. On this type of ground, it's much better to wait until what my Granny called 'good drying weather', when the land is starting to dry naturally. Catch it just right and it'll dig beautifully, but you might have to wait until late March or April at the latest. After initial cultivations on clay soil, I'd settle for adding a mulch of organic matter and grit each spring, thereby building up your own decent topsoil as the years go by. It works – I've done it.

WINTERIZE THE GARDEN

Now that autumns are longer and winters milder, you might think you don't need to bother tucking the garden up for the 'off season' – but you do. We might not have the regular snow, or soil frozen solid and ponds iced over for weeks that our grandparents had to contend with, but today's milder winters bring their own set of problems – not least of which are waterlogging, rotting, and a massive build-up of pests now there's no cold snap to cut down their numbers. So be prepared, and nip potential problems in the bud before they happen. The family will call you an old fuss-pot, but take no notice – you'll save time, money and a lot of aggravation in the long run.

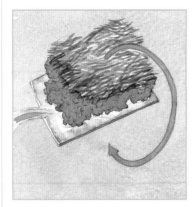

Bare ground needs digging over and enriching with plenty of organic matter.

HOW TO DIG OVER A BARE FLOWERBED OR VEG PATCH

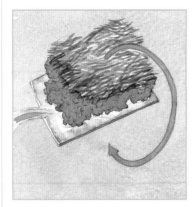

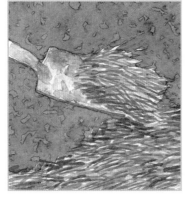

1 Spread organic matter over the area first, using a spade. Starting at one end of the plot, dig a complete row across it, turning each spadeful of earth over so it buries the organic matter.

2 Work over the entire plot in this way, a row at a time, until it's all done, leaving it looking slightly like a ploughed field, with all the organic matter now buried just below the surface.

Gales

Strong, wintry winds are a big problem in all but the most well-sheltered gardens.

- If you have fences, go to the base of the posts and check they're not rotting off – a replacement now can save you having to reinstate half your fence, plus whatever it smashed on the way down.

- Make sure all your garden gates and shed and greenhouse doors have good solid latches, and keep them firmly shut or they'll knock themselves to bits in the gales.

- Take your wind chimes down for the winter – they'll drive the neighbours barmy clanging flat out in windy weather.

- Look out for anything lying around loose in the garden that could blow against a window or the greenhouse. Dustbin lids are regular offenders, and they're easily fixed with one of those elasticated gizmos they sell in car accessory shops for holding luggage on to roof racks. Branches of nearby trees and unrestrained climbers can also break glass they slap against on a windy night, so have a look, and what you can't tie down, cut off.

- Check the stakes of newly planted trees and shrubs (see Trees, Shrubs and Climbers, p.276).

- Protect container plants from heavy winds (see Patios and Containers, p.282).

Heavy rain

Climate change means we're having much more rain in winter nowadays, so you need to watch out for problems caused by excess wet.

- One relatively 'new' problem caused by wet winters is that a lot of perfectly hardy plants, such as rosemary, lily bulbs and alpines, that normally come through the winter with no problems will often die off, simply because they don't like wet feet while they're dormant. If you garden on clay soil, or in a low-lying

HOW TO FORK OVER

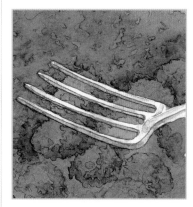 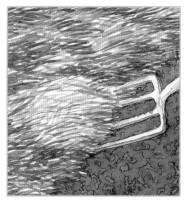

1 Poor ground is better forked over, rather than being dug and the poor subsoil brought to the surface. Fork it as deeply as you dare, and break down the clods with the back of the fork.

2 Spread well-rotted garden compost or manure on the surface and allow the worms to mix it in. That way you will create decent topsoil.

situation where water gathers, it's worth growing any plants that need good drainage in raised beds; alternatively, grow them in pots and move them under cover for the winter, and either 'plunge' them wherever they are wanted in summer, or use them as patio plants.

- Protect the lawn from damage in wet weather (see Lawns, p.274).

- Protect container plants from heavy rain (see Patios and Containers, p.282).

Cold snaps

Don't be fooled by a few mild winters into thinking we'll never have a hard frost. It'll usually happen with no warning, just when you least expect it.

- It doesn't take much to wreck your outdoor tap unless it's well lagged. You can buy a special insulated tap-cosy to slip over it, but a good wrapping of newspaper or bubble wrap with a plastic carrier bag tied over the top does the job just as well, even if it's not so pretty. If you need to keep the tap in use during the winter, there's no need to cover up until a sharp cold snap is forecast.

● Before freezing weather, lag your outdoor tubs (see Patios and Containers, p.282).

Mild weather

Since we stopped having 'proper' winters, pest problems are worse than ever.

● Snails are the big winners. They congregate in huge groups for the winter, at the foot of walls, and under planks or tubs, so hunt them out and you can usually dispose of enormous numbers. You might even put some clay pots or lengths of plastic drainpipe out specially to trap them. Sneaky but effective, and a darn site safer than rushing around with slug pellets in spring, when they surge out *en masse* and devour everything in sight.

● Look out for signs of mice and their larger relatives in your compost heaps, or tunnelling into the shed or greenhouse. Disturb everything regularly, and make sure there's nothing around they can eat; stored fruit and vegetables are bound to be a temptation. And cover your winter brassicas, if the pigeons are after them. Chances are if you don't net 'em you won't get 'em.

● Squirrels won't hibernate in a mild winter, so they will be out looking for food – anticipate them digging up spring bulbs and raiding your bird table. Mixing hot chilli pepper powder with bird seed and peanuts works wonders, as birds like the taste but squirrels don't (see August, p.217). Use wire netting to protect bulbs. Squirrels have also been known to chew up irrigation tubing that's left outside in borders all year round, so if it's the porous sort, it's worth burying it several inches underground with fine mesh wire netting over the top, otherwise I'd simply coil the lot up and bring it inside until it's needed next year.

Winter mowing tip
Do use a grass box for mowing in winter, even if you don't bother in summer, as the clippings won't dry up and disappear at this time of year. They'll just lie around looking messy and smothering the grass, before being trodden back indoors.

Wire netting placed over the tops of pots will keep squirrels from digging up bulbs.

LAWNS

PROTECT THE LAWN

Prolonged wet spells invariably make the lawn sodden, so it really is worth keeping off it as much as possible, otherwise your feet just sink in and the footsteps will wear a muddy path that sets solid in summer.

● If you're planning a day's gardening when conditions are a bit boggy underfoot, protect the lawn by unrolling a temporary path where you'll need to push your barrow to avoid leaving muddy tracks. If you have no alternative route to somewhere you have to go regularly, for example your shed or the back gate, then make a path.

● If you have patches of green slime or liverwort, or soft slippery places forming on the lawn, the quick fix is to sprinkle them with gritty horticultural sand to make the surface firmer and more non-slip – but make a mental note to do some serious lawn care next year.

CONTINUE MOWING

This is the time when, traditionally, we always stopped cutting the grass for the winter and sent the mower off for an expensive re-fit. Well, sorry if you were looking forward to a break, but today's milder winters mean that grass keeps on growing. You certainly won't need to mow it as often as in summer, but it'll need topping every 2–3 weeks right through the winter, or by the spring it'll be looking decidedly shaggy. Choose a day when the grass is dry and the ground isn't boggy. Don't cut too close between now and next April – shift your mower blades a notch or two higher.

LAWN MOWER CARE

If you have time to spare, or are looking for a job to do on a rainy day, you could get ahead with mower maintenance (see January, p.17).

MAKING LEAFMOULD AND HOMEMADE POTTING COMPOST

When you only have a couple of barrowloads of leaves to dispose of, you might just as well mix them with other ingredients and add them to your usual compost heap. But if you have lots, then it's worth making leafmould – particularly if they are oak or horse chestnut leaves, which take a long time to break down owing to their high tannin content. Use leafmould for top-dressing woodland plants, enriching your rock garden, and for filling containers in which you'll be growing alpines. You can also use 'neat' leafmould for top-dressing camellias and rhododendrons grown in containers, as an alternative to topping them up each spring with ericaceous compost. If you're lucky enough to have masses of leafmould to spare, you could use it as a mulch for perennials all around the garden, even under trees, although most people have to keep it for special plants that really need it.

- To make leafmould, push the well-damped leaves into a black plastic bin liner bag, prod a few air holes in the sides with a garden fork, and stack them anywhere out of the way for one year; allow two in the case of oak. At the end of that time, the contents will have turned into black crumbly 'super-loam', which makes a valuable home-grown substitute for peat.
- To make homemade potting compost, sterilize the leafmould in a roasting bag in the oven, set at the lowest temperature for an hour. Mix equal quantities John Innes potting compost No 2, well-rotted leafmould, and horticultural grit. This makes a very good home-made potting compost for filling pots or tubs, including sink gardens containing alpines or choice dwarf rockery bulbs. You could use the same mixture for filling raised beds and rock features outside in the garden, in which case you don't need to sterilize the leafmould and good topsoil could replace the John Innes.

CLEAR FALLEN LEAVES

One job that needs doing badly right now is sweeping up fallen leaves from the lawn. They might look picturesque at the time, but when they cover the grass completely, and stay put for weeks, the grass is starved of light and quickly becomes a martyr to fungal diseases and bare patches. Once you've cleared the leaves, you can use them to make leafmould (see box above).

- If you have a fairly tough breed of mower, such as a ride-on or a large powerful petrol mower, the easiest way to gather fallen leaves is by running it over the lawn, with the blades set up high and the grass box in place.

- If you have a hover mower, a small electric or hand mower that is not up to the job, then use a besom broom, a spring-tined rake, or an electric lawn-raker with its rotating teeth set to their highest setting.

- If you have a large area to clear, it might be worth hiring or buying a proper leaf-sweeper, which is like a pot-bellied pram with rotating bristles underneath, or a leaf blower to huff the leaves into convenient heaps and then clear them away in a barrow.

Left: A rubber-toothed rake is really efficient at clearing the lawn of leaves.

LAY TURF

If you didn't lay turf in October, you can still lay it now (see October, pp.250–1).

CONTINUE TO DIG OVER AREAS FOR NEW LAWNS

Take advantage of favourable soil conditions to prepare soil for new lawns you'll be sowing or turfing in spring (see September, p.227).

TREES, SHRUBS AND CLIMBERS

Hedge-planting tip
If you garden on really poor soil, it's worth making your trench well in advance so you can fill it gradually over the summer – throw in all your kitchen peelings, lawn clippings and annual weeds, covering them with a layer of soil each time. By autumn, it will have turned to decent planting compost that just needs weeding and stirring up before planting.

PLANT BARE-ROOT PLANTS

Autumn is the natural planting season for plants that are moved with bare roots. Once the leaves have fallen, and plants are preparing for winter dormancy, any deciduous woody plant that is dug up out of the ground with bare roots will move happily, so if there's anything in your garden that you want to dig up and move, now's the time to do it. If you want to plant an economical new hedge using bare-root plants, or you've ordered bare-root roses by post from a specialist nursery, this is the only time available.

Correctly speaking, you can actually plant bare-root plants any time between leaf fall (when deciduous plants shed their leaves) and bud burst (when they start to grow back again in spring), but autumn is best because soil conditions encourage new rooting, while in winter the ground is often too boggy or else frozen solid so they can often just rot. But if conditions are good you can keep going right through the winter, and as late as mid-March.

Successful planting techniques

The trick with planting bare-root plants is to prepare the soil well (see October, p.252) and make sure you don't keep the plants hanging about. Plants in pots can stand around for weeks or more, provided you keep them watered, but the roots of bare-root plants lack that protective layer of soil around them, so they dry out fast. If you can't plant them straight away, 'heel them in', which just means burying the roots in any empty patch of ground for now, to keep them moist (see January, p.20).

When you plant bare-root plants (see box below), you'll need to dig a much wider hole than for pot-grown plants, to accommodate their stiff, spreading root systems. I've seen people make a little hole and shove the plants in with the roots curled up in the bottom, just to get them out of the way – or even left draped over the edges of the hole so they're sticking out above the ground after they have been 'planted'.

PLANT A HEDGE

The kinds of plants you are most likely to buy bare-rooted nowadays are deciduous hedging plants, for example beech, hornbeam, hawthorn, rose species and field maple. As these are planted quite close together, it's much easier

HOW TO PLANT A BARE-ROOT SHRUB

1 Dig a hole that is wider than the plant's roots when they are well spread out. Work plenty of organic matter – well-rotted compost or manure – into the base of the hole and into the soil that has been removed.

2 Sit the plant in place and arrange the roots over the bottom of the hole.

3 Look for a soil mark near the base of the plant that shows the level it was growing at before, and aim to replant it to the same depth. Jiggle the plant up and down a bit as you start shovelling enriched soil around the roots, to adjust the depth slightly as well as settling the soil round the roots.

4 When you are happy, firm the roots into place, then lightly prick over the soil with a fork to relieve surface compaction. Water and mulch to finish off.

HOW TO PLANT A HEDGE

1 Mark out the line of your hedge with a length of string between two canes, to act as a guide and keep the row straight.

2 Dig the trench down to the full depth of your spade and fill it with organic matter, which you can stir into the soil at the bottom with a fork.

3 Space your plants out evenly. For a medium-sized hedge, a single row of plants spaced 30–45cm (12–18in) apart is fine, but if you want a hedge more than 1.2m (4ft) tall, plant a slightly staggered row, with the plants about 75cm (30in) apart.

4 Backfill around the roots with the original topsoil, after mixing it with plenty of organic matter, firm gently and water well. If the original plants were tall or non-branching, cut them down to about 15cm (6in) from the ground to make the new hedge branch out right from the base.

to dig a trench and plant the whole lot in bulk rather than put each plant down an individual planting hole.

PREPARE LARGE DECIDUOUS SHRUBS FOR MOVING

Large shrubs can often be moved if they outgrow their space, or if you need to reorganize the garden slightly. Regard them as bare-root plants, and move them when they are leafless and dormant, between late October/early November and mid-March. Since mature shrubs develop a few thick, hawser-like roots designed for support, you'll improve their chances of survival considerably if you 'train them' to grow a fibrous root system, similar to that of a young plant, which is better able to take in water and nutrients to help the plant get back on its feet. This naturally takes time, so you need to start preparing for the move well in advance – ideally a year before the move. The method is the same as for transplanting a large evergreen (see April, p.90), but there's no need to protect newly moved deciduous shrubs from wind or sun, since they don't have any leaves to lose water through, unlike evergreens.

STAKE NEWLY PLANTED TREES

Trees are planted in exactly the same way as shrubs, with one big exception – they need staking. There are two types of stake, and which kind you use depends on what you are planting.

Permanent stakes

The only trees that need permanent stakes are those with very frail or feeble root systems, which in practice means anything grown on very dwarfing rootstocks, such as fruit trees and some ornamental crab apples. Since the stake needs to last virtually the lifetime of the tree, we're talking about something pretty substantial, such as a 2m (6ft) chestnut stake. Tree stakes are pointed at one end so they're easy to hammer into the ground.

Temporary stakes

All other trees only need staking for the first couple of years after planting, while the roots take a hold. In this case, you only need a 1m (3ft) stake, which is just enough to hold the very base of the tree and stop the roots being rocked loose in a gale. Research has shown that young trees whose trunks are allowed to sway in the wind develop stronger trunks and roots

Make sure newly planted trees and shrubs are firmed back after frosts, which can lift them out of the soil.

Right: Trees with weak root systems, such as fruit trees and some ornamental crab apples, need permanent staking.

Improvised tree tie
If your tree stakes or ties are chafing the bark, then an old pair of tights makes a brilliant emergency tree tie.

that grip the ground better. By using long stakes, you only teach them bad habits – they use their stakes as crutches, and fall down years later, when the stake eventually rots away. Short stakes are easy to put in, and after a couple of years you can take them out.

- After planting your bare-root tree (see How to plant a bare-root shrub, p.276), hold the base of the stake about 30cm (1ft) away from the tree, and hammer it halfway into the ground at an angle of 45 degrees. Then use a single tree tie to fix the tree to the stake, about 30–45cm (12–18in) from the ground (see below).

KEEP AN EYE ON NEWLY PLANTED TREES AND SHRUBS

You can't expect just to plant trees and shrubs – even when conditions are perfect – and forget all about them afterwards. There are a lot of people who do just that, then feel very peeved when their plants die off. You still need to visit them regularly to check they are all right.

- The weather may do your watering for you, but if it's dry a good soaking tides them over.

HOW TO PLANT A TREE WITH A PERMANENT STAKE

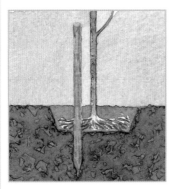

1 Prepare your planting hole, then knock the stake in vertically, keeping it perfectly upright.

2 Plant the tree next to it, so you aren't hammering the stake through the roots afterwards. Enrich and return the soil, then firm it into place and water well.

3 Secure the tree to the stake with two proper tree ties – not old bits of string – at the top and bottom of the trunk. Proper tree ties have a buckle so that you 'belt up' around the trunk and then fix the ends around the tree stake, so there's a buffer between the trunk and the stake to prevent the bark rubbing in windy weather.

HOW TO TAKE HARDWOOD CUTTINGS

1 Collect some strong, straight stems approximately 30–45cm (12–18in) long. They should already have lost their leaves.

2 Make a clean, straight cut across the base, just below a leaf scar, and a sloping cut about 20cm (8in) above it, just above a leaf scar, so you are removing several centimetres from the tip of each shoot.

3 Dip the bottom 2.5cm (1in) of the cutting into plain water and then dip it into hormone rooting powder. Make a slit trench in a sheltered bed or border and trickle sharp sand into the base (see illustration, p.280).

4 Push the cuttings, right way up, into the trench in your cuttings bed, about 15cm (6in) apart so that only the top 2.5cm (1in) of each shoot is left sticking out. Firm each side of the trench with your foot to close the soil around the cuttings.

• Strong winds can rock newly planted trees or shrubs loose, or even work them out of the ground, in which case firm them back with your heel. Similarly, you might find a mole has heaved the plants out of the ground by tunnelling under them, or frost has caused the ground to 'lift', in which case they need firming back in.

PROTECT PLANTS FROM WIND

Tie in long shoots of climbers and wall shrubs, and check tree stakes and ties after windy weather.

RENOVATE OLD SHRUBS, CLIMBERS AND HEDGES

Between now and spring, you can start renewal-pruning overgrown shrubs and climbers, and renovating deciduous hedges (see January, p.21).

TAKE HARDWOOD CUTTINGS

If you want shrubs for free, the easiest way is to grow your own from hardwood cuttings. It's a good way to produce plants in bulk when you want to grow yourself a new hedge, and it's also very handy if you or a friend or relative has a new garden that needs filling cheaply. Hardwood cuttings of roses have the advantage over garden-centre-bought roses in that they do not produce 'suckers', as they are grown on their own roots rather than a rootstock of briar. Unlike other types of cuttings, you don't need any equipment at all for hardwood cuttings – they root outside in the garden soil. Another advantage is there's not much work involved, since the weather takes care of them for you.

Which plants root from hardwood cuttings?

You can root the tougher shrubs this way, and although it is more a technique for deciduous shrubs, there are some evergreens that are relatively easy to root. Shrubs that propagate successfully this way include dogwoods, buddleia, euonymus, forsythia, kerria, philadelphus, spiraea, weigela, berberis, willow, hydrangea, flowering currant, rosemary, yew, box, pyracantha and *Euonymus fortunei*. In addition, this method also works for some roses (Hybrid Teas, Floribundas, and certain shrub and Patio roses), plus soft fruit bushes such as gooseberries, blackcurrants, redcurrants and whitecurrants.

When to take hardwood cuttings

It's very easy to tell when shrubs are in the right state to take hardwood cuttings – just wait

HOW TO MAKE A CUTTINGS BED

1 Prepare your ground well. Fork it over and work in some well-rotted organic matter, just as if you were going to sow vegetable seeds (see March, p.68), but don't bother with any fertilizer.

2 Make a slit trench by pushing a spade in and waggling it backwards and forwards to leave a V-shaped slit the full depth of the spade. Work your way along the row. Sprinkle about 2.5cm (1in) of sharp sand into the bottom of the trench before planting your cuttings (see illustration, p.279).

In a spare patch of soil heel in bare-root shrubs that arrive before you are ready to plant them.

until the leaves drop off in autumn. November is the time you'll have the highest success rate, although cuttings can be taken throughout winter, provided the soil is workable, right up until the first new leaves start unfurling in spring. Rose cuttings can be taken from October on, but for shrubs and soft fruit bushes you need to wait until November. (See How to take hardwood cuttings, p.279.)

Make a cuttings bed

It is useful to have a special cuttings bed, or 'nursery bed', where you can root cuttings and leave the young shrubs undisturbed for the following year (see illustration, left). A spare corner down the garden is fine, or use a couple of rows at one end of the vegetable patch. If you don't have room for a cuttings bed, just pop a few cuttings into any convenient bit of ground in the garden where you can prepare the soil, where cuttings won't be disturbed, and where you won't need the space for a year or so.

Cuttings aftercare

The following summer, when the cuttings start growing new shoots, nip the growing tips out after 10–15cm (4–6in) so they grow nice and bushy instead of just having two or three stems. Keep them weeded and watered, then this time next year dig up and space the young plants out so they have more room to grow, or pot them up, unless they are big enough to plant out in the garden by then. Wait until they are about the same size as the shrubs you buy at a nursery, otherwise they'll just be completely overwhelmed – it's like sending a boy to do a man's job.

SOW HARDY SHRUBS AND TREES

You can sow seed from hardy shrubs and trees now (see Under Cover, p.284), and can put pots of seed outdoors if you don't have a greenhouse or cold frame, but you do need to protect them from mice and wind. Sink pots to their rims in the ground, and maybe stand a soft drinks bottle with the bottom cut off to act as a cloche over the top.

FLOWERS

PLANT TULIPS AND HYACINTHS

If you didn't plant tulips and hyacinths last month, do so before the end of the month (see October, p.254).

DIVIDE FIBROUS-ROOTED PERENNIALS

Once the Michaelmas daisies (*Aster novi-belgii*), goldenrod (*Solidago*), perennial helianthus, or similarly rugged customers with fibrous roots are over, it's a good time to cut them down to about 10cm (4in) from the ground, dig them up and divide them – as long as you don't garden on really heavy clay soil. If you do, then it's probably better to leave it until spring (see March, pp.64–5), when new divisions have a much better chance of recovering and growing away well, since it'll be the start of their natural growing season. Most perennials divide best in the spring for the same reason. Whatever you do, don't disturb hostas and other plants with thick fleshy roots or a delicate disposition now.

LIFT AND STORE DAHLIAS

Dahlias are the flowers that have benefited most from our late autumns and mild winters – they'll keep flowering until the weather turns very cold, so nowadays they have an exceptionally long, late season. Once they've finished flowering, you'll need to lift and store the tubers, unless you live in a mild area with well-drained soil.

- Leave the plants alone until the foliage turns black, which won't be until they're hit by a 'proper' frost, then cut the plants down to about 15cm (6in) from the ground and dig the tubers up. Shake the worst of the soil off the roots, wash the tubers clean, and turn the plants upside down so the sap drains out of the hollow stems.

- When they've dried off as much as possible outside, take them into your shed or garage to continue the good work under cover. When they're completely dry, hang them up in nets in the roof, or store them in stacking

trays – use those plastic boxes with lots of holes in the sides, as you want plenty of air circulation.

- Once you have dahlia tubers in store, keep an eye on them; the dangers are mice having a nibble, or they'll quietly go rotten as soon as your back is turned. If you catch damage early enough, you can often save the tubers with minor surgery: cut out any rotted pieces and dust the open wound with powdered sulphur, and you'll most likely save the tuber.

- In mild areas where the soil is well drained, you can risk leaving dahlia tubers in the ground all winter. Cut the tops down and cover the area over with a 10cm (4in) thick layer of organic mulch, bark chippings or even gravel for extra insulation, and hope for the best. Four years out of five you'll get away with it.

PLANT LILY BULBS

Plant or divide and move lily bulbs (see October, p.254).

Dahlias are spectacularly colourful flowers for the autumn garden. This is 'Bishop of Llandaff'.

FINISH PLANTING BEDDING

If you didn't get it done last month, plant spring and winter bedding now, if weather permits.

PROTECT YOUNG AND SLIGHTLY TENDER PLANTS

Some slightly tender plants, particularly when newly planted, are especially vulnerable and need some protection.

- Protect any potentially slightly tender plants, such as 'hardy' fuchsias and phygelius, with a deep mulch of bracken or bark chippings in colder areas.

- Truss up tree-fern foliage on newly planted specimens into a 'haycock' with straw, tied loosely around with string; they get tougher as they get older, and from their second year onwards you might want to risk leaving them un-trussed unless heavy frost is forecast – it's a gamble.

- Cut off dead leaves of gunnera (young plants are specially prone to frost damage) and stand them over the crown of the plant like umbrellas for winter protection.

REMOVE LEAVES

Clear fallen leaves from the tops of plants.

Protect newly planted tree ferns from frost by surrounding the growing point with straw or bracken and tying up the fronds to hold it in place.

PATIOS AND CONTAINERS

PROTECT CONTAINER PLANTS

Wind, rain and continuous frost can cause damage to container plants.

- Tubs of top-heavy plants that stay outside all winter, for example potted patio fruit trees, can blow over and break on a windy night, so move them close to a wall for shelter. As belt and braces, I'd also tie them up to a trellis or a couple of wall nails.

- It's not until we've had weeks of steady rain that you discover your tubs of winter pansies are awash because they've been parked under a leaky gutter, or they're standing in a puddle. Any containers of winter plants and spring-flowering bulbs will be safest moved up close to the wall of the house, which keeps a lot of the rain and wind off. Stand them on a set of pot feet or a couple of bricks for drainage.

- The odd cold night is no problem for large containers of winter bedding and hardy patio plants left outside all year round, but a very long, continuous cold spell is different. If the compost freezes solid for long it kills the plants – even when they are perfectly hardy – because all the moisture in it turns to ice, so the plants die of drought. Well before a big freeze, lag your outdoor tubs by wrapping newspapers or plastic bubble wrap around them, or shift them into your porch, shed or garage. They'll be okay for a few days, even if it's dark, although they'd rather be in your sunroom, conservatory, carport or greenhouse if you have one.

PLANT UP CONTAINERS

Plant some evergreens and shrubs in containers for winter colour (see December, p.298).

VEGETABLES AND HERBS

GROW YOUR OWN GARLIC

If you're a garlic fan, why not try growing your own? It doesn't take up much room and, like overwintering onions, it occupies ground that would otherwise be sitting there doing nothing. Now, I know a lot of people don't plant garlic until spring, but unless you live in a very cold area, it's much better planted now. It'll take root and grow gently through the winter, so you'll have a much bigger, better and earlier garlic harvest, timed just right for summer salads and barbecues.

FORCE CHICORY

Continue forcing witloof chicory (see October, p.257).

HARVEST VEGETABLES

Continue to harvest leeks and Brussels sprouts. If you haven't used your carrots and parsnips by the middle of the month, dig up what's left of your crop and store them in the salad drawer at

Dig up leeks as you need to use them.

the bottom of your fridge or in a stacking tray in the shed. Don't leave them too long, and try and use them up as soon as you can.

DIG UP HERBS FOR FORCING

Dig up roots of chives and mint to force on a warm windowsill (see Under Cover, p.284).

HOW TO GROW GARLIC

1 Garlic specially sold for planting is available in garden centres, or you can order it from the autumn supplements that a lot of the big seed catalogues send out in late summer. Alternatively, you could use the biggest cloves taken from around the edge of garlic sold at the greengrocer, although this is usually less successful.

2 Prepare the ground as if you were going to sow vegetable seed (see March, p.68), then push each individual clove of garlic in so that only the very tip shows above the ground. Plant in straight rows, 10–15cm (4–6in) apart, so there's enough room between rows to run a hoe through later.

3 In no time you'll see grassy-green shoots growing, which sit through the winter and get the plants off to a flying start in spring. You'll be pulling 'wet' garlic in June, and by the end of July it'll be ready to lift and dry for storing. If you miss your chance now, you can always plant garlic in March, but you won't be using it until September onwards.

Types of garlic
Enthusiasts claim that violet or 'rose' garlic, which has pinky purple outer skin, has a much finer flavour than the usual white kind, although they are all the same colour inside. Giant 'elephant' garlic (which is actually a stem leek, but looks, tastes and behaves like garlic) is surprisingly mild for its size, and is excellent for roasting.

FRUIT

PLANT FRUIT TREES
Provided the soil isn't frozen or wet, you can plant fruit trees now.

PLANT SUMMER-FRUITING RASPBERRY CANES
Summer-fruiting raspberries are usually sold in late autumn and early spring as short, bare canes in bundles. Plant them as soon as possible after purchase, so the roots don't dry out.

- Dig a trench and work in as much well-rotted organic matter as you can before burying it with soil. Knock in a 2m (6ft) high fence post every 2m (6ft) along the trench and stretch three horizontal wires between them, spaced equal distances apart, as a 'fence' to support the plants later. Plant the canes in a straight line at the foot of the wires, spacing them 38–45cm (15–18in) apart.

TAKE CUTTINGS OF SOFT FRUIT BUSHES
Take hardwood cuttings of redcurrants, whitecurrants, blackcurrants, gooseberries and vines (see Trees, Shrubs and Climbers, p.276).

CHECK FRUIT IN STORE
Regularly check fruit in store, and use any that are showing even the first sign of bruising, damage or going soft. They won't keep, and if they start rotting it'll soon spread to all the rest nearby. Get them into a pie.

START WINTER PRUNING
If you're looking for a job, you could start winter pruning of standard apple and pear trees now (see January, p.23). However, it's something you can do any time through the winter, provided you get it done before the buds start bursting in March.

MULCH FRUIT TREES
Mulch all pruned fruit with organic matter, or leave the job until early spring, when mulching borders generally (see March, p.54).

Separate stored apples with paper so that if one fruit starts to rot it does not spread to the rest.

UNDER COVER

VENTILATION AND WATERING
Ventilate the greenhouse on sunny days and reduce watering to a bare minimum.

CHECK BULBS
Check any bulbs being forced for early flowering, and water if the compost is drying out, but don't overdo it. Begin checking weekly, so that pots can be moved into the house as soon as the buds begin to show the first hint of colour – but not before.

SOW HARDY PLANTS FROM SEED
Seeds of hardy plants need a chill before they'll germinate, so it pays to sow them at the start of winter, when they'll experience a natural cold spell. You can sow packets of bought seeds, or home-saved seeds of hardy trees, shrubs, conifers and rock plants, and the sort of perennials that need a cold spell before they'll come up (the instructions on the seed packets tell you which these are). The list of possibilities includes all sorts of interesting plants – lilies, Japanese maples and clematis – and it's a great way to grow a collection of trees and shrubs to train as bonsai specimens (see Project, p.77). If you belong to a specialist society, such as the Alpine Garden Society or the RHS, you're entitled to an allocation of seeds from them, and they are usually hardy kinds that need pre-chilling. The technique is dead easy.

Pre-chill seeds
- Use clay pots if possible, and John Innes seed compost with about 10–20 per cent gritty horticultural sand mixed in to improve the drainage. Scatter the seeds thinly over the surface, and cover them with a very thin layer of coarse grit or fine gravel. The idea is to hold the seeds down and keep moist air around them, but not totally swamp them – the beauty of grit is the way it lets light and air in between the bits.

WINDOWSILL SALADS

Home-grown herbs and salads are usually in pretty short supply in winter and early spring, but there's a lot you can grow on a windowsill indoors. Oh, I know you won't exactly be self-sufficient, but you can certainly grow enough to liven up your larder, and it'll give you a great sense of self-satisfaction. Start now, so you have some fresh produce lined up ready for Christmas.

Herbs

Herbs will grow happily indoors on a brightish windowsill, even if it's not actually all that sunny, and a small collection of culinary herbs gives a kitchen windowsill a distinct taste of the Med. To make the most of them, stand a row of pots inside a long, narrow planter. If you use some plants so much that they start looking a bit worn out, it's dead easy to lift them out and replace them to refresh the display.

- You can buy pots of fresh herb plants from the supermarket, right through the winter, long after most herbs in the garden have died down and they're no longer on sale at garden centres; they'll keep growing indoors if you keep them watered and cut them little and often.
- You can also raise your own favourite annual herbs, such as basil, chervil, pot marjoram, coriander, dill and parsley from seed. Sow them thinly in pots and don't bother pricking them out – let each potful grow as a group, and just thin the seedlings out a bit if they're very overcrowded. They'll quickly grow into a big, bushy clump that's much more productive than a single plant. Start cutting little bits as soon as they're big enough, and don't let them flower, or leaf-production grinds to a halt.
- To have fresh chives and mint in winter, dig up some roots from the garden now, pot them up, and keep them on a windowsill indoors – the warmth fools them into thinking it's summer already, so they start growing again.
- If you rooted cuttings of rosemary, sage and thyme in summer, pot them up and stand the young plants on a windowsill indoors; again, the warmth makes them grow when they'd normally be dormant, so you'll have some sprigs for cooking.

Sprouting seeds

They've been described in health-food circles as 'gardening in a jar', but you can hardly count it as horticulture, since there's no soil, compost or mess, and the end result is ready to eat in only a few days. You don't even need a windowsill – most people grow their crop in the airing cupboard, as the heat and dark bring them on fast, but it's not essential. Do buy seeds that are sold specially for sprouting, and not vegetable seeds intended for growing, as they may have been treated with fungicide. Plenty of seed catalogues offer quite a good range of seeds for sprouting, and so do organic specialists.

- The sprouted seeds most people know are Chinese bean sprouts, alias mung beans. At home, it's almost impossible to grow bean shoots as long, white and straight as the ones you buy in the shops, but it's fun to try and the result tastes good, even if home-grown bean shoots are short and bent. Soak a handful of mung bean seeds overnight, then rinse them well in fresh water and place them in a large glass jar. Don't screw the top of the jar back on, instead use a rubber band to fix a circle of clean white cotton fabric over the top. Stand the jar in a warm, dark place, and rinse them with fresh water twice a day. After about 4 days they're ready to eat.
- There are lots of other seeds you can sprout too. Alfalfa sprouts are fragile-looking and taste like petit pois; fenugreek sprouts taste of curry; and enthusiasts will even sprout adzuki beans, chickpeas, radish seeds and similar sprouting seeds, although some are rather – let's say – an acquired taste.

Seedling salads

Saladini, misticanza and Oriental saladini are mixtures of leafy salad plants that you grow rather like mustard and cress, to use in sandwiches or to add variety to shop-bought salads in winter. Again, they are quite fast-growing and productive, so you'll have a good crop from a windowsill. These special seed mixtures are available from seed firms by post.

- Sow a good pinch of seed in a trough of seed compost on a windowsill, water sparingly, and as soon as the seedlings are 2.5cm (1in) or so high, start snipping them just like mustard and cress. When you grow seedling salads in winter, they need good light and plenty of fresh air, and if they're very overcrowded, it's worth thinning them out a bit or you'll find some patches 'damping off'. When you've cut the lot, tip the container out, pull out the roots left behind, top it up with some more seed compost, and sow some more.
- Rocket, basil and land cress are worth growing as seedling salads when you can't be bothered to wait for them to grow bigger. Sow the seed thinly in a trough of seed compost on the windowsill, thin the seedlings out slightly if they grow very thickly, but treat them all rather like the pots of herbs you buy from the supermarket and start snipping what you want as soon as the leaves are big enough, leaving the rest of the plants to keep growing. There will be some re-growth, but if you cut heavily, sow a second batch when the trough is half used, to keep yourself supplied.
- You can grow watercress in pots on a windowsill by rooting 'cuttings' taken from a bunch from the greengrocers. Replace the old plants when they start to run to seed quickly – when that happens they stop producing leaves.
- Corn salad is another very fast-growing crop that's usable from the large-seedling stage onwards, and is also worth trying on a bright windowsill. If you grow it in perlite or vermiculite, you can just pull the seedlings out when they have about three true leaves, wash them well, and use them root and all. It's also worth sowing corn salad in the greenhouse, as it doesn't need much warmth.

Sow seeds for pre-chilling in pots and stand them outdoors, covering them with wire netting to discourage rodents.

Pool check
If you leave your pump and lights in the pool over winter, ensure you clean the filters regularly and check the condition of the cable.

• Sink the pots to their rim in the soil or in a bed of sand underneath your cold frame. If you don't have a cold frame, use a quiet corner of the garden and put small-mesh wire netting over the top to stop the seeds being eaten. Keep the pots watered, because they won't even start germinating if they stay dry.

• Nothing will happen during the winter, and some seeds will come up next spring, but some pots will just sit there doing nothing. Take these into the greenhouse for a warm season in late spring, which will often start slow seeds germinating. Any that still don't come up are best kept watered in summer (leave them in the greenhouse, or sink the pots back out into a cool, shady part of the garden and then leave them out throughout autumn and winter to give them a second winter chilling – some very slow-germinating kinds take two or three alternate cold and warm seasons before they do anything, so don't be in too much of a hurry to throw 'dead' pots away. They may surprise you yet.

• When seedlings eventually appear, pot them up in John Innes No 1 potting compost and grow them on in the greenhouse or a cold frame, or a safe place down the garden where you'll remember to keep an eye on them – they need regular feeding and watering. When they're roughly as big as plants you buy at a nursery, plant them out in the garden.

CREATE WINTER DISPLAYS
Winter is a quiet time in the garden, so you can afford to spend more time under glass. It can be quite cosy when the weather isn't up to scratch outdoors, so make the most of the opportunities the 'closed season' offers.

• Even in an unheated greenhouse, you can create some stunning seasonal displays of evergreen rock plants (e.g. sempervivums), early spring-flowering species (e.g. saxifrages and dwarf bulbs, such as *Iris danfordiae*), autumn-flowering crocuses and cyclamen in pots. Set them out now, and by the time you

want the space for other things next March or April you can move them back outdoors.

• An unheated conservatory usually traps enough heat from the house to suit nearly-hardy plants such as florists' cyclamen and indoor azaleas. It's also worth bringing pots of camellias under cover now; they make good conservatory or cold-greenhouse plants, and under cover they'll flower a month earlier and the flowers won't be ruined by bad weather, as they often can be outside.

• If you have a heated greenhouse with an electric propagator, you can use it to start all sorts of unusual houseplants and greenhouse pot plants that are slow to germinate, for example palms, cacti, bird of paradise flowers (*Strelitzia reginae*), yuccas, rubber plants (*Ficus* species), coffee (*Coffea arabica*), and spores of indoor ferns. So have some fun and grow yourself a treat, while there's time to 'play'.

CHECK STORED BULBS AND CROPS
Check stored fruit and veg and bulbs and corms for signs of rotting. Use fruit and veg from store.

WATER GARDEN

AUTUMN CLEAR-OUT
If you haven't already done your end-of-season clear-out, including cutting down marginal plants and covering the pond with a net, you can do so now (see October, p.262).

PLAN A NEW POND
If you're considering making a new pond, plan it in advance so you can do the digging during the winter, when there isn't a lot of routine gardening to be done (see January Project, p.29).

PROJECT Grow a living screen

A willow screen is like living trellis with leaves. A short length makes a fashionable feature for a wild or naturalistic-style garden – you could plant a length of it instead of a hedge, or use it to screen off part of the garden. It is very versatile, you can make it any height from about 1–2m (3–6ft), and you can even 'grow' your own arch if you want.

You'll need lots of long hardwood cuttings of willow, which you can buy in bundles in winter from basketry willow suppliers by post, or cut them from your own plants once the leaves have dropped off. Good varieties include *Salix alba* var. *vitellina* 'Chermesina' (carmine willow), *Salix daphnoides*, which has pewtery-purple stems, or *Salix* var. *vitellina* (golden willow).

What you need

Spade

Organic matter

Rustic fence posts, ideally 5–8cm (2–3in) thick and 2.2m (7ft) high for a 1.5–2m (5–6ft) high screen

Hardwood cuttings of willow

Fencing wire

1 Make a trench and fill it with organic matter. Work it into the soil, leaving the ground level, exactly as if you were preparing to plant a hedge (see p.276).

2 Knock a post in every 2m (6ft) along the trench, and run two horizontal rows of wires along to make a light framework.

3 Push one row of cuttings into the ground, spaced 60cm (2ft) apart, so they're leaning over at an angle, with the base of the cuttings about 15cm (6in) deep in the ground.

4 Push a second row of cuttings into the same trench, leaning in the opposite direction. Weave them in and out of the first row to make a light, open-basketwork-style pattern. Tie the willow cuttings to the wires to hold them in position.

5 The cuttings take root during the winter and start growing in spring, slowly fleshing out the shape with sideshoots and foliage. Once it thickens out, clip it once or twice a year, in spring and early autumn. Using hand shears or electric hedge-trimmers, trim enough to stop the screen growing more than a few inches wide to let it thicken out.

6 Once the screen is as tall as you want it, prune the tops of the original cuttings out to stop it growing any taller. Do that again each winter.

DECEMBER

Whatever else is going on in the garden this month, the things we notice most are those with a festive feel to them, because the garden is a great source of home-grown Christmas decorations.

In the days of grand Edwardian country house parties, Christmas was the time when the gardeners pulled out all the stops. The outdoor staff weren't just responsible for keeping the kitchen provided with enormous quantities of luxury vegetables and out-of-season fruit; they also had the job of cutting a huge Christmas tree from the estate and setting it up in the hall for the family to decorate, and then making huge displays of pot plants banked up with moss. These days, Christmas is a good excuse for being a tad more creative than usual with plants, flowers and other garden produce, but there's no need to make hard work for yourself. Have fun and enjoy it. Don't forget to make the most of the season by visiting great winter gardens – National Trust members will have full details in the members' handbook.

THE BIG PICTURE festive flowers and foliage

Helleborus niger, the Christmas rose (above), it has to be said, is pretty bad at clock-watching. If you want the big, round, flat-faced white flowers for Christmas, get yourself down to the garden centre a week or so beforehand and buy one with fairly advanced buds. Keep it in a warm room to bring it on, and it'll be perfect on the day. People often force pot-grown plants in a cold or frost-free greenhouse, but in the garden the timing all depends on the weather and other garden wildlife – if you don't see any buds on your Christmas rose, suspect slugs, who are probably making Christmas dinner of them. Plants make evergreen clumps about 30 × 30cm (12 × 12in).

PEAK SEASON December–February.
GROWING CONDITIONS Well-drained soil with plenty of organic matter, in light shade.

Sarcococca hookeriana* var. *digyna (above), with its common name of Christmas box, sounds like a seasonal back-hander for the postman, but it's actually an up-and-coming evergreen shrub. Years ago you'd never have heard of it, let alone seen one; today, you'd be unlucky not to meet it at this time of year in any good garden centre. It has purple-tinged stems with long, lean leaves interspersed with small, fluffy white flowers with a superb scent. In the garden, it'll reach about 1.5 × 1.5m (5 × 5ft), but use it in a tub on your patio for its first Christmas. ***Sarcococca confusa*** has shorter, glossy green leaves, is rather tighter growing, and has an even more powerful scent.

PEAK SEASON December–February.
GROWING CONDITIONS Most moist soils, in shade.

Hollies are available in dozens of varieties. ***Ilex aquifolium*** is the tough, wild holly that's so good in a windswept spot, but it's not the best for berries, and with many of its cultivated varieties the male and female flowers are produced on separate plants, so you need two to tango. If yours is an only holly, it's best to choose a hermaphrodite, such as ***Ilex aquifolium* 'Pyramidalis'** and **'J.C. van Tol'** (top) to be sure of Christmas berries. When there are others around the area, you can play the field. If yellow berries take your fancy, there's ***Ilex aquifolium* 'Amber'**. With blue hollies, for example ***Ilex × meserveae***, it's the foliage that's blue – a deep, glossy glaucous colour – rather than the berries; ***Ilex × meserveae* 'Blue Maid'** is a good one. Some of the best hollies to grow for Christmas are those with variegated foliage, such as ***Ilex × altaclerensis* 'Lawsonia'** (above). ***Ilex aquifolium* 'Golden Milkboy'** and **'Silver Milkmaid'** both have a coloured central splodge surrounded by an irregular edging of green. But for both berries *and* variegated foliage, the one you want is ***Ilex aquifolium* 'Pyramidalis Aureomarginata'**, which has good gold variegation and a generous crop of red berries. Most hollies will eventually reach 5 × 4m (15 × 12ft), but are very slow-growing.

PEAK SEASON December–January.
GROWING CONDITIONS Not fussy.

OLD FAITHFULS

Ivies come in an incredible range of varieties, many of which you never see outside a specialist nursery, but if you're serious about your Christmas decorations then it's worth investigating further. *Hedera helix* 'Fantasia' has cream and green speckled leaves in the traditional ivy shape; 'Melanie' has slightly flounced foliage with a faint mauve edge; 'Jake' has small, heart-shaped lime green leaves, and 'Calico' has a cream inkspot in the centre of dark green leaves with the texture of seersucker. 'Tripod' has large, dark green leaves in the shape of a spindly 'T', and 'Fluffy Ruffles' has extravagantly curled leaves that look as if they've had a perm. *Hedera colchica* 'Sulphur Heart' (above) has long, mid-green leaves, suffused with creamy yellow. Grow ivy in pots, tubs and hanging baskets, as ground cover under shrubs, for climbing up dead tree trunks or through large shrubs, or use it to cover walls of outbuildings.

PEAK SEASON All year round.
GROWING CONDITIONS Not fussy, although best in shade.

Viscum album (above) more commonly known as mistletoe, occasionally grows wild in this country, but it can be deliberately grown in the garden if you have a suitable host species, as it is parasitic. It's great fun to try. Save a few berries after Christmas and in February or March, when they are ripe and rotten, press them into a cut in the bark on the underside of an apple tree branch, plastering them in place with a spot of mud. It takes several years before you have much to show for it. Mistletoe berries only ripen in December, but for the rest of the year the evergreen clump makes a novel decoration hanging up in the tree – rather like a green, self-watering hanging basket.

PEAK SEASON December.
GROWING CONDITIONS Normally needs a mature apple tree to grow on; some mistletoes grow on poplar or oak.

Picea abies, Norway spruce, is the traditional Christmas tree. It's grown in commercial forestry plantations for timber – young trees are cut and harvested as a crop for Christmas, but small trees are also sold in pots with a full set of roots. The more expensive *Abies nordmanniana*, Nordmann fir (above), is increasingly popular, as it does not shed its needles so badly when brought indoors. There are more decorative conifers that can be bought growing in pots from the garden centre to use as Christmas trees. Some of the best include blue spruces (cultivars of *Picea pungens*), the dense, conical green *Picea glauca* var. *albertiana* 'Conica', and *Abies koreana*, with violet cones that look like natural candles, complete with wax dripping down them. You can also find exotic conifers, such as *Pinus montezumae*, the shitzu tree, or *Pinus patula*, the orang-utan pine, at a specialist nursery – beautiful trees, with exceptionally long, dangling bunches of soft needles, but very slightly tender, so after Christmas, treat them as trees for a cold conservatory unless you have a mild garden.

PEAK SEASON December.
GROWING CONDITIONS Keep in a cool room, and water well while they're indoors.

Arum italicum 'Marmoratum' (above) is a tuberous plant that is only above ground in winter, when it forms a 30cm (12in) tall thicket of large, cream and dark green variegated, arrowhead-shaped leaves. Mature plants also have pale yellow 'arum' flowers in spring, followed by clusters of red seedheads, which persist after the leaves have died down for the summer. Clumps spread slowly, and on clay soil it can become a bit too much of a good thing after a while. It produces useful foliage for festive flower arranging, and is good for winter interest under trees and shrubs.

PEAK SEASON November–March.
GROWING CONDITIONS Not fussy, best in shade.

SOMETHING SPECIAL

Taxus baccata, yew (above), is a favourite hedging conifer for stately homes and large country gardens, but the upright form, '**Fastigiata**', 4 × 1.2m (12 × 4ft), or the slow, compact golden form, '**Standishii**', 2 × 0.6m (6 × 2ft), are often used in a wide range of gardens as design statements. Actually, they're more like exclamation marks, handy as grow-it-yourself architecture, and they're good in pots by the front door over Christmas. All yews provide very useful foliage for making festive wreaths and garlands. The seeds inside the berries are poisonous.

PEAK SEASON All year round.
GROWING CONDITIONS Most well-drained soils in sun or light shade; good on chalk.

Lonicera × purpusii (above) is a shrubby honeysuckle, 2 × 2m (6 × 6ft), whose rounded, twiggy shape is outlined in white flowers in winter. If you look closely, you see each flower is the same shape as those of the better-known climbing honeysuckles, but instead of being grouped together in large, round 'wagon wheels', they grow singly so they aren't so spectacular. The best thing about winter honeysuckle is the scent, but at this time of year it wants planting somewhere close to the house, or somewhere you walk past regularly, as the fragrance doesn't travel well. This honeysuckle normally drops its leaves in winter, but it can be semi-evergreen in a mild, sheltered spot.

PEAK SEASON December–February.
GROWING CONDITIONS A sheltered spot with well-drained soil, in sun or light shade.

Chimonanthus praecox 'Grandiflorus', wintersweet (above), is a shrub you don't very often see – probably because it doesn't flower while it's young enough to be sold in full bloom in a pot at the garden centre. It takes several years to start flowering, but be patient, because the pale yellow flowers hanging from the bare stems have an unusual see-through quality, and the scent is delightful. It makes a big, rather open shrub, similar in shape and size to witch hazel (*Hamemelis*), so allow 2 × 2m (6 × 6ft), although given time it will grow bigger. Most folk grow it trained against a sunny wall.

PEAK SEASON December–March.
GROWING CONDITIONS A sheltered spot in fertile, well-drained soil and full sun.

Rhododendron **'Christmas Cheer'** (above) is worth growing for the name alone, but if you're lucky it really can flower at Christmas. It's a medium-sized shrub, growing 2 × 2m (6 × 6ft), with very pale pink flowers. It is pretty, and unbelievably early.

PEAK SEASON December–February.

GROWING CONDITIONS A sheltered spot with humus-rich, acid soil in light shade, or in a pot of ericaceous compost on the patio.

DECEMBER at-a-glance checklist

GENERAL GARDEN TASKS (p.294)
✔ Continue winter digging if soil is workable.
✔ Fork over vacant ground; turning the ground over several times reduces soil pests naturally by exposing them to birds.
✔ Plan and begin any landscaping jobs.
✔ Clear away debris to prevent harbouring slugs and snails.
✔ Rake up the last of the leaves.
✔ Send off for seed catalogues from adverts in newspapers and magazines.

LAWNS (p.295)
✔ Avoid walking on the lawn.
✔ Rake up fallen oak leaves.
✔ Carry out lawn repairs if conditions allow.

TREES, SHRUBS AND CLIMBERS (p.296)
✔ Move or plant deciduous trees or shrubs if soil is workable.
✔ Rejuvenate shrubs, climbers and hedges.
✔ Prune ornamental vines.
✔ Cut shoots for indoor decoration.
✔ Continue taking hardwood cuttings if you didn't last month.
✔ Organize your Christmas tree.

FLOWERS (p.297)
✔ Grow festive midwinter flowers.
✔ Sow seeds of hardy plants.

PATIOS AND CONTAINERS (p.298)
✔ Plant seasonal outdoor tubs and hanging baskets for Christmas.
✔ Prevent plant damage from wind and rain.

VEGETABLES AND HERBS (p.298)
✔ Harvest Brussels sprouts, Christmas broccoli, parsnips and leeks, and lamb's lettuce from the greenhouse. Store harvested vegetables in the shed.
✔ Continue forcing chicory.

FRUIT (p.300)
✔ Plant fruit trees and bushes, if you haven't already and if soil is workable.
✔ Finish off stored fruit.

UNDER COVER (p.300)
✔ Tidy plants in the greenhouse and conservatory, and water plants sparingly.
✔ Sow exhibition onions.
✔ Check bulbs in store.

WATER GARDEN (p.300)
✔ Make provisions to prevent the pond from freezing over.

Watch out for
● Chilled pot plants – pot plants that have been standing in the open outside shops and on market stalls may not be the bargain you think, since they'll have come straight from a warm sheltered greenhouse into biting cold wind, and probably won't last long when you get them home. Poinsettias are especially vulnerable.

Get ahead
● Clear up the shed, clean garden tools, wash pots and seedtrays, and store in plastic carrier bags hung up on the shed wall to keep clean ready for the spring propagating season.

Last chance
● Buy Christmas pot plants from nurseries and garden centres.

GENERAL GARDEN TASKS

Tie bubble wrap or newspaper around taps as protection from frost.

WINTER DIGGING

Provided the ground is workable, you can continue winter digging for new lawns (for spring construction), new beds and borders, and the vegetable patch (see November, p.272).

PLANNING AND LANDSCAPING

Continue with planning and begin any landscaping or garden redesign jobs you may have in mind. Start with hard landscaping (laying paving, making paths, walls and raised beds, digging ponds, etc). Delay any jobs that involve concreting until such time as there won't be a frost. Leave soil preparation until last, and wait until the ground is in workable condition before proceeding – there's no huge hurry, as you don't really want to be planting until March onwards.

FROST PROTECTION

Wrap insulation around outside taps if you didn't last month, and roll up the hosepipe and put it away in the shed for the winter.

INDOOR JOBS

As it's a quiet month, clear up the shed, clean garden tools, wash pots and seedtrays, etc.

CLEAR AWAY DEBRIS

Clear ivy from the bottom of hedges, and clear up any rubbish that's been left around the garden, as it offers good overwintering places for pests such as slugs and snails.

FORKING OVER

Fork over vacant ground, turning the soil over several times to reduce the likelihood of pests.

RAKE UP LEAVES

Rake up any remaining oak leaves from paths and lawns, and pull them out from among herbaceous plants. The garden should at last be free of fallen leaves – thank goodness!

SAVE PRUNINGS

When pruning apples and pears, save the prunings to use for plant supports for perennials or as pea sticks during the spring and summer.

ORDER AHEAD

Order manure if needed for winter digging and soil preparation, and send off for seed catalogues.

HOW TO BUILD A RAISED BED

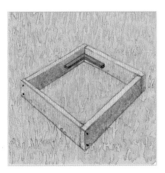   

1 Once you've decided where to put your bed, make sure that the ground is reasonably level. Using 15 × 5cm (6 × 2in) timber, position and then screw together the first layer, butt jointing the timbers and using a builder's square in the corners to make sure it's all straight.

2 Use this first layer as a template for fixing the position of the corner posts. For these, cut 7.5 × 7.5cm (3 × 3in) timbers 3cm (1in) longer than the final depth of the bed to allow for concreting them into the ground. Move your first layer out of the way while you dig the holes for the posts.

3 While the concrete is setting around the posts, replace the first level, making sure that it's still straight, and check that it's all level. Once set, you can build up the rest of the bed, layer by layer, staggering the joints and screwing the timbers to each other and to the corner posts as you go.

4 A depth of three boards gives a comfortable height to work at, and you'll find it's just right for sitting on too. For a really neat finish, top with a piece of 15 × 5cm (6 × 2in) timber, mitred into the corners. Place a couple of inches of gravel in the bottom to aid drainage before filling with topsoil.

GIFT IDEAS

When you're stuck for last-minute gifts for gardening friends, opt for something practical. Good stocking fillers that are always welcome include:

- Gardening gloves – the thin, vinyl kind for light jobs; the thick, soft leather type for serious pruning and handling prickly plants.
- Pocket knife – for taking cuttings, slicing open sacks of compost, etc.
- Secateurs – the scissor or parrot-beak type are preferred by enthusiasts for serious pruning and fruit tree training; the less expensive anvil type are best for general-purpose use all round the garden.
- Multi-tool – something like a superior Swiss army knife featuring a knife, pliers, and other gadgets; it folds down to pocket size and slides into a case.
- Labelling system – for the botanically minded, long-lasting plant name labels are a godsend.
- Hand tools – the very latest whizz-bang hand tools are always welcome by 'green' gardeners, and also by followers of fashion who like to be first with the latest idea off the telly. Look out for scaled-down versions of popular garden tools for children, and long-handled or ergonomically designed tools for anyone who finds it hard to bend or grip standard gardening kit. The latest thing is for reproduction antique hand tools; for collectors, obscure but real gardening antiques make unique shed decorations.
- Containers – large tubs, sets of pots, and smart self-watering containers for the conservatory are always useful.

LAWNS

KEEP OFF THE LAWN

Avoid walking on the grass as much as possible this month.

CARRY OUT LAWN REPAIRS

Repair lawn edges and bald, worn-out patches with turves if weather conditions allow (see September, p.226).

RAKE UP FALLEN LEAVES

Rake up any oak leaves lying on the lawn and use them to make leafmould (see November, p.275).

PARTY PARKING

Try to prevent people parking on your lawn during the party season. If there's no alternative, lay sheets of strong metal mesh over it to spread the weight and stop wheels sinking in and leaving ruts. If ruts occur, then resign yourself to a few hours of intensive lawn maintenance. Don't just fill ruts up with topsoil; the ground will be very compressed, so loosen up the soil with a fork, mix a little sharp sand or horticultural grit in and, if you're still short of material, then, yes, add some sifted topsoil. Keep off the lawn, and don't reseed until March or April.

The garden is magical in winter. The colour palette is limited, but the strong shapes and skeletal framework provide a stark kind of beauty.

Christmas tree spray ensures the needles stay on for longer.

Opposite: Frost-rimed berries on pyracantha.

TREES, SHRUBS AND CLIMBERS

MOVE DECIDUOUS TREES OR SHRUBS

You can move or plant deciduous shrubs at any time throughout the dormant season (see November, p.277), provided the soil is in a suitable state. However, the very best times are shortly after leaf fall and just before the start of the spring growing season (early March).

REJUVENATE SHRUBS, CLIMBERS AND HEDGES

Between now and spring, you can start renewal-pruning overgrown shrubs and climbers, and renovating deciduous hedges (see January, p.21).

PRUNE ORNAMENTAL VINES

You could prune ornamental vines now (see January, p.24).

CUT SHOOTS FOR INDOOR DECORATION

Winter jasmine, winter-flowering viburnum, holly and ivy are all worth cutting for indoor/decorative use.

CONTINUE TAKING HARDWOOD CUTTINGS

You can still take hardwood cuttings now, although they have a better chance of rooting in November (see November, p.279).

CHRISTMAS TREES

Going out to buy the Christmas tree is part of the build-up to the Big Day, and it should be fun, but most people are already so over-excited that their normal consumer caution is switched off. The last thing you want is a tree that is going to shed needles all over your floor; it'll just make a lot of work clearing up, and it'll already be looking a bit bald around the branches by Christmas Day.

If you're using fairy lights, you'll need to stand your tree close to an electric socket (do your watering when the lights are unplugged), and if you've bought a huge tree then copy the Edwardians and stand it in the stairwell, where there's plenty of space around the branches – don't cramp it in a corner where the tip is touching the ceiling. For the sake of festive looks, you can slip the pot inside a colourful pot cover, or else truss the original pot up with coloured crepe paper or wrapping paper.

Christmas trees are available in various forms:

Potted trees with roots

The sort of tree that's going to hang on to its needles best of all is a real live Christmas tree complete with roots, growing in a pot. Although it's a bit more expensive than a 'cut' tree, it's a very good buy, as you can keep it to use again another year. Traditional Norway spruces are sometimes grown in pots especially for the live Christmas tree

trade, but you can always go for something different and choose a conifer from the garden centre that you can plant in the garden afterwards.

A pot-grown tree can be bought 3 weeks or more in advance, but stand it in a sheltered spot in the garden until you're ready to bring it in and decorate it. From then on, treat it just like a giant pot plant – keep it regularly watered, and stand it in a cool room, well away from radiators or anywhere it's likely to be knocked.

Bare-root Christmas trees

Christmas trees sold with bare roots have been dug up from a forest where they're treated like a crop, in much the same way as a field of corn – so don't worry that you're denuding the countryside. Another batch will be replanted, and in the meantime they remove a lot of carbon dioxide from the air and nitrates from the soil, so they're doing a good recycling job.

Contrary to what you'll often hear, the roots of bare-root Christmas trees haven't been boiled to stop you growing them again another year, but they've lost so much root there's little chance of them surviving in the long term. Pot them anyway; garden soil is fine, as it's just to give them stability and keep the roots moist so the needles don't dry out too fast –dehydration is what makes them drop.

Don't buy this sort of tree until you're ready for it, and choose a fresh-looking one – check it over for any sign of browning or needle-drop. It's worth spraying this type of tree with Christmas tree spray when you get it home; it forms an invisible 'plastic' layer over the needles and prevents moisture loss, so the needles stay put longer, and keep the roots watered.

Cut Christmas trees

Christmas trees that are sawn off and sold without any roots behave more like cut flowers, so treat them in the same way.

Buy the trees at the last minute, and use one of the special stands available. This looks like a clamp at the base of the tree that holds it upright, with a 'vase' for the base of the trunk to stand it in. Slice about 2.5 (1in) off the base of the trunk when you sit it in the stand, then fill the 'vase' with water and keep it regularly topped up – it's amazing how much longer even a tree without any roots will last without shedding its needles if you remember to do this simple job. Misting the needles over with Christmas tree spray just before you decorate helps as well – think of it as hairspray for trees. Whatever you do, don't use real hairspray, as trees aren't keen on it and it's highly inflammable.

FLOWERS

GROW MIDWINTER FLOWERS

As a boy I always felt disappointed when we didn't have a white Christmas, but now winters are so much milder, one of the great joys for a lot of people is walking around the garden totting up all the different flowers they have in bloom on Christmas Day – the record is over a hundred.

For commuters, public holidays are often the only time they're home for any length of time during daylight hours in winter, so for goodness sake make the most of it. A tour of the garden gives you an appetite for lunch – you're allowed to take your festive G&T with you – and if you don't find the floral abundance you'd hoped for, then make yourself a mental note and do something about it as planting time comes round in March and April, so that next year's show is better.

The best places to position your midwinter flowers, strategically speaking, are trained out over walls, around the front door and over the porch, and in tubs on the patio – in short, places you can appreciate the scent and spectacle without having to wade knee deep in mud, or get dressed up specially and haul off down the garden.

SOW SEEDS

You can continue to sow seeds of hardy plants in fair weather (see November, pp.284–6).

CUT FLOWERS AND FOLIAGE

Make the most of what's available in the garden, particularly holly, ivy and conifer foliage, late berries, such as those of pyracantha (which are handy for putting with foliage to 'cheat' if you don't have any berried holly), and twigs of midwinter shrubs in flower, such as winter jasmine. Cut the stems with secateurs, then take them indoors and stand them in deep, tepid water until you're ready to arrange them. Re-cut each stem to length to suit your vase, using a sharp knife to make a long, sloping cut – this gives a larger surface area for water to be absorbed, so the flowers last longer.

Purchased cut flowers

Cut flowers from the florist really do need leaving until the last minute. Again, it's worth buying them from a shop that's kept them indoors and not a bucket on the pavement outside, where they'll have been badly chilled and blown about. Choose flowers that aren't fully open, with lots of buds to come.

To make cut flowers last, cut 2.5cm (1in) from the bottom of the stems as soon as you get them home, and stand them in a deep bucket of tepid water overnight, right up to their necks, before arranging them. That should stop even notoriously droopy flowers, such as roses and gerberas, keeling over at the necks. If you want flowers that'll really last a long time, it's hard to beat chrysanthemums (bottom right).

Foliage

Foliage from the garden is the way to make expensive, out-of-season flowers go further. If you grow flower arrangers' favourites, such as pittosporum, fatsia and phormium (above centre, in its variety 'Jester'), you're really in business, but even plants that are not that exciting in the garden take on quite a new personality when you use them creatively indoors. Pieces chopped out of your Leyland hedge, spotted laurel (above left), yew, privet, elaeagnus and ivy can really look quite glamorous.

Milder winters mean there's much more in the way of flowering material available from the garden than back in the days when Christmas day usually coincided with a foot of snow. You may be able to pick twigs of witch hazel (*Hamamelis* – top centre), Christmas rose (*Helleborus niger*), and winter jasmine (*Jasminum nudiflorum* – top right), which all look good in the middle of your dinner table combined with a few big leaves of bergenia, *Arum italicum* 'Marmoratum' (top left), or 'Paddy's Pride' ivy.

Holly and mistletoe are mostly bought from the florist or greengrocer, simply because so few of us grow them in the garden as they are both desperately slow. Again, to make them last longer, buy them as late as you can, cut 2.5cm (1in) off the end of the stems, and stand them in water overnight in a cool room.

PATIOS AND CONTAINERS

PLANT UP DECORATIVE OUTDOOR CONTAINERS

Although indoor plants and flowers are probably going to be the main thrust of your festive displays (see Under Cover, p.300), it's worth making a special effort with containers around the front door and porch or out on the patio. You'll be seeing a lot of them over the next few weeks, and they make a natural extension to your indoor Christmas decorations.

Garden centres will have plenty of suitable plants. Don't worry about using shrubs and other plants that aren't really suitable for growing in containers in the long term, as they'll only stay put until spring – just plant them out in the garden when their best display is over.

Clipped evergreens, like this half-standard bay tree, make good winter focal points on a patio or terrace.

- For hanging baskets, go for ivies and *Gaultheria procumbens* (see p.270) – a low, creeping evergreen with big red berries.

- In a mixed tub, winter-flowering heathers go brilliantly with skimmia – both the pink-budded *Skimmia japonica* 'Rubella' (see p.270) and the red-berried *Skimmia japonica* 'Veitchii' – and the bare red stems of dogwood (*Cornus*).

- For specimen plants, choose winter box (*Sarcococca hookeriana* var. *digyna* – see p.290), with fragile, off-white tubular flowers and curving 'canes' clad in purple-tinged oval leaves, or there's *Viburnum davidii* (see p.268), with turquoise berries and big oval, leathery leaves.

- If you want plants capable of staying in containers for several years, go for trained standard hollies, topiary trained box, and ivies trained around climbing frames.

PREVENT PLANT DAMAGE

Protect plants from wind and excessive rain (see November, p.282).

VEGETABLES AND HERBS

FRESH FOOD FOR THE FESTIVE SEASON

If you've planned carefully earlier in the year, it's possible to enjoy all your favourite festive vegetables fresh from the garden. You can have sprouts, leeks, parsnips and the earliest purple-sprouting broccoli down the garden, tasting all the better after the first serious frost. From the greenhouse or cold frame you can be picking salads such as lamb's lettuce; there will be fresh herbs on the kitchen windowsill, and stored spuds in the shed.

Store vegetables

A frost-free shed or garage is a good place to store sacks of carrots, onions and spuds, and a box of apples or citrus fruits will last there for weeks, as long as it's not damp and there are no rodents around. Even fresh vegetables with a relatively short shelf-life, such as salads, greens and roots, keep far better in a cool shed than in a hot kitchen over Christmas.

- When you bring vegetables back from the greengrocer's, re-pack them into a large cardboard box with several layers of newspaper placed around the inside for insulation; they should stay in good condition for as long as 7–10 days.

- If the weather turns freezing cold, simply lag your sacks and boxes of vegetables with newspaper or straw, or shift them indoors – the cupboard under the stairs is ideal if it's not too warm – or if there are only small amounts left, the salad drawer in the bottom of the fridge will keep the last of your stored roots in good condition for several weeks. But make sure they're dry when you put them away, or they'll just rot and stink the place out.

FORCE CHICORY

Continue forcing witloof chicory (see January, p.26 or October, p.257).

NATURAL CHRISTMAS DECORATIONS

Plants *make* Christmas, so this isn't the time to stint yourself; all I'd say is don't buy 'living decorations' too far in advance. Even the most durable natural materials will be over the top by 25 December if they've already been on duty in a hot living room for weeks. (See also p.296 for Christmas trees and p.297 for cut flowers and foliage for Christmas.)

Festive pot plants

Since you'll spend more time than usual at home indoors over Christmas, this is the time to plan a conservatory or living room display that really knocks your socks off in terms of flower power.

Buying and caring for festive pot plants

Choose pot plants wisely so they last.

- Buy them from a shop, garden centre or nursery that's kept them under cover, and choose plants with flowers that look fresh, with none going over.
- Have them wrapped so they don't catch cold when you take them home – a windy journey or a sudden drop in temperature wrecks the flowers in no time.
- At home, to keep them fresh, water lightly but regularly and keep them in good light, at an even temperature, well away from open fires and radiators.
- Keep pot plants and cut flowers well away from bowls of fruit. Ripe fruit gives off ethylene gas that will shorten the life of anything in bloom.

Poinsettias

Poinsettias are *the* modern Christmas classic, and now you can get pink, cream and variegated poinsettias as well as the traditional red. The 'flowers' are actually coloured bracts; the true flowers are just the little tufts of yellow tucked away in the middle.

Poinsettias have only been on the pot-plant scene in the last 20–30 years. They don't have any real-life connection with Christmas – they've only caught on because of their red colour combined with the holly-shaped leaves and bracts – and they don't even flower naturally at Christmas. Growers 'fool' them into flowering out of season by a complicated process of artificial lighting and blackout curtains, which they start bringing into play months beforehand. Left to their own devices, poinsettias flower when the days and nights are of equal length, which in the UK normally happens around Easter. In the wild, poinsettias grow into 10m (30ft) trees, so to make them short enough for pot plants, the growers use chemicals to dwarf them. As Christmas favourites go they are quite fussy, so keep them in a warm room, at an even temperature of 16–24°C (60–75°F) and out of draughts.

Old favourites

Indoor azaleas, cyclamen, Christmas cactus and pot chrysanthemums are old Christmas favourites. Since they are all very nearly hardy, they are happiest in a cool room, making them ideal for a chilly hallway or out in your conservatory, porch or sunroom where there's little or no heating. They all like regular watering so that the compost doesn't dry out, and in the case of Christmas cactus, don't turn the pot around or move it to another room once the buds have formed, as they tend to drop off if the plants undergo a major change of lifestyle.

The Christmas azalea is the only pot plant that can be watered every day so that the rootball remains moist. Stand it in a filled bowl for half an hour, then tip away the excess.

Cineraria and calceolaria, whether home-grown from your greenhouse or bought from a shop, are also happiest in coolish conditions – again a conservatory or enclosed porch is ideal. Short-lived annuals such as these two are good for temporarily brightening up darker places than you'd risk a long-term pot plant in, because they're only going to be thrown away once they're over.

Forced bulbs

Forced hyacinths and daffodils are available in the shops in the run-up to Christmas and they're no trouble. Just treat them like annual flowers – enjoy them while they're at their best and throw them away afterwards, because once they've been forced they're no good for anything else.

If you've grown your own out-of-season bulbs, keep a close eye on them from late November onwards. As soon as the buds have developed and show the first signs of their true colour, move them inside. If you bring them in too soon, they often 'go wrong', producing flowers on short, stunted stems that get lost in the foliage.

When you've grown or bought forced bulbs in individual pots, you can pick out those that are all the same size and stage of development to put together in a larger container, such as a bowl or a planting trough. There's no need to tip them out of their pots – simply stand them inside and pack damp moss between them. Simple but very effective, and perfect for Christmas.

Orchids

Orchids are the latest new thing for Christmas. Prices have come down a lot recently, but they still have an aura of being special. You'll find no end of them about, as they peak at this time of year. Bought as the flowers first open, orchids are incredibly good value, as the flowers can last 3 months or more.

Phalaenopsis, the moth orchid, is very reliable and long-flowering (they can repeat-flower almost the whole year round), with arching spikes of large flowers resembling pink or white butterflies hovering over compact plants. *Paphiopedilum*, slipper orchids, are also quite compact, with spotty foliage and enormous, pouch-shaped flowers in greens, white and purple. Cymbidiums are the biggest, and have tall tussocks of thick, grass-like stems and typical 'corsage orchid' flowers.

As a general rule, during the winter all indoor orchids need a steady temperature of 16–21°C (60–70°F) and high humidity, which is best provided by standing the pot on a dish of damp pebbles. Orchids must never be over-watered: it's much better to give them a good soak once a week and then let the pot drain. Being potted in very open compost, often consisting of large bits of bark, most of the water runs straight through if you try and water them in the normal way, so what I find works best is to plunge the pot almost to the rim in a deep bowl of tepid water for a few minutes and then lift it out. Don't use tap water for orchids, as they hate the chlorine and chalk in it. Instead, save the water that's left in the kettle after you've boiled it to make a cup of tea, let it cool and use that, as most of the chalk and chlorine have dispersed. They don't like a lot of feeding, just add a drop of orchid fertilizer to the water every 2 or 3 weeks.

FRUIT

PLANT FRUIT TREES AND BUSHES

I wouldn't choose to be planting pot-grown plants right now (ideally, wait until March), but if you've ordered bare-root trees and bushes, and this is when they happen to be delivered, get them in as soon as you can. If the ground is too wet or frosty to plant them, or you simply don't have time to do the job properly, heel them in temporarily and plant them later (see January, p.20).

EAT STORED FRUIT

You'll probably make big inroads into your fruit over Christmas, and that's no bad thing since you can't expect it to keep for a lot longer.

UNDER COVER

GREENHOUSE JOBS

When the festivities are approaching their noisy peak, the kids are over-excited and the dog has just been lavishly sick, that's the moment when a lot of chaps are overcome with an irresistible urge to do good works down the garden.

It's a little-known fact that late December is a great time for tidying your shed (see January, p.17), sorting out the dahlia tubers (see November, p.281), and picking dead leaves off the plants in the greenhouse. There are very sound horticultural reasons why these invaluable jobs must be done now, without even waiting to help with the washing up.

Sow exhibition onions

The job that comes top of keen vegetable growers' lists is sowing their exhibition onions. If you don't get that done as soon as possible after the shortest day, you'll automatically be wasting valuable growing time, which could make all the difference between taking a well-deserved first and coming nowhere in the running at your local show next summer.

Real enthusiasts use artificial light to push early sowings along – you can buy suitable kinds from specialist greenhouse supply catalogues, but it's a lot of trouble and expense to go to if your main aim is to avoid yet another game of Scrabble with the relatives.

PLANT MAINTENANCE

Tidy plants in the greenhouse and conservatory, and water greenhouse and conservatory plants sparingly.

CHECK BULBS

Check bulbs in store and remove any going mouldy or soft before the rot spreads to their neighbours.

WATER GARDEN

PREVENT THE POND FROM FREEZING OVER

In a cold area where there's any risk of ice forming for more than a few days at a time, float a rubber ball on the pond surface so that should ice form you can lift it out and leave a ready-made breathing hole for fish. Alternatively, melt a hole by standing a hot saucepan on it for a few minutes. Whatever you do, don't crack the ice with a hammer, as the shockwaves are too much for semi-dormant fish.

Right: If frost seems likely, float a ball on the pond surface to prevent it from freezing over.

PROJECT Make a Christmas wreath from garden materials

An evergreen wreath is the traditional front door decoration, and if you have suitable plants in the garden it's not difficult to make your own. You can adapt the same basic technique to make evergreen swags to drape down the banisters, festoon around a disused fireplace, or outline your party buffet table; it's all very much in the Victorian and Edwardian gardening tradition.

You can also make various shapes out of chicken wire stuffed with artificial moss to use as the base for all sorts of Christmas floral decorations. A pillow shape is easiest to make, and it can be placed in a shallow plant container and used to hold fresh or dried flowers, or coloured shrub stems and foliage from the garden. It doesn't have to be elaborate and complicated to look good.

Treat yourself, after all this, to a darned good read by the fire – glass in hand. There should be no shortage of seed catalogues and gardening books this Christmas.

What you need

Stiff garden wire

String

Raffia

Synthetic green moss (the sort sold for lining hanging baskets)

Sprigs of evergreen shrubs, such as rosemary, euonymus, ivy, holly, bay, laurel, spruce, yew or hedging conifers

Decorations such as fir cones, dried flowers, crab apples, berry sprigs

Thin florist's wire

1 Coil some stiff garden wire into a circle several thicknesses deep and tie the coils in place with string to hold the shape, or cheat and buy a ready-made wire wreath base from a florist.

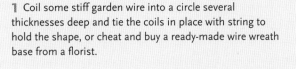
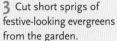
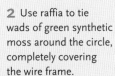
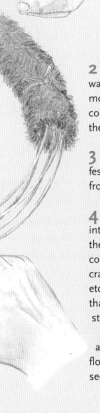

2 Use raffia to tie wads of green synthetic moss around the circle, completely covering the wire frame.

3 Cut short sprigs of festive-looking evergreens from the garden.

4 Tuck the ends firmly into the mossy base, then add some contrasting red berries, crab apples, fir cones, etc. to taste. Anything that does not have a stem of its own can be impaled or tied to a thin length of flexible florist's wire used to secure it in place.

INDEX

Page numbers in *italics*
refer to illustrations

ACKNOWLEDGEMENTS

My thanks to Sarah Reece, the editor of this book, for her wisdom, her good nature and her patience, and to Nicky Ross for, as ever, being an inspiration. Thanks also to Polly Boyd for her editorial expertise and Amanda Patton for her beautiful illustrations. Sue Phillips has done sterling research over a long period of time and I am tremendously grateful for her input. To Isobel Gillan, the designer, and Jonathan Buckley, who has photographed me (and the plants and flowers) in fair weather and foul, I offer my sincere thanks for their skills, their dedication to this project and their company (and also for Isobel's chocolate brownies).

David and Claire Asher, who own the garden used in the making of the television series, and Gill and Chris Siddell, whose garden has been used for photography, deserve especial thanks for their forbearance and good will, and I only hope they like what they are now looking at!

Thanks to all the cameramen, sound recordists, editors and production staff involved in *The Gardener's Year* television series, especially Helga Berry and Kath Moore who pushed me around on a daily basis. Without their expertise, patience, good humour and thermal underwear I doubt there would have been anything to laugh at at all. I wouldn't have missed it for anything.

Jonathan Buckley would like to thank the many garden owners and designers who have allowed him to take photographs in their gardens. The following gardens appear as wider shots:

Peachings, Hampshire (Gill and Chris Siddell): 56, 116b, 135, 137b, 146, 162b, 166r, 168r, 169t, 171, 172, 188, 213, 280, 300.

Well Cottage, Hampshire (David and Claire Asher): 2, 9, 14, 33, 49, 69, 81, 114t, 119, 126, 128r, 132t, 134, 151, 158, 159b, 164, 167, 177, 185t, 191b, 201, 207, 209t, 211b, 221, 226, 243, 249, 250b, 267.

Almeida Street, London (Marie Clarke) 183; Beth Chatto Gardens, Essex (Beth Chatto) 56b, 121r; Castelnau, London (Dan Pearson) 293r; Causeway, Sussex (June Streets) 287; The Dingle, Welshpool 10c; Eastgrove Cottage, Worcestershire (Malcolm and Caroline Skinner) 19; East Ruston Old Vicarage, Norfolk (Alan Gray and Graham Robeson) 238r; Glebe Cottage, Devon (Carol Klein) 260b; Glen Chantry, Essex (Sue and Wol Staines) 114t, 172b, 228, 253, 258; Great Dixter, East Sussex (Christopher Lloyd) 28, 50tr, 72, 105, 281; Heron's Bonzai, RHS Chelsea Flower Show 77; Ketley's, East Sussex (Helen Yemm) 295; Lady Farm, Somerset (Judy Pearce) 120c, 262; Peerley Road, Sussex (Trudi Harrison) 239; Perch Hill, East Sussex (Sarah Raven) 15, 21, 76t, 99, 107, 173 both, 256, 301; Rofford Manor, Oxfordshire 258; Roger's Rough, Sussex (Richard Bird) 166l; Sandy Lane, Manchester (Maureen Sawyer) 76b; Serge Hill, Hertfordshire (Mrs Stuart-Smith) 103; Upper Mill Cottage, Kent (David and Mavis Seeney) 95, 289; West Dean Gardens, Sussex (Sarah Wain and Jim Buckland) 212b, 284.

This book is published to accompany the television series
The Gardener's Year, produced for BBC2 by BBC Bristol.
Series producer: Kath Moore

Published by BBC Books, BBC Worldwide Limited, Woodlands,
80 Wood Lane, London W12 0TT

First published 2005
Reprinted 2005, 2006
Text copyright © Alan Titchmarsh 2005
The moral right of the author has been asserted.

Photographs copyright © Jonathan Buckley 2005

Except the following photographs from: Ardea 145br; BBC Worldwide/Susan Bell
148r, 284; BBC Worldwide/Tim Sandall 277 both; David Austin Roses 152l; Garden
Picture Library 52tl, 62r, 80tr, 118tl & tc, 122tl & cl, 123tl, 134tl, 143bl & bc, 146cl,
150tc, 154tr, 222tr, 286tc, 291tcr, 293tl, 296tl; Harpur Garden Library 18, 34tl, 180,
245tr, 246tc; Andrew Lawson Photography 51tc, 62l, 115bl, 122tr, 134tlb, 150c, 180tr,
266tr, 292tl

BBC Worldwide would like to thank the above for providing photographs
and for permission to reproduce copyright material. While every effort
has been made to trace and acknowledge all copyright holders, we would
like to apologize should there be any errors or omissions.

ISBN-13: 978 0 563 52167 9
ISBN-10: 0 563 52167 8

Commissioning editor: Nicky Ross
Project editor: Sarah Reece
Copy editor: Polly Boyd
Designer: Isobel Gillan
Illustrator: Amanda Patton
Picture researcher: Joanne Forrest Smith
Horticultural consultant: Tony Lord
Production controller: Kenneth McKay

Set in Fairfield and Scala Sans
Colour origination and printing by Butler & Tanner Ltd, Frome, Great Britain

For more information about this and other BBC books,
please visit our website at www.bbcshop.com or telephone 08700 777 001.